MEMORY

MEMORY
An Anthology

Chatto & Windus
LONDON

Published by Chatto & Windus 2008

2 4 6 8 10 9 7 5 3 1

Selection, introductions and edition copyright © Harriet Harvey Wood and
A.S. Byatt 2008

First published in Great Britain in 2008 by
Chatto & Windus
Random House, 20 Vauxhall Bridge Road,
London SW1V 2SA

www.rbooks.co.uk

Addresses for companies within The Random House Group Limited can be found at:
www.randomhouse.co.uk/offices.htm

The Random House Group Limited Reg. No. 954009

A CIP catalogue record for this book is available from the British Library

ISBN 9780701177379

The Random House Group Limited makes every effort to ensure that the papers used
in its books are made from trees that have been legally sourced from well-managed
and credibly certified forests. Our paper procurement policy can be found at:
www.randomhouse.co.uk/paper.htm

Mixed Sources
Product group from well-managed
forests and other controlled sources
www.fsc.org Cert no. TT-COC-2139
© 1996 Forest Stewardship Council
FSC

Typeset by Palimpsest Book Production Limited, Grangemouth, Stirlingshire
Printed and bound in Great Britain by CPI Mackays, Chatham ME5 8TD

Contents

The Idea of Memory

The Art of Memory

Memory and Science

Memory and Imagination

You have to begin to lose your memory, if only in bits and pieces, to realise that memory is what makes our lives. Life without memory is no life at all . . . Our memory is our coherence, our reason, our feeling, even our action. Without it, we are nothing.

Luis Buñuel, *Memoirs*

'It's a poor sort of memory that only works backwards,' the Queen remarked.

Lewis Carroll, *Through the Looking-Glass*, Chapter 5

Nessun maggior dolor
Che ricordarsi del tempo felice
Nella miseria.

Dante, *Inferno*

I remember
Those are pearls that were his eyes:

T.S. Eliot, *The Waste Land*

Introduction

A.S. Byatt

Memory is not quite the same thing as consciousness, but they are intricately, toughly and delicately intertwined. Someone once said that we consist of the pure, theoretical instant of awareness, and everything else is already memory. When we think of our selves we immediately begin to sort and arrange memories, which we then rearrange. We are fascinated by those who have – through wounds or brain damage – lost all or part of their memories. A terror of our time is living with dementia – either in ourselves, or in those we share our lives with. Memories can be polished, like objects taken out, burnished, and contemplated, or they can flitter just out of reach, like lost threads of broken webs. To remember is to have two selves, one in the memory, one thinking about the memory, but the two are not precisely distinct, and separating them can be dizzying.

I have a memory I think of as The Memory. It is seen from the point of view of a small person just seeing over the wall of a playground in East Hardwick Elementary School. The stone is hot, and is that kind that flakes into gold slivers. The sun is very bright. There is a tree overhead, and the leaves catch the light and are golden, and in the shade they are blue-green. Over the wall, and across the road is a field full of daisies and buttercups and speedwell and shepherds'-purse. On the horizon are trees with thick trunks and solid branches. The sky is very blue and the sun is huge. The child thinks: I am always going to remember this. Then she thinks: why this and not another thing? Then she thinks: what is remembering? This is the point where my self then and my self now confuse themselves into one. I know I have added to this Memory every time I have thought about it, or brought it out to look at it. It has acquired notes of Paradise Lost, which I don't think it had when I was five or six. It has got both further away and brighter, more and less 'real'. I always associate it with one of my very few good memories of my maternal grandmother – a perpetually cross person, who never smiled. The year she died, she began to forget, and forgot to be irritated. She said to me, sitting by the fire at Christmas, 'Do you remember all the beautiful young men in the fields?' And she smiled at me like a sensuous young girl. She may have been talking about the airmen who were billeted on her in the war – or she may have been remembering something from long before my mother was born. I shall never know. But I can see the young men in the fields.

Memory is an anthology of the ways people have thought about memory – and, to a lesser extent, of things they have remembered. Harriet Harvey Wood and I have tried to cover as many fields – philosophical, aesthetic, scientific, psychological, personal, social – as we could, and this has inevitably meant that each section is inconclusive and suggestive, rather than offering anything like coverage. The anthology is in two parts. The first is a collection of substantial essays on memory, most of them specially commissioned, by scientists, artists, and thinkers from several fields. The second is a collection of extracts, arranged thematically. Harriet Harvey Wood's Introduction to that section describes the principles of arrangement.

Craig Raine says in his essay in this book that 'Memory is like metaphor in its operations.' He goes on 'Memory is sexual in its operations.' (He is referring partly to the use of the word 'coming' in describing sexual pleasure, which does certainly bear some relation to the pleasure of finding the desired memory from inside.) Memory is like metaphor and humans have always needed metaphors to think about memory. There is a long tradition, starting with Plato, which uses the metaphor of the mind as a soft wax surface, on which an image can be impressed, or as a gemstone, in which it can be engraved or scratched. St Augustine thought of his memory as palaces full of spaces in which he encountered thoughts and people. Memory can be a pit or well from which things rise to the surface. Lately I have once or twice, searching for names I 'know I know' (and *how* do we know we know if we can't remember?) found myself looking down into an inky depth in which there was only absence, no elusive flickering fish. We invent machines to assist and fortify our memories, and then use these machines as metaphors for thinking about how memory works. Ulric Neisser, in a fine essay on deceptive certainties of remembering, points out that photographs record indifferently everything present to them, whereas no live memory works like that. He discusses the effects of using the images of recording machines and video cassettes, and of the 'flashbulb' memory – so bright and shocking that it is felt to be burned into the brain. We have computers which remember what we cannot, to which we bolt on added memory, or into which we insert 'memory sticks'. We have the idea that we shall be able to insert a language, or a map, or mathematical skills, into our brains as we can into machines. But cognitive scientists like Neisser and Steven Rose, who work with the 'wet stuff', with the chemistry and biological organisation of the brain, have taught us to be wary of machine metaphors for bodily thought. Steven Rose's essay in this anthology is both a lucid description of the history of the scientific study of memory, and a fascinating description of his own experimental work – and that of others – on understanding changes in the substance of brains as they make memories.

Remembering is a bodily activity, taking place in the brain, and also in the connections between the brain and the nervous system. When I was young there was a philosophical theory that the brain would never be able to study itself – an unease associated with the indivisible self who 'has' a memory. But now immense advances are being made in the study of how our brains map and store our thoughts and experience, and communicate with the rest of our bodies. Forests of dendrites, millions and millions of neurones connected into living and changing networks along axons that meet at synapses, arrange both our conscious and our unconscious lives. The word 'dendrite' itself is a precise metaphor – it comes from 'dendron', the Greek word for a tree, and the dendrites spread and join in branch-like forms. I think metaphor itself, and our pleasure in metaphor, may be the result of two objects or concepts meeting and fusing in these threads of living cells. Not only do we need metaphor to remember – it is a basic part of the process of thinking.

Surprising discoveries have been made. Students of living brains can now see which precise areas are excited by stimuli. As Antonio Damasio tells us, it turns out that if we think of a hammer we are exciting many different and physically separated areas – those that think of visual images of hammers, those that remember the *feeling* of how a hand clasps a hammer, those that remember words and groups of words, and those that can translate 'hammer' into different languages. We remember colour words in a different part of the brain from the place where we store the ability to see and recognise colours. We know now that London taxi drivers seem to develop an enlarged area of the hippocampus to remember the Knowledge of the streets.

Memory, language, and the body are intertwined in a very complex way, and this can arouse violent debate. I was once on a committee studying the teaching of English language which contained opposing camps about the virtues of 'learning by heart' – a phrase I like, partly because it reminds me of Wordsworth, remembering sensations 'felt in the blood and felt along the heart', and partly because the basic unit of English verse, the iambic pentameter, contains as many heart beats as we make during one breath. The writers on the committee needed this idea of committing poetry and grammar to memory – a kind of bodily memory that became a human resource. Many of the teachers felt that 'rote learning' was a form of punishment, and unnecessary in the days of calculators, computers and recorders. George Steiner once said that human nature had changed – that there was a generation of teenagers that could find out anything – on the Internet – and remembered nothing, because they did not need to. Poetic rhythms, and grammatical forms, and more complicated and deliberately artificial structures of mnemonics are part of the history and interest of the subject of memory. We have a section on the elaborate memory theatres and weird systems of clues-by-verbal-juxtaposition of mediaeval and Renaissance thinkers – my favourite example is the remembering of a witness, or a testament, by visual-ising bulls' testicles. It is interesting that many of the linguistic students of memory refuse to believe that anyone can have a memory that is not put into words. I 'know' I have a very early memory of the square rim of a pram hood, and the blue sky beyond, and the 'feel' of working out that my body was lying in a space framed by the rim of the hood and the edge of a blanket. It is slightly painful to me to put this into words. When I 'remember' it, I do so with my blood and limbs and skin, I don't use or need words.

There have been theories of memory which tested the idea that the DNA, which carried the handed-on forms of a species, might also be the organ of memory. Rats, and nematode worms, were trained to remember and perform tasks, and then slaughtered and fed to other rats and nematode worms, which were thought to have ingested the learned behaviour and to react more quickly in the next generation. Scientists searched for the 'engram', a ghostly descendant of Plato's impression on the wax, the Form of Memory that mys-teriously persists in a creature's brain when every molecule in that brain has decayed and been replaced several times. The image we have now – which 'feels' to me like a good image – is one of constant communication and reinforcement and pruning (to use J.P. Changeux's useful word) of the network of cells in the brain, which is simultaneously a structure of molecules, and a system of electrical signals. This gets rid of the imagined infinite regression of homunculi observing either 'representations' or reproductions 'in' the brain. Nevertheless, even if the DNA is not the vehicle of Memory, there is a complex and delicate relation, suggested in an elegant essay by Patrick Bateson, between what animals may learn or remember, and their fitness, and therefore survival and handing on of their genes. The example he begins with is the cheetah who learns, or remembers, that gazelles who 'stot' vigorously are less worth-while to pursue than feebler ones. Here memory reinforces natural selection and works with it.

Memory, or Mnemosyne, was, the Greeks believed, the mother of the Muses. Art is all, at some level, both a mnemonic and a form of memory. Frank Kermode, in an elegant essay compares St Augustine's contemplative form of memory as a search for God with Wordsworth's *Prelude*, an autobiographical poem about the Growth of a Poet's Mind, which has some of the subtlest recordings of the feeling of thinking in English, and with Freud's analysis of the psyche as a system for hiding and disguising desires and individual histories – and then of repeating the patterns of desire and disguise. Malcolm Bowie is interested in what he calls remembering forwards – the way in which a composer, or a painter, can envisage and then make something new, by remembering and reshaping something earlier – Beethoven remembering Bach's variations, Titian remembering Ovid's Marsyas. Bowie is extremely subtle about the way the mind moves forward and back, elaborating and discarding. His essay reminded me of what a painter once said to me when he was halfway through reading Thomas Mann's *Magic Mountain*. You can feel the form of what is to come, he said, weighing on you. Or *in* you. I think the felt form of the part of an unfinished work – a novel half written, say, that has found its shape – is not unlike the search in the memory for something you know you know. And culturally, of course, the same mixture of remembering and reinventing is always going on. Our anthology includes a passage from a recent book by Milan Kundera in which he meditates on the fact that no reader – not even another novelist, a professional – can ever hold in the memory the whole of a complex novel, by Flaubert, say, or by Kafka. The work is formed, and no single memory will ever be adequate to think about it.

Frances Yates studied the intricate and strange Memory Theatres of the Renaissance, where an argument, or a poem, could be remembered by arranging it in an imaginary building, in floors and alcoves and stages, which the professional thinker then revisits. This solidifying of remembered ideas or objects turns out to be very similar to the techniques used by professional mnemonists – such as the one studied by the Russian psychologist, Luria – who attach things to be remembered to buildings and gates along a path. This also resembles what the London taxi drivers appear to do – they associate words with buildings – they 'see' a Crystal Palace or an Odeon and attach routes to fixed points.

One of the great memory-connected systems of recent times is of course psychoanalysis. Freud's metaphorical map of the psyche, a building with storeys, with the Superego, the Ego, and the shapeless dark sea of the Id rising above each other, is a different kind of memory theatre. Frank Kermode quotes Adam Phillips, who says the patients of analysts are people haunted by memories they want to rid themselves of. Freud discovered the device of screen memories – memories which disguise, or cover, memories the subject wants to forget or hide. But these screen memories at the same time point to the lost incident, or love object, or fear, and the skilled analyst can resurrect the lost memory by the method of asking the 'patient' to make free associations to dreams, or waking fears, until, it is hoped, the form of what is lost can be brought to the surface, contemplated reasonably, and understood. Here the Unconscious has done the work of the unnaturally conscious mnemonist, and attached meanings to apparently arbitrarily chosen objects. This particular map of the soul and its workings has been a great resource for all sorts of artists, literary, visual, and in film and theatre. Ignês Sodré, a psychoanalyst with an acute literary intelligence, has written on Freud's study of 'Mourning and Melancholia' and has related it to George Eliot's profound understanding, in *Silas Marner* of the processes of remembering, clinging on to, internalising and fetishising a lost object.

Psychoanalysis deals with the subtleties of the relation between memory and forgetting. Recent uses of psychoanalytic techniques to 'bring to the surface' lost abuses from childhood, or traumas suffered and suppressed, have also aroused a considerable interest in false, or created, or invented memories. The usefulness of dredging up lost (or imagined) terrors from the deep well of unconsciousness has been called in question for various reasons. Studies have recently suggested that survivors of a catastrophe who have been professionally debriefed

and encouraged to remember often fare less well than those who
have gone through a more natural process of forgetting and adjusting.
We need to forget, in order to survive. Both psychologists and psychi-
atrists have studied our propensity to make up memories, to create,
or add, or subtly change what we remember. Studies of 'false memory
syndrome' show that suggestion – by therapists or others – can bring
into being the memories they are looking for. Ulric Neisser made an
illuminating study of the inaccuracy of firmly held memories of, say,
the day Kennedy died, or the day the Shuttle exploded. People asked
to write down their memories at the time of an event, and to write
them down again some time later, were found radically to have altered
their accounts – and to believe firmly that the later account was
'true'. Neuroscientists can now study the process of putting together
a memory as neurones and axons are reinforced. It has been suggested
that every time we, so to speak, take out, or visit a memory to look
at it, we repeat the process of putting it together in the brain. This
would lead logically to the inference that there is no 'true' or 'original' memory to be reconstructed or discovered. And this in turn, as
Neisser says, should make us worried about the whole idea of giving
evidence in law courts, of our reliance on people recalling the truth
under oath. Good witnesses are quite probably creative constructors
of memories.

What is true about the relations between invention, imagination
and ideology in individual processes of remembering is of course also
true of public, and communal memory. Nations put up public memor-
ials to events that are part of a desired history. They construct history
books for children. They prune and reinforce desiderated narratives.
Sudhir Hazareesingh has been carrying out research in the French
National Archive on the image and memory of Napoleon Bonaparte
in the nineteenth century. He writes very lucidly about the construction of a national memory and identity by the use of markers such
as street names – a political Memory Theatre – flags, and songs. He
is interested in what the French chose not to remember about what
went on in Vichy France, and are now revisiting. It is possible for
states to erase, and reinstate, people in common memories, as politicians in Kundera's *Unbearable Lightness of Being* are airbrushed out
of photos when out of favour, and put back when the climate changes.
The German people after the Second World War are very different
from Germans before it, and have a very complex relation to their
common memories. The painter, Anselm Kiefer, deliberately trans-

gresses public proprieties of memory by revisiting images that have been consigned to oblivion. He ranges from the Nazi salute to the bombastic architecture of the 1930s, from Teutonic myths to Wagnerian Nuremberg. He paints with doubleness – the images are seen partly through the beauty and terror of the poems of Paul Celan. But they are there – not to be forgotten.

There is a public analogy to George Steiner's clever, resourceful, unremembering teenagers. Manfred Osten, in a thoughtful book, *Das geraubte Gedächtnis*, [*Stolen Memory*], argues that precisely the aids to memory we have constructed in machines – the memory banks which have replaced card indexes, the CDs that have replaced diagrams and drawings – are taking away our inhabited public memory. This is both because – as in the case of the teenagers – everything is indiscriminately available, and, which is a problem the big memory institutions, the great libraries and museums are encountering – the technology becomes rapidly obsolete, and as it becomes inaccessible the memories are lost. Thomas Hobbes, in one of the quotations I most love about memory, remarks severely that imagination is nothing but decaying sense, and that when the decaying sense is 'fading, old and past' we call it memory. Obsolescent technology gives a whole new terror to the decay of sense, imagination and memory itself.

In our anthology we have – including Hobbes – many literary evocations of memory and memories. We have autobiography – including Augustine and Wordsworth, and a splendid essay by that most subtle of biographers and autobiographers, Richard Holmes, who ranges from the 'memory boxes' used to arouse fading memories in the old, to Mole's stream of sudden memory in *The Wind in the Willows*, to Coleridge's wonderful image of the memory or mind as an insect winning its way along the surface of a stream 'by alternate pulses of passive and active motion'. We have the Woolfs, and Proust, and Nabokov who Craig Raine says is a greater writer than Proust. Raine may be right when he says Proust's attempts to make philosophical definitions of memory don't quite work. (He claims that Proust's description of involuntary memory – as opposed to the willed act of memory – elevates the former to a religious experience: '[It] restores reality in its entirety, with all its qualia intact, and is therefore a form of resurrection. It is further a kind of 'immortality'. I agree with Raine that this doesn't quite work, that the religious joy it bestows is suspect.)

But the glory of Proust is the precision with which he renders the moment of the recall of lost time, even if we may have reason to suspect that he is creating, or recreating the past.

I shall end by picking out one example, which is from Tennyson's *In Memoriam,* a poem whose greatness is still not sufficiently recognised. It is one of the most powerful meditations on loss and recall, time, and the movement and construction of the human mind in time. The passage we chose is a precise meditation on the nature of consciousness, which would have satisfied Freud and Melanie Klein. It describes the conundrum with which I began, the identity and difference between the self who remembers, and what is remembered. It is written in a stanza which is both a mnemonic and a mimicry of the way thought composes and turns on itself.

> The baby new to earth and sky
> What time his tender palm is prest
> Against the circle of the breast,
> Has never thought that 'this is I:'
>
> But as he grows he gathers much,
> And learns the use of 'I' and 'me'
> And finds 'I am not what I see,
> And other than the things I touch.'
>
> So rounds he to a separate mind
> From whence clear memory may begin,
> As through the frame that binds him in
> His isolation grows defined.

The two editors of this collection started from very different interests and preoccupations. Harriet Harvey Wood is a mediaevalist, and a classicist, with an interest in Scottish literature and thought. In that context I am a Romantic, with an intense, if necessarily amateur, interest in neuroscience and psychology. These preoccupations – which are also to a certain extent limitations – can be seen in our choice of texts. But the collaboration has been inventive and wide-ranging because of the differences of emphasis. All sorts of strange connections and coincidences have been discovered. We should like to thank our contributors – who have been patient and understanding during illnesses of both editors. And we hope readers will find things that surprise them, and things they remember and revisit with pleasure.

Part I

Frank Kermode, 'Palaces of Memory'

Whether it is a question of a single person, or a multitude of persons falsely represented by the self-biographer (selves-biographer?) as one, there is no avoiding the question of memory, as Augustine was the first to understand. We are warned that he used the term in a much wider sense than we do. For him it was the very instrument of personal continuity, the basis of self-identity, and 'the stomach of the mind' (*Confessions* X.8). And it was also the means of access to grace. Since his narrative is of a delayed self-opening to grace, memory is in every sense the basis of it.

Memory also offers the clue to the way the world at large functions, for the world is also fallen into materiality and sense, so that its redemption must be a matter of history, of a cosmic memory. One sees why Augustine follows his narrative with the philosophical enquiry into memory that occupies the tenth book of the *Confessions*. Here are some of the famous words:

I come to the fields and vast palaces of memory, where are the treasuries of all kinds of objects brought in by sense perception. Hidden there is whatever we think about, a process which may increase or diminish or in some way alter the deliverance of the senses and whatever else has been deposited and placed on reserve and has not been swallowed up and buried in oblivion. When I am in this storehouse, I ask that it produce what I want to recall, and immediately certain things come out; some require a longer search, and have to be drawn out as it were from more recondite receptacles. Some memories pour out to crowd the mind, and when one is searching and asking for something quite different, leap forward into the centre as if saying, 'Surely we are what you want?' With the hand of my heart I chase them away from the face of my memory until what I want is freed of mist and emerges from its hiding places. Other memories come before me on demand with ease and without any confusion in their order. Memories of earlier events give way to those which followed, and as they pass are stored away available for retrieval when I want them. And that is what happens when I recount a narrative from memory. (X. viii)

This is a simple model, basically rather like a library, and it does distinguish easy-access books from books on reserve. However, the books interact. What the senses have collected and stored is modified by association with 'whatever we think about'. Some items come easily, even too easily, so some must be waved away. Some are deep in the stacks or in special collections. The section that follows describes a sort of cataloguing system, in which acquisitions are organised according to the sense that introduced each of them: sight, sound, smell, taste, touch. Access to these resources enables one to enjoy and compare images of the world: 'I distinguish the odour of lilies from that of violets without smelling anything at all' (X. viii) and in these halls of memory 'I meet myself and recall what I am, what I have done, and when and where and how I was affected when I did it'; moreover, with those recollections other images less immediate to that self-meeting may in their turn be blended and combined.

To see what Augustine meant by self-exploration amid the contents of memory one needs to reflect that it is not merely sensory images that are collected and combined. Ideas are stored in the memory before one has learned them. As in Plato's *Meno*, though with the important difference that Augustine does not admit prenatal knowledge, learning is remembering. Similarly stored, part of the original deposit, are 'the affections of my mind'. Thus the rememberer can identify affective experiences when he or she has them later; but, as preserved in the memory and reported to the enquirer, they may differ strangely from what they were as primordial experience; and here the doubling effect is obvious: 'I can be far from glad in remembering myself to have been glad, and far from sad when I recall my past sadness. Without fear I remember how at a particular time I was afraid ... I remember with joy a sadness that has passed and with sadness a lost joy' (X. xiv).

Forgetfulness in Augustine's *memoria* is treated as a fact of memory: 'memory retains forgetfulness ... So it is there lest we forget what, when present, makes us forget' (X. xvi). I must remember forgetfulness, even though it destroys what I remember. One further point: how is it possible to aspire, as everybody does, to a felicity which, though we have the idea of it, we have never actually experienced? We have no memory, in the ordinary sense of the word, of any earlier happiness on which to model such hopes. Yet where else can they come from, if not from memory? The notion of happiness must be there, put there by some prior agency, innate. God, too, is in the memory, but by his own inter-vention, to be found there perhaps very late, when fascination with his creation gives way to love of him. Here comes the requirement of continence, a degree of abnegation, achievable only by grace. *Da quod iubes.* God must give the continence he commands. Only then will he be found, and the enquiring spirit enabled to meet itself.

From this remarkable passage we can derive the idea of a neces-sary doubleness, and also the notion that the experience as remem-bered is not, affectively, of the same quality as the experience itself; or, as one almost needs to say, the experience as remembered is not the same as the experience remembered. Here is another aspect of difference in doubleness. A pain recalled is recognised as a pain, yet it may be recalled with pleasure; a past joy can be remembered with intense sadness (a point perhaps remembered by Dante, in a famous passage, as well as by Wordsworth). Augustine is sure, as many of his successors have been, that what memory celebrated is not, in tone or significance, identical with the actual moment remem-bered. For, as he remarks in Book XI. xviii, meditating on past and future: 'the memory produces not the actual events which have passed away but words conceived from images of them, which they fixed in the mind like imprints as they passed through the senses . . . when I am recollecting and telling my story, I am looking on its image in present time . . .' This image belongs to what he calls 'the present of things past'. Other memories have worked on the image, and Augustine here anticipates the Freudian *Nachträglichkeit*, or deferred action (Freud spoke of 'memory-traces being subjected from time to time to a rearrangement in accordance with fresh circumstances – to a retranscription'). Forgetfulness affects memo-ries, of course, but memories can do the work of forgetfulness by modifying the original deposit, which is further changed when the product of time and much reworking must suffer a translation into language.

For Augustine any such translation must be a fall. Language, in its nature successive, is part of the fallen world, the world of time. He sets the word against the Word; the Word belongs to the simultaneous present, the *nunc stans*, of eternity. In a famous passage (XI. xxviii) Augustine speaks of reciting a psalm. Before he begins to do so he has an expectation directed towards a whole. Verse by verse, as he recites, it passes into memory; so there is a blend of memory and expectation. But his attention is on the present, through which the future passes into the past. As he goes on, memory expands and expectation diminishes until the whole psalm has been said, and all is in the memory. The same action occurs in the life of the individual person, 'where all actions are parts of a whole, and also of the total history of the "sons of men" (Ps. 30: 20) where all human lives are but parts'. So one's life, in this respect like all other lives, passes into memory and has a typical near-completeness which, so long as we remain alive, we can seek in the memory; always remembering that when we report it in words we have in some measure to undo that completeness, both because we are using words, and because memory always entails forgetting.

Although he stresses certain dualisms in the action of memory, Augustine does not doubt the continuous individuality of the 'I' which is doing the remembering and the forgetting. Nevertheless, he sees his life, and the life of all the fallen, as a collection of scattered fragments. But he is far from wanting to represent the memory-image and his own report of it as such; for in achieving closure, totality, it has taken on a kind of intemporality, it imitates the eternal Word. His story is in fact of the unification of those fragments by his conversion, the terminus of his narrative, the conquest of division. So in this matter of fragmentation and dispersal of the self you could say he is aware of the problems of memory and subjectivity, but not that he would have recognised his problem as expressed in the language of Nietzsche or that he could have accepted the rhetorical and formal solutions offered by Roland Barthes or Paul Valéry in the *Cahiers*. Augustine recognises fragmentation but his whole drift is to mend it. He is thus antithetical to these writers, and also to Henry Adams, who expressly wanted to deny the illusion of unity in his life, to bring it back 'from unity to multiplicity'. This is the counter-Augustinian trend in modern autobiography. But the Augustinian strain remains strong.

Our modern assumptions about memory are likely to refer more directly to the Freudian tradition. In a recent paper called 'Freud and the Uses of Forgetting' the psychoanalyst Adam Phillips begins by remarking that 'People come for psychoanalytic treatment because they are remembering in a way that does not free them to forget.' Symptoms are involuntary and disguised memories of desire, unsuccessful attempts at self-cure. Those memories need to be forgotten, but desire, for Freud, is unforgettable. Repression is simply a way of seeming to get rid of things by keeping them. There is no cure for memory, though we try to use it to forget with, as in screen memories, devices designed to enable us to forget memories of a forbidden desire. Psychoanalysis attempts a cure by inducing the kind of remembering that makes forgetting possible. The only certain cure is death.

Here are paradoxes on remembering and forgetting that represent the two as a doublet and in that respect are faintly reminiscent of Augustine's; but the differences are at least as marked. Phillips can think of the logic of Freud's psychoanalytical process as being the reverse of what we take to be the autobiographer's: 'Either the most significant bits of one's past are unconscious, and only available in the compromised form of symptoms and dreams; or the past is released through interpretation into oblivion.' Forgetting is the only way to remember; remembering is the only way to achieve benign forgetting. The product of analysis is not autobiography but evacuation. And Phillips finds in the analyst's ideal state of 'free-floating' or 'evenly suspended attention' a parallel use of forgetting; the analyst must learn not to mind not having things in mind, he works by not trying to remember. This is not, to most people's way of thinking, at all like the practice of attentive reading (though it is sometimes held to be the correct practice, as in the writings of André Green and some others).

So the concept of memory offered by psychoanalysis is at first sight hostile to the truth of autobiography. What we profess to remember is what we have devised to protect us from the truth; and this will be the case even when, or perhaps especially when, the attempt to hide nothing is exceptionally strenuous and well advertised, as with Jean-Jacques Rousseau. The concept of *Nachträglichkeit* explains how a past is recovered in a distorted form; a childhood memory becomes a trauma, a trauma not directly associated with a 'real' childhood memory. Memory invents a past.

Its reworkings defend us against the appalling timelessness of the unconscious. What we remember we may remember because we are forgetting in the wrong way; our remembering then takes the form of repetition, of acting out. If the analyst cures this repetition by fostering 'the work of remembering' he is not doing it because the memories thus elicited are valuable, but because he wants to dispose of them as bad for the patient, as what he needs to forget.

Here the timeless is not, as in Augustine, eternity, but the unconscious, and we struggle against its forces, using substitute memories, writing about what ought to be disposed of precisely because of its inauthentic link to the unconscious. There are deposited anterior memories, and Augustine had those, but his were related to felicity and to God, not to incest and murder. Augustine needs access to the timeless, but our need is rather to forget it as totally as possible. We achieve access to its contents by the dual imaginative activity of the transference, but we do so with the object not of verifying them but of destroying them: to remember them, or even seem to do so, is a stratagem to relinquish or dispose of them. But Augustine needed them alive, because he sought the timeless for reasons having nothing to do with destruction; he wished to account for his life as a whole, given shape, made so by the action of memory and the timelessness into which it passes when it is finished.

There seems little doubt that the dominant myth of autobiography is still Augustinian rather than Freudian. Of course it may be that all autobiography is in Freudian terms defensive or resistant, that to totalise, to close, to advertise a psychic structure that cannot on a strict view be authentic, is false and evasive. But it seems to be true that what excited many writers is to achieve some measure or simulacrum of closure, and thus a substitute timelessness. Tolstoy got over being impressed by Rousseau's *Confessions* when he decided that, far from demonstrating the love of truth, Rousseau lied and believed his lies, which of course made him incapable of the truth to which he claimed to aspire. Rousseau himself admits that he left things out – from very pure motives – and occasionally made things up. Nabokov's artful autobiography is full of elegantly rendered and various detail, but, as he once remarks, what gives such a work its formal value is thematic repetition. John Sturrock is especially interested in the phenomenon, so often repeated in autobiography as to be endoxically recognisable, of what he calls the 'turn' – the point of epiphany or conversion, seen as the moment when the person under description individuates or selves himself, as it were, finds the point from which all can be seen to cohere, and so achieves a kind of closure. This moment is present in some form virtually everywhere. It draws on or constitutes the memory of a deviance, often apparently quite slight, from some norm of experience or behaviour, a deviance that makes the writer, in his own eyes at any rate, worth writing about as a single person. In the process he cannot avoid providing relevant material on what he takes himself to be deviating from, so that autobiography appeals to our notions of normality as well as to our interest in the myriad possible devian-cies; and to our interest also in wholeness, a quality we seek when recounting to ourselves our own lives. Everybody takes these things for granted, and if they want confirmations they will look for their best expression not in the narratives of analysands, which require a different and specialised form of attention, but in the works of people who understand the conditions of art: say, in poets such as Wordsworth. For to communicate persuasively the experience of the turn it is necessary to practise an art.

Kinds of memory are subject to various sorts of classification, but we are familiar, largely on the evidence of works of art, with the idea that there is a rough, recognisable distinction between two kinds of memory, roughly voluntary and involuntary. Those 'turns', those hinges or fulcra on which a whole narrative depends and which justify the very existence of the narrative, are a very conspic-uous, very 'placed', treatment of involuntary movements of consciousness momentarily present in some more accessible area of the memory, brought, as Augustine might have said, from special collections to open shelves, and then displayed against a back-ground of simpler recollection. Now, their subtly fine bindings, gleaming against the drab covers of commonplace recollections, they stand out, and seem worthwhile recounting. Though they are the sort of thing that can, perhaps does, occur to everybody, these privileged moments are not easy to put into words; they are not only what the author is really about but also a test of whether he ought to be an author.

I will borrow from Barrett J. Mandel a neat little illustration from Edmund Gosse's *Father and Son*. The author describes it as one of the many 'trifling things' that make up a life, but still 'a landmark'. The boy's fundamentalist father wanted him to decline an invitation to a party, and suggested that he pray for guidance from the Lord as to whether he should go. Asked what the Lord's answer was, the boy, well knowing his father's confidence that God's response would favour his own view, nevertheless replied, 'The Lord says I may go to the Browns.' The father 'gazed at me in speechless horror' and left the room, 'slamming the door'. Mandel admires this and calls it genuine autobiography, but adds that the writer Gosse knows more about the father and his thoughts than the boy Gosse can have done, and for that reason is able to pinpoint this moment as one of significant rebellion, a type of such resistance, and set it in a larger context that explains why it was significant, a landmark and not a trifle – or, perhaps better, despite its *seeming* a trifle, and getting called that by an author who wished us to understand that he can now see how things hang together in a larger view of his remembered life. It is the mature, hindsighted record of an important stage in the widening gulf between father and son, part of a narrative designed to chart that process. We allow without demur that Gosse could not possibly be remembering his father's precise words; we already know, from our own memories, the nature of the relation of such a moment to truth and memory. As Mandel expresses it, the author is saying to the reader: 'My life was as this tale I am telling.' This is a satisfying formula, and it implies a claim that in this form (as this tale) it will have power to indicate landmarks and confer meaning on what would otherwise be mnemonic trifles.

We can add that an episode of this sort could have been worked over, told and retold to the author himself and perhaps to others; as the memory of a memory, of many memories perhaps, it acquires those associations of which Augustine speaks. To give this degree of centrality, of totality, to a memory, or to 'thematise' in the way recommended by Nabokov, is to seek to confer on the narrative a power to eliminate the restrictions of time; to institute its own laws of causality, to endow it with totality by invoking what W. B. Yeats called 'the artifice of eternity'. Much autobiography presumes to imitate that power.

Wordsworth offers an account of his life as 'this tale I am telling', though he might have accepted both the ultimate relation of time-dispersed elements to eternity, as adumbrated by Augustine, and the apparent triviality of some of the scattered episodes in themselves. Certain elements in this exercise in self-distinguishing are worth mention. Like Rousseau, Wordsworth is aware of the double consciousness all autobiographers must contend with. Childhood days have 'self-presence' in his mind (*The Prelude*, ii. 30–32); but more generally it is the present consciousness that speaks of a remote past recreated, remembered sometimes without his being able to give simple reasons for the memory. The most memorable of these memories, I suppose, are those spots of time: the gibbet, the girl with the pitcher, the bleak music of an old stone wall. These are the memories that count, and they count because the language that expresses their freight of emotion is, so to speak, adequately inadequate: it cannot verbalise what was not verbal, and so devoted itself to mystery and even discomfort.

There are other escapes; one of the great things about Wordsworth, as with Augustine, is that one sees them as constituents of that calm society he could, at the end of this story, with pained rejoicing, detect in himself. For loss, and these insistent premonitions of further loss, he needs consolation, a word that occurs, in company with a 'strength' that endures, as early as *The Prelude*, iii. 108 (1805). Yet the fulcrum, the moment of illumination, comes a little later, when, after a night of dancing, he moves through 'a common dawn' and recognises, although making no vows, that nevertheless 'vows were then made for me'; that henceforth he would be, 'else sinning greatly, / A dedicated spirit. On I walked / In blessedness, which even yet remains' (*The Prelude*, iv. 337–45).

The *kind* of experience, here so delicately rendered, recurs in most autobiographies, always as a claim to distinction, to the stigma of individuality, of election, though as a rule far less distinguished. For in the end what distinguishes is not the experience itself but the force and authority of the language claiming it. The religious tone is unmistakable, the sense of involuntary vocation calmly accepted; the boldness and pathos of that 'even yet remains'. It is, we say, pure Wordsworth.

The Prelude is the greatest and most original of English auto-biographies, but it is so not because Wordsworth's intention is so different from most others. What we see particularly clearly in his prose is his desire to break through the assumptions and habits controlling or limiting normal introspection, as they limit poetry. The forces that break through, and enable deeper self-examination, are all anterior in origin to the formation of customary and habitual behaviour, shades of the prison-house; they are deep in the memory and hard to reach because of the distracting mist and clamour of ordinary life. But the memory, for a time at any rate, is accessible, its records can be reached, brought up from the deep store. It is not surprising that Wordsworth used the Platonic trope of anamnesis [the idea that the soul had existed before, in a purer state, where it gained its ideas], for, as Augustine also knew, the memory contains what seems not to have been put into it by the senses. Probably many vocations are discovered by some such process. These deep, vertiginous mnemonic plunges most of us know about from literature rather than from ourselves – not because we are denied them, but because they have to be given appropriate expression or enactment. The question as to what sorts of people are capable of doing this – what sorts of people should be writing autobiography anyway – I must, for the moment, leave unanswered.

Index on Censorship 30 (2001)

Malcolm Bowie, 'Remembering the Future'

'Interessantere Lebenserscheinugen', erwiderte er, 'haben wohl immer dies Doppelgesicht von Vergangenheit und Zukunft, wohl immer sind sie progressiv und regressiv in einem. Sie Zeigen die Zweideutigkeit des Lebens selbst.'

'Life's more interesting phenomena,' he replied, 'probably always have this Janus face towards the past and the future, are probably always progressive and regressive in one. They reveal the ambiguity of life itself.'

Thomas Mann: Doktor Faustus (1947)

Mnemosyne, the goddess of memory and mother of the muses, has enjoyed high prestige as an intellectual aid ever since her appearance in Plato's *Phaedrus* and *Theaetetus*. Divinised or not, memory has been seen as the fountainhead of human knowledge, and the protector of all those who seek wisdom, virtue and truth. What is it about memory that nevertheless makes me uneasy, and willing, with all due modesty, to dissent from the judgement of the centuries? As a technical term it is one of the least threatening items in any psychological or philosophical lexicon. Whether we think of memory as a mental faculty or as a stored and retrievable mental image, it has important tasks of definition to perform. In the former case it helps us to characterise the humanity of human beings, for men and women are by far the most skilful remembering organisms, and in the latter it helps the individual to sustain a continuous sense of personal identity: only I possess exactly these memories arranged in exactly this mobile mosaic. You and I may both take 'blue remembered hills' around with us as mental traces, and we may both see them through the filter of that celebrated phrase from A. E. Housman's *A Shropshire Lad*, but only I have those hills woven together with the bus ticket, the mint imperial and the ominous bank statement that were in my pocket when I stepped out eastwards from the ruins of Cluny Abbey on 3 April 1982. Memory is so closely woven into the texture of our lives that it would be madness to seek ways of unpicking and expelling it. Having qualms about memory makes no more sense than having reservations about air, water or bread, or worrying about the tilt of the earth's axis.

Yet uneasy I remain, and worried. In part this strain of feeling is just a personal rebellion against the commodification of memory that currently rages in publishing, the media and academic research. Perhaps it is memoirs rather than memories that I dislike so, and the rising tide of 'life-writing' in its many lucrative sub-genres. Perhaps the thing that bothers me most is the sentimental sheen that the remembered past so often acquires, the rosy-hued patina that so readily descends on life-events once the machinery of retrospection is set in motion. Tragic awareness is in danger of being lost. And just look at what has happened to nostalgia, I am inclined to grumble when this mood is upon me. It started out as an affliction, a morbid and insistent homesickness. It was to the human sense of belonging to a native place what neuralgia was to nerve tissue and myalgia to muscle: it hurt. But now nostalgia is the slightest and flimsiest of sensations. It is what we feel when we allow ourselves to be tickled by memories, and caressed by a past that has had its claws removed. Modern nostalgia is so obviously delusional and demeaning as a habit of mind, and so shoddy when turned into merchandise, that men and women of good will and discrimination will, one hopes, have no truck with it.

What is happening when memory or one of its main emotional derivatives begins to cause me such an excess of indignation? Am I merely exciting myself with the thought of my own singularity, prancing along in my moral solitude like the man who broke the bank at Monte Carlo, or am I taking a roundabout route to the simple truth that too much memory is a debilitating thing? The answer, I suppose, is that I want memory to be drained of its sentiment, and to prepare itself for a life of action. I want memory to have a prospective dimension, to inhabit the future tense, to bring new worlds into being. And to complete this wish-list, let me add that the new kind of memory I am calling for will, while hurling itself forward in time, remain true to the past, fully able to celebrate its achievements and mourn its losses.

All this will seem a tall order until we remind ourselves that some such cross-weave between past, present and future already exists and is available for inspection. It is to be found in the experience of art, and in those complex acts of remembrance that works of art invite us to perform. A novel, a sonnet or a symphony is a mnemonic device inside which, intricately coiled and coded, is an elaborate set of instructions. These tell us, time-bound creatures that we are, how to handle the time dimension in which all artworks unfold: when to look back, when to look ahead in expectation, and how to layer and interconnect different time-levels inside the onrush of artistic experience. Recognising these instructions in one encounter with art, we are soon able to apply them elsewhere. Listening to Byrd's polyphony prepares us for our first acquaintance with Palestrina's, and becoming accustomed to the tension between forward movement and the vertical layering of voices in Renaissance choral music at large may prepare us for similar-seeming tensions elsewhere: between linear narrative and simultaneous pictorial patterning in a fresco by Masaccio, or between sound-echoes and propositional structure in a Mallarmé sonnet. From one encounter to the next, we become more adept as readers, listeners or viewers, and our increasing proficiency soon begins to supply a further reward. We are able to take the hesitations and two-way pulls of art experience back into our ordinary lives. In the conviction that an exhilarating rather than a maundering style of remembrance is to be found in certain artworks, I shall now examine some cases of strong, future-directed artistic memory, beginning with a late work of Beethoven's.

Labouring at his Thirty-three Variations in C major on a Waltz by Anton Diabelli, Opus 120 (1819–23), Beethoven remembered Mozart's Leporello, and the laborious life of which he sings in the opening measures of *Don Giovanni* (1787):

> Notte e giorno faticar
> Per chi nulla sa gradir;
> Pioggia e vento sopportar,
> Mangiar male e mal dormir!

Slaving night and day/for one whom nothing pleases/enduring rain and wind/ill fed and short of sleep!)

Looking back over the twenty-one variations already composed, and ahead to the deeply expressive culmination of his drama, Beethoven discovered not only a moment of fellow feeling with

Don Giovanni's aggrieved servant but a new potentiality of Diabelli's undistinguished tune. Guided by the hand of a master, the tune turns into Mozart as we listen, or so it seems. From the composer's own viewpoint, it would be more accurate to say that he had noticed the near-identity between Leporello's brief solo and the left hand of Diabelli's piece, stored the resemblance away, and released it on cue when a *coup de théâtre* was called for in the plotting of his own work.

Beethoven's borrowing from Mozart in the twenty-second variation of his Diabelli set prepares the way for a much more elaborate act of homage. As he moves forward to the climax of the work in variations 29–31, his retrospection takes him further back in the eighteenth century, to the mighty summation of baroque variation form that is to be found in J. S. Bach's Goldberg set, BWV 988 (1741). The relationship between the two works is complex. At one level, Beethoven is fired by a sense of creative rivalry with an admired predecessor: he writes thirty-three variations to Bach's thirty, and rises to his high summit of tragic declamation from a much lower starting point than the one that Bach had chosen for himself. Where Bach begins with an exquisite aria that already foretells the tragedy of his variation 26, Beethoven begins with a jaunty waltz of limited predictive power, and moves by slow stages to his final outpouring of grief. Modelling himself on Bach, and placing his lament at exactly the point that Bach had pre-ordained for it, Beethoven nevertheless presents himself as the hero of an improbable process of discovery. Reverence and rebellion are finely balanced.

The Goldberg and Diabelli sets are both encyclopaedic in their range, and bold in their yoking together of disparate styles and conventions. In each the variation principle is relentlessly foregrounded over a very long span of musical invention, and each, considered alone, is a formidable art of memory. In each case a major source of pleasure for the listener is in the gradual saturation of the space of possibility. The rhythmic, melodic, harmonic and dynamic potentialities inherent in the preliminary theme are explored with an insolent display of thoroughness and method. The acoustic domain fills with echoes and reminders as the time of hearing passes. And being able to remember well, across the spectrum of feelings and forms, is an essential skill for the listener. If he already has this skill his advantage is clear. If not, the work itself will school him in the required gambits during successive rehearings. Simpler variations, for all the respite from contrapuntal ingenuity they seem to offer, bring a rich texture of recollected earlier material in their wake. Complex variations seem to be striving for their own effects of extremity and exhaustiveness by way of the multiple resonances they keep in play. The basic picture in each of these capacious works is, therefore, of a forward-driven linear drama wreathed around in silent or inwardly sounding grace-melodies. Each is alive with reminiscence and self-reference.

The Beethoven set becomes still more extraordinary when its underlying Bach-derived template is brought to life. Equipped with knowledge of the Goldberg variations, the listener remembers not only the accumulated previous states of the Beethoven/Diabelli theme but a previous moment in the tradition from which the whole work grew. We not only measure Beethoven's virtuosity against Bach's, and a later against an earlier sequence of bravura exercises, but we superimpose one cumulative and irreversible emotional contour upon another. We hear double, and in so doing move beyond any rivalry between composers towards a limitless absorption of the one into the other. Beethoven thinks within and against the Bach keyboard manner, and invites us to do likewise. Remembrance has become a first-hand medium of artistic expression; the future of the later work, its propulsive power, the individuality of its intentional movement, the new sonority it propounds, have been found in an eager and acquisitive backward leap.

To some, all this will sound too didactic to be a major element of the compositional process, and much too indirect as a route towards aesthetic rapture. It will sound more like a critical history of music in sound than a spontaneous adventure of the acoustic imagination. Those who hesitate in this way are unlikely to be persuaded to change their listening habits by being reminded that Bach and Beethoven themselves are unashamedly learned composers. What is more likely to convince them is the simple fact that remembering under controlled conditions is an essential aim of artistic form, and that memory-events occurring inside the individual artwork are replicated in large format on the wider stage of cultural history.

Beethoven starts from a waltz, and ends with a transcendentalised minuet. His last variation is a recapitulation of his own work seen as a catalogue of dance and other rhythms; it both extends an argument and, summarising it, closes it off. It would make little sense to confine the recapitulatory process to this single work, however, for the work occupies a public world in which musical forms pass freely from hand to hand. Dance-rhythms, to speak only of those, are common property and available off the shelf to any composer who needs them. What is more, Beethoven will have known, without being excessively erudite, that Bach in his instrumental suites and elsewhere had been the dancing master of his age; he had taken jigs, minuets and sarabandes from the dance-floor and made them into staples of the recital room. Remembering Bach's dances was not very different from remembering his own. For the listener, the pleasure to be taken from complex interrelations such as these often feels remarkably simple and direct: the music in performance is haunted by voices, the composer's own and those of his predecessors. Those the performer plays and those the listener silently adds grow together to yield an unparalleled sense of fullness in the time-bound transformational process that the musical work comprises.

For the critic or analyst, the relations between one instrumental work and another may be difficult to construe, but at least a common language exists in which to map their exchanges and divergences. Whether by Bach or by Beethoven, the work is all notes, reverberations and silences; under the sign of Goldberg or of Diabelli, it all takes place at the keyboard. The picture, initially at least, is very different when two art-forms are brought together and when the ambient voices that a given work summons up are from another artistic workshop. When the language of poetry meets pigments and brush-strokes, for example. Here, the critic and the analyst become notably squeamish.

For the most part, we can forget about plenitude and creative memory when scholarship gets to work on meetings of this kind. Titian, for example, belongs firmly to art history, and Ovid to literature and mythography. When the former turns to the latter in search of pictorial subjects, as he does in the great *poesie* commissioned by Philip II of Spain, the craft of the painter overshadows that of the poet, who is reduced, in many learned accounts, to the rank of anthologist or copywriter. Ovid in this view was no poet, and there is no need for the Titian specialist to honour him as one. Ovidians, in the same way, can easily condescend to Titian and treat him as no more than an illustrator, one among hundreds who have swarmed around the *Metamorphoses* for centuries. Yet when the supreme painter plucks Venus and Adonis, Bacchus and Ariadne,

Diana and Actaeon or the contest between Apollo and Marsyas from Ovid's poem an uncanny event begins to unfold. Ovid finds a new reader of extraordinary energy and originality, and an absorbing transitional realm between the arts opens up. A new intermediate species is called into being: a reader-viewer, a recipient of art whose eyes are literate, as Titian's were.

What happens when a viewer brings the experience of literature to the panel or the canvas before him? What kind of manifold event takes place when, looking at Titian's *Perseus and Andromeda* (1554–56) in the Wallace Collection, for instance, the visitor has before his or her mind's eye *Metamorphoses* IV. 660–714 rather than the descriptive label supplied by the gallery? Both artists depict Andromeda chained to a rock, threatened by a sea-monster, and about to be rescued by Perseus. Ovid dwells upon the moment of rapture that propels the slayer of Medusa towards further heroic action:

> quam simul ad duras religatam bracchia cautes
> Vidit Abantiades, nisi quod levis aura capillos
> Moverat et tepido manabant lumina fletu,
> Marmoreum ratus esset opus; trahit inscius ignes
> Et stupet et visae correptus imagine formae
> Paene suas quatere est oblitus in aere pennas (672–7)

(Andromeda was pinioned to a rock./When Perseus saw her, had a wafting breeze/Not stirred her hair, her eyes not overflowed/With trembling tears, he had imagined her/A marble statue. Love, before he knew,/Kindled; he gazed entranced; and overcome/By loveliness so exquisite, so rare,/Almost forgot to hover in the air.)

Titian follows his source closely in producing a visual equivalent to these lines. Breezes waft about Andromeda's person, although it is her modest veil rather than her hair that bears the impress of the wind; her pose and flesh colour recall marble statuary; and the ungainly dive that Perseus launches against the monster suggests that his winged ankles are indeed losing thrust. Cross-referring between the canvas and the verse narrative, tracking not only the painter's adherence to the Ovidian template but also his self-willed departures from it, the reader-viewer begins to take possession of a teasing in-between world.

Yet this is only the start of his adventure, for the works unsettle each other profoundly; each introduces instability and syncopation into the other's characteristic behaviour as an artistic proposition. At the simplest level, Titian rediscovers real cruelty in setting the captive's naked skin against the lacerating teeth of the beast, and in allowing a shape-echo to pass between those teeth and the hooked sword that Perseus wields. By an opposite vein of suggestion, the lightness and comedy of Ovid's verse may prompt us to see the three main actors in Titian's drama as three versions of a single spiralling, insinuating dance. A richer form of interaction between the two works, however, is to be found in their combined play with narrative time.

The painting, if we read it from left to right, as if it were a gigantic printed page, retains Ovid's original order of events: imprisoned Andromeda on the extreme left is followed by the preying monster, which is followed in turn by the flying ace who will destroy the monster and set the victim free. But the painting differs from the verbal narrative in that the rightwards movement of the viewer's eye can be reversed at will, or abandoned in favour of an impatient to-and-fro scansion of the scene. The picture surface is alive with refrain and recall: against the onward flow of events, human gestures, including the artist's brush-strokes, are caught in a rhyme-scheme and a time-scheme of their own. In paint, the outcome of the drama is for ever uncertain, even if we consult Ovid to remind ourselves that this mythical story ends well. At any moment narrative time can be brought to a standstill and the human protagonists left hovering in the face of violent death. A benign sea-rhythm runs through Ovid's lines: images of water and wave carry the story forward through extreme danger to eventual triumph. Titian gives us instead a remorseless ocean that laps indifferently against Andromeda's rock and the scaly sides of a predatory serpent. His heroine in her radiant nakedness is both the victim of an unjust decree and a trophy bride for Perseus, and in both capacities she has her origin in the *Metamorphoses*. Titian insists on the ambiguity, compresses two potential outcomes into a single supercharged instant and restores a tragic resonance to what might otherwise have remained a swaggering romantic exploit. His depiction of elemental force and animal savagery keeps death perpetually in play.

Brush in hand, Titian remembers Ovid, and his act of memory

is easier to grasp, and more rewarding to contemplate, if we remember that brush, and think of the act primarily in painterly terms. Subsidiary questions about the painter's role in this particular encounter between the arts can of course sometimes be rewarding. How much Latin did Titian have, and which of his learned friends helped him to read Ovid in the original? Which vernacular translations of the *Metamorphoses* did Titian know? How familiar was he with the various attempts to 'moralise' or Christianise Ovid that had been produced from the fourteenth century onwards, and to what extent did he rebel against these? In what sense was he himself a moraliser of pagan antiquity? But such questions are much less absorbing than the face-to-face interrogation of one great artist by another. If we allow Ovid and Titian to meet in their own *intermundium*, if we are brazen enough to create such a space for them by our exertions as combined reader and viewer, we can begin to uncover memory as a kinetic principle and creative force. Poetic and pictorial meanings interweave contrapuntally; two rhythms run at once through the time-dimension of art.

The *poesie* for Philip II have no standard format, even though Titian seems to have planned certain of the paintings as pairs, and their Ovidian source materials are used in a variety of ways. One of the projects to which Titian turned in extreme old age takes its cue from the brief and oddly skewed retelling of the Marsyas story to be found in Books VI and XI of the *Metamorphoses*. The satyr Marsyas, having been defeated in a musical contest with Apollo, is flayed alive by the victor. Ovid dwells on this punishment with gruesome relish and comic bravado:

> clamanti cutis est summos direpta per artus,
> nec quicquam nisi vulnus erat; cruor undique manat,
> detectique patent nervi, trepidaeque sine ulla
> pelle micant venae; salientia viscera possis
> et perlucentes numerare in pectore fibras. (VI. 387–91)

(and as he screamed/ Apollo stripped his skin; the whole of him/Was one huge wound, blood streaming everywhere,/Sinews laid bare, veins naked, quivering/And pulsing. You could count his twitching guts,/And the tissues as the light shone through his ribs.)

A new beauty, at once optical and arithmetical, is to be found inside the victim's dissected frame. Ovid then adds an emollient coda: the shepherds who had witnessed the satyr's ordeal wept so profusely that a new, limpid river sprang from their tears. Titian in 1570, on the other hand, will have none of this consolation, and reinforces the horror of the scene by ringing Marsyas round with sharply individualised vignettes of cruelty in action. In the top left corner of the canvas, a beautiful youth clasps his viol in self-absorbed rapture; just below him an artisan specialising in skin removal goes to work with professional application, and lower still Apollo, who kneels, busies himself with his flaying as if this were an act of benevolent homage to his prey; on the right, King Midas reflects disconsolately on the cruelty of gods and men, as a bucket of blood travels past his knee.

This terrifying work has visual as well as literary sources, but compacts and reinvents these in a way that is startlingly original. The viol-player alludes to the youthful musicians who appear often in the paintings of Titian's great Venetian predecessor Giovanni Bellini; Midas re-enacts the pose and replicates the features of Michelangelo's Jeremiah in the Sistine Chapel; and, above all, representations of the Crucifixion are an inescapable reference-point: the agony of Marsyas repeats those of Christ and of St Peter, whose upside-down slaughter, as depicted by Michelangelo in the Cappella Paolina, is likely to have been seen by Titian during his Roman stay in the mid-1540s. The main actors in this scene, including the bearer of the bucket, are all present in the Ovid room of the Palazzo Te in Mantua: Giulio Romano and his assistants had roughed out the immolation of Marsyas almost fifty years before Titian began work on his own version. Yet the mere enumeration of these earlier works does not take us far in understanding the rapaciousness of Titian's memory, and the extremity of his recreative act. He takes artistic practice to a dangerous brink beyond which lie, in the words of A. D. Melville's translation, a 'quivering, pulsing and twitching' of painted surfaces; a cult of gesture and rhythm seems about to supersede the intentional life of individuals; and perspective threatens to dissolve into a picture surface that is either all figure or all ground. The 'argument' of the painting is still more alarming, in that all those who attend upon Marsyas behave either cruelly towards him or with active indifference to his plight. The musician plays on, the philosopher-king cogitates, the workmen flex their muscles, and the young god, as he wields his scalpel, discovers a new politeness and decorum. No one escapes the painter's critique, least of all himself, whose artistry is as much on display as the viol-player's and involves an ecstatic musicalising of paint. This theatre of cruelty would be unthinkable without its backcloth of inherited Christian imagery, but this is the Crucifixion with all trace of catharsis and redemption removed.

One urgent question, however, still needs to be put: where exactly is the future in this interplay between later and earlier works of art? The in-between world of which I have spoken brings Beethoven into dialogue with Bach, Titian into dialogue with Ovid and Michelangelo, and, one might add, Racine with Euripides, Verdi with Shakespeare, Picasso with Velázquez. The list is endless. But surely such dialogue, and the energetic, many-levelled perception that it encourages in enthusiasts for art, is still mainly a backward-looking affair, and likely to be profitable to those who study the predecessors rather than the descendants of a great artist. What about the work of art in its progress through time, in its becoming and its forward flight? One rather limited and over-familiar account of the matter involves the propensity that strong artworks have to call their own progeny into being. Imitation, pastiche, and the sheer staying power of highly individualised artistic styles do indeed allow us to see futures being created before our eyes. One way of beginning to understand the singularity of, say, Leonardo or Caravaggio is to follow the fortunes of the *leonardeschi* in Lombardy or of the *caravaggisti* across Europe as a whole. Bohemian music in the late eighteenth and early nineteenth centuries is a tribute to the diffusive power of the classical style consolidated by Haydn and Mozart and centred on Habsburg Vienna.

When it comes to individual works, these migrations into the future can offer a powerful incitement to fresh awareness. Titian's Marsyas, for example, reappears as an informative background in Tom Phillips's portrait of Iris Murdoch (1984–86): Apollo's dissecting arm and hand, appearing over Murdoch's head, allude to the charismatic cruelty of many of her principal male characters. Those who travel back to Titian's work with this modern portrait in mind will perhaps find themselves reflecting anew on the closeness of meditative Midas to the scene of torture. Midas like Murdoch is a philosopher who does his thinking inside the force-field of unspeakable deeds; perhaps their serenity as thinkers is obscurely connected to the smell of blood. On the broad canvas of cultural history, time has its own elasticity: works of art travel forward into the future, and later works alter the past by retroaction. Kafka can help us reread the Dickens of whom he only half approved. The book of Exodus is never quite the same again for those who expose their nervous systems to the speech-song and the orchestral tumult of Schoenberg's *Moses und Aron*. Even where there is no documented link between a later and an earlier work, this circling back from future to past can still take place: Rodin's *Le Penseur*, for example, could be just as potent as Michelangelo's Jeremiah to anyone seeking dialogue-partners for Titian's dejected king.

Yet the dialectic of past and future to be found in cases like these, even if it points us in the direction of a general rule about artistic experience, is too bland to be useful as an exploratory tool when the inner grain of an individual work comes into view. At this level, the future is created word by word, note by note, dab by dab of colour, and the aggregation of these micro-elements in the *facture* of the work as a whole offers a serviceable bridge between the author and the receiver of that work, for both travel from poverty to plenty as time passes.

I spoke earlier about the variation principle, and the two grandest keyboard works embodying it that Europe has produced. But other formal conventions offer an equally arresting perspective on the becomingness and 'futurality' that inheres in the art of music. In a baroque ritornello movement, in a sonata argument on the classical Viennese model, or in the articulation of a tone-row by composers of the second Viennese school, musical time is governed by two conjoined imperatives. Continuity and change are both insisted upon, and development proceeds in such a way that material from the past is both recapitulated and superseded by an ever-incipient future. In each of these conventions the work is Janus-faced moment by moment. As the clock or the metronome ticks, implications are made explicit, potentialities are actualised and a fullness previously merely glimpsed is brought to birth in sound. A pressure towards completion runs as a magnetic force through the incomplete propositions that the work sets forth and interlaces. The future is the open arena into which artistic memory surges.

Describing in these terms the forward motion of the remembering mind might at first seem to confine us to the realms of music or literary narrative, those time-dwelling arts *par excellence*. But painting, too, is dynamic and propulsive even when it seeks to dissociate itself from the storyteller's art. Wherever we begin our viewing of a Titian canvas, we enter a world of promises, prefigurations and echoes. As the eye travels across the painted surface, inventing depths and three-dimensional layerings as it goes, the beholder rediscovers the time-axis both of his formal preferences and of his underlying appetites. In the wake of the painter, he moves from incompleteness to plenitude; he realises possibilities, tries out internal relations – discarding some, accepting others – and segment by segment refashions his memories of the work in order to collude with its becoming. If Titian characterised in this way begins to sound like Cézanne, Mondrian or Jackson Pollock, so much the better – for we are talking about that indwelling in the stuff of time that great artists across the ages do indeed share.

My own temporal preferences will by now be clear. I want the Janus-time of art's unfolding to flow back variously into the time of ordinary living and, in doing so, to protect me from the complacencies and sentimental trappings of the merely nostalgic backward gaze. Strict border controls will not serve these wishes well, especially as I am greedy and want my pantheon of art experiences to be as large and richly populated as possible. So far, and not altogether helpfully, I have admitted to my discussion long works and long-drawn-out processes of elaboration, as if time were more time-like when it arrived in an immense convoy of moments. But there is no need to reach for the *Divine Comedy*, the Sistine ceiling, or Wagner's *Der Ring des Nibelungen* in order to find clinching support for what is, after all, a modest enough claim.

Brief or small-scale works – miniatures, maxims, Cycladic statuettes, Beethoven's bagatelles rather than his epic Diabelli soundscape – have their own intentional life, their own sprung rhythms, and their own effects of copiousness and completion. Act IV of *Measure for Measure*, for example, begins with a brief song of singular beauty:

> Take, oh take those lips away,
>   That so sweetly were forsworn,
> And those eyes, the break of day,
>   Lights that do mislead the morn;
> But my kisses bring again, bring again,
> Seals of love, but sealed in vain, sealed in vain

and Giuseppe Ungaretti in 1917, also writing about the impact of morning light, went even further in the art of reduction:

> m'illumino
> d'immenso.

In both these cases a strong temporal pulse is created by the sparest of grammatical means. Shakespeare's lines travel from the removal to the restoration of the beloved's body, and from an earlier to a later imagined future. And both events, the taking away and the bringing back, are sensuously realised: the mouth is sweet, and the eyes bright, even as they are cast aside; and the lovers' lips are sealed together even as a warning voice, enlisting a different meaning of the verb 'to seal', hints at subsequent loss and betrayal. An intimate rhythm of desire has been rediscovered in the space between two contrasted imperatives. Nothing happens in the poem, apart from a clash between two virtual events. Ungaretti finds his pulse in the indicative rather than the imperative mood. His four words, sealed together in a sumptuous display of assonance and alliteration, are the point at which two times, two meanings of the present tense, converge. The poet summons up an instant that is singular and un-repeatable on the one hand, and endlessly able to reproduce itself on the other: I do this once; I do this continually; I do this indefi-nitely often. A galvanic spasm passes between two temporalities as we read. In miniature, both poets give us the whole of desire-time.

The future is ubiquitous, then, in desire-driven works of art, and the future is assembled from whatever contingent materials happen to be at hand. The new work emerges from memories, from sense-impressions, from the whole rag-and-bone shop in which the acquis-itive artist lodges. Its looking back is a looking forward. Writers quote and misquote each other. Painters and musicians readily turn to literature as a spur to their creativity. Choreographers turn melody and instrumental colour into silent dance-steps. This limit-less criss-cross of influence is familiar enough, and can be alarming when certain monumental works are at issue. Virgil's *Aeneid*, for example, begins to levitate in a dazzling prismatic display when we bring to mind its transformation at the hands of Dante, Ariosto, Purcell, Ingres, Berlioz, Hermann Broch and so many others from across the artistic genres and media.

One class of artistic practitioner seems, however, especially worth acknowledging at the end of this brief homage to art inflamed by the future. I am thinking of those writers who, far from simply nodding to their predecessors or signalling their approval of other art-forms, set out in headlong pursuit of works not their own, write for their lives about the achievement of others, and rediscover the time of creation in the fever of their own prose. Everyone will have his or her favourite examples of this style of verbal performance, and I shall confine myself here to a handful of passages relating directly to artists I have already mentioned. Walter Pater writing about Leonardo's *Mona Lisa* and Freud describing the intellectual passion that sustains Leonardo's *œuvre* as a whole are both touched by the demon of poetic invention. Vasari in his life of Giulio Romano writes about the Palazzo Te with more than mere enthusiasm: his sparkling words seem to lift Giulio's building blocks into position and cover the interior walls with the erotic panorama of his frescos. And no one has written more searchingly about Beethoven than Thomas Mann in the early chapters of *Doktor Faustus*, where the last piano sonata – Opus 111 in C major – is re-performed in prose. Mann's language offers at once a critical reading of the work, a tribute to its strangeness, and an engaging comedy of intellectual manners.

In all these cases, the memory of an earlier artwork is the trigger that sets a new artwork going. The new work is not a gloss, an exposition or a commentary but the reinvention of an experience, with all its risks and hazards left in place. The writers I have mentioned, even as they celebrate a new birth and make possible worlds real, are unillusioned about the human future in the longer term. They do not idealise it. They know that it will contain very bad news as well as good, and this knowledge gives their writing about art its precarious beauty and its disconsolate joy.

Craig Raine, 'Memory in Literature'

In *A la recherche du temps perdu*, Proust says many acute things about memory – about physical memory in the body, for instance, in *Du côté de chez Swann*. One assents and thinks of Robert Frost's 'After Apple-Picking': 'My instep arch not only keeps the ache, / It keeps the pressure of a ladder-*round* [my italics].'

Proust is good, too, on memory's inaccuracy and its arbitrariness. Think of Albertine's wandering beauty spot in *A l'ombre des jeunes filles en fleurs* or Marcel's observation in *Le temps retrouvé* that one forgets the duel one nearly fought but remembers the yellow gaiters one's opponent wore as a child in the Champs-Elysées. A strikingly dramatic but implausible illustration, this, almost worthy of Henry Carr's slippage and distortion in Stoppard's *Travesties* – where sartorial details, reveres and darts and flares, are given a Wodehousian precedence over world events. Less good, though, than Henry V's prediction that soldiers at Agincourt will remember their part in the battle 'with advantages'.

I prefer, too, T.S. Eliot's more sober sense of arbitrariness in the 'Conclusion' to *The Use of Poetry and the Use of Criticism*: 'Why, for all of us, out of all we have heard, seen, felt, in a lifetime, do certain images recur, charged with emotion, rather than others? The song of one bird, the leap of one fish, at a particular place and time, the scent of one flower, an old woman on a German mountain path, six ruffians seen through an open window playing cards at night at a small French railway junction, where there was a water-mill: such memories may have symbolic value, but of what we cannot tell, for they come to represent the depths of feeling into which we cannot peer.'

They are, then, these memories, super-charged with sensation – sensation which is powerful, but indescribable. This sensation – of significance, of occluded feeling – is the subject of this essay. Can we describe it? Can we say what it means?

Proust is interested in the particular sensation that accompanies remembering. The tea-soaked madeleine loses its force when it is repeatedly tasted. Tom Stoppard recorded something similar in the first issue of *Talk* magazine when he wrote 'On Turning Out to be Jewish' (September 1999). He meets in Czechoslovakia a woman whose cut has been stitched decades before by Doctor Straussler, the father he never knew: 'Zaria holds out her hand, which still shows the mark. I touch it. In that moment I am surprised by grief, a small catching-up of all the grief I owe. I have nothing that came from my father, nothing he owned or touched, but here is his trace, a small scar.' A moving moment. But Stoppard has recorded unsentimentally that its power to move diminishes every time he tells the story.

Is the sensation simply nostalgia – like the nostalgic regret of Nicholas Bulstrode in *Middlemarch* for the time when he was an effective Methodist preacher in Islington's Upper Row with an ambition to be a missionary? Or is it something more profound – like Proust's meditation, in *A l'ombre des jeunes filles en fleurs*, on his Aunt Léonie's sofa in the brothel? On that same sofa, Marcel has first experienced love with a girl cousin. Proust gives us a stereoscopic irony as the seedy and the pre-sexual amalgamate. There seems to be a hidden message in the coincidence. Is the coincidence merely a coincidence? Or has the coincidence been arranged? Elements of this supernatural innuendo emerge repeatedly in Nabokov's *Speak, Memory*. General Kuropatkin is showing the young Nabokov tricks with matches on a sofa, when he is summoned away: 'the loose matches jumping up on the divan as his weight left it'. Fifteen years later, the disguised, fugitive general asks Nabokov's father for a light . . . Nabokov says the true purpose of autobiography is 'the following of such thematic designs through one's life'.

In Book XI of *The Prelude*, Wordsworth writes about significant yet insignificant memories as 'spots of time':

> There are in our existence spots of time
> Which with distinct pre-eminence retain
> A vivifying Virtue, whence, depress'd
> By false opinion and contentious thought,
> Or aught of heavier or more deadly weight,
> In trivial occupations, and the round

> Of ordinary intercourse, our minds
> Are nourished and invisibly repair'd . . .

This explanation isn't an explanation at all. It is a statement of intrigued bafflement: 'the hiding places of my power / Seem open; I approach and then they close.' And the example that Wordsworth gives is interestingly drab. It has a few meagre components – a 'naked Pool, / The Beacon on the lonely Eminence, / The Woman and her garments vex'd and toss'd' – and its power is largely retrospective. It is 'in truth, / An ordinary sight'. Looked back on, though, the dreariness becomes a 'visionary dreariness' that Wordsworth would need colours and words unknown to man to paint. The discrepancy here, in Eliot, and in Proust, is between the original experience and that experience when it is hallowed by remembrance.

The effect is something like cropping in photography. Though each of these writers professes to be *bouleversé* by the detail of the experience, actually the experiences are vital because they exist cropped of context, shorn of explanation. At the beginning of *The Waves*, Virginia Woolf gives us the childhood memories of Rhoda, Louis, Bernard, Susan and Neville as highlights, ordinary epiphanies: Mrs Constable pulling up her black stockings; a flash of birds like a handful of broadcast seed; bubbles forming a silver chain at the bottom of a saucepan; air warping over a chimney; light going blue in the morning window. These mnemonic pungencies are different from the *Bildungsroman* of Joyce's *A Portrait of the Artist as a Young Man* as that novel gets into its stride. They resemble rather the unforgettable anthology of snapshots Joyce gives us at the novel's beginning – a snatch of baby-talk; the sensation of wetting the bed; covering and uncovering your ears at refectory. Or Bellow's *Augie March*, when Augie is a kind of shipboard unofficial counsellor, the recipient of emotional swarf: 'Now this girl, who was a cripple in one leg, she worked in the paint lab of the stove factory'; 'He was a Rumania-box type of swindler, where you put in a buck and it comes out a fiver'. Cropped for charisma.

Of course, memory itself is naturally cropped, as Stendhal records in Chapter 13 of *Vie de Henri Brulard*, where he notes that some memories are undated, vivid as fragmented frescoes, but surrounded by the blank brickwork of oblivion.

Actually, *anything* fragmented, as the romantics knew from

Percy's *Reliques*, is granted a penumbra of suggestion that we mistake and read as vividness of outline. A perfect example is Auden's 'Journey to Iceland':

> The site of a church where a bishop was put in a bag,
> the bath of a great historian, the fort where
> an outlaw dreaded the dark,
>
> remember the doomed man thrown by his horse and crying
> *Beautiful is the hillside. I will not go,*
> the old woman confessing *He that I loved the*
> *best, to him was I worst.*

Memories are more effective than memoirs. Isolation counts for more than continuity. The Paris of Hemingway's *A Moveable Feast* is less vivid than the same material telescoped in 'The Snows of Kilimanjaro'.

This is *A Moveable Feast*: 'All of the sadness of the city came suddenly with first cold rains of winter, and there were no more tops to the white houses as you walked but only the wet blackness of the street and the closed doors of the small shops, the herb sellers, the stationery and the newspaper shops, the midwife – second class – and the hotel where Verlaine had died, where I had a room on the top floor where I worked.' It isn't just the clumsiness of the three 'where's. It's the automatic, sentimental cliché that poisons *A Moveable Feast* – the *flyblown* yellowed poster, the unknown girl at the café 'with a face fresh as a newly minted coin if they minted coins in smooth flesh with rain-freshened skin, and her hair was black as a crow's wing and cut sharply and diagonally across her cheek'.

Nostalgia, as Kundera redefines it in *Ignorance*, is 'the suffering caused by an unappeased yearning to return'. In *A Moveable Feast*, Hemingway fails to return to his past, he is exiled from his memories, because his prose is writing itself and he is having a hard time keeping up.

In 'The Snows of Kilimanjaro', on the other hand, the detail is seen and hand-picked: 'There never was another part of Paris that he loved like that, the sprawling trees, the old white plastered houses painted brown below, the long green of the autobus in that round square, the purple flower dye upon the paving, the sudden drop down the hill of the rue Cardinal Lemoine to the River, and the other way the narrow crowded world of the rue Mouffetard. The street that ran up toward the Pantheon and the other that he always took with the bicycle, the only asphalted street in all that quarter, smooth under the tyres, with the high narrow houses and the cheap tall hotel where Paul Verlaine had died.' By 1964, Hemingway has forgotten the flower dye and the round square. His memory fails. So his memories fail.

Nostalgia, of course, has a non-Kunderan meaning, less connected with suffering and more with emotional indulgence. As in, 'they wallowed in nostalgia'. Here the territory is thick with shared memories, with mnemonic solidarity. For example, Ursula in *Women in Love* remembers 'the servant Tilly, who used to give her bread and butter sprinkled with brown sugar'. In one of Edna O'Brien's novels, the heroine sits on the step of the back door, eating sugar on bread.

In *Le temps retrouvé*, Marcel floats a theory of involuntary memory which he opposes to the willed act of memory. The theory is founded on three rapidly consecutive examples less famous than the madeleine in *Du côté de chez Swann*.

They are as follows. Two uneven paving stones outside the Princesse de Guermantes's mansion recall two particular paving stones in the Baptistry of San Marco in Venice. The *ting* of a teaspoon against a plate recalls the noise of a railway man's hammer testing the wheels of the Paris train as it stood outside a wood – when Marcel (twenty pages earlier) reflected on his lack of talent for literature, a verdict based on his apparent indifference to nature. 'I am in the midst of nature. Well, it is with indifference, with boredom that my eyes register the line which separates your radiant foreheads from your shadowy trunks.' Now the formerly tedious scene dazes Marcel with its previously unmentioned specifics – opening a bottle of beer, hearing the tapped wheels. The experience is experienced with its accessories. And, lastly, the texture of a napkin brings back the very texture of Marcel's bathing towel at Balbec. The napkin contains the towel, which contains an ocean green and blue as a peacock's tail – *the* ocean, since involuntary memory never recalls the indefinite article.

Involuntary memory, in this account, restores reality in its entirety, with all its qualia intact, and is therefore a form of resurrection. It is, further, a kind of 'immortality'. Marcel, accordingly, feels joy that makes death a matter of indifference to him. His faith in his literary talent is restored by the intensity with which he recalls these essentially banal experiences.

The idea is shared, or perhaps borrowed, by Nabokov, a much greater writer, in Chapter 3 of *Speak, Memory* (Part VI): 'I see again my class-room, the blue roses of the wallpaper, the open window. Its reflection fills the oval mirror above the leathern couch where my uncle sits, gloating over a tattered book. A sense of security, of well-being, of summer warmth pervades my memory. That robust reality makes a ghost of the present. The mirror brims with brightness; a bumblebee has entered the room and bumps against the ceiling. Everything is as it should be, nothing will ever change, nobody will ever die.' In Nabokov's account, memory is complete, beyond process, exempt from change. The reasoning here is coherent.

Proust's exposition of 'fragments of existence withdrawn from Time' is somewhat muzzy by comparison: 'the truth surely was that the being within me which had enjoyed these impressions had enjoyed them because they had in them something that was common to a day long past and to the present, because in some way they were extra-temporal, and this being made its appearance only when, through one of these identifications of the present with the past, it was likely to find itself in the one and only medium in which it could exist and enjoy the essence of things, that is to say: outside time'.

In any case, Proust's laborious explanation is partial. He has not elucidated the mechanism of memory properly. The mystery that needs explanation is why the recalled experience should bring such acute pleasure when the actual, original experience was 'tedious', and therefore unapprehended.

Proust's 'answer' is that we experience intimations of immortality. It is possible, though, that we simply enjoy the act of remembrance – and that this requires no explanation. It is a fact, the way we are, part of any human being's hard-wiring.

On the other hand, the pleasure is extraordinary. It is comparable to 'the constant readiness to discern the halo round the frying pan or the likeness between a weeping-willow and a Skye terrier'. That simile from Nabokov's *The Real Life of Sebastian Knight* is a clue to the true nature of memory's mechanism, as I hope to explain.

Memory is like metaphor in its operations.

Memory is sexual in its operations.

In English we speak of 'coming' when we speak of orgasm. 'I'm coming' means that the sexual partner is arriving at the predestined place, the site of pleasure. The journey can be long or short but the elusive destination is known in advance.

The words Marcel uses to describe the pleasure that accompanies his three involuntary memories are 'a shudder of happiness', 'avec un tel frémissement de bonheur'. Not that this is explicitly or exclusively sexual. The word 'frémissement' can be applied to fear, anger, as well as pleasure. It is, too, according to my *Petit Robert*, a light (*léger*) sensation, rather than Eliot's 'blood shaking the heart'. The other word Marcel uses is 'joie'. In French, another word for joy, 'jouissance', is also the word for coming, for 'plaisir sexuel'. 'Jouissance' seems less pedestrian than 'coming'. But having an orgasm – or 'orgasme' – is '*parvenir* à la jouissance'. And 'parvenir' means to arrive at a predetermined point.

In English we use the French word 'parvenu' to suggest someone who is socially ambitious, someone who has only recently achieved social prominence, social *heights* – an assiduous social corkscrew, someone who isn't a someone, but someone who is a nobody. 'One of the low on whom assurance sits / As a silk hat on a Bradford millionaire.'

Our other word, also French, for such a person is an *arriviste*[1] – someone who has just arrived at the desired destination.

I suggest that the pleasure, the joy *really* experienced by Marcel, and by the rest of us, is bound up with the sensation of imminence, suspense and arrival – common to sex and simile.

Memory is metaphorical in its operations. The pleasure experienced by Marcel is primarily the actual act of remembrance, and only secondarily in the recovered detail of what is remembered. In each of these three involuntary memories, Marcel experiences a delay. The paving stones are like . . . what? The teaspoon is like . . . what? The texture of the napkin is exactly like . . . what? Marcel claims the recall is instant, but it isn't. As he tests the uneven paving stones, he has to repeat the initial movement exactly: 'Every time that I merely repeated this physical movement, I achieved nothing;

---

[1]. When Paul Pennyfeather marries Margot Beste-Chetwynde in Waugh's *Decline and Fall*, his social elevation, from schoolmaster to millionaire, is marked by his shopping: 'Paul, with unaccustomed prodigality, bought two new ties, three pairs of shoes, an umbrella, and a set of Proust.'

but if I succeeded, forgetting the Guermantes party, in recapturing what I had felt when I first placed my feet on the ground in this way, again the dazzling and *indistinct* [my italics] vision fluttered near me, as if to say: "Seize me as I pass if you can, and try to solve the *riddle* [my italics] of happiness I set you." '

The pleasure of memory is the pleasure we experience when we read a good simile – the pleasure of difference between the two things being compared, the pleasure we take in the justice of the comparison and the sensation of comprehension. Every good simile is a kind of riddle. X is like Y. Why is X like Y? The mind sifts the evidence for and against, seeking the evidence for. Why is a Bang and Olufsen television set like Darth Vader? Because it has a dark screen, unlike most conventional television sets. There are a million ways in which a B & O television set *isn't* like Darth Vader. The fractional delay in any simile occurs while the mind works out the way in which the B & O television *is* like Darth Vader. Marcel solves the riddle of what the paving stones remind him of. He arrives at a solution, he *comes* to the occluded destination, to the only conclusion retrospectively possible.

At its most banal, this process is what Bloom experiences in the 'Lestrygonians' episode of *Ulysses* when he tries to remember a name across twenty-odd pages. Finally, it comes to him: 'Pen. Pen. Penrose.' The itch is scratched. The search has come to a conclusion.

At its most complex, it is Molly's recollection at the end of *Ulysses* of losing her virginity to Bloom on Howth Head. Whereas in Proust, the present provokes a specific memory of the past, Molly's memory of Howth is underlaid with an earlier memory, and, surrendering to Bloom, she surrenders also to an earlier lover: 'yes when I put the rose in my hair like the Andalusian girls used or shall I wear a red yes and how he kissed me under the Moorish wall and I thought well as well him as another . . .' Molly's first proper kiss and her first full act of intercourse are conflated. Lieutenant Jack or Joe or Harry Mulvey (Molly can't remember his Christian name) is twinned with Leopold Bloom. Memory as multiple orgasm, so to speak.

In 1948, Vladimir Nabokov began *Speak, Memory* with a phrase that was later lifted by Samuel Beckett and vulgarised in *Waiting for Godot*: 'the cradle rocks above the abyss'. (In Beckett, 'we give birth astride the grave'. Twice.) The word 'remember' is itself an implicit rejoinder to death. Its etymology counters dismemberment. It is very rare therefore to encounter a flat rejection of memory like Ursula Brangwen's in *Women in Love*: 'She wanted to have no past. She wanted to have come down from the slopes of heaven to this place, with Birkin, not to have rolled out of the murk of her childhood and her upbringing, slowly, all soiled. She felt that memory was a dirty trick played upon her. What was this decree that she should "remember"! Why not a bath of pure oblivion, a new birth, without any recollection or blemish of past life.'

Of course, Lawrence had a low opinion of Proust: 'too much jelly-water: I can't read him.' As did Evelyn Waugh, who wrote to Nancy Mitford (16 March 1948): 'I am reading Proust for the first time – in English of course – and am surprised to find him a mental defective. No one warned me of that. He has absolutely no sense of time. He can't remember anyone's age. In the same summer as Gilberte gives him a marble & Françoise takes him to a public lavatory in the Champs-Elysées, Bloch takes him to a brothel.' Nor was Joyce keen to be matched against Proust. On 24 October 1920, Joyce wrote to Frank Budgen: 'I observe a furtive attempt to run a certain M Marcel Proust of here against the signatory of this letter. I have read some pages of his. I cannot see any special talent but I am a bad critic.'

On the whole, though, Proust's influence makes itself felt wherever memory is important.

In spite of his confession in 1948 that he hadn't read *A la recherche*, Waugh's *Brideshead Revisited* (1945) is clearly influenced by an *idea* of Proust's novel. Not only is there a reference to Charlus – the toady don Mr Samgrass spends 'a cosy afternoon with the incomparable Charlus' – but there are several uncharacteristic extended metaphors stretching for a paragraph at a time. Uncharacteristic of Waugh – and though a famously Proustian trope, one less frequent, it is my impression, in the later volumes of *A la recherche*, where the sentences themselves are pithier, more Waugh-like. And Charles Ryder, Waugh's narrator, encapsulates his theme at the beginning of Book III: 'My theme is memory ... These memories, which are my life – for we possess nothing certainly except the past – were always with me. Like the pigeons of St Mark's ...' An extended metaphor ensues. Is it a coincidence or a Freudian slip that the pigeons are situated in San Marco, a locus central to *Le temps retrouvé*?

I should say, too, that Virginia Woolf's *The Years* – with its time range from 1880 to 1937, its repeated motifs, its chronological gaps during which characters alter dramatically – was an attempt to emulate Proust in English. Delia's party at the end of *The Years* gathers all the narrative's aged survivors in one place, just as Proust assembles his survivors at the Princesse de Guermantes's, where their aged appearances are ironically and famously described as fancy dress – an extended conceit that begins brilliantly but soon shows signs of strain, like a man with asthma holding his breath.

Of course, Virginia Woolf idolised Proust: on 6 May 1922 she wrote to Roger Fry, 'Proust so titillates my own desire for expression that I can hardly get out a sentence. Oh if I could write like that! I cry. And at the moment such is the astonishing vibration and saturation and intensification he procures – theres [*sic*] something sexual in it – that I feel I *can* write like that and seize my pen and then I *can't* write like that. Scarcely anyone so stimulates the nerves of language in me: it becomes an obsession. But I must return to Swann.' Fulsome praise, though in October she is still on Volume 1. Three years later, on 9 February 1925, Woolf tells Margaret Llewelyn Davies that she's only read three volumes. No obstacle to her claim on 21 April 1927 to her sister Vanessa that Proust is 'far the greatest novelist'.

She seems, however, never to have actually finished reading *A la recherche*. In a 1928 newspaper piece, 'Preferences', she writes 'I have also bought and propose to read should my life last long enough the final volumes of Proust's masterpiece.' (*Le temps retrouvé* was published in 1927.) On 27 April 1934, she tells Ethel Smyth she's reading *Sodom et Gomorrhe*. And on 21 May 1934, again to Ethel Smyth: 'I cant [*sic*] write myself within its arc; that's true; for years I've put off finishing it.'

And yet in April, May, June of 1929, her three-part essay 'Phases of Fiction'[2] claims that Proustian psychology is an advance on Henry James, while adding the qualification that the 'expansion of sympathy' is almost self-defeating. Everything in Proust, however trivial, provokes an extended meditation. 'Proust is determined to bring before the reader every piece of evidence upon which any

---

2. The only two specific citations in 'Phases of Fiction' are both to Volume 3 *Le coté de Guermantes* – to p. 385 (Marcel saying he is not asleep as he is woken by his mother to go to his grandmother's deathbed) and to p. 688 (Swann telling the Duchesse de Guermantes that he will be dead in three or four months as she gets into her carriage to go out to dinner).

state of mind is founded.' The risk is that the commentary is surplus to requirements, that there is no hierarchy of importance – that the footnotes bury the trickle of text, as it were. 'We lose the sense of outline.'

How do we account for Virginia Woolf's high opinion of Proust if it is so precariously founded? It is partially explained by this hyperventilating assessment to Roger Fry on 3 October 1922: 'One has to put the book down with a gasp. The pleasure becomes phys-ical – like sun and wine and grapes and perfect serenity and intense vitality combined. *Far otherwise is it with* Ulysses: *to which I bind myself like a martyr to a stake, and have thank God, now finished – My martyrdom is over. I hope to sell it for £4.10.* [my italics]'[3] Joyce was right when he told Budgen: 'I observe a furtive attempt to run a certain M Marcel Proust of here against the signatory of this letter.' For Virginia Woolf, Proust was a way of putting her rival Joyce in his place – and a way, too, of acceding easily to the preferential judgements of homosexual Bloomsbury.

One is queasy, however, at her little litany of praise – grapes, Evian water, pinot noir and the seafront at Cannes! – because its blowsy imprecision suggests impeccable ignorance. And although her essays refer often to Proust, one sometimes wonders if she had read as little as Evelyn Waugh.

Her essay, 'Pictures', invokes a Proustian scene in a theatre, in which 'we have to understand the emotions of a young man for a lady in the box below'. Andrew McNeillie, the editor of the essays, does not identify this minutely, yet vaguely, invoked incident. Nor can I find it. (When Marcel goes to see Berma in *Le côté de Guermantes*, he is in the stalls looking *up* at the boxes.) It is, in any case, dangerously close to nonsense: 'At the same time our senses drink in all this our minds are tunnelling, logically and intel-lectually, into the obscurity of the young man's emotions which, as they ramify and modulate and stretch further and further, at last penetrate so far, peter out into such a shred of meaning, *that we can scarcely follow any more* [my italics] were it not that suddenly, in flash after flash, metaphor after metaphor, the eye lights up that cave of darkness, and we are shown the hard, tangible, material shapes of bodiless thoughts hanging like bats in the primeval dark-ness where light never visited them before.' As I type this out, I

---

3. Very different from her public assessment in the *Times Literary Supplement* (23 May 1918), where she lauded the spirituality of *Ulysses*.

am hardly surprised it corresponds exactly to nothing factual in
Proust. It is an *hommage* to Proust's obscurity.

Beckett wrote a brief (and intermittently unreadable) monograph
about Proust and *Krapp's Last Tape* is a kind of dwarf *A la
recherche*, shrunk in the wash. On the one hand, there is the unforgettable (but ironically forgotten) physical memory of the black
ball in the dog's mouth: 'a small, old, black, hard. Solid rubber
ball. (*Pause.*) I shall feel it, in my hand, until my dying day.' On
the other hand, there is the hypnotic memory of the punt and the
girl. Ruth Miller, an early Bellow biographer, remembered Bellow
reading to her the passage in *Le temps retrouvé* when Marcel is
stuck in his train in a field. In *Herzog*, Herzog persecutes his friend
Nachman with 'the engine of his memory'. And Bellow's *The
Adventures of Augie March* owes a debt to Proust as well as a
more obvious debt to Twain's *The Adventures of Huckleberry Finn*
and the American vernacular. When Augie announces that he 'will
go at things' in his 'own way', 'free-style', and that his memories
will be set down as they arrive, 'first to knock, first admitted', he
is not in fact going at things entirely in his own way. It is also the
Guermantes' way, Swann's way, and Proust's way – the way of
involuntary memory.

Ignês Sodré, 'Where the Lights and Shadows Fall: on not being able to remember and not being able to forget'

Thus the shadow of the object fell upon the ego.

(Freud, Mourning and Melancholia)

It was the whiteness of the whale that above all things appalled me.

(Melville, *Moby Dick*)

As the child's mind was growing into knowledge, his mind was growing into memory: as her life unfolded, his soul, long stupefied in a cold narrow prison, was unfolding too, and trembling gradually into full consciousness.

(George Eliot, *Silas Marner*)

'As the child's mind was growing into knowledge, his mind was growing into memory': in this amazing phrase George Eliot describes Silas Marner's emergence from a state of severe melancholic withdrawal into full lively consciousness. The connection between the availability of significant emotional memories to conscious thought and the sense of the very existence of the self and its relation to others is central to her conception of the mind when creating her character. The direct parallel with the development of the child's mind implies that this transformation from what she calls an 'insect-like' state into full humanity, this 'trembling gradually into consciousness', is a psychological rebirth: a new 'stepping into the light', in Damasio's inspiring phrase.

In this essay I will examine, from a psychoanalytical point of view, this particular kind of lack of 'illumination' in the conscious mind, a regression to a memory-less state of almost complete darkness, of being psychically reduced to the faint glow of candlelight. I will also examine the emotional inability to forget, as these apparently opposite psychological problems in fact belong to the same area of the psychopathology of memory. I am thinking about the problem of an excessive 'illumination' of particular events in the mind which compulsively steal the limelight, which can be the consequence of trauma, that is to say, of the ego being overwhelmed by an experience it cannot deal with. Traumatic experience may return unmodified to the conscious mind as if it is never transformed into a proper memory, psychologically remaining perpetually in the present.[1] Excessive fear, excessive grief, or an excessive sense of grievance create situations where ordinary forgetting cannot take place.

When considering the lack of habitual connection to autobiographical memory portrayed in *Silas Marner*, I am not thinking about what was Freud's first and monumental discovery in the early days of psychoanalysis, the mechanism of repression which made disturbing memories unavailable to consciousness, with noxious effects on psychic functioning: 'hysterics suffer from (unconscious) reminiscences', neurotic symptoms could be resolved through the recovering of a disturbing memory. Silas's melancholic withdrawal into what George Eliot calls 'this Lethean influence of exile, in which the past has become dreamy because its symbols have all vanished, and the present too is dreamy because it is linked to no memories', is a state in which all good experience has become unreal and irrelevant, rather than unconscious or obliterated; the past can be retrieved in a minimal, half-dead way, but can only be brought back in full, integrated, organic form through a powerful emotional connection that infuses it again with symbolic relevance.

In normal functioning, the present is fully itself and at the same time illuminated by relevant bits of the past; one's sense of identity is dependent on one's autobiographical self: my being who I am depends on experiencing an emotionally connected 'now' whilst being who I was at all different stages throughout my life. (These memories are partly conscious and partly implicit in one's way of

---

[1.] What Freud discovered in relation to war trauma, and we know so well now in post-traumatic stress disorders, is that an indigestible, overwhelming event keeps re-invading the mind with the fresh impact of an experience in the present; fear and horror are there as if the inimical person or thing is present in the room. We also know that infantile trauma can be repeated through a re-enactment of the abuse situation, but with the roles reversed: child abusers are often abused children, who are compelled to repeat the unbearable violence through identification with the aggressor, in an (unconscious) attempt to master the trauma by projecting it into a new victim. In this case, the disturbing memory remains unconscious but so concrete that it needs to be re-enacted in external reality.

being.) The existence of a multi-faceted future in the present of the mind (what Damasio calls 'memory of the future') is of course also dependent on intrinsic connections with multiple, flexible versions of past selves. Silas's absent memories weren't unconscious: but they had ceased to inform in a flexible lively way his moment-to-moment relationship with others and, even more fundamentally, with himself. His consciousness had become so rigidly reduced that his meaningfully connected self was constantly in a penumbra. This is clearly portrayed in the novel as a consequence of the loss of his loved objects, of trust, of his religion: a loss he was psychically unable to deal with and therefore to recover from until the point in the novel in which he is saved by the resurgence of his capacity to love a little child.

These pathological states are connected to the incapacity to mourn unbearable losses, and the consequent melancholic states that such a disturbance produces in the mind. Remembering too much – the incapacity to allow a particular event in the past to be past, as in excessive persecutory guilt, excessive grievance, or trauma – is equally a failure of mourning; but this time a particular memory remains in the limelight of the mind, obscuring all other relationships and pursuits. These continue to exist at the fringe of consciousness, made irrelevant. The wound of grief remains unhealed, and the pain is for ever as alive and raw as in the moment of injury: one thinks of the Ancient Mariner ('and ever and anon throughout his life an agony constraineth him to travel from land to land', for ever compelled to tell his tale) and of his direct descendant Captain Ahab, similarly crossing the whole world from sea to sea in his 'monomaniacal' quest for Moby Dick. Melville reverses the direction of the guilt, so that revenge rather than atonement is the driving force informing the compulsive behaviour; but grief and grievance are in this context two sides of the same coin; the Albatross and the White Whale are for ever centre stage, in the limelight of the mind.

Marner, a figure inspired by George Eliot's childhood memory of a linen-weaver, a man carrying a heavy bag, moving from place to place, had his name possibly chosen because of its link to the Ancient Mariner, a poem she admired.[2] Although he settles next to the Stone Pit near Raveloe, he cannot, like the Mariner, be part

---

[2.] Terence Cave, introduction to *Silas Marner* (1996).

of the ordinary life of the community. He remains in exile until his redemption; and although his world is as minuscule as the Mariner's and Ahab's are never-ending, he, too, is dominated by one idea only. We could argue, of course, that from a psychological point of view, Silas's almost total forgetting, the limitation of his consciousness to a tiny spot of light surrounded by constant obscurity, is also a form of unconsciously never forgetting the absence of the loved objects: a feeling memory of the overwhelming presence of absence ('darkness visible', illuminated by what Nerval called 'le soleil noir de la melancholie').

In *Mourning and Melancholia* (1917),[3] one of Freud's most revolutionary works, he discovered the unconscious mechanism through which we internalise our lost love object and identify with it; the successful work of mourning, which is a painful and lengthy process, leads to the giving up of the object, accepting its death, thus locating it in the 'past' region of the mind, so that it can remain in our inner world as a symbolic presence that informs our life as a memory, both consciously and unconsciously. Failure to mourn creates an internal situation by which the lost object is excessively identified with, and the self lives in the shadow of an internal death, leading to pathological depression.

Freud describes this primitive introjection leading to melancholia in two strikingly different ways:

> Thus the shadow of the object fell upon the ego, and the latter could henceforth be judged by a special agency [i.e. the superego], as though it were an object, the forsaken object.[4]

And:

> The ego wants to incorporate this object into itself, and, in accordance with the oral or cannibalistic phase of libidinal development in which it is, it wants to do so by devouring it.[5]

He further explains the process by saying:

3. The discussion of *Mourning and Melancholia* which follows is also part of my paper, 'The Wound, The Bow and the Shadow of the Object' in *Freud: A Modern Reader*, ed. R. J. Perelberg (2005).
4. *Mourning and Melancholia* (1917), p. 249.
5. Op.cit., pp. 249–50.

If the love for the object – a love which cannot be given up though the object itself is given up – takes refuge in narcissistic identification, then the hate comes into operation on this substitutive object, abusing it, debasing it, making it suffer and deriving sadistic satisfaction from its suffering.

This description has the emotional atmosphere of my second quote above: 'cannibalistic devouring' goes with the sadistic abusing and killing of the object (and of the self identified with it).
Later he says:

[W]hen the ego finds itself in an excessive real danger which it believes itself unable to overcome by its own strength . . . it sees itself deserted by all protecting forces and lets itself die. Here, moreover, is once again the same situation as that which underlay the first great anxiety-state of birth and the infantile anxiety of longing – the anxiety due to separation from the protecting mother.[6]

This has the emotional tone of the first quote about 'the shadow of the object'. What Freud is discovering here is that in relation to catastrophic loss the self feels totally possessed by, and in possession of, the object; as if quite concretely consumed by it; and at the mercy of powerful and contradictory emotions, intense sorrow and intense hatred. The successful work of mourning will eventually transform the lost object into a proper memory. If loss is experienced as so overwhelming that it cannot be mourned, melancholia (and the defence against it, mania) gets established.

Although it may seem odd to write about a story by one of the editors of this anthology, I would like to discuss A.S. Byatt's 'A Stone Woman', since it illustrates Freud's thoughts about the work of mourning and the processes involved in the transformation of the lost loved object into memory in a particularly illuminating way.
'A Stone Woman' starts with a woman mourning the death of her mother; as with many of Byatt's stories, it occupies a territory in which the atmosphere of fairy tale and myth overlaps with carefully observed reality through the use of images and metaphors intensely real in their detail, yet conveying an imaginary other

6. Freud, *The Ego and the Id* (1923), p. 58.

world. For a psychoanalyst they directly communicate the experience that our internal world, the world of dreams and unconscious phantasy (psychoanalysts call it the world of internal object relations), is at least as real as external reality. I will quote from this story of painful bereavement, touching as it does on one's earliest, most primitive attachment, to illustrate what I have just described as Freud's analysis of the unconscious processes involved in mourning and its potential for developing into melancholia.

The story begins:

> At first she did not think of stones. Grief made her insubstantial to herself; she felt herself flitting lightly from room to room, in the twilit apartment, like a moth. The apartment seemed constantly twilit, although it must, she knew, have gone through the usual sequences of sun and shadow over the days and weeks since her mother died.[7]

This is what Freud was trying to describe with his phrase 'Thus the shadow of the (lost loved) object fell upon the ego': 'grief made her insubstantial to herself', both because the loved object takes her 'substance' away and also because she becomes like a ghost herself, insubstantial like the departing spirit, a mother who is present only in absence.

A few lines down, there is too much light, and a need to try again and again to take in the reality of death: rage and ashes, violence and sorrow, and the hurrying foam of Time moving, towards the frightening loneliness of the future, but also backwards into the past:

> She drew the blinds because the light hurt her eyes. Her inner eye observed final things over and over. White face on white pillow amongst white hair. Colourless skin on lifeless fingers. Flesh of my flesh, flesh of her flesh. The efficient rage of consuming fire, the handfuls of fawn ash which she had scattered, as she had promised, in the hurrying foam of a Yorkshire beck.
>
> She went through the motions, hoping to become accustomed to solitude and silence. Then one morning pain struck her like a sudden beak, tearing at her gut. She caught her breath and sat down, waiting

7. A.S. Byatt, *Little Black Book of Stories* (2003), p. 129.

for it to pass. It did not pass, but strengthened, blow on blow. She rolled on her bed, dishevelled and sweating. She heard the creature moaning. She tried to telephone the doctor, but the thing shrieked raucously into the mouthpiece, and this saved her, for they sent an ambulance, which took the screaming thing to a hospital, as it would not have taken a polite old woman. Later they told her she had had at the most four hours to live. Her gut was twisted and gangrenous.[8]

This is what Freud was describing by his phrase 'cannibalistic devouring' of the object, characteristic of the early stages of mourning. What one experiences as acute, devouring pain is in unconscious phantasy exactly that: a concrete creature that devours you from inside with its horrible beak. In the unconscious, the baby self has devoured the mother, and also feels devoured by her; at the most primitive level the object is a 'creature' in horrible pain, as is the primitive, infant self who cannot yet fully digest the experience. The loss at this level is not experienced as an absence, but as a tearing, gut-devouring presence.

Byatt's imagery of the bereaved woman's rotting insides links in my mind to Coleridge's imagery: the guilt about killing the Albatross causes the Mariner to feel his whole world is rotting, dominated not by death-as-absence but by Life-in-Death with all its horrors:

> The very deep did rot: O Christ
> That ever this should be!
> Yea, slimy things did crawl with legs
> Upon the slimy sea.

After her near-death experience of her 'very deep rotting', Byatt's character begins to notice that she is gradually turning into stone: bits of her body become transformed into various kinds of colourful stones and jewels. In a similar way, when the Mariner's process of regeneration starts, the rot and the slimy things turn into beautiful jewel-like creatures:

[8.] Ibid., pp. 130–31.

Beyond the shadow of the ship
I watched the water-snakes:
They moved in tracks, of shining white,
And when they reared, the elfish light
Fell off in hoary flakes.

Within the shadow of the ship
I watched their rich attire:
Blue, glossy green, and velvet black,
They coiled and swam; and every track
Was a flash of golden fire [...]

The self-same moment I could pray;
And from my neck so free
The Albatross fell off and sank,
Like lead into the sea.

I will quote again from 'A Stone Woman', a few pages down:

When would she be, so to speak, dead? When her plump flesh heart
stopped pumping the blue blood along the veins and arteries of her
shifting shape? When the grey and clammy matter of her brain
became limestone or graphite? When her brainstem became a column
of rutilated quartz? When her eyes became – what? She inclined to
the belief that her watching eyes would be the last thing, even though
fine threads on her nostrils still conveyed the scent of brass or coal
to the primitive lobes at the base of the brain. The phrase came into
her head: Those are pearls that were his eyes. A song of grief made
fantastic by a sea-change. Would her eyes cloud over and become
pearls? Pearls were interesting. They were a substance where the
organic met the inorganic, like moss agate. Pearls were stones secreted
by a living shellfish, perfected inside the mother-of-pearl of its skeleton
to protect its soft inward flesh from an irritant. She went to her
mother's jewel-box, in search of a long string of freshwater pearls
she had given her for her seventieth birthday. There they lay and
glimmered; she took them out and wound them round her sparkling
neck, streaked already with jet, opal, and jacinth zircon.[9]

9. Ibid., pp. 145–6.

In this passage, the bereaved woman moves towards death by identification with the dead mother, and simultaneously moves towards memory and differentiation from her. The eyes (which are both the self's most effective organ for 'taking in' the object, and simultaneously that which makes the infant aware of the separation between himself and the mother) are potentially dead and yet very much alive in her self-observation and in her curiosity: 'Pearls were interesting. They were a substance where the organic met the inorganic'. Internal objects are organic and inorganic at the same time; she is delicately poised between life and death. Moving towards mother's jewel-box recreates mother-in-the-past, memory-of-mother; there is both differentiation and closeness: *her* pearls, *my* neck (and 'freshwater' . . . no slimy things at this particular moment?). And yet the double meaning of *wound* brings back the operation, the scars turned into dead jewels, the pain of loss; also perhaps a more actively suicidal thought, perhaps a reference to unconscious guilt: the mother as her Albatross hanging from her neck.

This is Freud's description of what happens to memory during mourning; his 'jet, opal, and jacinth zircon':

> [The reality of death can only be accepted] bit by bit, at great expense of time and cathectic energy, and in the meantime the existence of the lost object is psychically prolonged. *Each single one of the memories and expectations in which the libido is bound to the object is brought up and hypercathected*, and detachment of the libido is accomplished in respect of it. [my italics][10]

And now, back to Silas Marner, who finds a place near an expanse of water which, even though it is just a Stone Pit, will hide an important secret and a corpse (its deep did rot); there he creates a tiny mournful Sicilia on the fringes of an incomprehensible, alien Bohemia, where he spends his insect-like existence until one day a daughter will bring him to life again.[11]

In the beginning of the story, Silas Marner the weaver has become a recluse as a consequence of a very painful situation; he had been

---

[10.] *Mourning and Melancholia*, pp. 244–5.
[11.] The connection between the creation of Marner and *A Winter's Tale* has often been discussed; see, for instance, Cave, *op. cit.*

betrayed by his girlfriend and his best friend, and falsely accused
of stealing money. As this accusation was considered by the religious community in his primitive church as 'proven' by drawing
lots, he also suffered a loss of religious faith; in essence, all his
good objects deserted him, and he felt condemned to go away to
a foreign place, and live a life of total isolation. In psychoanalytic
terms, we could say that he suffered such catastrophic loss that he
was unable to mourn it, and became melancholically withdrawn.
He had nothing left but work; gradually he became addicted to
the gold coins he earned and started to build up his treasure. 'He
had seemed to love it little in the years when every penny had its
purpose for him; for he loved the *purpose* then. But now, when all
purpose was gone, that habit of looking towards the money and
grasping it with a sense of fulfilled effort made a loam that was
deep enough for the seeds of desire; and as Silas walked home-
ward across the fields in the twilight, he drew out the money and
thought it was brighter in the gathering gloom.' When his gold is
stolen, he becomes desperate: Silas's 'had been a clinging life; and
though the object round which its fibres had clung was a dead
disrupted thing, it satisfied the need for clinging'.

One night, as he stood outside his house, disconnected from
reality in a 'cataleptic fit', a two-year-old girl, whose mother had
just died in the snow, comes in, attracted by the light from the
door, and sits near the fire, just where the gold had been buried
before it was stolen. When he comes in and sees the child's bright
blond hair, his first thought is: 'my gold has returned to me!'

This is not just what is needed for the development of the plot;
it also conveys the meaning of an unresolved mourning, which
would remain so unless a symbolic metamorphosis can take place;
the presence of the unconscious link with his coins experienced as
his 'familiars' and, as the word suggests, his family in his internal
world, ('bright faces which were all his own') makes psychic recovery
possible. The implication is that the 'dead disrupted things' still
have a deep emotional connection, through unconscious memory,
with the lost love objects, especially with his dead little sister, and
that the belief in the transformation of something dead into something alive – which can repair the wrong committed against him –
allows his own process of resurrection to begin. The memory of
the lost love object 'unfolding' into psychological light allows for
the return of the symbolic functioning: this child is not the sister,

but she symbolises the sister, and can therefore be invested with the emotions that belonged to the loved object in the past, starting the reparative process.

Very early in the novel George Eliot portrays movingly how pity and compassion redress momentarily the situation of emotional isolation by connecting Silas to the past, bringing to illuminated focus a particular aspect of his autobiographical memory:

> About this time [i.e. when he started falling in love with the gold coins] an incident happened which seemed to open a possibility of some fellowship with his neighbours. One day, taking a pair of shoes to be mended, he saw the cobbler's wife seated by the fire, suffering from the terrible symptoms of heart disease and dropsy, which he had witnessed as the precursors of his mother's death. He felt a rush of pity at the *mingled sight and remembrance*, and, recalling the relief his mother had found from a simple preparation of foxgloves, he promised Sally Oates to bring her something that would ease her, since the doctor did her no good. In his office of charity, Silas felt, for the first time since he had come to Raveloe, a sense of unity between his past and present life, which might have been the beginning of his rescue from the insect-like existence into which his nature had shrunk. [my italics]

There he was, with his sick mother fully imagined/remembered, as well as his healthy mother of earlier times when she could make good medicine from herbs, and good emotional medicine for her little boy through compassion – when she consoled him for his losses. He symbolically helps his suffering (internal) mother through helping Sally Oates, and (temporarily) retrieves her through 'mingled sight and remembrance'.

What makes this fascinating for a psychoanalyst is this sense that several levels of memory are operating in a vital integrated way at the same time: the sick, dying mother, bringing alive his compassion and also a re-experience of the bereavement; the mother of his youth, who was capable of a particular expertise and could help and heal others and teach him useful life skills; and ultimately, in implicit (not conscious) memory, he is also the once-loved child, 'cured' of pain, who will therefore be able to 'cure' a 'mother'. The identification with a good mother is there to be re-awakened at the sight of the bereaved child.

Another moving passage displays Silas's unconscious memory of the warm, nurturing link between mother and child:

Yet even in this state of withering a little incident happened, which showed that the sap of affection was not all gone. It was one of his daily tasks to fetch his water from a well a couple of fields off, and for this purpose, ever since he came to Raveloe, he had had a brown earthernware pot, which he held as his most precious utensil among the very few conveniences he had granted himself. It had been his companion for twelve years, always standing on the same spot, always lending its handle to him in the early morning, so that its form had an expression for him of willing helpfulness, and the impress of its handle on his palm gave him a satisfaction mingled with that of having the fresh clear water. One day as he was returning from the well, he stumbled against the step of the stile, and his brown pot, falling with force against the stones that overarched the ditch below him, was broken in three pieces. Silas picked up the pieces and carried them home with grief in his heart. The brown pot could never be of use to him any more, but he stuck the bits together and propped the ruin in its old place for a memorial.

With her usual psychological brilliance George Eliot had already shown that, in the melancholic state, love itself doesn't do the trick, without the 'mingled sight and remembrance': before the appearance of Eppie, Marner is befriended by Dolly Winthrop, but she can't cure his melancholia – even though she imagines that the sight of a lovely child might do this; Marner can't but be brought to life by seeing and hearing her little son Aaron singing a Christmas 'carril':

She stroked Aaron's brown head, and thought it must do Master Marner good to see such a 'pictur of a child'. But Marner, on the other side of the hearth, saw the neatly-featured rosy face as a mere dim round, with two dark spots in it.

In his emotional withdrawal, Marner relates to Aaron as an autistic person might. What he sees is entirely lacking in emotional significance; the image perfectly conveys what happens to sight when not 'mingled' with memory, when devoid of symbolic connection. George Eliot also shows us the opposite process to this 'turning into stone': as Eppie's mind develops, she makes alive what is inanimate. Dolly describes how Eppie will

> 'get busier and mischievouser every day – she will, bless her . . . but I'll bring you my little chair, and some bits o' red rag and things for her to play wi': an' she'll sit and chatter to 'em as if they was alive'.

Marner can only engage again in the life process through Eppie, so life acquires meaning with the symbolic return of the lost loved object, now a vivid memory constantly informing the new relationship. The trigger for the restoration of emotional sight is the linking of the live child/sister with the fantasy of recovering the gold, standing for the treasured, buried internal objects; as in Byatt's story, where every aspect of mother has turned into jewels, buried in the Stone Woman's body.

Even at his most miserly, which is the same as his most amnesic, Marner wouldn't exchange his gold coins for others with different faces – in other words, in unconscious memory he discriminates between his loved ones and strangers – and when particularity is preserved, something human remains. By transforming the Stone Woman not into just a massive piece of stone but into many different very particular kinds of stones – different colours, textures, shapes, ages, etc. – Byatt shows the discrimination in the internal world between the hundreds of very particular, distinct memories of various aspects and functions which compose the internalised lost object, and therefore the multi-faceted nature of the process of identification.

The process of making the world alive depends on 'mingled sight and remembrance', actual experiences in external reality coloured by projections of our own emotions and of memories of our objects (as in Eppie transforming rags into people). In pathological over-remembering, a similar but sinister version of this occurs, as for instance in Captain Ahab's invention of an inner world of motives and personality for Moby Dick through the projection of his own hatred into his enemy: Ahab's imagination is not used for play but to feed his obsession, and it transforms his memories in a destructive way. He could be said to hoard the one distorted and over-illuminated memory, killing off in the process all other memories.

By 'petrifying' countless Wedding-Guests throughout his life, the Ancient Mariner hangs on possessively to his Albatross: not allowing the past to be mended through allowing space for other, different memories.

Steven Rose, 'Memories are Made of This'

'If any one faculty of our nature may be called more wonderful than the rest, I do think it is memory. There seems something more speakingly incomprehensible in the powers, the failures, the inequalities of memory, than in any other of our intelligences. The memory is sometimes so retentive, so serviceable, so obedient – at others, so bewildered and so weak – and at others again, so tyrannical, so beyond controul! [*sic*] – We are to be sure a miracle in every way – but our powers of recollecting and forgetting, do seem peculiarly past finding out.'

Thus Fanny Price, Austen's long-suffering heroine in *Mansfield Park*. It took more than half a century from the writing of that novel for psychologists to attempt to bring the discipline of the laboratory to bear on this tyrannical and uncontrollable memory, and nearly another before it was to become subject to the molecular probes and confident claims of a resurgent neurobiology. Today's neuroscience seizes not on Austen but on the poet Emily Dickinson for its claim to knowledge, its leading figures gleefully quoting her verse:

> The Brain – is wider than the Sky
> For – put them side by side –
> The one the other will contain
> With ease – and You – beside

Yet after my own lifetime of research, in charting the biochemical cascades and cellular remoulding that even the simplest of learning experiences seems to generate in my young chicks (the experimental animals which have participated, albeit involuntarily, in more than three decades of my study of memory) I have to confess that I still don't feel we have done more than deepen some of its mysteries. Fifteen hundred years before Fanny Price, in his *Confessions*, St

Augustine listed some of the phenomena that needed explaining: Memory, he says, is a 'spacious palace, a storehouse for countless images'. But memory is capricious. Some things come spilling from the memory unwanted, whilst others are forthcoming only after a delay. Memory enables one to envisage colours even in the dark, to taste in the absence of food, to hear in the absence of sound. 'All this goes on inside me in the vast cloisters of my memory.' Memory also contains 'all that I have ever learnt of the liberal sciences, except what I have forgotten ... innumerable principles and laws of numbers and dimensions ... my feelings, not in the same way as they are present to the mind when it experiences them, but in a quite different way ...' and things too, such as false arguments, which are known not to be true. Further, he points out, when one remembers something, one can later remember that one has remembered it. No wonder that the mind seemed to soar outside the physical confines of mere brain-goo. For Augustine, unlike Emily Dickinson, it is the mind, not the brain, which is wider than the sky, and I am inclined to agree.

What the experimental sciences have tried to do, of course, is to operationalise memory, to reduce and control 'learning experiences' in such a way that their parameters could be studied. The process was begun by Hermann Ebbinghaus, whose book, *Uber das Gedächtnis* (On Memory), published in 1885, broke new ground by asking whether there were general laws of memory formation. To explore these general laws, he invented the simple technique which in various forms has been a staple psychologist's tool ever since – that of the nonsense syllable, a series of three letter sets each composed of a vowel between two consonants, as for instance: HUZ; LAQ; DOK; VER; JIX. Using himself as subject Ebbinghaus then explored the conditions required to remember such lists; numbers of readings, spacing and so forth, until he could make two errorless readings of the entire list. Once the list was learned, he could then test how successful he was at recalling it at various subsequent times from minutes to days. To quantify this process of recall, all that he had to do was to note how many readings of the list were necessary, at any given time after it had been learned, to once again be able to repeat it without error.

A number of general rules could be derived from such observations. For instance, in any such list of a dozen nonsense syllables, some are easier to remember than others – in particular, those at the beginning and at the end of the list. These are the so-called primacy and recency effects. They may seem obvious when described so simply, but what Ebbinghaus did was to demonstrate clearly that in this case at least common sense was supported by science. In addition, he showed that if a list is once learned, it becomes easier to relearn subsequently. A comparison of the number of trials required to learn it the second time with those required first time round provides a calculation which has become known in the psychology literature as *savings* – the measure of memory. The use of the savings score enables one to specify more precisely the loss and stabilisation of memory with time. He found that most of the memory loss occurred within the first minutes after training; once the memory had survived that hurdle it seemed much more stable, leading to the temporal distinction between short- and long-term memory which has become a staple of subsequent research.

Ebbinghaus's was the first step in developing the taxonomy of memory that has provided much of the focus of subsequent psychological research. In the 1930s Frederick Bartlett famously showed how the content of even remembered items becomes transformed and simplified over time. And in the 1980s and 90s, Alan Baddeley drew a distinction between working memory – that is memory dredged up from past experience for current use, so to say – and the more deeply stored reference memory. Meanwhile, based in part on evidence from patients with identifiable brain lesions, Endel Tulving, and later Larry Squire, added a further taxonomical distinction, that between various classes of memory. Procedural memory is remembering *how* to do something – to ride a bicycle for instance. Declarative memory is remembering *that* – that a particular two-wheeled drivable object is called a bicycle. Declarative itself becomes divided into semantic (Augustine's numbers and dimensions) and episodic or autobiographical memory – recall of episodes in one's own life.

For a neurobiologist, the crucial questions are about how these forms of memory are instantiated in the brain. Do the categories reflect the engagement of different brain regions, and different molecular processes, or are they higher-level distinctions, without matching brain correlates? Until recent decades, the only effective way of addressing these questions in humans was by observing the effects of various forms of brain lesion and disease on memory. Classical disease-induced losses of memory, notably from what used to be called senile dementia but more frequently now Alzheimer's disease, can't answer these questions because the brain damage they cause is both progressive and very general. But some consequences of stroke, or accident – or surgically induced damage – can be instructive. The most famous case of iatrogenic memory loss is of an epileptic patient, known to every neuroscientist by his initials, HM, who was operated on in the 1950s to remove regions of his temporal cortex and hippocampus so as to eliminate the epileptic focus. The result was a catastrophic loss in his ability to transfer memory from short to long term. HM, who has continued to be a subject of research for the subsequent half-century, can remember events up to the time at which he was operated on, but forgets any new experience within minutes. Although he can show some procedural learning of new skills, he cannot retain declarative – especially episodic, autobiographical – memory. Events, as he himself puts it, simply fade away; he says 'every day is by itself'. This observation, soon matched by studies in animals, suggests that the hippocampus has a crucial role to play in the registration of new experience, and that without it and adjacent brain regions items can no longer be transferred into longer-term memory.

Within the last decades, the possibility of studying ongoing memory processes in the living human brain has been transformed by the advent of new technologies, notably the windows opened by functional magnetic resonance imaging (fMRI) and magnetoencephalography (MEG). The former makes possible the measurement of changes in blood flow to small regions of the brain, the assumption being that the higher the rate of blood flow the more active that region is under any particular circumstance, such as performing a learning or memory task. The latter takes advantage of the fact that signalling within the brain is primarily electrical, and electrical current flow is accompanied by tiny changes in the magnetic field surrounding the current. Both techniques require rather formidable instrumentation; fMRI is better at localising sites of change, MEG is most helpful in charting the temporal dynamics, making it possible to plot changes in brain activity millisecond by millisecond.

Two examples reveal what can be learned from such techniques. Eleanor Maguire and her colleagues studied London taxi drivers asked, whilst under fMRI, to recall a complex journey within the city. The act of recalling the route activated their hippocampi. In our own experiments, using MEG, we took subjects on a virtual supermarket tour, asking them to make choices of items to purchase based on their past experience and preferences. Faced with a choice, say of three brands of coffee, subjects took about two seconds to press a key indicating their choice. But in those two seconds, there was a flurry of brain activity. Within 80 milliseconds, the visual cortex became active; by 300 milliseconds, the left inferotemporal cortex, assumed to be a site of memory storage. At 500 milliseconds, Broca's area, a region associated with speech, was engaged as the subjects silently vocalised the range of choice items – and at 800 milliseconds, as they made their final decision as to which item they preferred – assuming they preferred any – the right parietal cortex, associated with affect-laden decisions, was active. These dynamics reveal the many regions of the brain involved in even a simple act of episodic and semantic memory; even primary sensory regions like the visual cortex are more active when people are performing a memory-related task than when they see the same images but are asked simply to make a cognitive choice – for instance of which item is the shortest of those displayed. Thus Baddeley's working memory does not seem to be simply localisable to one brain region.

Revealing though such studies are – and they are as yet in their infancy as the techniques and instrumentation mature – there are limits to the types of answer they can provide. If learning and the making of memory demand cellular and molecular changes, these cannot be studied except in animals. To do this demands developing models of learning and memory in these animals that may serve in some sense as a surrogate for the same processes in humans. The doors to such an approach were opened early in the last century by Ivan Pavlov's well-known experiments with dogs. Pavlov trained them to associate the ringing of a bell with the arrival of food, and hence to salivate (a learned or, in the jargon, a conditioned reflex). In the 1930s B.F. Skinner developed a different learning model (operant conditioning) in which animals had to perform some act, such as pressing a lever to obtain food, or to escape an electric shock. If after one or more trials the animal's behaviour changes appropriately – for instance, by salivating to the bell or by pressing the lever sooner in response to a signal or running a maze faster and with fewer errors – the animal is said to have learned from the experience. And, when it performs the learned task in an error-free way, it is said to be remembering the experience. The unspoken assumption is that whatever the brain processes that are involved in such changes in the animal's behaviour may be, they will be similar to those occurring in the human brain when we learn and remember. The Skinnerian view was that all creatures learn and remember in the same way: that there are general laws of learning that are as universally applicable as the gas laws or gravitation in physics.

Of course, there are problems with such an assumption. What and how an animal will learn is species-specific. Some food-storing birds, such as scrub jays, can recall during winter the many thousands of sites at which they cached edible seeds the previous summer. Others – songbirds like zebra finches – cannot learn such tasks but readily acquire new songs. Further, an animal can only inform a human experimenter that it is learning or remembering by way of some change in its performance of a task. It may 'remember' its previous experience but choose not to perform the task appropriately – a point made in the 1950s in a famous critique of Skinnerian approaches, a paper called simply 'The Misbehaviour of Animals'. Despite heroic attempts at complex experimental designs, the taxonomic distinctions between procedural and declarative learning and memory are always going to be confounded in animal studies.

Yet, if learning from some new experience results subsequently in a change in the behaviour of the animal when presented with a similar situation, one must assume that something has changed in the brain to support the changed behaviour. This inferred intervening variable is regarded as a memory 'store,' 'trace' or 'engram', which is formed when learning is taking place, and reactivated when that learning is later recalled. The challenge for neurobiologists then became that of identifying the anatomical, cellular, molecular or physiological nature of the trace. The temporal distinction between short- and long-term memory, the evidence that short-term memory is labile and easily disrupted, whereas long-term memory seems relatively protected, suggested that it must depend on some structural remodelling of the patterns of neural connection within the brain, engraving the memory in the brain in a manner analogous to that of inscribing a magnetic trace on a tape or a CD which can subsequently be replayed, invoking the original material. The seductive metaphorical power of computer 'memory' has been very influential in shaping thought on this question.

The myriad nerve cells in the brain (a hundred billion in the human cortex alone) communicate by way of up to ten-thousand-fold (a hundred trillion) more junctions, known as synapses. It is at the synapses that electrical signals travelling down one nerve axon trigger the release of chemical signals – neurotransmitters – that in turn carry the message across a small gap to an adjacent nerve cell, stimulating a response in the second cell. Maybe learning results in some change in synaptic connections, so as to create novel signalling pathways? In 1948 the Canadian psychologist Donald Hebb framed the hypothesis that has shaped all subsequent biochemical and physiological research in the field, that learning involves the remodelling of such synaptic junctions. In his own words (and indeed his own italics):-

> *Let us assume then that the persistence or repetition of a reverberatory activity (or 'trace') tends to induce lasting cellular changes that add to its stability. The assumption can be precisely stated as follows: When an axon of cell A is near enough to excite a cell B and repeatedly or persistently takes part in firing it, some growth process or metabolic change takes place in one or both cells such that A's efficiency, as one of the cells firing B, is increased.*
>
> *The most obvious and I believe much the most probable suggestion concerning the way in which one cell could become more capable of firing another is that synaptic knobs develop and increase the area of contact between the afferent axon and efferent [cell body]. There is certainly no direct evidence that this is so ... There are several considerations, however, that make the growth of synaptic knobs a plausible perception.*

By the 1960s, neuroscientists had become sufficiently confident in the power of their technologies to attempt to verify Hebb's hypothesis experimentally. But after an initial burst of enthusiasm the field became mired in controversy. Claims that training rats on some simple task resulted in increases in RNA [ribonucleic acid] and protein synthesis in their brains and, even more extravagantly, that when the RNA was extracted and injected into the brain of a recipient the memory was transferred too, achieved great publicity but were technically flawed. Research funds dried up and even to suggest that one was working on the biochemistry of memory became somewhat disreputable.

More patient experiments in the 1970s began to revive confidence, and Hebb's plausible perception became tangible evidence. Two disparate approaches helped. One seems very remote from memory as we might understand it. The physiologists Tim Bliss and Terje Lomo placed stimulating and recording electrodes into cells in the rat hippocampus, and found that if they fired a train of electrical pulses into the cells, their output properties were permanently modified; the cells showed a 'memory' of their past experience. The phenomenon, called long-term potentiation, became intensely studied as either a mechanism or a model for memory over the succeeding decades. At around the same time, the psychiatrist turned neuroscientist Eric Kandel began exploring the physiological properties of the neurons in the giant sea slug *Aplysia californica*. Aplysia has two useful properties. One is that it can be trained on a simple task, to contract its gills (rather as a land slug rolls into a ball) in response to a jet of water being applied to its tail. The second is that many of its nerve cells are giant and the 'same' cell is easily identifiable from slug to slug. Kandel was able to map the neural circuitry involved in the withdrawal reflex, and to identify some specific synapses whose electrical properties and biochemistry changed as the slug learned. With a reductionist rhetorical flourish, Kandel offered the research community 'memory in a dish'.

Over the decades that followed, evidence from a variety of labs, including my own, showed that indeed, when an animal – in my case a young chick – is trained on some novel task, there are increases in the size and strength of specific synaptic connections in particular brain regions. Under the microscope, the connections are structurally larger and the efficacy of the neurotransmitters within them is enhanced. The experimental problem was to prove that these changes were in some way associated with the storage of the putative memory trace, rather than a consequence of other aspects of the task and its performance. For example, in the task we use, young chicks are offered a small bright bead. Almost invariably, they will peck at such a bead within a few seconds of seeing it. If the bead is made to taste unpleasant (we dip the bead in a rather bitter, curryish tasting liquid), the chick will peck once, and then demonstrate its distaste by shaking its head energetically and wiping its bill on the floor of its pen. If it is subsequently – any time up to several days later – offered a similar but dry bead, the chick will not peck it, but back away, sometimes replicating the earlier pattern of head shaking and bill wiping. We infer that the chick has learned, after a single experience, that this particular colour, shape and size of bead tastes unpleasant – at least in this specific context – and that when the bead is presented once more, this memory is reactivated. For the initiates, this is described as one-trial passive avoidance learning.

The passive avoidance task has a number of experimental advantages. It is quick and reproducible, and builds upon a normal aspect of the young chick's behavioural development – that is, to spontaneously explore its environment by pecking at small objects. Because the training event – the peck at the bead – takes only a few seconds, one can readily separate the immediate consequences of the bitter taste from the subsequent cascade of events during the transitions between shorter- and longer-term memory. Advantages have corresponding disadvantages. Is what we discover about learning in such a young animal, where the brain is developing rapidly, relevant to learning in adulthood? Do the molecular events involved when a chick learns in a single trial to peck a bead in any way correspond to those during the many trials a rat needs to learn to run a maze – still less those when a child learns the names of the days of the week or what to expect on its birthday?

Even setting these queries aside, can we be sure, even for the chick, that the change we find in the synapses is actually some form of memory trace? That is, that it is a necessary, sufficient and exclusive change in the brain which in some way 'represents' the memory, enabling it later to be recalled? Could the change not have occurred simply as a result of some aspect of the initial experience, such as the taste or sight of the bead, or the learned motor activity of pecking? Or, as we cannot know whether the chick has learned the task without testing it, maybe it is a consequence of the recall experience rather than the learning itself? I don't intend here to reprise the decade-long series of control experiments that enabled us to distinguish between general experience-induced and learning-induced changes. I have discussed these at some length in my book *The Making of Memory*. But it may be of more than merely technical interest to outline the sorts of approach one can use.

There are broadly two approaches to identifying the molecular processes that occur in the minutes to hours following training on a simple task such as passive avoidance and which are presumed to be required for the maintenance of short-term memory and to underpin the transition to long-term memory, a process called memory consolidation. One can train the animal on the task and look for changes in some putative biochemical measure – the activity of an enzyme, the concentration or rate of synthesis of a molecule. Or one can attempt to disrupt the consolidation process by administering an inhibitor – some drug or anti-metabolite, known to block a specific biochemical process believed to be necessary for consolidation. If the drug blocks such a process, then the animal should subsequently not recall the task; that is, it should show a specific amnesia. Observing the changes in the suspected biochemical measure over time, or the time window during which the administered amnesic agent is effective, makes it possible to plot a temporal sequence of molecular events – a biochemical cascade – occurring over the hours following training and which seem to culminate in the lasting modulation of synaptic strengths. Since the 1980s I have used both methods in tandem in elucidating this cascade in my chicks.

Within the minutes following the onset of the training experience, there are changes in the release of neurotransmitters at the synapses in specific brain regions. As well as activating the post-synaptic nerve cell to fire, these increases also stimulate a wave of biochemical activity in the cell, which in due course results in the synthesis of a family of proteins, called cell adhesion molecules, destined to be transported to the synapses. Cell adhesion molecules are a bit like Velcro. They are located in the cell membrane, for instance at the synapse, with one end (the Velcro end) sticking out into the space between one nerve cell and the next, holding the two sides, pre- and post-synaptic, together. The newly synthesised adhesion molecules that are produced as a result of the training experience are dispatched to the activated synapses (a process that takes some 4–6 hours in chicks and rats), and inserted into their membranes, altering the strength of connections between the two sides of the synapse. This would seem precisely to confirm Hebb's hypothesis for how memory might be coded and stored in the brain.

The distinguished Nobel prize winning biochemist, Hans Krebs, in whose Oxford lab I was based during a post-doctoral period in the early 1960s, once told me that for every biological problem, God had chosen an appropriate organism in which to tackle the problem. I have argued that, for the study of the molecular processes involved in memory formation, the chick is indeed God's organism. Others have made different choices, ranging from fruit flies and sea slugs to the more familiar laboratory rats and mice. In 2001, the Nobel Committee opted for the slug – although the prize they gave its developer, Eric Kandel, was not so much for his memory work with the slug (*Aplysia californica*) as for his studies of its neurotransmitters. What is interesting and encouraging is that despite the differences and learning paradigms, a sequence of broadly similar molecular processes has been shown to occur in the brains or nervous systems of these varying species during and following the training experience.

So can we conclude that we have found the engram – or at least identified the processes whereby engrams are constructed? The suggestion that memories are encoded in terms of changed synaptic connectivities has certainly proved attractive to a new breed of researcher, who call themselves computational neuroscientists, interested in making mathematical and computer models for how learning might occur in a distributed neural network connected by a mesh of synapses. In such a theoretical network, each memory (or association) is represented by activity in a specific set of synapses, a unique pattern, but any one synapse can be involved in many different such associations. On this basis, and estimating the number of synapses that it contains, Edmund Rolls has calculated that the hippocampus can store some 36,500 memories.

But a calculation of this sort is based on a prior set of assumptions: that biological memories can be decomposed into isolated monads and measured in terms of the bits and bytes with which computer people calculate the power of their machines. It is this that is so unrealistic; how many bits of information does the variety of memories listed by St Augustine require? For that matter, how many bits of information do my chicks need to remember to avoid pecking at a small red bead but know that it is safe to continue pecking at a yellow one? The chick categorises the experience of pecking the bitter bead in terms of the colour, shape and size of the bead, the context in which it was pecked, its own past experience of pecking other beads, and probably many other features as well, any one of which may provide the cue for its subsequent behaviour. I am far from sure that, for the chick, this complex of meanings within which any subsequent sight of and response to the bead is embedded is simply decomposable into information theory's bits.

Indeed, this theoretical concern is rapidly confirmed by experiment. The linear cascade that the biochemical and pharmacological experiments demonstrate, leading from transient changes in the release of neurotransmitters to seemingly permanent structural changes in the synapse, was no sooner established than paradoxes began to appear in the data. Memory traces apparently firmly located in one brain region seem over the subsequent hours and days to migrate to others – as indeed might have been suspected from HM's experience. His hippocampal damage did not erase old memories, only prevent new ones being formed. Furthermore, there is no single site for 'the memory' as if it constituted a discrete entity. The MEG experiment I referred to above shows that many brain regions are involved in the dynamic process of recalling and responding to prior experience. And even for my chicks we have been able to show that different aspects of the memory of the bitter bead – its colour, shape, size – engage different ensembles of nerve cells and synapses distributed in different regions of the brain.

Furthermore, memory involves more than just synapses, or even just brains. How well a person or a chick learns and remembers depends on many other aspects of body state. Alertness and attention depend on physiological processes such as blood flow and hormonal level. Memory involves emotion as well as cognition, and hormones produced outside the brain, notably adrenaline and its neurotransmitter relative noradrenaline, are engaged in determining what is remembered. When chicks peck a bitter bead, there is a surge of steroid (corticosterone, the chick's equivalent of cortisol in humans) release into the bloodstream. Too little or too much corticosterone, and the chick will not remember the experience, and will peck the previously bitter bead when tested later. In this sense learning and remembering – memory – is a property not of individual synapses or nerve cells or brains, but of the entire organism, the person.

Nor is this all. Hebb's model is one of learning: what happens when an animal, or human, registers some new experience. Implicit in it is also a theory of recall: that remembering the experience involves reactivating the novel pathways that learning has generated. Memories are stored as in computer files, and remembering would seem to be no more than pulling these files out of deep store and reopening them. But this mechanical model won't do. Each act of recall is itself a new experience. Reactivated memories are subtly changed each time we recall them. Classroom experiments beautifully illustrate what we all know to be the case. Thus in the aftermath of the disaster which destroyed the US *Challenger* rocket and killed the astronauts in it, a group of psychology students were encouraged to write down their recollections of the event. The records were stored, and a year later they were asked to write the account again. The huge discrepancies between their first and second accounts indicated just how labile memories of quite dramatic events are. Far from passively recording the past, we in our memories actively reconstruct it.

Very recently, neurobiology has begun to catch up with common experience and the psychologists. Many labs, including our own, have now shown that when an animal is given a reminder of a previously learned experience, the memory becomes labile once more, and can be disrupted by drugs and biochemical inhibitors rather as it can be during initial consolidation. Some researchers have begun to speak of this as 'reconsolidation'. However, the temporal dynamics of reconsolidation are rather different from those during consolidation; different brain regions are involved, and the biochemical changes do not exactly recapitulate those of consolidation.

Of course, being reminded of a past experience is itself to some extent a novel experience. We don't step into the same stream twice, and memory depends on history. That neurobiologists have only so recently come to realise this shows just how blinkered and reductionist their – our – paradigms have been. We are trapped by the experimental need for simple and reproducible designs, for operationalising our definitions of 'learning', 'memory' and so on as if these complex processes could be trapped within small boxes, sealed off from everything else that is going on in a living, behaving, learning and remembering organism throughout every moment of its existence. Our experiments capture only a small part of such complexity, and we are at fault if we mistake this small part for the whole.

Half a century ago, neuroscience saw the brain as composed of discrete centres, regions responsible for vision, audition, pain, memory and so forth. Superimposed on all these different regions was a super-coordinating centre, the association cortex. Separate regions reported upwards to this coordinator, which assembled them and instructed the motor regions of the brain how to respond.

This homunculus inside the head was the source of identity, individuality, the 'I' located a few centimetres behind our eyes.

Alas for simplicity, there is no such homunculus. As Gertrude Stein said about, I believe, downtown Los Angeles, there is no there there. Brains don't have a central processor, a super-manager controlling everything. Rather they are distributed networks of cellular ensembles, richly interconnected, which between them create the illusion of coherent experience that we all in our normally functioning moments share. The enigma of memory, as with so many aspects of brain processes, seems to be that it is both localised and non-localised. Remembering is at once sure and certain, as when we recall the names of the days of the week, or mount and ride off on a bicycle for the first time for many years, and as evanescent and elusive as a soap bubble, as when we try to remember the first moment we saw a lover and compare our own memory of that event with his or hers.

Fanny Price was surely right. Which is why we neurobiologists of memory must from time to time come out of our labs, reflect on our own varied procedural, declarative, episodic and autobiographical memories, and turn to the work of those philosophers, poets and novelists who can illuminate and interpret our experience so much more richly and meaningfully than can the most ingenious experimenter.

Patrick Bateson, 'Memory and Evolution'

If you are lucky enough to visit one of the great game parks of East Africa and witness a cheetah stalking a gazelle, you may see something very surprising. The gazelle on which the crouching cheetah has fixed her gaze may suddenly jump into the air. The cheetah relaxes and turns her head, searching for other gazelle. The curious leap of the gazelle when approached by a predator is known as 'stotting'. The leap indicates to the cheetah, or so we suppose, that she is less likely to catch that gazelle than one that does not jump or does not jump so high.

What has this to do with memory and evolution? Anyone brought up on popular accounts of biological evolution will have been told that the record of what made ancestors successful lies in the genes and that the genes, being immortal, are the drivers of change. In this case, however, the cheetah does not have to change genetically. All that individual animals have to do in each generation is to profit from their experiences. Chasing gazelle that leap into the air is a waste of breath. Genetic change in the gazelle will occur because the important thing is to stand out from the crowd. Those animals that signal ineffectively to the predator that they have spotted the predator will be less likely to survive. By degrees, the standard for jumping will be raised even though at any one time the young, the sick and the lame will always be prime targets for the cheetah. The evolutionary pressure on the gazelle to make their jumps ever more conspicuous than those of their peers will be driven by the cheetah's preferences and these will be driven by her memory of past failures. I should make clear at this point that by memory I do not mean 'represented in the genes' in some metaphorical sense. I mean memory in its generally accepted sense of experience represented in the nervous system. The experienced cheetah's choice of prey depends on such memory.

The role of choice in evolution was clearly recognised by Charles

Darwin in his principle of sexual selection.[1] His idea was that the female peacock, say, chose the male with the biggest tail. She would have sons with bigger tails. These sons in their turn would subsequently be chosen by females with similar preferences for males with the largest tails. The evolutionary pressure would be for bigger and bigger tails since the males with the biggest tail would mate with the most females. Moreover the females that made such choices would have more grand-offspring than those that did not. Eventually the trend to produce ever greater tails would halt when the male could no longer carry it safely. Males with tails that were too large could no longer rise from the ground quickly enough to escape the jaws of a fox. Most biologists suppose that the evolutionary process of sexual selection, as Darwin called it, involves two genetic changes, one in the male giving rise to a bigger tail (or whatever) and one in the female giving rise to a preference for an ever more striking adornment. If that is the case, then no memory is involved. However, another possibility is that the female's choice is affected by her memory, as in the case of the cheetah.

The activities of animal breeders can be used to illustrate the effects of memory in mate choice. The appearance of the Siamese cat has changed astonishingly in a hundred years as the result of human intervention. From being an apple-headed animal with a robust body it has become long-muzzled and cadaverously thin. My guess is that this change was not the result of a conscious desire to alter the breed with a particular pre-determined goal in mind. Rather, judges at cat shows grew bored with the appearance of ever more perfect apple-heads and awarded prizes to animals that were slightly different from what they had seen so often. Cat breeders were quick to note the judges' preferences and picked from among their kittens those that most nearly matched the new fashion. In fashion, things never stand still. As with the plunging hemline, the Siamese cat's nose became longer as the breeders attempted to catch the judge's eye with their latest would-be champions. What is helpful about the analogy is that trend over time only requires

[1.] This idea was presented in his book *The Descent of Man and Selection in Relation to Sex* published in 1871. Darwin first used the metaphor of selection in 1859 in *On the Origin of Species*, opposing natural selection to the artificial selection employed by plant and animal breeders. The extension of the metaphor to evolutionary processes driven by preference has caused difficulties and what animals do has frequently been confused with the consequences in terms of evolutionary change. Muddle is avoided if the preferential mating behaviour of animals is referred to as mate choice.

genetic changes in the cats. The drivers of the change are the judges' memories and their interest in slight novelty.

Just as genetic changes in the judges are not required to explain the astonishingly rapid changes in pedigree cats, so genetic changes in female peahens are not required to explain the extremely large tails of the males. Females may not know who their fathers are but they certainly will recognise their brothers. When they become sexually mature, they will do what so often happens in mate choice, preferring mates who are a bit different but not too different from the brothers who are most familiar to them.

The interest in slight novelty need not lead to a consistent trend over generations. However, if the attention of the female is drawn to the male who is not only slightly different from her brothers but is also more conspicuous, then an evolutionary trend is likely. In the case of the peacock the more successful male is characterised not only by a larger tail but also by a tail with more eye spots on it. Birds find eye spots especially attention-grabbing and, indeed, some of their prey such as moths use the sudden flashing of eye spots on their wings as a means of deterring an attack by startling their insectivorous avian predators. The essence of the argument is that a startling evolutionary change in male form can be driven by female memory. To be sure, genetic change is required to produce ever more conspicuous males, but the evolutionary process is rapid because improvements in their ornaments do not need to be locked into genetic changes in the females' preferences.

Whether or not my conjectures about the role of memory are correct, biologists are generally agreed that animals make active choices and the results of their choices have consequences for subsequent evolution. Three additional proposals have been made for the ways in which an animal's behaviour could affect the subsequent evolution of its ancestors. First, by their behaviour, animals change the physical or the social conditions with which they and their descendants have to cope and thereby affect the subsequent course of evolution – sometimes referred to as 'niche construction'. Secondly, by their behaviour animals often expose themselves to new conditions that may reveal heritable variability and open up possibilities for evolutionary changes that would not otherwise have taken place. Finally, and perhaps most interestingly, animals are able to modify their behaviour in response to changed conditions; this allows evolutionary change that otherwise would probably have been prevented by the death of the animals exposed to those conditions. The last one is most relevant to my general theme of the role of memory in biological evolution.

Modern thinking about the importance of behavioural plasticity in evolution is usually thought to stem from James Baldwin, but the Russell family's tutor, Douglas Spalding, advanced very similar ideas twenty-three years before him,[2] and in 1896 two others, Lloyd Morgan and Osborn, independently developed ideas about 'organic selection', as the subject was called at the time, at the same time as Baldwin.[3] Lloyd Morgan's account of the process was particularly clear and may be paraphrased as follows:

(a) Suppose that a group of organisms that are capable of change in their own lifetimes are exposed to new environmental conditions.

(b) Those whose ability to change is equal to the occasion survive. They are modified. Those whose ability is not equal to the occasion are eliminated.

(c) The modification takes place generation after generation in the changed environmental conditions, but the modification is not inherited. The effects of modification are not transmitted through the genes.

(d) Any variation in the ease of expression of the modified character which is due to genetic differences is liable to act in favour of those individuals that express the character most readily.

(e) As a consequence, an inherited predisposition to express the modifications in question will tend to evolve. The longer the evolutionary process continues, the more marked will be such a predisposition.

(f) Thus plastic modification within individuals might lead the process and a change in genes that influence the character would follow; the one paves the way for the other.

It is obvious, from this outline of the proposed process, that Lloyd Morgan was not suggesting a Lamarckian genetic inheritance of

2. D. A. Spalding, 'Instinct with Original Observations on Young Animals', *Macmillan's Magazine*, 27 (1873).

3. J. M. Baldwin, 'A New Factor in Evolution', *American Naturalist*, 30 (1896). C. Lloyd Morgan, 'On Modification and Variation', *Science*, 4 (1896). H. F. Osborn, 'Ontogenic and Phylogenic Variation', *Science*, 4 (1896).

acquired characters as a mechanism. Nor, less obviously and less consistently, were Osborn or Baldwin. The crucial postulate is a cost of operating the original process of phenotypic adaptation, a cost that can be subsequently reduced by genotypic change, enabling Darwinian evolution to occur. Adaptability to new conditions might be physiological, such as coping with high altitudes by enhancing the oxygen-carrying capacity of the blood. Alister Hardy, a much-loved Professor of Zoology in the middle of the twentieth century, did more than most in the intervening years to pick up on this point and stress that the process could be of great significance. He put it as follows:

> If a population of animals should change their habits (no doubt often on account of changes in their surroundings such as food supply, breeding sites, etc., but also sometimes due to their exploratory curiosity discovering new ways of life, such as new sources of food or new methods of exploitation) then, sooner or later, variations in the gene complex will turn up in the population to produce small alterations in the animal's structure which will make them more efficient in relation to their new behaviour pattern; these more efficient individuals will tend to survive rather than the less efficient, and so the composition of the population will gradually change. This evolutionary change is one caused initially by a change in behaviour.[4]

Hardy envisaged a cascade of changes flowing from the initial behavioural event. Even without structural change, control of behavioural development might alter over time. A requirement for this to happen is that adapting to the new conditions be more costly than doing it easily without active modification. One instance might involve differential responsiveness to particular types of food. Many cases of choice of an unusual food for a given species are probably not due to genetic changes, but to the functioning of normal mechanisms in unusual circumstances. A group of animals might be forced into living in an unusual place after losing their way, but they cope by changing their preferences to suitable foods that are locally abundant. Later, those descendants that didn't need to learn so much when foraging might be more likely to survive than those that could show a fully functional behavioural repertoire only by

4. A. Hardy, *The Living Stream* (1965), p. 170.

learning. A cost was incurred in the time taken to learn. As a consequence, what started as a purely learned difference between animals of the same species living in different habitats became a difference that developed without learning.

The influential child psychologist Jean Piaget, who began his career as a biologist and was much influenced by Baldwin, provided an early example of how the process might work.[5] He studied pond snails in different Swiss lakes that differed in how much wave action occurred. When he transferred snails from one lake to another, the morphology of the shell was changed in response to the musculature required for the wave action of that lake. The descendants of the transferred snails eventually inherited the changed morphology without needing to be exposed to the wave action of that lake. In the terms used by Lloyd Morgan, the initial change could involve adaptability by the individual snail; the adaptability is won at some cost so that descendants expressing the character more efficiently would be more likely to survive. Piaget believed that he had found a clear example of the inheritance of acquired characteristics and never seems to have realised how his supposed Lamarckian effect could be Darwinised.

A well-known palaeontologist, George Gaylord Simpson, coined 'the Baldwin effect' as a term for organic selection, but he did so in order to disparage it.[6] He and many others who forged the new synthesis of Darwinism did not think that behaviour played an important role in evolution and this became the standard line of neo-Darwinists. The dispute is about whether individual adaptability provided the leading edge for evolutionary change or whether it was both unimportant and, if it occurred, involved no new principles. As one critic of organic selection put it: 'If learned behaviors are so effective in getting a useful trait passed from generation to generation at the cultural level, there will be presumably be no selection pressure for the spread of genetic factors favoring the trait.'[7] In other words, if learning is so useful, why dispose of it? My view is that this criticism is based on an impoverished understanding of how behaviour is changed and controlled. The answer

---

[5.] Piaget's work did not come out in book form until 1979, near the end of his life, in *Behaviour and Evolution*.

[6.] G. G. Simpson, 'The Baldwin Effect', *Evolution*, 7 (1953).

[7.] Bruce H. Weber and David J. Depew, *Evolution and Learning: The Baldwin Effect Reconsidered* (2003).

to those who think that the proposed evolutionary change would lead to a generalised loss of ability to learn is to state quite simply that it would not. Learning in complex organisms consists of a series of sub-processes. At the very least it involves detectors that respond to many different features such as lines, movement and more complex patterns such as eyes and faces; on the other side it involves particular motor systems that execute functionally coherent patterns of behaviour; and in between is a parallel array of inter-mediate systems that allow features to be combined in a host of different ways and connected to any of the executive systems control-ling behaviour.[8] Even in the simplest systems an array of detectors is linked directly to an array of executive mechanisms as well as indirectly through an intermediate layer and all connections are plastic. With such networks a particular feature detector can become non-plastically linked to an executive system in the course of evolu-tion without any further loss of plasticity. The effect is that after organic selection, automating behaviour that was previously learned would have a trivial and unnoticeable effect on the animal's capacity to learn new things.

The critics of organic selection also argued that if a character-istic form of behaviour were valuable then the species would acquire it anyway by natural selection, so invoking adaptability to set the process in motion was unnecessary. Once again the critics miss the point. The existence of a new pattern of behaviour, acquired by learning, sets an end-point against which the same pattern, devel-oped without learning, must be compared. Dan Dennett surmised that he could artificially select a population of parrots to say 'Boo Chomsky' without instruction, but throughout the evolutionary process the goal would have to be specified.[9] The chances that all the necessary mutations and genetic recombinations would arise at the same time are very small indeed. In the natural world, if an unlearned pattern of behaviour is not as good as the learned one in the sense that it is not acquired more quickly or at less cost, then nothing will happen. If it is better, evolutionary change is possible. The question is whether the unlearned behaviour could evolve without the comparison. If learning involves several sub-processes or several sequences then the chances against an unlearned

[8] P. Bateson and G. Horn, 'Imprinting and Recognition Memory: a Neural Net Model', *Animal Behaviour*, 48 (1994).
[9] Dennett in Weber and Depew, *Evolution and Learning*.

equivalent appearing in one step are very small. However, with the learned behaviour as the standard, every small step that cuts out some of the plasticity with a simultaneous increase in efficiency is an improvement.

As an example of how the setting of an end-point might work, suppose that the ancestor of the Galapagos woodpecker finch, that pokes sharp sticks into holes containing insect larvae, did so by trial and error and its modern form does so without much learning. In the first stage, a naïve variant of the ancestral finch, when in foraging mode, was more inclined to pick up sharp sticks than other birds were. This habit spread in the population by Darwinian evolution because those behaving in this fashion obtained food more quickly. At this stage the birds still learn the second part of the sequence. The second step is that a naïve new variant, when in foraging mode, was more inclined to poke sharp sticks into holes. Again this second habit spread in the population by Darwinian evolution. The end result is a finch that uses a tool without having to learn how to do so. Simultaneous mutations increasing the probability of two quite distinct acts (picking up sticks and poking them into holes in the case of the woodpecker finch) would be very unlikely. Learning makes it possible for them to occur at different times. Without learning, having one act but not the other has no value. It goes without saying that learning involves memory, so memory becomes a crucial part of what I call 'the adaptability driver' of evolution.[10]

Before exploring further the importance of the adaptability driver I shall briefly discuss a concept called 'genetic assimilation'[11] often confused with organic selection. Frequent references are made in the biological literature to learned behaviour becoming an instinct by genetic assimilation. The claims are made casually and without much thought being given to the way in which the evolutionary process is meant to work. How is it supposed that a shake-up of development in one generation leaves the developmental process more likely to be shaken up in the next? The nature of this cumulative process is not explained. By contrast, the adaptability driver of organic selection involves necessary compensation for the effects

---

10. P. Bateson, 'The Active Role of Behaviour in Evolution', *Biology and Philosophy*, 19 (2004).

11. The term was first used by Conrad Waddington and he provided the first empirical evidence for what he had in mind in 1953 in *Evolution*, 7.

of a new set of conditions and immediate response by the individual to the challenge. The accommodation is not inherited and differential survival of different genotypes may arise from subsequent differences in the ease with which the new adaptation is expressed. The empirical findings on which genetic assimilation was based also involve expression of a novel character in a new environment, but the character is not an adaptation to the triggering condition, even though in the regime of artificial selection used in the experiments, the character conferred some advantage on its possessor. The novel characters do not bear any functional relation to the conditions that disrupted normal development. Nor need there be such a relationship under natural conditions. All that is required initially is that the environmental conditions trigger the expression of a character that can be repeated generation after generation so long as the environmental conditions persist. The initial response of the animal in organic selection is fast whereas the developmental effects of exposing animals to abnormal environment were not seen until they were adult. Since most individuals will be adaptable, most will survive in the initial stages of organic selection. In the experiments giving rise to the idea of genetic assimilation those animals expressing the novel character, a subset of the total population, were artificially selected for further breeding. Finally, in the case of organic selection described by Lloyd Morgan, fresh phenotypic variation presumably arises by mutation that allows the adapted character to be expressed more easily and thence leads to differential survival. In Waddington's experiments mutation was neither postulated nor needed.

By contrast, organic selection involves necessary compensation for the effects of a new set of conditions and immediate response by the individual to the challenge. The accommodation is not inherited and differential survival of individuals with different genes may arise from subsequent differences in the ease with which the new adaptation is expressed. The evidence offered for genetic assimilation also involves expression of a novel character in a new environment, but the character is not necessarily an adaptation to the triggering condition, even though it may confer some advantage on its possessor. In the case of organic selection most individuals will be adaptable and will survive through the initial stages of the evolutionary process. In the examples of genetic assimilation only a subset of the total population develops the new character, and these were artificially selected for further breeding. Finally, in the case of organic selection fresh phenotypic variation presumably arises by genetic mutation, allowing the adapted character to be expressed more easily and thence leading to differential survival. In the experiments used to discuss genetic assimilation mutation was neither postulated nor needed.

Returning to the adaptability driver, it is worth considering its relevance to human evolution. Why did the hominoid line double the relative size of the brain in two million years? Why is the linguistic capacity of a modern human so much greater than that of a chimpanzee? Where did consciousness come from (if such a question is amenable to a coherent answer)? The critical issues are not so much whether the various conjectured links between adaptability and evolution could work, but whether they could have driven evolution so hard and so fast as seems to be the case with the hominoid line. The combination of existing characteristics to provide something new may provide an answer.[12] Non-human primates are known to make signals that are reliably linked to their internal state. A variant might have arisen, producing new signals when in a certain state not previously associated with a signal. This could matter a lot in situations where the success of the group depended on co-operation and trust. In these circumstances, a powerful upward evolutionary drive could be generated. If members of a group were able to link the signal by an individual to the context in which it was produced and then could predict the behaviour of the signaller, the capacity to generate new signals linked to the signaller's state could spread in the population. This enhanced capacity could then have the emergent effect that individuals would be able to create signals in contexts that were both novel and abstract. At each stage, social learning could spread the benefits within the population, thereby accelerating the evolutionary process. New signals could be copied and linked to context and thence to internal state. Here again learning and memory are crucial in driving the evolutionary ratchet.

Another line of thought also linking memory to evolution is that play boosted the evolution of cognitive capacity. The playful use of objects can lead to discovery and result in their proving useful as tools. In what is metaphorically called the adaptive landscape,

[12.] See Deacon in Weber and Depew, *Evolution and Learning.*

a species may be trapped on a low hill when a higher one (and better, in terms of the image) can only be reached by going down before starting to climb to the more beneficial place. The exuberance of play may enable an individual to discover the route because play will often involve leaving the hilltop on which the species is trapped. Once discovered, the behaviour patterns that led to the beneficial outcome can then be automated piecemeal along the lines suggested for the tool-using in the Galapagos woodpecker finch. On this argument those aspects of play that are creative or break out of local traps are especially promising candidates for driving evolution. Once again memory is the crucial link in the driving process. When complex sequences of behaviour appear, their components are gradually automated by Darwinian selection. The spontaneously expressed improvements in what could be readily perceived as cognitive ability would not have evolved by genetic recombination or mutation since the probability of the simultaneous occurrence of all the rare necessary events is vanishingly small. Thus aspects of play can increase the total sum of spontaneously developing behavioural structure that serves to solve complex problems. The adaptability driver of play increases the cognitive tool kit available to the young animal.

As with other aspects of evolution, no necessary link need exist between adaptation and the predictability of behaviour. The evolutionary process can establish rules that affect how the individual changes its behaviour in response to new conditions. To understand the opportunities that this regularity opens up, consider a rule-governed game like chess. It is impossible to predict the course of a particular chess game from a knowledge of the game's rule. Chess players are constrained by the rules and the positions of the pieces in the game, but they are also instrumental in generating the positions to which they must subsequently respond. The range of possible games is enormous. The rules may be simple but the outcomes can be extremely complex. Once the route to a particular outcome has been found, it can be automated.

The most important conclusion here is that the adaptability driver involving memory provides a ladder in evolution. Clearly, complex structures can develop without such a process, but the driver is important when intermediates provide no benefit and a combination of simultaneous mutations needed to provide a functional whole is improbable. Whole organisms survive and reproduce differentially and the winners drag their genes with them. This is the engine of Darwinian evolution and the reason why it is so important to understand the role of learning and memory in biological evolution of complex behaviour.

Ulric Neisser, 'Memory with a Grain of Salt'

In a tradition that goes back to ancient Greece, popular accounts of memory tend to be metaphors. Plato himself likened it to the writing on a wax tablet, which was the information technology of his time. His tablet metaphor is just one version of *memory as writing*, which we still use today when we speak of remembering something 'literally,' i.e. exactly, by the letters. But real remembering is almost never literal: people soon forget the exact language they may have heard. At best they remember the 'gist,' and even that is far from certain.

The next significant memory metaphor to appear was based on photography, invented early in the nineteenth century. Photographs reproduce scenes accurately and completely, but also with a curious indifference: every blade of grass that was projected to the lens ends up in the picture, whether the photographer was interested in it or not. Does anybody have *photographic memory* in that sense? I doubt it. The term is occasionally used, but I think that's only because the metaphor is so readily available. Before photography nobody described remembering as if it were a kind of looking at mental pictures, or claimed that they could recall every blade of grass in a scene. To be sure, some people had good memories. Some people have good memories today too, and they may even claim that they can see past scenes in their 'mind's eye.' But no matter how vivid and clear those images may be, the reports that go with them are not necessarily accurate. Even the best memory image is nothing like a photograph.

The next relevant bit of technology, a century or so after the camera, was the *tape recorder*. Is there perhaps a recorder in the brain, such that our every experience is somehow preserved on its tape? The Canadian neurosurgeon Wilder Penfield, working in the 1940s, became convinced of this by observations he made while electrically stimulating the brains of conscious epileptic patients.

When a certain cortical locus was stimulated, such a patient might say that she heard a familiar piece of music playing, or perhaps a child calling. Despite years of study, none of those experiences was ever validated as being an accurate recall or even as having the characteristics of a remembered episode (as opposed to, say, a dream image). Penfield nevertheless attributed them to an automatic neural tape recorder, the 'permanent record of the stream of consciousness.'[1] The newly available tape-recorder metaphor was irresistible.

Nowadays, of course, we have videotapes as well as audiotapes. Professional hypnotists, occasionally hired by the police in criminal investigations, may tell hypnotised witnesses that they need only 'zoom in' on the relevant 'frames' of their memories to see again what they saw before. But in fact there are no videotapes in our brains, just as there are no wax tablets. What such witnesses may say is just their idea of how to respond in a manner driven by the metaphor. Happily, most American jurisdictions no longer allow hypnotically obtained testimony to be used in court.

All these metaphors compare memory to some permanent medium of storage: written documents, photographic film, magnetic tape. Such a comparison seems harmless enough, but once the metaphor is in play we tend to endow memory itself with properties that only the medium really has: permanence, detail, incorruptibility. Cautious skepticism would be an appropriate response when the witness gives a highly detailed report of what the perpetrator was wearing, describes a once briefly seen object in great detail, or recalls the special tone of someone's voice on a given occasion. Unfortunately the usual response is just the opposite: jurors are much more likely to believe a richly elaborated recall than a bare-bones account of what happened. They say 'Listen to all those details! He couldn't be making it all up!' But he could: data show that there is no consistent relation between the amount of detail reported in a memory and its accuracy.

Misleading as they may be, there is still something comforting about such metaphors. Our past experiences are the very life we lived; how wonderful if they were really on tape somewhere! This line of thought is encouraged by the occasional occurrence of unexpected recollections. We say, 'I haven't thought of that in years! If one long-lost memory like that is still somewhere in my head,

1. W. Penfield, 'The Permanent Record of the Stream of Consciousness', *Proceedings of the 14th International Congress of Psychology* (1954).

couldn't everything else be in there too?' Rhetorical questions are difficult to answer; sometimes the best reply is just another metaphor. Imagine buying an old house, tearing up the floorboards, and unexpectedly finding a copy of a newspaper dated forty years earlier. You would probably be amazed and interested, read every page, tell your friends. But would you conclude that every issue of that newspaper ever printed was somewhere in your house? I think not.

Whenever newspapers turn up, it is wise to bear in mind that not everything they say is true. The same principle applies to memories. To illustrate this point, consider a relatively recent version of the photographic metaphor that is called 'flashbulb memory.' According to Roger Brown and James Kulik, who coined that phrase, some life experiences are so important that the brain takes a sort of indelible flash photo of the scene.[2] Their best example – very plausible to Americans of my generation – was the moment in 1963 when one first learned that President Kennedy had been shot. In a study undertaken twelve years after the event, almost everyone in the sample still recalled that ghastly moment. At least, that's how Brown and Kulik described their results. But of course the actual finding was only that everyone still *claimed* to recall it, which is not at all the same thing. How can we tell whether such claims are justified?

My suspicions on this point were aroused by a flashbulb memory of my own. I long remembered how I had heard the news of the Japanese attack on Pearl Harbor on December 7, 1941 – the day before my thirteenth birthday. I was listening to a baseball game on the radio, in the living room of the house where we lived that year. The announcer interrupted the game to report the attack, and I ran upstairs to tell my mother. A perfectly good flashbulb memory, one would think. I thought so myself for twenty or thirty years, until one day it occurred to me that no one plays baseball in December!

After I described this mistake in my 1982 book *Memory Observed*,[3] several readers noted that a professional football game between two teams called the New York Giants and the Brooklyn Dodgers had in fact been broadcast on that day. So my memory was perhaps only wrong about the sport, an error that would make

[2] R. Brown and J. Kulik, 'Flashbulb Memories', *Cognition*, 5 (1977).
[3] U. Neisser, 'Snapshots or Benchmarks?' in U. Neisser (ed.), *Memory Observed: Remembering in Natural Contexts* (1982).

perfect sense for a baseball fan like me. I listened to baseball broadcasts all through my adolescence and still do so today; for me, baseball is the true American sport. So the real fact of the matter (listening to a football game) had yielded to my beliefs about myself, and the 'flashbulb memory' had changed accordingly.[4]

Many years later, I had an opportunity to study such memories more systematically. The occasion was the explosion of the space shuttle *Challenger* on January 26, 1986. Like John Kennedy's death, the *Challenger* disaster was a stunning tragedy for which America was quite unprepared. It seemed likely, then, that the moment of first hearing about it might become a 'flashbulb memory' for many people. To study those memories effectively, I would need accurate records of what had actually happened. With this in mind I distributed a short questionnaire to a class at Emory University (where I was teaching at the time) on the morning after the explosion. The students were asked to describe how they had first learned about the disaster: where they were, what they were doing, who told them, who else was present, what time it was. Given that the event had occurred less than 24 hours before, it seemed likely that these accounts would be accurate.

The completed questionnaires were put away until the freshmen of 1986 had become seniors in 1989. I then enlisted the aid of a graduate student, Nicole Harsch, and we contacted 44 original participants who were still on campus. They filled out a questionnaire just like the one they had completed three years earlier, and rated their confidence in each aspect of their memory. Their responses were then scored against their earlier reports on an eight-point scale: zero meant that nothing was remembered correctly, seven that every aspect of the report was right.

Here's an example. In 1989, subject RT gave this account of hearing the news:

> When I first heard about the explosion I was sitting in my freshman dorm room with my roommate and we were watching TV. It came on a news flash and we were both totally shocked. I was really upset and I went upstairs to talk to a friend of mine and then I called my parents.

4. See C.P. Thompson and T. Cowan, 'A Nicer Interpretation of a Neisser Recollection', *Cognition*, 22 (1985) and also U. Neisser, 'Remembering Pearl Harbor, *Cognition*, 23 (1986).

This was a very clear and definite memory, and RT's confidence ratings hit the top of the scale. Consider, however, what she had written on the morning after the event:

> I was in my Religion class and some people walked in and started talking about [it]. I didn't know any details except that it had exploded and the schoolteacher's students had all been watching which I thought was so sad. Then after class I went to my room and watched the TV program talking about it and I got all the details from that.

Comparison of these accounts shows that RT's confident flashbulb memory was wrong on every point. She was not unique in this: eleven of our 44 subjects scored zero, and five of the zeros nevertheless gave very high confidence ratings. These results surprised even me. I had expected to find small errors – football games turned into baseball games, perhaps – but not highly confident memories that were completely wrong.

To explore this finding further, Harsch interviewed the participants individually a few months later (in the spring of 1990). All of them repeated their 1989 stories – including the fabrications – even when she hinted that other possibilities should be considered. Finally, as a sort of ultimate hint, Harsch showed each subject his or her original 1986 questionnaire. We had expected that many of them would change their stories in response to this irrefutable evidence – that they would say 'Oh yes, now I remember. That's how it was.' To my surprise, no one did this. Many of the low-accuracy, high-confidence subjects were shaken and disturbed, but they did not back down. Instead they said things like 'This is my handwriting, so it must be right, but no matter – I still remember everything just the way I told you!' A few even argued that they must have been wrong the first time (on the day after the event) because they were surely right now![5]

The *Challenger* study was an early example of what has become a standard paradigm: asking people to describe their personal experience of some public event on two separate occasions, once just after it happened and again some time later. Further research in

[5] U. Neisser and N. Harsch, 'Phantom Flashbulbs: False Recollections of Hearing the News about *Challenger*', in E. Winograd and U. Neisser (eds), *Affect and Accuracy in Recall* (1992).

this paradigm has clarified a number of issues. One might wonder, for example, whether such memories grow weaker with the passage of time. Brown and Kulik thought not: they described their JFK flashbulbs as permanent, 'unchanging as the slumbering Rhinegold.'[6] A finding by Schmolck *et al.*,[7] who studied college students' memories of how they had heard the news of the 1995 O.J. Simpson verdict, shows that this is not the case. Schmolck and his collaborators obtained one set of responses within three days of the event and a second set after a delay that was 15 months for some subjects and 32 months for others. The 15-month group committed few serious errors, but the 32-month group (a delay comparable to our *Challenger* study) produced a substantial number of them.

If the passage of time creates vulnerability to error, where do the erroneous details themselves come from? Here there are many possibilities, some obvious. For example, RT's error – switching from actually hearing about *Challenger* in class to 'remembering' that she first heard about it via TV – is not difficult to explain. She surely watched television coverage later that day (as everyone did), and may have subsequently assumed that the TV images she still remembered were her first contact with the event. A number of the *Challenger* subjects made this switch (i.e. toward TV as the news source), but some of their other errors are more difficult to interpret. Subject GA, who actually had first heard the news in the cafeteria (it made her so sick that she couldn't finish her lunch) later recalled that 'I was in my dorm room when some girl came running down the hall screaming "The space shuttle just blew up!"' There is no reason to believe that such a screaming-girl episode ever took place; it seems more like a fantasy than a real event. Perhaps GA first imagined *herself* screaming through the dorm, and only later projected her emotions on to 'some girl.'

I do not know if this interpretation is correct, but GA would not be the only person who ever changed what began as a fantasy into what seemed like a memory. In the 'recovered memory' craze of the 1980s/1990s, patients in psychotherapy often experienced what seemed to be recovered memories of sexual abuse, sometimes even memories of hideous Satanic practices. At the height of the

---

6. Brown and Kulik, 'Flashbulb Memories', p. 86.
7. H. Schmolck, E. A. Buffalo and L.R. Squire, 'Memory Distortions Develop Over Time: Recollections of the O.J. Simpson Verdict after 15 and 32 Months', *Psychological Science* 11 (2000).

craze these patients often brought accusations against their own families, causing much disruption and grief. It is now clear that most or all of these 'memories' were sheer fabrications, made plausible only by then-popular theories of repression and the unconscious.

It's hard to predict what will become a plausible memory error; everything depends on the specifics of a given situation. Suppose, for example, that a widely viewed public event consisted of two similar sub-events in succession, the second of these being televised. One type of error that might occur in later recollections would then be to 'remember' seeing both sub-events, when in fact only the second was available for viewing. Exactly this sequence occurred in the terrorist attacks on the World Trade Center on 9/11 2001. Many people 'remember' seeing the first plane hit the first tower and then seeing the second plane hit the second tower, but this is impossible: no videotape of the first impact was shown on TV that day.

Among those who apparently hold this false belief is President George W. Bush, who has occasionally given public accounts of how he first learned of the 9/11 attacks. On one such occasion (12/4/2001), answering a child's question, Bush said:

> I was sitting outside the classroom [of a reading program in Florida] waiting to go in, and I saw an airplane hit the tower – the TV was obviously on, and I used to fly myself, and I said 'There's one terrible pilot.' And I said 'It must have been a horrible accident.' But I was whisked off there – I didn't have much time to think about it, and Andy Card . . . walked in and said 'A second plane has hit the tower, America's under attack.'[8]

It is always wise to take memory with a grain of salt, even when the rememberer is President of the United States.

All the rigid-medium metaphors – film, audiotape, videotape, even computer storage – suggest levels of permanence and accuracy that memory does not really possess. But they also mislead in another way, tempting us to misinterpret the nature of memory even when it happens to be accurate. This latter point is often overlooked, so it may be worth illustrating with one more study. That

---

[8.] D.L. Greenberg, 'President Bush's False "Flashbulb Memory" of 9/11/01', *Applied Cognitive Psychology*, 18 (2004).

study, based on a California earthquake, was originally motivated by an obvious weakness of the Brown and Kulik paradigm – namely, that the participants are not personally involved in the event. No matter how upset you may be on hearing the news of a distant assassination or disaster, it still didn't happen to *you*. So when an earthquake rocked northern California on October 17, 1989, a group of us decided to study the memories of people who had actually experienced it.[9] (Living in Atlanta at the time, how did I learn about an earthquake 3,000 miles away? From a baseball broadcast, of course: I was waiting for the World Series game scheduled for that evening in San Francisco!)

Altogether, my colleagues and I studied three sets of subjects. A control group consisted of students at Emory University in Atlanta, interviewed not long after they had first heard the news of the earthquake. A second group – the most important – consisted of students at the University of California in Berkeley who had experienced it themselves. (The quake was distinctly felt in Berkeley, across the bay from San Francisco, even though it did relatively little damage there.) These subjects, interviewed a couple of days after the event, were asked to describe their experiences: where they were when the earthquake hit, what they were doing at the time, etc. They also rated their emotional reactions. A third group, students in Santa Cruz where the physical impact of the quake was much greater, were initially interviewed only after a couple of weeks had passed. All the subjects were retested a year and a half later in the usual way.

The results showed a clear effect of personal involvement. The Atlanta controls, 3,000 miles from the quake itself, behaved much like the subjects of earlier 'flashbulb' studies. By the time of the retest, they had begun to make serious memory errors. In contrast, both California groups got very high scores; their earthquake recalls were essentially perfect. Given this result, it is all too tempting to fall back on some hard-copy metaphor. Isn't this just what one would expect of a 'flashbulb memory'? The earthquake experience was evidently so emotional that it became indelible and permanent.

Perhaps surprisingly, the data do not support this interpretation

9. U. Neisser, E. Winograd, E.T. Bergman, C.A. Schreiber, S.E. Palmer, and M.S. Weldon, 'Remembering the Earthquake: Direct Experience vs. Hearing the News', *Memory*, 4 (1996).

at all. The high retest scores of the California groups did *not* result from strong emotion: the Berkeleyites actually reported rather low arousal levels. Most had experienced earthquakes before, and they took this one in their stride. None of them was in actual danger; at first, many did not realise that this had been a 'big one.' Things were somewhat more stressful at Santa Cruz, but nowhere was there any correlation between reported arousal and later accuracy. Given this result, my colleagues and I prefer a different interpretation. What did happen, we think, is that people told their earthquake stories over and over again.

Personal experience of a major earthquake is definitely worth talking about. Friends and relatives call to find out how you survived, acquaintances want to compare your story with their own. Once you realise that you have a story to tell, it's hard to stop. After a while there were T-shirts for sale that said 'Thank you for not sharing your earthquake experience.' My favorite bit of data comes from the three subjects in the Berkeley sample who had not even noticed the quake as it was happening. A year and a half later, all three of them still knew just where they were and what they were doing while not noticing it!

Here, then, is an alternative to the hard-copy metaphors. Remembering is not like playing back a tape or looking at a picture; it is more like telling a story. The consistency and accuracy of memories is therefore an achievement, not a mechanical production. Stories have lives of their own. Some memory stories do achieve a kind of stability – especially if they have been frequently repeated – but their accuracy cannot be presumed simply because they are vivid and clear. With this in mind, it's always a good idea to take memory with a grain of salt.

Sudhir Hazareesingh, 'Remembering Badly and Forgetting Well: History and Memory in Modern France'

In January 2003, the National Assembly passed a law making it a criminal offence to dishonour the two principal emblems of the French Republic: the tricolour flag and the 'Marseillaise'. Spearheaded by the bullish Minister of the Interior [now President], Nicolas Sarkozy, and voted for even by the parliamentarians of the Left, this piece of legislation is a textbook example of French law-making at its most perverse. It was a response not to some general social disorder, but to a recent football match in Paris between France and Algeria, in which the national anthem was booed by young Algeria supporters, many of whom were French nationals. Its critics have pointed out that this law will not only be impossible to enforce, but will also prove fundamentally counter-productive, being if anything far more likely to provoke further incidents of this kind than to deter them. Indeed a petition condemning this legislation's 'narrow nationalism' is already in circulation. Invoking the *droit à l'outrage*, its signatories are urging the French people to carry out public acts of desecration against the national emblems in question.

Over the past year, I have been working in France's national and departmental archives, carrying out research on Napoleon Bonaparte's image and memory during the nineteenth century; and this story carries striking resonances of that earlier epoch. Above all, the parallel lies in the French state's self-appointed role as the guardian of 'national memory'. Since the Revolution of 1789, public institutions have taken the lead in articulating the meaning of French historical and cultural identity, utilising public space to surround citizens with symbols representing their collective identity and political trajectory as a nation: these emblems range from public monuments and statues of 'great men' to civic festivities and commemorations of political anniversaries, as well as street names (walking through Paris is a lesson in modern French political history). Symbols, in other words, have been regarded as key instruments in shaping collective consciousness, and establishing a 'civic link' between otherwise atomised citizens. But this frantic and somewhat obsessive concern with these emblems also reveals another aspect of French elite sentiment: its abiding sense of vulnerability. In contemporary Britain, a law to protect the Union flag would seem absurd – above all because it would appear inconceivable that such a monument of Britishness could be threatened by the activities of a few mindless vandals. In France, however, the fear is there, because in the collective political imagination the nation is a fragile entity, always tottering on the brink of disintegration; hence the need to nurture its various constituent elements. The state is not alone in performing this role of *chien de garde*; this defensive nationalism has wider cultural roots. It manifests itself both in the Académie Française's puritanical control of all foreign imports into the French language, and in the widespread public support for French struggles against the 'Americanisation' of their culture.

Yet, for the political and cultural historian, what is most striking about the state's attempts to protect its national symbols is how poorly French public authorities seem to understand their own history. Throughout the nineteenth century, successive French regimes – royalist, Bonapartist, republican – sought to legitimise their power by filling public space exclusively with their own symbols, and systematically expurgating those of their opponents. Thus, until the late 1820s, the Bourbon authorities prosecuted all those who mocked or insulted the King or any member of his family; any attempt to desecrate the royalist flag was also severely punished. Despite the harshness of the sentences (up to three years in jail in some cases), the French people found all sorts of ways of expressing their political dissent – lampooning the monarchy and its various emblems by direct insults (the well-proportioned Louis XVIII was popularly known as 'le mangeur de patates'), smashing or defacing busts of the King (a common tactic was to pour red wine over them), or writing seditious messages on the white flag (a good clean surface which almost invited such inscriptions as 'Long live the Republic'). At the same time, the archives show that political dissent was creatively expressed through a whole range of 'counter-symbols'.

Banned by the State, Napoleon's image became the badge of political resistance, and throughout the period between 1815 and

1830 the French police fought a losing battle trying to track down the Emperor's image: Napoleon found his way on to busts, statues and portraits, but also jackets, ties, breeches, walking sticks, tobacco boxes, scarves, handkerchiefs, knives, sweets and cakes. For every such object which was destroyed, thousands made their way through into private and public spaces, threatening the symbolic legitimacy of the Bourbon regime and revealing it for what it was: an authoritarian and repressive regime, contemptuous and fearful of its own people. The message from the archives is simple, if only M. Sarkozy wished to hear it: respect for public institutions and their emblems can neither be generated nor maintained by the State; it has to be earned.

So why, it might be asked, is such a simple lesson from history ignored by a State which constantly invokes the concept of 'memory'? The first answer is that 'memory' is not really a neutral category in France, but an ideological one. It has generally been used in French public discourse for instrumental rather than scientific reasons, in order to celebrate the particular heritage of the Republic, the regime which has been governing France almost without interruption since the late nineteenth century. 'Memory', in this sense, entails the exclusion of all those political forces which do not belong to the Republican tradition. The contribution of Bonapartism to the making of modern France is an excellent case in point. The French are still obsessed with Napoleon, and every year dozens of books, articles, exhibitions and works of creative fiction are devoted to this remarkable figure. One recent film is Antoine de Caunes's *Monsieur N*, a period drama set in the final years of Napoleon's life on the island of St Helena (which, in a characteristic piece of Gallic wishful thinking, sees the imprisoned Emperor outwit his English jailers). This film is in one sense a good reflection of Napoleon's status in French collective imagination: he is greatly admired, but he almost belongs outside history, in the realm of political legend and mythology. . . .

While such an instrumentalisation of 'memory' is perhaps understandable on the part of the Republican State, it is also important to note that it has received strong support from the French historical establishment. The living embodiment of this symbiosis is the historian Pierre Nora, the father of the modern concept of 'memory' in France, and one of the country's foremost intellectual barons; since 2001 he has been a member of the Académie Française. *Les lieux de mémoire* [*The Places of Memory*], the seven-volume work which brought him this promise of immortality, was published under his direction between 1984 and 1992 (it has recently been translated into English and published by Columbia and Chicago University Presses). The appearance of this monumental piece of work was heralded as a major landmark in France's reconstruction of its recent past. But Nora's approach is as interesting for what it leaves out of the remit of 'memory' as for what it includes. The volume in English devoted to 'The State', for example, focuses on the way in which French collective identity has been fashioned by public institutions; among the topics analysed are the emergence of national borders, the political and symbolic attributes of monarchical power, the Napoleonic Civil Code, and the memoirs of great statesmen. And yet this is only one side of the story. One of the distinctive features of the modern French experience is that the State has often directed its violence against its own citizens. But there is little mention of such unpleasantness in Nora's work. In his 'pantheonisation' of French national memory, there is no room for the victims of state violence and their 'memories' – workers beaten up by the police, Algerians thrown into the Seine, or women excluded from the public sphere. It is not in Nora's collection, either, that we should expect to find a chapter on the Drancy concentration camp, through which thousands of Jews transited during the Second World War on their way to Nazi death camps – even though it is a physical site, and the object of much remembering by those who survived their internment there (I once heard Nora actually deny that death camps were 'sites of memory'). The subtext underlying all this, of course, is that we are not dealing with 'memory' in the abstract, but with a particular form of ideologised memory. As wielded by Pierre Nora and his disciples, 'memory' has effectively become a history of national good deeds, a sort of virtual Republican theme park which rivals the concrete version built by EuroDisney in Marne-la-Vallée.

It is not all bad. The study of 'memory' has brought some positive consequences for French history, most notably perhaps the collective (and ongoing) reassessment of the Vichy years – not only in terms of the events themselves, but their wider significance. After subscribing for decades to the convenient myth of a nation united behind the Resistance – peddled by both Gaullists and Communists – France has finally awakened to confront the realities of the 1940–44 period. The specificities of French collaboration, the role of Vichy in the deportation of Jews, the deep strain of xenophobia in certain sections of French society, and the authoritarian under-pinnings of the political culture of the late Third Republic – all this is now the subject of debate and controversy, further kindled by the trials of Klaus Barbie, Maurice Papon and Paul Touvier (at the last, a number of historians were invited to give testimony). This is not a purely academic phenomenon, either: an important mass of testimonies on the Vichy era has been published over the past decade, and numerous associations (of *résistants*, victims of deportation, etc.) are also extremely active at national and local levels.

In this specific area, memory has genuinely enabled a more comprehensive understanding of France's recent past – even though there have been some perverse consequences: most notably the tendency in some circles to view the entire Vichy experience through the prism of the Holocaust, thereby forgetting the other victims of the regime (notably the Communists and other Republicans who resisted).

But in overall terms, French memory remains highly selective. If Vichy has re-entered French public consciousness, the Algerian War (1954–62) and its social and political consequences have remained essentially buried. Since 1999, this conflict has been officially recog-nised as a 'war' – a belated acknowledgement of the obvious, perhaps, but in fact a testimony to the French collective reticence to face up to one of the most sinister episodes in its modern history. Every now and then, it is true, a specific event brings the matter to public attention – most recently the publication of the memoirs of General Paul Aussaresses ... who freely admitted to the wide-spread use of torture and summary executions by the French Army in its fight against the FLN resistance fighters. But there is no 'collective memory' of this conflict in France; many aspects remain under-researched (the relevant archives are still very difficult to get hold of) and there is little ongoing public discussion. A recent study illustrated this by examining the place of the Algerian War in the Modern History curriculum in French secondary schools. The find-ings were edifying: in most textbooks, French colonialism continues to be presented as a 'globally positive' phenomenon, with little mention of how locals were treated as second-class citizens. As for the Algerian War itself, the textbooks offer no explanation or contextualisation of the conflict from a wider anti-colonial perspective (the FLN resistance is generally described as 'Muslim' or 'terrorist'); the French Army's practices of torture are mentioned, but invariably minimised or even justified on grounds of acceptable retaliation or military necessity. Why this schizophrenia between Vichy and the Algerian War, between remembering and forgetting events which are separated by barely a decade? There are several answers, which take us to the heart of contemporary French collective imagination: Vichy was an authoritarian regime which is now part of 'history', whereas the Algerian War was fought by the Fourth and Fifth Republics; the indelicacies of Vichy were part of a wider European phenomenon of war and occupation, whereas the Algerian War was distinctively (and almost uniquely) French; and the perpetrators of state torture and violence in Algeria were not sinister Fascists or mindless thugs, as in the Vichy years, but soldiers and officers of a French Army which included a considerable number of Resistance heroes. Above all, the victims of this violence were different in the two cases: under Vichy, they were essentially Europeans, while in Algeria they were Arabs. France is still not ready to confront its historical and contemporary quandaries in dealing with 'its' Arab populations.

The Times Literary Supplement (21 March 2003).

Richard Holmes, 'A Meander through Memory and Forgetting'

[1]

There is a goddess of Memory, Mnemosyne; but none of Forgetting. Yet there should be, as they are twin sisters, twin powers, and walk on either side of us, disputing for sovereignty over us and who we are, all the way until death.

[2]

For example, right now I am a sixty-one-year-old biographer and writing this at a tin table under an olive tree, on the banks of a tiny streamlet known as La Troubadore. In April La Troubadore gushes over a bed of shimmering white shingle, through the young vine fields, until it vaults into the River Droude, a minor tributary of the River Gardon.

Actually the Gardon is several rivers – *Les Gardons* – though no one can agree on quite how many. But they all flow out of the wild hills of the Hautes Cévennes, the two main branches emerging at Anduze and at Alès (famed for its municipal fountains). Both are much subject to spring and autumnal flooding (*la crue*), and regularly carry off the cars and houses of the plain. They join forces further south, near Avignon, and as one mighty waterway sweep under the Pont du Gard, the noble Roman bridge built by the emperor Augustus, with its fifty-three striding stone arches, one row balancing airily upon another, like some brilliant troupe of performing circus elephants, those creatures that never forget.

Paradoxically this famous Roman bridge is really an aqueduct, and the river beneath it never becomes the Gard. Indeed there is no River Gard at all, except possibly, momentarily, at the point where it goes under Le Pont du Gard. I have heard a local fisherman quote Heraclitus on this subtle question. Certainly, when it comes out the other side, the river is still Le Gardon and flows on

down to join the stately River Rhône near Arles and Tarascon, and
so out into the Mediterranean, untroubled by its many identities.

Yet they change constantly. By August my sparkling young
Troubadore is quite dry and silent. Its shingle is hot and dusty, like
a line of white bones laid along a ditch. The cheerful Droude has
dwindled to a fretful ghost, green and malodorous, skulking under
the trees. Even the two muscular Gardons have fallen into a brown
study, a long slack chain of slumbering rock pools, barely threaded
together by a trickle of live water, marooning thousands of tiny
distracted fish. So, it seems, are the seasons of Memory and
Forgetting, for ever alternating between flood and drought.

[3]

Here at my tin table, with the cicada beating their jazzy Django
Reinhardt sound, I am flooded with memories of the Cévennes of
forty summers ago. I arrived on the night train from Paris, with
its dark creaking woodwork and circular windows, and the pink
dawn coming up over Pont-Saint-Esprit and Orange. Getting out
at Avignon, I was told that all the autocars were 'en Grève'. I
studied my map for some time to find this desirable place, Grève.
Later it was explained that Grève was not a location, but a condition. To be *en grève* meant to be 'on strike'. It now occurs to me
that to be *en grève* could also be a state of mind.

So I hitch-hiked instead to Uzès in the van from the Cave Co-
operative. We drove past the *cimitière*, to the Mas St.-Quentin,
where Monsieur Hugues was ploughing between his vine rows with
his grey horse called Mistral. He completed his row and came over
to the side of the field, pushing his cap on to the back of his head,
and shook my hand with a certain caution. 'Un jeune Anglais,
pardee!' I stayed with his family in the mas for the next five months,
and, in a series of long walks westwards, discovered the Cévennes.

But just here memory falters, and runs dry. I see Monsieur Hugues
so clearly at that moment at the field's edge, the walnut-brown
face, the outstretched arm, the shy glance from under the cap, the
big old leather belt with the army buckle, and the red-check handkerchief pulled out to wipe his face. But red-check – was it? Or
did that belong to the other farmer who, weeks later, I met in a
high, alpine field near Mont Lozère in the Cévennes, under a burning
midday sun. The farmer who stopped his hay-making to give me

an ice-cold swig of water from his canteen, tucked under the tractor seat, and wrapped in a damp cloth to keep it cool. A red-check cloth perhaps? Was it his?

Or was it even the neckerchief that belongs to Monsieur Rolland, the farmer who lives across the track from us now, a seventy-year-old, who adores his vines, his dog and his grandchildren, and shakes my hand across the stone wall, bringing us grapes. Whose red-check handkerchief, whose walnut-brown face, whose eternal shy kindness of the Midi, am I actually remembering? And was that horse that I used to groom in the evenings in the courtyard of the Mas St.-Quentin, to the smell of roasting chicken and rosemary, really called Mistral?

So here is Memory mixed with Forgetting, and maybe combined with what the neuroscientists call confabulation, or 'unconsciously making it up'.[1] Two sparrows dive down and brawl in the dust under the apricot tree. Little bursts of hot wind from the south scrape the big, heart-shaped leaves of the *murier d'Espagne* across the terrace. I listen to this drowsy orchestration of the leaves, the cicada, the fountain, the tractor, the mid-afternoon bell from the village. I fall asleep for a few moments while making these notes. I dream, something about rivers and flooding. But when I wake I cannot remember what it was. I find myself wondering if the rivers used to dry up like this, forty years ago, when I was young?

[4]

Later I discovered the answer in my battered copy of Napoléon Peyrat's *Pasteurs du Désert*. This was Robert Louis Stevenson's favourite book about the Cévennes, which forms the haunting background to his *Travels with a Donkey*. Peyrat vividly recounts the history of the Camisard rebellion of 1702–5, and the memoirs of the visionary young soldier-prophets who came down from the hills to fight against their royalist oppressors on the plain. It was a Protestant insurrection against Catholic authority, but also a mountain people's insurrection against the centralised power of the city and the plain.

In the opening chapter of Volume 2 there is a passage describing the dashing Camisard leader, Jean Cavalier. It recounts his successful

---

[1.] Daniel C. Dennett, *Consciousness Explained* (1991), p. 250.

ambush of the King's dragoons at the Pont de Ners, just five kilo-
metres from my olive tree, where the Droude meets the Gardon
below Anduze. But Peyrat also makes a remarkable observation
about the fluctuating state of the rivers, and what they might
symbolise.

> In springtime during *la crue*, the river Gardon often bursts its banks
> and sweeps like an inland sea towards the village of Boucarain. But
> in the growing heat of summer, all this mighty torrent shrinks back
> again to expose a huge dry plain of sand and pebbles. Its panting
> ardour expires upon the banks of shingle (*grève*), until it is little
> more than a tiny pulse of water which the burning sun of the Midi
> soon dries up completely. So the Gardon is symbolic of the Cevenol
> revolt, as excessive in its triumphs as in its defeats. Moreover, the
> river would never countenance a bridge to be maintained at Ners.
> It would ruthlessly wash away each successive set of arches, as soon
> as they were built. Beside their eternally ruined stonework, a simple
> ferry boat, plying between one bank and the other, remained the
> most reliable method for travellers.[2]

So the Gardon had always fluctuated violently; and sometimes even
became the River Lethe too.

[5]

Here is something one of my students at the University of East
Anglia, Marisse Clarke, told me about forgotten memories. Marisse
was completing her MA in Life-Writing, and working on a project
to reconstruct the domestic history of pre-war Norfolk. It was a
jump-back of sixty years or more to the pre-fridge era, as she called
it. There was lots of written material, especially letters and diaries
in the Norwich archives, but she was interested in something more
direct and intimate, an oral history. Her main source became groups
of old age pensioners, many of them women, who met once a week
for 'Reminiscence sessions'. Initially they were shy, their memories
were very scattered, and it was difficult to get more than a few
well-worn tales. On subjects such as 'Christmas', Marisse suspected
many memories were made up of 'fanciful images', unconsciously

---

[2.] Napoléon Peyrat, *Les pasteurs du désert* (1842), 2 vols, II, p. 50. Translation R.H.

adapted from popular Christmas tales, films or Christmas cards (confabulation again).

Then a colleague told her about the Memory Boxes which had been taken along to other Reminiscence sessions. A Memory Box typically consisted of a large suitcase containing a number of perfectly humdrum domestic objects from the 1930s – a bar of Lux soap, a packet of Swan Vesta matches, an Ovaltine tin, a tortoise-shell hair-clip, a small mangle, and so on. For a 'Wash Day and Bath Night' session, things like stone hot water bottles and men's old razors were added – and the Memory Box itself became an old zinc bath.

According to Marisse, what many of us would regard as 'old junk' now became 'little treasures' of stored-up memory, with a high symbolic value. The effect of the Memory Boxes was often magical. The old women, many in their seventies and eighties, slowly began to handle, identify (eyesight not always so good) and discuss these familiar objects. Amazement was soon followed by laughter, delight and not infrequently indignation, and even some tears. Each physical object began to 'trigger' a long chain of recollections. Gradually an extraordinary stream of shared memories, anecdotes, jokes and stories would emerge. The flow – the flood – soon became unstoppable. It was quite unlike anything Marisse or her colleagues had heard before, and the memories had a knock-on or chain-reaction effect, each memory setting off another. Sometimes, it seemed, the evenings would explode into a party, a Memory party.

This was the starting point for a brilliant paper on oral history, old age and community memory: '*Wash Day and Bath Night: Uncovering Women's Reminiscences*'.[3] What did it demonstrate? Certainly that Marisse was a very good researcher, and knew how to wait, how to listen, and how to gain trust. But also that Memory and Forgetting are subject to the law of Association.

[6]

The concept of the association of ideas is at least as old as Aristotle writing in the fourth century BC. The argument was taken up by

3. Marisse Clarke, 'Wash Day and Bath Night: Uncovering Women's Reminiscences of Domestic Life in Norwich and its Surrounds, 1930s to 1940s.' Unpublished MA dissertation, September 2003, School of Literature and Creative Writing, University of East Anglia. By kind permission of the author.

Pascal and Hobbes, and later elaborated by David Hume in his *Treatise on Human Nature* (1738). Hume suggested that ideas were naturally linked by three qualities: 'resemblance, contiguity in time or place, and cause and effect'.[4] But it took an eighteenth-century doctor to transform these metaphysics into a scientific theory of memory.

One of the great, forgotten books of English Romanticism is David Hartley's *Observations on Man, His Frame, His Duty and His Expectations*, first published in 1749. Hartley was a successful physician, who turned his hand to philosophy and psychology. Born in Yorkshire, he practised largely in London and Bath, where he developed a theory of consciousness based on his own medical observations of his patients. Hartley's great originality was to consider memory primarily as a physiological process. It was something that occurred not only in the 'mind', but physically in the structure of the brain. He combined the empirical philosophy of Locke with his own views of the human nervous system. He argued that all memories were formed by 'clusters' or sequences of associated impressions and ideas. These were physiologically encoded in the brain in an enormous network of medullary 'vibrations', or smaller 'vibratiuncles', similar to electrical impulses moving through the brain tissue or 'medullary substance'.

Although Hartley had not carried out dissections of the cerebral cortex, and had no effective map of the human brain, his theories strikingly anticipate much speculative modern neuroscience. For example Francis Crick's study, *The Astonishing Hypothesis* (1994), with its characteristically provocative subtitle 'The Scientific Search for the Soul', proposes '40-Herz oscillations' within the brain and 'reverberations' within the cortex, as the possible basis of human consciousness. 'Consciousness depends crucially on thalmic connections within the cortex. It exists only if certain cortical areas have reverberatory circuits . . . that project strongly enough to produce significant reverberations.'[5]

In their most basic form Hartley's associative clusters were linked to simple impressions of pleasure or pain, but eventually organised themselves hierarchically. They evolved into all the higher forms of remembered knowledge, learning and reason. They evolved into

4. David Hume, *A Treatise on Human Nature* (1738), I, iv, 19.
5. Francis Crick, *The Astonishing Hypothesis* (1994), pp. 246, 252.

notions of imagination, ambition, conscience and love. They even evolved into a belief in God, what Hartley called 'theopathy'.

Hartley was a philanthropist, a vegetarian, a Christian and a believer in a mystical kind of Paradise. Yet in effect, he was putting forward a theory of the entirely physical or 'material' evolution of the human brain. He saw no sign of the traditional division between mind and body. He detected no separate interjection of a 'spirit', a divine 'spark' or a soul. Memory was a form of electrical or chemical motion. As he put it in his famous Proposition 90: 'All our voluntary powers are of the nature of Memory'.[6]

Hartley also had an unusual theory of dreams. Far from being coded messages from the unconscious, they were simply part of the brain's system of waste disposal. When we dreamed, we abandoned the useless memories and associations of the day. Dreaming was a functional form of forgetting, that prevented the machinery of the brain from becoming overloaded. Without forgetfulness, we would become mad. 'The wildness of our dreams seems to be of singular use to us, by interrupting and breaking the course of our associations. For if we were always awake, some accidental associations would be so cemented by continuance, as that nothing could afterwards disjoin them; which would be madness.'[7]

These ideas strongly attracted the eighteenth-century scientist and free-thinker, Joseph Priestley. Priestley was fascinated by various forms of chemical and electrical energy, and suspected that the human brain contained both. (He had a taste for daring innovations, and was the first to isolate, though not to identify, oxygen gas consumed in combustion.) In 1774 Priestley edited a new edition of the *Observations* with his own preface. 'Such a theory of the human mind . . . contains a new and most extensive *science*,' he wrote. 'It will be like entering upon *a new world*, affording inexhaustible matter for curious and useful speculation.'[8]

But others were profoundly shocked. Thomas Reid, a professor of moral philosophy from Edinburgh, observed that 'the tendency of Hartley's system is to make all the operations of the mind mere mechanism, dependent on the laws of matter and motion'. The horrific idea of human memory as a 'mere mechanism' inspired

---

[6.] David Hartley, *Observations on Man, His Frame, His Duty and His Expectations* (1749), I, 90.
[7.] Ibid., I, 3; Richard C. Allen, *David Hartley on Human Nature* (1999), p. 24.
[8.] Quoted ibid., p. vii.

Reid with a superb passage of polemic science fiction. 'If one should tell of a telescope so exactly made as to have the power of feeling; of a whispering gallery that had the power of hearing; of a cabinet so nicely framed as to have the power of memory; or of a machine so delicate as to feel pain when it was touched; such absurdities are so shocking to common sense that they would not find belief even among savages . . .'9

It does not weaken Reid's metaphysical outrage to observe that three hundred years later most of these 'absurd' and incredible machines do exist. Certainly one could argue that the laparoscope (introducing carbon fibre optics within the body), the mobile phone, the desktop computer and the MRI scanner demonstrate respectively many of the impossible features Reid describes.

[7]

More surprisingly, Hartley's *Observations* deeply impressed a Romantic poet. In his extraordinary effusion of 1796 entitled 'Religious Musings' (a sort of intellectual *tour d'horizon* written at the age of twenty-four), Coleridge grouped David Hartley with Newton and Priestley as one of the three visionary English scientists who had truly glimpsed a 'renovated Earth'. He described Hartley as the 'wisest' among scientific thinkers, who had fearlessly explored the human mind, and become (in a prophetic image)

> . . . The first who marked the ideal tribes
> Up the fine fibres through the sentient brain.

Many of Coleridge's finest early poems, such as 'Frost at Midnight' (1798), with its complex patterns of memory association, are explorations of Hartley's theories. Like a Memory Box, this poem contains a series of physical objects and sensations – an owl's cry, a flickering fire, a baby's cradle, the sound of church bells – which reverberate into an ever-expanding orchestration of memories. These also produce, like complex harmonies, several layers of past and future identity. The adult Coleridge becomes a child again; while the child remembers he has become a father; and the father blesses the child. It is no coincidence that the actual baby in this poem is

9. Thomas Reid, *Essays on the Intellectual Powers of Man* (1785), p. 95.

Coleridge's eldest son, Hartley, born near Bristol in 1796 and named in honour of the philosopher-doctor.

Coleridge's later *Notebooks* have many passages exploring the phenomenon of memory association, such as those connected with his beloved Asra, Sara Hutchinson. In March 1810 he wrote down an enormous catalogue of all the objects which by 'the Law of Association' reminded him of her – from a piece of music to a waterfall, from a bedroom door ajar to the delicious white sauce on a joint of meat. He described them as forming a powerful cluster of ideas, almost unbearably strong and vivid, 'that subtle Vulcanian Spider-web Net of Steel – strong as Steel yet subtle as the Ether – in which my soul flutters enclosed with the Idea of your's.'[10]

Here Hartley's 'vibrations' have been subtly transformed back into a 'flutter' of the soul; a word that also occurs at a key place in 'Frost at Midnight'. In this beautiful and observant passage, Coleridge uses the faint flicker of convected air above his fire (the mirage-like 'film', not the visible flame) to produce a remarkable image of human consciousness itself. It is essentially unstable, dynamic and playfully inventive.

> . . . the thin blue flame
> Lies on my low-burnt fire, and quivers not,
> Only that film, which fluttered on the grate,
> Still flutters there, the sole unquiet thing.
> Methinks, its motion in this hush of nature
> Gives it dim sympathies with me who live,
> Making it a companionable form,
> Whose puny flaps and freaks the idling Spirit
> By its own moods interprets, every where
> Echo or mirror seeking of itself,
> And makes a toy of Thought.

Coleridge would go on to dedicate three entire chapters of his *Biographia Literaria* (1817) to the history of Associationism 'traced from Aristotle to Hartley'. In one place he remarked that Hartley's theory of memory could be compared to 'a broad stream, winding through a mountainous country with an indefinite number of

10. S. T. Coleridge, *Notebooks*, ed. Kathleen Coburn (1957—), III, 3708 (1803).

currents, varying and running into each other according as the gusts chance to blow from the opening of the mountains'.[11]

[8]

In one form or another the theory of Associationism remained hugely influential throughout the Romantic period. The radical idea of memory as a physiological process was seen to provide a possible link between human consciousness and the rest of the living world, however remote. Coleridge had written of 'dim sympathies' with 'companionable forms'. More than seventy years after Hartley's *Observations*, the great chemist, Sir Humphry Davy, was exploring Associationism in connection with freshwater fishes in his book *Salmonia, or Days of Fly-Fishing*, published in 1828.

He was investigating the mysterious memories of fish, which he regarded as quite as interesting a phenomenon as those of human beings. For example, once a trout was caught and thrown back into the river, could it remember being hooked? Could it remember *the pain* of being hooked? Could it feel – or remember – pain at all? And if so, was trout-fishing inherently cruel? – an astonishingly modern question. 'But do you think nothing of the torture of the hook, and the fear of capture, and the misery of struggling against the powerful rod?'[12]

Davy debates these issues in a series of dialogues, which gain an added poignancy from the fact that he himself was ill, in pain and near death at the time he wrote them. 'My only chance of recovery is in entire repose,' he wrote from the shores of Lake Constance in July 1827, 'and I have even given up angling, and amuse myself by dreaming and writing a very little, and studying the natural history of fishes . . . I now use green spectacles, and have given up my glass of wine per day.'[13]

He concludes that although a trout may not feel pain in a human sense, it does remember being hooked, and afterwards may subsequently 'refuse an artificial fly day after day, for weeks together'. Davy thought the reason for this was that the trout associated the pain with the place. 'The memory seems local and associated with

---

[11.] Coleridge, *Biographia Literaria*, ed. Engell and Bate (1983), I ch. 6, p. 110.
[12.] Humphry Davy, *Salmonia, or Days of Fly-Fishing* (1828), in *Collected Works* (1840), IX, pp. 13–14.
[13.] Humphry Davy, *Fragmentary Remains, Literary and Scientific* (1847), p. 287.

surrounding objects; and if a pricked trout is chased into another pool, he will, I believe, soon again take the artificial fly. Or if the objects around him are changed, as in Autumn, by the decay of weeds, or by their being cut, the same thing happens.'[14]

[9]

One afternoon about five years ago I was walking around a favourite flower bed in Norfolk, which Rose and I had dug and planted from scratch. Every plant and shrub was an old friend – iceberg roses, Hidcote lavenders, blue hydrangeas, magnolia, purple berberis, red-tipped photinia, Japanese anemones, scarlet crocosmia, white potentilla. Then I came to a pleasant, green tufted shrub which had once been the size of a modest pincushion and was now more like that of a plump *chaise-longue*. I had often fed it, clipped it, hoed uxoriously under its skirts. I had, frankly, often wished to sprawl full length on its springy, inviting mattress of minute green foliage and tiny white flowerets.

But on this particular afternoon I gazed down at its familiar, cheery, hospitable shape and realised that I had totally forgotten its name. For several uncomfortable minutes I stared down at it, reaching into the pocket of my memory and finding it alarmingly empty, just as if I had suddenly lost a set of car keys. Only when I turned to walk back up the lawn, and was momentarily distracted by the flight of a pigeon above the beech trees, did the name 'hebe' spring effortlessly to mind.

Of course this is a common phenomenon among the middle-aged. (Is it called 'nominative aphasia'? I can't remember.) It applies particularly to the names of specific things – people, places, books, or – in my case – plants. It can be combated, especially by child-like mnemonic devices. 'Hebe-jeeby' has rarely failed me since. Nevertheless it tends to spread steadily and insidiously once it has begun. No one has quite explained its causes. I know a computer expert who calls it the 'disk full' effect; while others speak of senior moments, or hardening cerebral arteries, weakened synaptic links, alcohol, tea-drinking, metaphysical distraction, existential anxiety, or just the middle-aged mind generally 'on other things' – though not necessarily higher ones.

This kind of Forgetting certainly belongs to the goddess who has

[14.] *Salmonia*, p. 27.

no name. Yet it is not so much a failure to remember: more a failure to *recollect*. Moreover the act of recollection worked in a curious way. When I actively tried to recollect, it was as if I was constantly on the brink of remembrance, or as if I was stuttering with a word, or slipping back from the last few inches of a rope-climb. But the moment I stopped trying, the moment I looked up and admired the pigeon in his evening swoop over the beech trees, the word 'hebe' arrived without effort, without strain, like a free gift.

Coleridge was one of the first people to describe this phenomenon of 'active and passive recollection' in his *Biographia*. It appears in Chapter 6, where he compares the mental law of Association with that of the physical law of gravitation: 'it is to Thought the same, as the law of gravitation is to locomotion'. Sometimes we actively strive for memory, sometimes we passively yield to forgetfulness. When someone is 'trying to recollect a name', he uses 'alternate pulses of active and passive motion'. The surprising analogy Coleridge gives for this mental process is that of a tiny water-beetle swimming up a stream. He adds that a very similar active-passive is at work in the composing of poetry. The passage, with its impression of Coleridge himself bending over the surface of the water (or the mind), minutely observant, half poet and half scientist, is itself a kind of mnemonic image.

> Now let a man watch his mind while he is composing; or, to take a still more common case, while he is trying to recollect a name . . . Most of my readers will have observed a small water-insect on the surface of rivulets, which throws a cinque-spotted shadow fringed with prismatic colours on the sunny bottom of the brook; and will have noticed how the little animal *wins* its way up against the stream, by alternate pulses of active and passive motion, now resisting the current and now yielding to it in order to gather further strength and a momentary *fulcrum* for a further propulsion. This is no unapt emblem of the mind's self-experience in the act of thinking. There are evidently two powers at work . . .[15]

[10]

The power of what has been forgotten can sometimes be as great as that which has been remembered. In Edward Thomas's poem,

[15.] *Biographia Literaria*, Ch. 6, p. 125.

'Old Man', the unnamed bush that stands outside his cottage door has a tiny leaf with a dark, bitter, haunting smell. It evokes something he can never quite place or explain. Each time he rubs it between his fingers, the scent sweeps him back to the borders of a primitive memory, which is never quite rediscovered.

> As for myself
> Where first I met the bitter scent is lost.
> I, too, often shrivel the grey shards,
> Sniff them and think and sniff again and try
> Once more to think what it is I am remembering.
> Always in vain. I cannot like the scent,
> Yet I would rather give up others more sweet,
> With no meaning than this bitter one.
> I have mislaid the key. I sniff the spray
> And think of nothing; I see and hear nothing;
> Yet seem, too, to be listening, lying in wait
> For what I should, yet never can, remember . . .
> Only an avenue, dark, nameless, without end.

Thomas's poem also reminds one of the peculiar power of smell to summon up – to call back – specific memories (especially of places). I have an aftershave which instantly recalls a certain room in a motel in Pacific Grove, near Monterey, in California.

Proust observed in *A la recherche du temps perdu* that the smell and taste of things were 'more faithful' than visual images. They remained suspended in the mind for a long time, 'like souls ready to remind us, waiting and hoping for their moment to come amid the ruins of all the rest; they bear unfaltering, in the tiny and almost impalpable drop of their essence, the vast structure of recollection'.

That was written in 1913, as Proust reflected in Paris on the extraordinary power of the madeleine dipped in the tea, to call back the memories of his country childhood in Combray. It has become the classic literary reference to the power of smell and taste to summon memories. But five years earlier, in a dark lane near the River Thames, another equally powerful summons – with the force of 'an electric shock' – had already been recorded.

We others, who have long lost the more subtle of the physical senses, have not even proper terms to express an animal's intercommunication with his surroundings, living or otherwise, and have only the word 'smell' for instance, to include the whole range of delicate thrills which murmur in the nose of the animal at night and day, summoning, warning, inciting, repelling. It was one of those mysterious fairy calls from out of the void that suddenly reached Mole in the darkness, making him tingle through and through with its very familiar appeal, while as yet he could not clearly remember what it was. He stopped dead in his tracks, his nose searching hither and thither in its efforts to recover the fine filament, the telegraphic current, that had so strongly moved him.

This of course is the Mole from *The Wind in the Willows* (1908), trudging along one freezing December night on his way back to Ratty's snug, riverside burrow, when suddenly ambushed by olfactory memory. He too does not know for some moments what he is smelling, only that its associations are bewilderingly strong. Then finally comes 're-collection in the fullest flood'. What he is smelling is 'Home!' and his own past life there (back in the spring). 'Now, with a rush of old memories, how clearly it stood up before him in the darkness!'

Smell can be piercingly direct in its transporting power. In his autobiography, *Something of Myself* (1937), Rudyard Kipling describes a particular pungent kind of woodsmoke, made up of burning tar, old ammunition boxes and railway-sleepers, with which he says he could move an entire battalion of men to the veldt of South Africa, by reactivating their memories of the Boer War. Yet the precise action of smell on the human memory still remains mysterious.

In 2004 the Nobel Prize for Physiology was presented to two American scientists, Richard Axel and Linda Buck, for a brilliant paper on the connection between the nose and the brain. They established that the human nose has nearly a thousand separate 'receptors' (ten times more than a fish, though forty times less than a dog). These have complex connections with the cortex, involving no less than 3 per cent of our genes. They form unique clusters or 'olfactory patterns', which are capable of holding 'memories of approximately 10,000 different odours', a truly astonishing resource. Yet when asked, in the course of an interview on BBC World Service, what light their prize-winning work threw on Proust's experience, Richard Axel answered simply: 'None at all'.[16]

16. Nobel Prize press release, 4 October 2004.

[11]

In her popular science book, *The Human Brain: A Guided Tour* (1997) Susan Greenfield concludes, in a way that David Hartley would surely have recognised, that 'Memory is a cornerstone of the mind'. But writing as a Professor of Pharmacology, she still emphasises how little can be said definitely about the relationship between its 'phenomenological and physical' functioning. There is no generally accepted theory of how the brain produces the mind, or the mind generates consciousness, or of how consciousness depends on memory. The human brain has 100 billion cells, and their infinitely complex interaction remains much more mysterious than the functioning of an entire galactic star system. Perhaps there is something oddly reassuring about this.

Neurological experiments have proved that there is a short-term memory (which seems to be connected to the hippocampus and lasts up to thirty minutes). There is also a separate long-term memory which may last over ninety years, and seems to be distributed throughout the cerebral cortex. Amazing feats of memory have also been accurately studied and measured in the performance of chess-players, musicians, actors, sports aficionados (entire Wisdens committed to memory), or autistic patients. One recalls the Memory Man in the film of John Buchan's *The Thirty-Nine Steps* (1935, Alfred Hitchcock, but not in fact in the original novel of 1915).

Nevertheless, the actual way a single discrete memory (if there is such a thing) is 'recorded' in the human brain remains bafflingly obscure. Writing of Wilder Penfield's open-brain surgical experiments in Canada, Greenfield observes, 'The clinical cases reported by Penfield would also suggest that memory is not stored simply: it is not laid down directly in the brain. Rather, as seen in Penfield's studies, a cache of memories would be more like a nebulous series of dreams. One immediate problem was that the memories themselves were not like highly specific recordings on a video and were a far cry from the memories on a computer. Another problem was that if the same area was stimulated by Penfield on different occasions, different memories were elicited. Conversely, the same memories could be generated from stimulating different areas. No one has yet shown definitively how these phenomena can be explained in terms of brain functioning.'[17]

17. Susan Greenfield, *The Human Brain: A Guided Tour* (1997), p. 170.

Nevertheless, the basis of all memory still seems to be conceived as the establishment of 'associations' through clusters or 'networks' of neuronal links. 'We know that long-term memory is accompanied by an increase in the number of presynaptic terminals, and we know that memory involves establishing new associations.'[18] Chemical transmitters, voltage changes and synaptic 'circuits' have partly replaced Hartley's speculative 'vibrations', although the old imagery of flood and drought is still hauntingly present. Explaining the role of calcium in forming a neuronal connection, Greenfield writes of the glutamate receptor cell 'opening the channel for calcium ions to flood in', and subsequently of the 'large influx of calcium' strengthening the synapse by releasing 'a chemical cascade within the target cell'.[19]

Neuroscience also recognises many types of forgetting, though most of these are pathological. They include numerous kinds of brain damage; various forms of post-traumatic amnesia; Korsakoff's syndrome (based on severe dietary deficiency); alcoholic blackouts and lapses; Wernicke's aphasia in which speech itself is unlearned; Parkinson's (in which the brain forgets physical co-ordination); and of course Alzheimer's, which is not a natural consequence of old age, but a very specific degenerative disease of the medial temporal lobe.[20]

Forgetting as a more positive, constructive, or even healing process – both for individuals and for whole societies – receives scant attention. So does the 'benign protective amnesia' of old age, as reflected in Groucho Marx's memorable aside: 'I never forget a face, but in your case I am prepared to make an exception.'

[12]

Old age brings one particularly enigmatic feature of the lifelong exchange between Memory and Forgetting. It is the striking, but apparently paradoxical fact that, as old people begin to forget their immediate past, they often begin to remember their distant childhood with startling vividness. What possible metaphysical or physiological explanation can be given for this phenomenon?

Susan Greenfield calls it, among all the common processes of

[18.] Ibid., p. 186.
[19.] Ibid. p. 181.
[20.] David Samuel, *Memory: How We Use It, Lose It, and Can Improve It* (1997), pp. 75–7.

human memory, 'the most mysterious issue of all'. Characteristically, she sees the problem in terms of cellular loss and renewal. 'We know that some people can remember what happened to them ninety years ago, but by then every molecule in their body will have been turned over many times. If long-term changes mediating memories are occurring continuously in the brain, how are they sustained?'[21]

This paradox had already been observed by Leonardo da Vinci, in one of his Notebooks known as the *Codex Atlanticus*, at the beginning of the sixteenth century. 'Things that happened many years ago often seem close and proximate to the present time, and many things that happened recently seem as ancient as the long-gone days of youth.'[22]

Coleridge saw the problem in psychological terms. He suggested shrewdly that memories of childhood had a high visual content, with strong associated moods, but lacked linguistic or spoken elements. 'If I were asked how it is that very old people remember *visually* only the events of early childhood, and remember the intervening spaces either not at all or only verbally, I should think it a perfectly philosophical answer that old age remembers childhood by *becoming a second childhood!*'

He expanded this in a letter to his friend Robert Southey in August 1803. 'I hold that association depends in a much greater degree on the recurrence of resembling *states of feeling* than in trains of ideas; that the recollection of early childhood in latest old age depends on and is explicable by this.' He added that if flows of feelings, rather than discrete chains of ideas, formed the essential structure of memory, then Hartley's system was too atomistic and passive: 'Hartley's system totters.'[23]

In fact Coleridge came to consider (like Bergson, like Proust) that perhaps nothing was really ever forgotten. Perhaps movements of feeling, vibrations of emotion, were capable of resurrecting almost anything from our past lives. 'For what is Forgetfulness? Renew the state of affection or bodily Feeling, same or similar – sometimes dimly similar – and instantly the trains of forgotten thought rise up from their living Catacombs!'[24]

[21.] Greenfield, *Human Brain*, p. 176.
[22.] Charles Nicholl, *Leonardo da Vinci: the Flights of the Mind* (2004), p. 16.
[23.] Coleridge, *Letters*, ed. E.L. Griggs (1956) I, pp. 427–8.
[24.] Coleridge, *Notebooks*, I, 1575 (1803).

[13]

Yet in the Preface to his unfinished 'Kubla Khan' (1816), Coleridge described the most famous incident of creative forgetting in English literature. Retired to a lonely farmhouse near Exmoor in the autumn of 1797, he took opium and dreamed a poem of 'not less than from two to three hundred lines'. On awaking, he wrote down the first 54 lines (as we now know 'Kubla Khan') but was interrupted by 'a person on business from Porlock'. He could never recall the rest of the poem.

The analogy Coleridge uses for this moment of forgetfulness is, once again, water. '. . . On his return to his room, [he] found, to his no small surprise and mortification, that though he still retained some dim recollection of the general purport of the vision, yet, with the exception of some eight or ten scattered lines and images, all the rest had passed away like the images on the surface of a stream into which a stone had been cast, but, alas! without the after restoration of the latter!'

Most modern critics and biographers think that Coleridge invented the Person on business from Porlock, to hide the fact that he simply could not finish the poem. But I think he was visited first by Mnemosyne, and then by the other goddess. It was just that he could not remember her name.

Part II

. . . fragilis hominum memoria recedit et traditio litterarum semper ad memoriam reducit.

. . . the frail memory of man slips away and the written record always restores memory.

Charter of King Alfred

Introduction

Harriet Harvey Wood

Dennis Enright, himself a great anthologist, once remarked that for every existing anthology there are at least four other possible anthologies – things uncollected, directions not followed. We have come to the order and arrangement of ours after much thought and discussion – we are very aware of how much has been excluded because we had no more space, or not included because we hadn't found it.

We have concentrated on the writings of the western world, starting with Plato and ending close to the work of the present day, though we realise that new publications on the subject appear monthly, almost daily. We have been involved in a kind of White Queen race, running hard to stay in the same place. Aristotle made a good point, when, in the first book devoted to the subject, he made a distinction between memory and reminiscence, and on the whole, we have tried to observe his distinction and given priority to extracts which illustrate the ways in which memory works (and its more notable and extraordinary aberrations) – and also writings which try to define or illustrate what memory is. We have of course also included many reminiscences. Definitions start with illustrations, and reminiscence is a form of human self-definition.

The first section, 'Childhood Memories', does consist of reminiscences and was originally called 'Personal Memories'. We discovered that what we had gathered were all childhood memories, with the clarity and mystery good writers give to early memories. They include John Clare, Sigmund Freud, both the Woolfs and a passage from the autobiography of Eric Kandel, the great student of the biology of memory. All illuminate and are illuminated by the writings in later sections. They are what most people immediately think of when they think of memory. It would have been possible to fill an entire volume with these pieces alone. So many of them are the ones which stick longest in the imagination: Virginia Woolf's memory of seeing her holiday nursery in

Cornwall as if 'lying in a grape', Chesterton's vivid scarlet vision of Cardinal Manning.

Our second section contains extracts partly from what can be thought of as a classical tradition of writings on memory, starting with Plato, Aristotle and St Augustine. It includes Cicero's story of Simonides, the anonymous *Ad Herennium* treatise, Kim's Game from Kipling, and of course Frances Yates on Renaissance Memory Theatres, A.R. Luria's study of the mind of a mnemonist, and Borges's classic, 'Funes the memorious'.

'Memory and Science' starts with Aristotle on animals, and ends with Antonio Damasio and Kandel on their research in the neuroscience of memory. It includes classic thinkers and experimental workers like Pavlov and Bartlett. We also included Francis Galton's eccentric and comical study of his own thought processes. There are examples of the study of animal memory, as it is related to the study of 'instinct', with work by Konrad Lorenz and Nicolaas Tinbergen. And we have extracts from the huge and rapidly growing field of the study of the brain itself, from J.Z. Young to Semir Zeki, from Francis Crick to Vilayanur Ramachandran.

'Memory and Imagination' includes thinking by writers, artists and others about how we put the imagined world together, and the way the memory works in this process. Proust and Wordsworth are there of course – and we have included Freud in this section, both on screen memories, and in his analysis of a childhood memory Goethe recorded in his autobiography, *Dichtung und Wahrheit*. We have two passages from George Eliot, from *Middlemarch* and *Daniel Deronda*, in which it is clear that she is using rooted memories of her own childhood in her art. In *Daniel Deronda* the absence of such memories is a clue to the unsettled character of Gwendolyn Harleth.

We move from memory as a constructive power to the vexed and fascinating problem of false memories – memories constructed, for all sorts of reasons, which are not memories at all, but lies, or fantasies, or mistakes. And from invented memories we move to a section on the construction of public memory – communal mnemonics as a political act, street names as 'history', the 'official stories' of states. And we end with 'Forgetting' – from Cicero to Billy Collins. We cannot remember well if we have no capacity to forget.

The arrangement within chapters is in general chronological, by date of first publication. This principle has occasionally been abandoned when it resulted in an obvious absurdity, such as the separation of Leonard and Virginia Woolf by nearly half a century owing to the posthumous publication of the latter's memoirs. In such a case it seemed right to reunite husband and wife. The chronological structure, both in the philosophical and the scientific sections, helped to illustrate the development of research and the interplay of ideas. Sometimes the accident of this arrangement served to highlight unexpectedly serendipitous coincidences, such as the scarlet fever which formed the background of the childhood memories of both Samuel Butler's Henry Hoare and Leonard Woolf. More significant was the chance neighbourhood, within a couple of pages of each other, of Antonio Damasio's present-day discussion of what he has described as the '*as-if-body-loop*' mechanism and a striking illustration of it in the fifteenth-century Scottish poet, Robert Henryson's *Testament of Cresseid*. Troilus, riding back into Troy, does not recognise his lost love, Cresseid, in the disfigured leperwoman begging for alms, any more than she, blinded by her disease, recognises him. He certainly feels nothing for her; but something in her recalls Cresseid to his mind, and instantly he feels again the love she once inspired. In Damasio's words, he experiences again 'the configuration that our body assumed during a particular kind of emotion in the past'.

General themes emerge throughout the book. There is the development through time and technological improvements of metaphors for the memory, from the wax tablet of Plato's day (remarkably persistent over 2000 years) through St Augustine's university library and Locke's blank slate to the card index and computer technology of the nineteenth and twentieth centuries. Now we have audio and video tape recorders and digital cameras (as in the phrase, 'snapshot memories'), all used as metaphors for the act of memory, all promoting the very questionable idea, addressed by Ulric Neisser in part I, that an incorruptible memory of an event can be preserved.

Our collection shows memory as storytelling. We form memories into stories as we remember, and we polish the stories. The childhood memories that we take with us into later life are what define us to ourselves: they make us understand that, as Anthony Powell puts it, 'I was me'. The accuracy of what we remember is in a sense secondary. For most of us, our childhood memories are happy memories, to be looked back at with nostalgia, whether they have the dreamlike quality of which de Quincey writes or the sharp clarity of G.K. Chesterton. Most of the childhood memories here are happy ones. For some, like D.H. Lawrence, to remember childhood from a painful present is distressing. The classic statement of memory as pain is Francesca's words to Dante from the whirlwind in Hell, remembering young, adulterous love. '*Nessun maggior dolor che ricordarsi del tempo felice nella miseria*'; there is no greater grief than to remember happy times when one is in misery. But for most of us such memories, sad, happy, nostalgic, are our validation of ourselves, of our place in the world, of the roots that tie us to it.

It does not seem to matter that such memories are frequently inaccurate and that those who profess to remember them in many cases know them to be inaccurate. As William Maxwell says, 'In talking about the past we lie with every breath we draw'. If there is near unanimity on the extent to which these early memories are responsible for a sense of identity, there is also a general acknowledgement of the fact of their unreliability. What matters to their owners is what is significant. Gabriel Garcia Marquez summarises it well: 'Life is not what one lived, but what one remembers and how one remembers it in order to recount it.' The recognition of the different parallax from which a different member of a family or a group will recall a common experience will account for some variation in the retelling of it; I was recently told of a childhood event in which three children took part, all of whom in later life recalled it quite differently. But there is also a conscious element of continuous story-telling in which a significant memory is constructed and developed in the mind, or in which a number of flashes of early memory interact with each other to produce an artefact which may not be strictly true but which, perhaps because it is composed of ingredients which are, answers a need. Some such need underlies the screen memories of which Freud wrote so memorably.

The idea of the 'art of memory' recurs in all sorts of forms and contexts. The possession of a good memory has always been regarded as a desirable attribute. Almost every biography of a great man lays emphasis on his unusual powers of memory. It is no wonder, therefore, that the cultivation and improvement of the memory has been a preoccupation throughout history. How early this preoccupation started is not known, almost certainly long before there is any recorded evidence of it. The first man who is known to have discovered a method of impressing facts on the memory is a poet, Simonides of Ceos (c.556–468 BC). An entry in the *Parian Chronicle* (c.264 BC) describes him as 'the inventor of the system of memory aids'; but it is highly unlikely that he was in fact the first to discover his system.

It was here that we particularly regretted our inability to look at, for example, early Chinese or Sanskrit literature for similar records. The accidental circumstances in which Simonides developed the methods which were to make him famous and become so influential in the classical and mediaeval periods are told by Cicero in his treatise, *De Oratore*, and the context in which he tells the story indicates why the discovery was to be so assiduously cultivated by Simonides' successors. Orators, lawyers, politicians, anyone who was expected to be able to speak at length on subjects of considerable complexity and sophistication without the assistance of notes or any other visual aids, desperately needed some sort of system which would enable them to carry the points of their argument clearly in their heads. Simonides' idea of inventing a series of easily-remembered places or *loci* and then placing the points to be remembered in them (so that a speaker, by walking round a house or a room in his head, could retrieve the points of his argument in order from the lobby, the hall, the coat-rack, etc.) provided it. The anonymous Roman, of the same period as Cicero, who addressed a textbook on rhetoric to an equally unknown Herennius, elaborated the system still further, and his work provided the foundation on which mediaeval (and indeed later) writers were to build. Their further development of it, mostly in monasteries where philosophical and patristic tomes were being produced without the benefit of copyright libraries or the internet, appears to carry the system into the realms of fantasy. The treatise on the artificial memory of Thomas Bradwardine, the fourteenth-century theologian and mathematician known as the Profound Doctor, may raise a smile today; the point is that the system worked and, indeed, for many people is still working.

The best indication that Simonides may only be the first recorded practitioner of the artificial memory and not its true begetter is the consideration of how many people since the Middle Ages have worked out the system for themselves without the benefit of their classical or mediaeval predecessors. Frances Yates, in *The Art of Memory*, tells the story of a professor whose favourite parlour game was to ask each of his students to name an object, and later astonish them by repeating the list in the right order, simply by placing the objects, as they were named, on the windowsill, on the desk, in the waste-paper basket. He had never heard of the classical mnemonic, she says, but had discovered the technique quite independently, as did A.R. Luria's famous patient, S., as have done many others down to the present day. Yates goes on to describe how, during the Renaissance, the original simple system was further developed and refined in the hands of scholars like Giulio Camillo, Giordano Bruno and Robert Fludd into a series of magical and occult memory theatres of extraordinary complexity. The painter and sculptor, Anselm Kiefer, has carried the system one step further in the late twentieth century, in using it to construct a kind of symbolic memory theatre of German icons and images from German history, and especially from the Second World War.

There are, of course, a large number of pieces which have no other justification for being there than the fact that they caught our imagination and we could not bear to exclude them. Most of our choices, in the last analysis, were personal choices. Our best hope was to suggest some of the aspects and angles from which the subject could be approached. But there was the discipline of space. We have been obliged to sacrifice many pieces that we would have liked to include and we have been obliged to cut rigorously even those which we have included. The editorial knife is red with the blood of Plato, Augustine, Freud, Proust and others. On some occasions we have been obliged to make a different kind of choice. It is right that writers and publishers should receive some kind of return for use of the work which they have brought into print, but editors of anthologies work to tight budgets. This is a suitable place to record our deep gratitude to many publishers and copyright holders who have generously reduced or waived their normal charges to enable us to include extracts to which we attached importance. But not all have been so understanding. The chapter on public memory would have looked very different if we had not had at the last moment to withdraw from it an extract from E.H. Gombrich's life of Aby Warburg on Warburg's ideas about inherited memory. This we regretted; but the charge demanded for it was exorbitant.

We spent much time deciding how the material should be arranged. Not the least of the challenges was the fact that almost everything could be placed in more than one category. St Augustine would fit as well into 'Memory and Imagination' as into 'The Idea of Memory'; Freud's search for his mother in the wardrobe would be as suitable for 'Memory and Science' as for 'Childhood Memories'. Edwin Muir, who started in 'Childhood Memories', ended up much more appropriately in 'Memory and Imagination' but either would have done. The different chapters do not represent hard-and-fast categories; the material of one flows naturally into another.

The fundamental importance of memory is admirably described by Antonio Damasio in his *Looking for Spinoza*: 'What we do not know cannot hurt us. If we had the gift of consciousness but were largely deprived of memory, there would be no remarkable anguish either. What we do know, in the present, but are unable to place in the context of our personal history could only hurt us in the present. It is the two gifts combined, consciousness and memory, along with their abundance, that result in the human drama and confer upon that drama a tragic status, then and now. Fortunately, the same two gifts also are at the source of unbounded enjoyment, sheer human glory.'

Annotations. Footnotes from the original extracts are indicated by numbers: editorial footnotes by symbols.

Childhood Memories

From WILLIAM SHAKESPEARE, *The Tempest* I. ii

Prospero:	Canst thou remember
	A time before we came unto this cell?
	I do not think thou canst, for then thou wast not
	Out three years.
Miranda:	Certainly, sir, I can.
Prospero:	By what? by any other house or person?
	Of any thing the image tell me that
	Hath kept with thy remembrance.
Miranda:	'Tis far off,
	And rather like a dream than an assurance
	That my remembrance warrants. Had I not
	Four or five women once that tended me?
Prospero:	Thou hadst, and more, Miranda. But how is it
	That this lives in thy mind? What see'st thou else
	In the dark backward and abysm of time?
	If thou rememb'rest aught ere thou camest here,
	How thou camest here thou mayst.
Miranda:	But that I do not.

From THOMAS DE QUINCEY, *Confessions of an English Opium-Eater* (1822)

The minutest incidents of childhood, or forgotten scenes of later years, were often revived. I could not be said to recollect them; for, if I had been told of them when waking, I should not have been able to acknowledge them as parts of my past experience. But, placed as they were before me in dreams like intuitions, and clothed in all their evanescent circumstances and accompanying feelings, I *recognised* them instantaneously. I was once told by a near relative of mine that, having in her childhood fallen into a river, and being on the very verge of death but for the assistance which reached her at the last critical moment, she saw in a moment her whole life, clothed in its forgotten incidents, arrayed before her as in a mirror, not successively, but simultaneously; and she had a faculty developed as suddenly for comprehending the whole and every part. This, from some opium experiences, I can believe; I have, indeed, seen the same thing asserted twice in modern books, and accompanied by a remark which probably is true – viz. that the dread book of account which the Scriptures speak of is, in fact, the mind itself of each individual. Of this, at least, I feel assured, that there is no such thing as ultimate *forgetting*; traces once impressed upon the memory are indestructible; a thousand accidents may and will interpose a veil between our present consciousness and the secret inscriptions on the mind. Accidents of the same sort will also rend away this veil. But alike, whether veiled or unveiled, the inscription remains for ever; just as the stars seem to withdraw before the common light of day, whereas, in fact, we all know that it is the light which is drawn over them as a veil, and that they are waiting to be revealed whenever the obscuring daylight itself shall have withdrawn.

THOMAS HOOD, 'I remember, I remember' (1826)

I remember, I remember
The house where I was born,
The little window where the sun
Came peeping in at morn;
He never came a wink too soon
Nor brought too long a day,
But now, I often wish the night
Had borne my breath away!

I remember, I remember
The roses, red and white,
The violets, and the lily-cups,

Those flowers made of light!
The lilacs where the robin built,
And where my brother set
The laburnum on his birthday, –
The tree is living yet!

I remember, I remember
Where I was used to swing,
And thought the air must rush as fresh
To swallows on the wing;
My spirit flew in feathers then,
That is so heavy now,
And summer pools could hardly cool
The fever on my brow!

I remember, I remember
The fir trees dark and high;
I used to think their slender tops
Were close against the sky:
It was a childish ignorance,
But now 'tis little joy
To know I'm farther off from heaven
Than when I was a boy.

JOHN CLARE, 'Remembrances' (1832)

Summer pleasures they are gone like to visions every one
And the cloudy days of autumn and of winter cometh on
I tried to call them back but unbidden they are gone
Far away from heart and eye and for ever far away
Dear heart and can it be that such raptures meet decay
I thought them all eternal when by Langley Bush I lay
I thought them joys eternal when I used to shout and play
On its bank at 'clink and bandy' 'chock' and 'taw' and ducking
    stone
Where silence sitteth now on the wild heath as her own
Like a ruin of the past all alone

When I used to lie and sing by old eastwells boiling spring
When I used to tie the willow boughs together for a 'swing'
And fish with crooked pins and thread and never catch a thing
With heart just like a feather – now as heavy as a stone
When beneath old lea close oak I the bottom branches broke
To make our harvest cart like so many working folk
And then to cut a straw at the brook to have a soak
O I never dreamed of parting or that trouble had a sting
Or that pleasures like a flock of birds would ever take to wing
Leaving nothing but a little naked spring

When jumping time away on old cross berry way
And eating awes like sugar plumbs ere they had lost the may
And skipping like a leveret before the peep of day
On the rolly polly up and downs of pleasant swordy well
When in round oaks narrow lane as the south got black again
We sought the hollow ash that was shelter from the rain
With our pockets full of peas we had stolen from the grain
How delicious was the dinner time on such a showry day
O words are poor receipts for what time hath stole away
The ancient pulpit trees and the play

When for school oer 'little field' with its brook and wooden brig
Where I swaggered like a man though I was not half so big
While I held my little plough though twas but a willow twig
And drove my team along made of nothing but a name
'Gee hep' and 'hoit' and 'woi' – O I never call to mind
These pleasant names of places but I leave a sigh behind
While I see the little mouldywharps hang sweeing to the wind
On the only aged willow that in all the field remains
And nature hides her face where theyre sweeing in their chains
And in a silent murmuring complains

Here was commons for the hills where they seek for freedom
    still
Though every commons gone and though traps are set to kill
The little homeless miners – O it turns my bosom chill
When I think of old 'sneap green' puddocks nook and hilly
    snow
Where bramble bushes grew and the daisy gemmed in dew

And the hills of silken grass like to cushions to the view
When we threw the pissmire crumbs when we's nothing else to do
All leveled like a desert by the never weary plough
All vanished like the sun where that cloud is passing now
All settled here for ever on its brow

I never thought that joys would run away from boys
Or that boys would change their minds and forsake such
  summer joys
But alack I never dreamed that the world had other toys
To petrify first feelings like the fable into stone
Till I found the pleasure past and a winter come at last
Then the fields were sudden bare and the sky got overcast
And boyhoods pleasing haunts like a blossom in the blast
Was shrivelled to a withered weed and trampled down and done
Till vanished was the morning spring and set that summer sun
And winter fought her battle strife and won

By Langley bush I roam but the bush hath left its hill
On cowper green I stray tis a desert strange and chill
And spreading lea close oak ere decay had penned its will
To the axe of the spoiler and self interest fell a prey
And cross berry way and old round oaks narrow lane
With its hollow trees like pulpits I shall never see again
Inclosure like a Buonaparte let not a thing remain
It levelled every bush and tree and levelled every hill
And hung the moles for traitors – though the brook is running
  still
It runs a naked brook cold and chill

O had I known as then joy had left the paths of men
I had watched her night and day besure and never slept agen
And when she turned to go O I'd caught her mantle then
And wooed her like a lover by my lonely side to stay
Aye knelt and worshipped on as love in beautys bower
And clung upon her smiles as a bee upon her flower
And gave her heart my poesys all cropt in a sunny hour
As keepsakes and pledges to fade away
But love never heeded to treasure up the may
So it went the comon road with decay

SAMUEL BUTLER, *Note Books*, 'Henry Hoare's Torn Finger-Nail' (1878)

When Hoare was a young man of about five-and-twenty, he one day tore the quick of his finger-nail – I mean, he separated the fleshy part of the finger from the nail – and this reminded him that many years previously while quite a child he had done the same thing. Thereon he fell to thinking of that time, which was impressed upon his memory partly because there was a great disturbance in the house about a missing five-pound note, and partly because it was while he had the scarlet fever.

Having nothing to do he followed the train of thought aroused by his torn finger, and asked himself how he tore it. After a while it came back to him that he had been lying ill in bed as a child of about seven years old at the house of an aunt who lived in Hertfordshire. His arms often hung out of the bed and as his hands wandered over the wooden frame of the bed he felt that there was a place where a nut had come out so that he could stuff his fingers in; one day, in trying to stuff a piece of paper into this hole, he stuffed it so far and so tightly that he tore the quick of his nail. The whole thing came back so vividly, though he had not thought of it for twenty years, that he could see the room in his aunt's house, and remembered how his aunt used to sit by his bedside writing at a little table from which he had got the piece of paper which he had stuffed into the hole.

So far so good; but then there flashed upon him an idea that was not so pleasant. I mean it came upon him with irresistible force that the piece of paper he had stuffed into the hole in the bedstead was the missing five-pound note about which there had been so much disturbance. At that time he was so young that a five-pound note was to him only a piece of paper; when he heard that five pounds were missing he had thought it was five sovereigns; or perhaps he was too ill to know anything, or to be questioned. I forget what I was told about this – at any rate he had no idea of the value of the piece of paper he was stuffing into the hole but now that the matter had recurred to him at all he felt so sure it was the note that he immediately went down to Hertfordshire where his aunt was still living, and asked to the surprise of every one to be allowed to wash his hands in the room he had occupied as a child. He was told there were friends staying with them who had the room at present, but, on his saying he had a reason, and particularly begging to be allowed to remain alone a little while in this room, he was taken upstairs and left there.

He immediately went to the bed, lifted up the chintz which then covered the frame, and found his old friend the hole.

A nut had been supplied and he could no longer get his fingers into it.

He rang the bell and, when the servant came, asked for a bed-key. All this time he was rapidly acquiring the reputation of being a lunatic throughout the whole house, but the key was brought, and by the help of it Hoare got the nut off. When he had done so, there sure enough, by dint of picking with his pocket-knife, he found the missing five-pound note.

See how the return of a given present brings back the presents that have been associated with it.

From SIGMUND FREUD, *The Psychopathology of Everyday Life* (1901), translated by James Strachey

I would like to cite one more example illustrating the significance that an apparently random childhood memory can acquire through analytical study. In my forty-third year, when I became interested in the remnants of my own childhood memories, I recollected a scene which had come into my mind now and then over a long period – for ever, as it seemed to me – and there were reliable indications that it must date from before the end of my third year of life. I saw myself standing in tears in front of a wardrobe [in Austrian usage: *Kasten*] and demanding something, while my half-brother, twenty years older than me, was holding its door open, and then my mother suddenly came in, beautiful and slender, as if just coming home from a walk through the streets. I had used these words to describe the three-dimensional scene, but I could take it no further. I had no idea whether my brother was going to open or close the wardrobe – in the first translation of the image into words I called it a *Schrank* ['wardrobe' in standard

German] – or why I was crying, or what my mother's arrival had to do with it; I was tempted to explain it to myself as a memory of my older brother's teasing me and being interrupted by our mother. Such misinterpretations of a remembered childhood scene are not at all unusual; we remember a situation, but it is unfocused, and we do not know exactly where the psychic emphasis lies. My analytical investigations led me to an entirely unexpected interpretation of this image. I had been missing my mother, and began to suspect that she might be shut up in the wardrobe – the *Schrank* or *Kasten* – so I asked my brother to open it. When he did, and I could see that my mother was not inside, I began screaming; that was the part I remembered, along with my mother's appearance immediately afterwards, which calmed my fears and longings. But what made me, as a child, think of looking for my absent mother in the wardrobe? Some of my dreams from the same period relate vaguely to a nursemaid of whom I had certain other memories, for instance that she consistently used to make me hand over to her the small change people gave me as presents, a detail which itself could claim to figure as a screen memory for later events. This time, I decided to facilitate the task of interpretation, and I asked my now elderly mother, about the nursemaid. I learned a good deal, including the fact that this clever but dishonest character had stolen from the household on a large scale while my mother was lying in, and my half-brother had insisted on bringing legal charges against her. This information, casting a sudden bright light on my childhood memory, helped me to understand it. The nursemaid's sudden disappearance had affected me quite deeply, and in fact I had turned to that same brother to ask where she was, probably because I had noticed that he had something to do with her removal from the household. Evasively playing on words, as he commonly did, he had told me that she was 'in the clink [German: *eingekastelt*, a colloquial expression for 'in jail']'. I understood this answer in a purely childish way [as meaning 'in the wardrobe' – *Kasten*] and asked no more questions, since there seemed no more to learn. When my mother went out a little later I was anxious, fearing that my bad brother had shut her up too, just like the nursemaid, and I made him open the wardrobe for me. And now I also understand why my mother's slender figure, which seemed to have been just restored, featured so prominently in my visual version of this childhood scene; I am two and a half years older than my sister, who was born at this time, and when I was three years old my half-brother left our household.[1]

From EDMUND GOSSE, *Father and Son* (1907)

Out of the darkness of my infancy there comes only one flash of memory. I am seated alone, in my baby-chair, at a dinner-table set for several people. Somebody brings in a leg of mutton, puts it down close to me, and goes out. I am again alone, gazing at two low windows, wide open upon a garden. Suddenly, noiselessly, a large, long animal (obviously a greyhound) appears at one window-sill, slips into the room, seizes the leg of mutton and slips out again. When this happened I could not yet talk. The accomplishment of speech came to me very late, doubtless because I never heard young voices. Many years later, when I mentioned this recollection, there was a shout of laughter and surprise:

'That, then, was what became of the mutton! It was not you, who, as your Uncle A. pretended, ate it all up, in the twinkling of an eye, bone and all!'

I suppose that it was the startling intensity of this incident which stamped it upon a memory from which all other impressions of this early date have vanished.

[1.] Anyone with an interest in the mental processes of childhood will easily understand the deeper conditioning of my demand to my big brother. At the age of not quite three, I realised that my recently born sister had grown in my mother's uterus. I was not at all pleased about the new baby and suspected, gloomily, that my mother's body might be harbouring yet more children. The wardrobe symbolised the maternal womb to me; I therefore demanded to see inside the cupboard, and to that end I applied to my big brother. As other material shows, an older brother can replace a father as a little boy's rival. Apart from my well-founded suspicion that this brother was responsible for putting the absent nursemaid in prison, I also feared that he had somehow implanted the new-born child in my mother's body. My sense of disappointment when the wardrobe proved empty arose from the superficial motivation of my childish demand, and was misplaced in relation to my deeper level of feeling. On the other hand, my great satisfaction at noting my mother's slender figure on her return is fully comprehensible only on that deeper level.

D.H. LAWRENCE, 'Piano' (1913)

Softly, in the dusk, a woman is singing to me;
Taking me back down the vista of years, till I see
A child sitting under the piano, in the boom of the tingling
    strings
And pressing the small, poised feet of a mother who smiles as
    she sings.

In spite of myself, the insidious mastery of song
Betrays me back, till the heart of me weeps to belong
To the old Sunday evenings at home, with winter outside
And hymns in the cosy parlour, the tinkling piano our guide.

So now it is vain for the singer to burst into clamour
With the great black piano appassionato. The glamour
Of childish days is upon me, my manhood is cast
Down in the flood of remembrance, I weep like a child for
    the past.

W.H. HUDSON, *Far Away and Long Ago* (1918)

... when a person endeavours to recall his early life in its entirety
he finds it is not possible: he is like one who ascends a hill to
survey the prospect before him on a day of heavy cloud and shadow,
who sees at a distance, now here, now there, some feature in the
landscape – hill or wood or tower or spire – touched and made
conspicuous by a transitory sunbeam while all else remains in obscurity. The scenes, people, events we are able by an effort to call up
do not present themselves in order; there is no order, no sequence
or regular progression – nothing, in fact, but isolated spots or
patches, brightly illumined and vividly seen, in the midst of a wide
shrouded mental landscape.

It is easy to fall into the delusion that the few things thus distinctly
remembered and visualised are precisely those which were most
important in our life, and on that account were saved by memory

while all the rest has been permanently blotted out. That is indeed how our memory serves and fools us; for at some period of a man's life – at all events of some lives – in some rare state of the mind it is all at once revealed to him as by a miracle that nothing is ever blotted out.

It was through falling into some such state as that, during which I had a wonderfully clear and continuous vision of the past, that I was tempted – forced I may say – to write this account of my early years. I will relate the occasion, as I imagine that the reader who is a psychologist will find as much to interest him in this incident as in anything else contained in the book.

I was feeling weak and depressed when I came down from London one November evening to the south coast: the sea, the clear sky, the bright colours of the afterglow kept me too long on the front in an east wind in that low condition, with the result that I was laid up for six weeks with a very serious illness. Yet when it was over I looked back on those six weeks as a happy time! Never had I thought so little of physical pain. Never had I felt confinement less – I who feel, when I am out of sight of living, growing grass, and out of sound of birds' voices and all rural sounds, that I am not properly alive!

On the second day of my illness, during an interval of comparative ease, I fell into recollections of my childhood, and at once I had that far, that forgotten past with me again as I had never previously had it. It was not like that mental condition, known to most persons, when some sight or sound or, more frequently, the perfume of some flower, associated with our early life, restores the past suddenly and so vividly that it is almost an illusion. That is an intensely emotional condition and vanishes as quickly as it comes. This was different. To return to the simile and metaphor used at the beginning, it was as if the cloud shadows and haze had passed away and the entire wide prospect beneath me made clearly visible. Over it all my eyes could range at will, choosing this or that point to dwell upon, to examine it in all its details; or in the case of some person known to me as a child, to follow his life till it ended or passed from sight; then to return to the same point again to repeat the process with other lives and resume my rambles in the old familiar haunts.

What a happiness it would be, I thought, in spite of discomfort and pain and danger, if this vision would continue! It was not to be expected: nevertheless it did not vanish, and on the second day I set myself to try and save it from the oblivion which would presently cover it again. Propped up with pillows I began with pencil and writing-pad to put it down in some sort of order, and went on with it at intervals during the whole six weeks of my confinement, and in this way produced the first rough draft of the book.

And all this time I never ceased wondering at my own mental state; I thought of it when, quickly tired, my trembling fingers dropped the pencil; or when I woke from uneasy sleep to find the vision still before me, inviting, insistently calling to me, to resume my childish rambles and adventures of long ago in that strange world where I first saw the light.

It was to me a marvellous experience; to be here, propped up with pillows in a dimly-lighted room, the night-nurse idly dozing by the fire; the sound of the everlasting wind in my ears, howling outside and dashing the rain like hailstones against the window-panes; to be awake to all this, feverish and ill and sore, conscious of my danger too, and at the same time to be thousands of miles away, out in the sun and wind, rejoicing in other sights and sounds, happy again with that ancient long-lost and now recovered happiness!

During the three years that have passed since I had that strange experience, I have from time to time, when in the mood, gone back to the book and have had to cut it down a good deal and to reshape it, as in the first draft it would have made too long and formless a history.

From SIEGFRIED SASSOON, *Memoirs of a Foxhunting Man* (1928)

Among a multitude of memories my 'dream friend' has cropped up with an odd effect of importance which makes me feel that he must be worth a passing mention. The fact is, that, as soon as I began to picture in my mind the house and garden where I spent so much of my early life, I caught sight of my small, long-vanished self with this other non-existent boy standing beside him. And, though it sounds silly enough, I felt queerly touched by the recollection of that forgotten companionship. For some reason, which I cannot explain, the presence of that 'other boy' made my childhood unexpectedly clear, and brought me close to a number of things which, I should have thought, would have faded for ever. For instance, I have only just remembered the tarnished mirror which used to hang in the sunless passage which led to my school-room, and how, when I secretly stared at my small, white face in the mirror, I could hear the sparrows chirping in the ivy which grew thickly outside the windows. Somehow the sight of my own reflection increased my loneliness . . .

And now, as I look up from my writing, these memories also seem like reflections in a glass, reflections which are becoming more and more easy to distinguish. Sitting here, alone with my slowly moving thoughts, I rediscover many little details, known only to myself, details otherwise dead and forgotten with all who shared that time; and I am inclined to loiter among them as long as possible.

From G. K. CHESTERTON, *Autobiography* (1936)

Of this positive quality, the most general attribute was clearness. Here it is that I differ, for instance, from Stevenson, whom I so warmly admire; and who speaks of the child as moving with his head in a cloud. He talks of the child as normally in a dazed day-dream, in which he cannot distinguish fancy from fact. Now children and adults are both fanciful at times; but that is not what, in my mind and memory, distinguishes adults from children. Mine is a memory of a sort of white light on everything, cutting things out very clearly, and rather emphasising their solidity. The point is that the white light had a sort of wonder in it, as if the world were as new as myself; but not that the world was anything but a real world . . .

At this time, of course, I did not even know that this morning light could be lost; still less about any controversies as to whether it could be recovered. So far the disputes of that period passed over my head like storms high up in air; and as I did not foresee the problem I naturally did not foresee any of my searches for a solution. I simply looked at the procession in the street as I looked at the processions in the toy theatre; and now and then I happened to see curious things, twopence coloured rather than a penny plain, which were worthy of the wildest pageants of the toy theatre. I remember once walking with my father along Kensington High Street, and seeing a crowd of people gathered by a rather dark and narrow entry on the southern side of that thoroughfare. I had seen crowds before; and was quite prepared for their shouting or shoving. But I was not prepared for what happened next. In a flash a sort of ripple ran along the line and all these eccentrics went down on their knees on the public pavement. I had never seen people play any such antics except in church; and I stopped and stared. Then I realised that a sort of little dark cab or carriage had drawn up opposite the entry; and out of it came a ghost clad in flames. Nothing in the shilling paint box had ever spread such a conflagration of scarlet, such lakes of lake; or seemed so splendidly likely to incarnadine the multitudinous sea. He came on with all his glowing draperies like a great crimson cloud of sunset, lifting long frail fingers over the crowd in blessing. And then I looked at his face and was startled with a contrast; for his face was dead pale like ivory and very wrinkled and old, fitted together out of naked nerve and bone and sinew; with hollow eyes in shadow; but not ugly; having in every line the ruin of great beauty. The face was so extraordinary that for a moment I even forgot such perfectly scrumptious scarlet clothes.

We passed on; and then my father said, 'Do you know who that was? That was Cardinal Manning.'

Then one of his artistic hobbies returned to his abstracted and humorous mind; and he said: 'He'd have made his fortune as a model.'

From HENRY GREEN, *Pack My Bag: A Self-Portrait* (1940)

If I say I remember, as it seems to me I do, one of the maids, that poor thing whose breath smelled, come in one morning to tell us that the *Titanic* had gone down, it may be that much later they had told me I *should* have remembered, at the age I was then, and that their saying this had suggested I did remember. But I do know, and they would not, that her breath was bad, that when she knelt down to do one up in front it was all one could do to stand there.

From GWEN RAVERAT, *Period Piece: A Cambridge Childhood* (1952)

Long after I have forgotten all my human loves I shall still remember the smell of a gooseberry leaf, or the feel of the wet grass on my bare feet; or the pebbles in the path. In the long run it is this feeling that makes life worth living, this which is the driving force behind the artist's need to create.

From CYRIL HARE, *He Should Have Died Hereafter* (1958)

How fantastic to suppose that he had forgotten all about it! With the scent of the heather in his nostrils, the sound of the horn fresh in his ears, gazing across the valley at two distant hummocks which suddenly revealed themselves as the very oldest of old acquaintances, Pettigrew found his memory opening up like some monstrous flower, fold within fold. He saw himself, a small boy, jogging uncomfortably to the meet along a road innocent of motor traffic but thick with dust on a hard-mouthed, self-willed pony that could not accommodate its pace to that of the big hunter alongside ... The boy was wearing what struck him now as fantastically uncomfortable clothes – a hard hat that seared his forehead, breeches that pinched his flesh below the knees, gaiters that never quite spanned the gap between the breeches and the heavy black boots. In his leather gloves he clutched a thonged hunting crop that was at once his greatest pride and an appalling encumbrance. One pocket was weighed down with a vast pocket knife equipped among other things with a hook designed to take stones out of horses' hooves; another bulged tightly over the packet of sandwiches which, when eaten later in the day, would prove, whatever their composition, to taste of leather gloves and smell of sweating pony . . .

By now the picture of the small boy was becoming overlaid in Pettigrew's mind with a host of other images – his father's old-fashioned, full-skirted hunting coat, the Henry Alken prints in the Sallowcombe dining-room, the echo of the peculiar wail of the Vicar's voice at Mattins. With an effort he came back to the present and looked for inspiration across the valley towards Tucker's Barrows. (How could he have forgotten that household name for an instant? he asked himself.) But the view gave him no help in self-expression . . .

In the silence that fell between them he became aware of a variety of small sounds – the buzzing of an intrusive fly, the plash of water from the stream in the combe below, and finally the sound for which, without realising it, he had been straining his ears for minutes past – the faint whimper of hounds. It came for a moment only and was not repeated. Pettigrew was not surprised. Wherever they were running, he reflected, it was an even chance that it was uphill and through long heather or bracken. They would have little breath to spare to give tongue on a warm afternoon like this. It was, of course, a matter of complete indifference to him whether they were running, or in what direction; but he found himself none the less concentrating his attention upon a particular part of the skyline where the ground dipped to form a saddle between the Barrows and another, less prominent eminence. The latter point he recognised at once, in his mood of reawakened sensitivity to the past. It was called Bolter's Tussock; and astonishingly enough, the absurd name evoked a thoroughly disagreeable sensation in his mind. Alone in that wide prospect of familiar friendly scenes the place stood for something vaguely but unquestionably sinister. Something had occurred there so unpleasant that he had long since buried the recollection of it deep in his subconscious mind. Painfully and perversely he struggled to disinter it. He was almost on the point of success when the present intruded upon the past, and temporarily blotted it out.

From LEONARD WOOLF, *Sowing* (1960)

This looking back at oneself through middle age, youth, childhood, infancy is a curious and puzzling business. Some of the things which one seems to remember from far, far back in infancy are not, I think, really remembered; they are family tales told so often about one that eventually one has the illusion of remembering them. Such I believe to be the story of how as an infant I fell into a stream near Oban which I heard so often that eventually it became part of my memory. What genuine glimpses one does get of oneself in very early childhood seem to show that the main outlines of one's character are moulded in infancy and do not change between the ages of three and eighty-three. I am sure that my attitude to sin was the same when I lay in my pram as it is today when I sit tapping this out on the typewriter and, unless I become senile, will be the same when I lie on my death-bed. And in other ways when I can genuinely remember something of myself far off and long ago, I can recognize that self as essentially myself with the same little core of character exactly the same as exists in me today. I think that the first things which I can genuinely remember are connected with an illness which I had when I was about three. It was a very severe attack of scarlet fever which also affected my kidneys and in those days scarlet fever was a dangerous disease. I can remember incidents connected with the illness and I think they are genuine memories; they are so vivid that I can visualize them and myself in them.

The first is of a man coming into the room and applying leeches to my back. I insisted upon seeing the leeches and was fascinated by them. Twenty-five years later, one day in Ceylon during the rainy season, I was pushing my way through thick, wet grass in the jungle. I was wearing shorts and suddenly looking down I saw that my two bare knees were black with leeches. And suddenly I was back, a small boy of three, lying in bed in the bedroom high up in the Lexham Gardens house with the kindly man rather reluctantly showing me the leeches. I doubt whether in the intervening twenty-five years I had ever recalled the man with the leeches, but there in a flash the scene and the man and the leeches and my feelings were as vivid to me as the leeches on my knees, the gun in my hand, and the enveloping silence of the jungle.

When I look into the depths of my own mind (or should one say soul?) one of the characteristics which seems to me deepest and most persistent is a kind of fatalistic and half-amused resignation. I never worry, because I am saved by the feeling that in the end nothing matters, and I can watch with amusement and detachment the cruel, often undeserved but expected, blows which fate rains upon me. In another incident of my scarlet fever, which I think I do genuinely remember myself (though it became a family story), I seem to see this streak in my character already formed in the three-year-old child. At one moment my illness took a turn for the worse and I was, so it was said, upon the point of death. They called in Sir William Jenner, the Queen's doctor and a descendant of the Jenner who invented inoculation. He was a kindly man and I was fascinated by the shape of his nose. He prescribed a draught of the most appalling taste. I drank it down, but on his second visit – presumably next day – I sat up in bed with a second dose in the glass in my hand unable to drink it despite all the urging of my mother and Sir William. At last I said to them – according to my mother, with considerable severity – 'If you will *all* go out of the room, I will drink it.' I do not really remember that, but I do vividly remember the sequel. I remember sitting up in bed alone and the resignation with which I drank the filthy stuff, and the doctor and my mother coming back into the room and praising me. Sir William sat down on my bed and said that I had been so good that I would be given what I wanted. What did I want? 'A pigeon pie', I said, 'with the legs sticking out.' 'You cannot', he explained and his explanation was not unexpected by me, 'be given a pigeon pie with the legs sticking out just yet, but you will be given one as soon as you are quite well. But isn't there something – not to eat – which you would like now?' I remember looking carefully into his kindly old face and saying: 'I should like to pull your nose.' He said that I might, and gently, not disrespectfully, but as a kind of symbol or token, serious but also, I believe, deep down amused, I pulled Sir William Jenner's nose.

From VIRGINIA WOOLF, *Moments of Being*
(published 1976)

Two days ago – Sunday 16th April 1939 to be precise – Nessa said that if I did not start writing my memoirs I should soon be too old. . . . There are several difficulties. In the first place, the enormous number of things I can remember; in the second, the number of different ways in which memoirs can be written. As a great memoir reader, I know many different ways. But . . . without stopping to choose my way, in the sure and certain knowledge that it will find itself – or if not it will not matter – I begin: the first memory.

This was of red and purple flowers on a black ground – my mother's dress; and she was sitting either in a train or in an omnibus, and I was on her lap. I therefore saw the flowers she was wearing very close; and can still see purple and red and blue, I think, against the black; they must have been anemones, I suppose. Perhaps we were going to St Ives; more probably, for from the light it must have been evening, we were coming back to London. But it is more convenient artistically to suppose that we were going to St Ives, for that will lead to my other memory, which also seems to be my first memory, and in fact it is the most important of all my memories. If life has a base that it stands upon, if it is a bowl that one fills and fills and fills – then my bowl without a doubt stands upon this memory. It is of lying half asleep, half awake, in bed in the nursery at St Ives. It is of hearing the waves breaking, one, two, one, two, and sending a splash of water over the beach; and then breaking, one, two, one, two, behind a yellow blind. It is of hearing the blind draw its little acorn across the floor as the wind blew the blind out. It is of lying and hearing this splash and seeing this light, and feeling, it is almost impossible that I should be here; of feeling the purest ecstasy I can conceive. . . .

But of course there was one external reason for the intensity of this first impression: the impression of the waves and the acorn on the blind; the feeling, as I describe it sometimes to myself, of lying in a grape and seeing through a film of semi-transparent yellow – it was due partly to the many months we spent in London. The change of nursery was a great change. And there was the long train journey; and the excitement. I remember the dark; the lights; the stir of the going up to bed.

But to fix my mind upon the nursery – it had a balcony; there was a partition, but it joined the balcony of my father's and mother's bedroom. My mother would come out onto her balcony in a white dressing gown. There were passion flowers growing on the wall; they were great starry blossoms, with purple streaks, and large green buds, part empty, part full.

If I were a painter I should paint these first impressions in pale yellow, silver, and green. There was the pale yellow blind; the green sea; and the silver of the passion flowers. I should make a picture that was globular; semi-transparent. I should make a picture of curved petals; of shells; of things that were semi-transparent; I should make curved shapes, showing the light through, but not giving a clear outline. Everything would be large and dim; and what was seen would at the same time be heard; sounds would come through this petal or leaf – sounds indistinguishable from sights. . . . When I think of the early morning in bed I also hear the caw of rooks falling from a great height. The sound seems to fall through an elastic, gummy air; which holds it up; which prevents it from being sharp and distinct. The quality of the air above Talland House seemed to suspend sound, to let it sink down slowly, as if it were caught in a blue gummy veil. The rooks cawing is part of the waves breaking – one, two, one, two – and the splash as the wave drew back and then it gathered again, and I lay there half awake, half asleep, drawing in such ecstasy as I cannot describe.

The next memory – all these colour-and-sound memories hang together at St Ives – was much more robust; it was highly sensual. It was later. It still makes me feel warm; as if everything were ripe; humming; sunny; smelling so many smells at once; and all making a whole that even now makes me stop – as I stopped then going down to the beach; I stopped at the top to look down at the gardens. They were sunk beneath the road. The apples were on a level with one's head. The gardens gave off a murmur of bees; the apples were red and gold; there were also pink flowers; and grey and silver leaves. The buzz, the croon, the smell, all seemed to press voluptuously against some membrane; not to burst it; but to hum round one such a complete rapture of pleasure that I stopped, smelt; looked. But again I cannot describe that rapture. It was rapture rather than ecstasy. . . .

At times I can go back to St Ives more completely than I can this morning. I can reach a state where I seem to be watching things happen as if I were there. That is, I suppose, that my memory supplies what I had forgotten, so that it seems as if it were happening independently, though I am really making it happen. In certain favourable moods, memories – what one has forgotten – come to the top. . . .

But the peculiarity of these two strong memories is that each was very simple. I am hardly aware of myself, but only of the sensation. I am only the container of the feeling of ecstasy, of the feeling of rapture. Perhaps this is characteristic of all childhood memories; perhaps it accounts for their strength. Later we add to feelings much that makes them more complex; and therefore less strong; or if not less strong, less isolated, less complete.

From SAMUEL BECKETT, *Happy Days* (1961)

What now? [*Pause.*] What now, Willie? [*Long pause.*] There is my story of course, when all else fails. [*Pause.*] A life. [*Smile.*] A long life. [*Smile off.*] Beginning in the womb, where life used to begin, Mildred has memories, she will have memories, of the womb, before she dies, the mother's womb. [*Pause.*] She is now four or five already and has recently been given a big waxen dolly. [*Pause.*] Fully clothed, complete outfit. [*Pause.*] Shoes, socks, undies, complete set, frilly frock, gloves. [*Pause.*] White mesh. [*Pause.*] A little white straw hat with a chin elastic. [*Pause.*] Pearly necklace. [*Pause.*] A little picture-book with legends in real print to go under her arm when she takes her walk. [*Pause.*] China blue eyes that open and shut. [*Pause. Narrative.*] The sun was not well up when Milly rose, descended the steep . . . [*pause.*] . . . slipped on her nightgown, descended all alone the steep wooden stairs, backwards on all fours, though she had been forbidden to do so, entered the . . . [*pause*] . . . tiptoed down the silent passage, entered the nursery and began to undress Dolly. [*Pause.*] Crept under the table and began to undress Dolly. [*Pause.*] Scolding her . . . the while. [*Pause.*] Suddenly a mouse – [*Long pause.*] Gently, Winnie. [*Long pause. Calling.*] Willie! [*Pause. Louder.*] Willie! [*Pause. Mild reproach.*] I sometimes find your attitude a little strange, Willie, all this time,

it is not like you to be wantonly cruel. [*Pause.*] Strange? [*Pause.*]
No. [*Smile.*] Not here. [*Smile broader.*] Not now. [*Smile off.*] And
yet . . . [*Suddenly anxious.*] I do hope nothing is amiss. [*Eyes right,
loud.*] Is all well, dear? (*Pause. Eyes front.* To *herself.*] God grant
he did not go in head foremost! [*Eyes right, loud.*] You're not stuck,
Willie? [*Pause. Do.*] You're not jammed, Willie? [*Eyes front,
distressed.*] Perhaps he is crying out for help all this time and I do
not hear him! [*Pause.*] I do of course hear cries. [*Pause.*] But they
are in my head surely. [*Pause.*] Is it possible that . . . [*Pause. With
finality.*] No no, my head was always full of cries. [*Pause.*] Faint
confused cries. [*Pause.*] They come. [*Pause.*] Then go. [*Pause.*] As
on a wind. [*Pause.*] That is what I find so wonderful. [*Pause.*] They
cease. [*Pause.*] Ah yes, great mercies, great mercies.

From VLADIMIR NABOKOV, *Speak, Memory* (1967)

How small the cosmos (a kangaroo's pouch would hold it), how
paltry and puny in comparison to human consciousness, to a single
individual recollection, and its expression in words! I may be inor-
dinately fond of my earliest impressions, but then I have reason to
be grateful to them. They led the way to a veritable Eden of visual
and tactile sensations. One night, during a trip abroad, in the fall
of 1903, I recall kneeling on my (flattish) pillow at the window of
a sleeping car (probably on the long-extinct Mediterranean Train
de Luxe, the one whose six cars had the lower part of their body
painted in umber and the panels in cream) and seeing with an inexplicable pang, a handful of fabulous lights that beckoned to me
from a distant hillside, and then slipped into a pocket of black
velvet: diamonds that I later gave away to my characters to alle-
viate the burden of my wealth. I had probably managed to undo
and push up the tight tooled blind at the head of my berth, and
my heels were cold, but I still kept kneeling and peering. Nothing
is sweeter or stranger than to ponder those first thrills. They belong
to the harmonious world of a perfect childhood and, as such,
possess a naturally plastic form in one's memory, which can be set

down with hardly any effort; it is only starting with the recollections of one's adolescence that Mnemosyne begins to get choosy and crabbed. I would moreover submit that, in regard to the power of hoarding up impressions, Russian children of my generation passed through a period of genius, as if destiny were loyally trying what it could for them by giving them more than their share, in view of the cataclysm that was to remove completely the world they had known. Genius disappeared when everything had been stored, just as it does with those other, more specialised child prodigies – pretty, curly-headed youngsters waving batons or taming enormous pianos, who eventually turn into second-rate musicians with sad eyes and obscure ailments and something vaguely misshapen about their eunuchoid hind quarters. But even so, the individual mystery remains to tantalize the memoirist. Neither in environment nor in heredity can I find the exact instrument that fashioned me, the anonymous roller that pressed upon my life a certain intricate watermark whose unique design becomes visible when the lamp of art is made to shine through life's foolscap.

To fix correctly, in terms of time, some of my childhood recollections, I have to go by comets and eclipses, as historians do when they tackle the fragments of a saga. But in other cases there is no dearth of data. I see myself, for instance, clambering over wet black rocks at the seaside while Miss Norcott, a languid and melancholy governess, who thinks I am following her, strolls away along the curved beach with Sergey, my younger brother. I am wearing a toy bracelet. As I crawl over those rocks, I keep repeating, in a kind of zestful, copious, and deeply gratifying incantation, the English word 'childhood,' which sounds mysterious and new, and becomes stranger and stranger as it gets mixed up in my small, overstocked, hectic mind, with Robin Hood and Little Red Riding Hood, and the brown hoods of old hunch-backed fairies. There are dimples in the rocks, full of tepid seawater, and my magic muttering accompanies certain spells I am weaving over the tiny sapphire pools.

From PENELOPE LIVELY, *Going Back* (1975)

Remembering is like that. There's what you know happened, and what you think happened. And then there's the business that what you know happened isn't always what you remember. Things are fudged by time; years fuse together. The things that should matter – the stepping-stones that marked the way, the decisions that made one thing happen rather than another – they get forgotten. You are left with islands in a confused and layered landscape, like the random protrusions after a heavy snowfall, the telegraph pole and hump of farm machinery and buried wall. There is time past, and time to come, and time that is continuous, in the head for ever.

From ANTHONY POWELL, *Infants of the Spring* (1976)

After the park and the street the interior of the building seemed very silent. A long beam of sunlight, in which small particles of dust swam about, all at once slanted through an upper window on the staircase, and struck the opaque glass panels of the door. On several occasions recently I had been conscious of approaching the brink of some discovery: an awareness that nearly became manifest and then withdrew. Now the truth came flooding in with the dust-infested sunlight. There was no doubt about it. I was me.

From WILLIAM MAXWELL, *So Long, See You Tomorrow* (1980)

I seem to remember that I went to the new house one winter day and saw snow descending through the attic to the upstairs bedrooms. It could also be that I never did any such thing, for I am fairly certain that in a snapshot album I have lost track of there was a picture of the house taken in the circumstances I have just described, and it is possible that I am remembering that rather than an actual experience. What we, or at any rate what I, refer to confidently as memory – meaning a moment, a scene, a fact that has been subjected to a fixative and thereby rescued from oblivion – is really a form of storytelling that goes on continually in the mind and often changes with the telling. Too many conflicting emotional interests are involved for life ever to be wholly acceptable, and possibly it is the work of the storyteller to rearrange things so that they conform to this end. In any case, in talking about the past we lie with every breath we draw.

From RICHARD COE, *When the Grass was Taller* (1984)

Freudian psychology . . . is irremediably one-dimensional, posi-tivistic . . . and utilitarian; it takes no account of that 'second reality', as Gide terms it, which is the essence of childhood revisited, nor is it in any way concerned with intuitive meanings and ultimate significances. For the poet . . . thin meaningfulness demands to be situated in a context outside himself; otherwise it is futile. It must be felt to relate, if not to a transcendental dimension in the usual sense, then at least to other human beings and other experiences: to a communal subconscious perhaps, to an inheritance from past generations, to an all-embracing mythology . . . more real than any 'real' experience, and more mysterious in its workings than any run-of-the-mill psychological determinism.

TED HUGHES, 'Fingers' (1998)

Who will remember your fingers?
Their winged life? They flew
With the light in your look.
At the piano, stomping out hits from the forties,
They performed an incidental clowning

Routine of their own, deadpan puppets.
You were only concerned to get them to the keys.
But as you talked, as your eyes signalled
The strobes of your elation,
They flared; flicked balletic aerobatics.
I thought of birds in some tropical sexual
Play of display, leaping and somersaulting,
Doing strange things in the air, and dropping to the dust.
Those dancers of your excess!
With such deft, practical touches – so accurate.
Thinking their own thoughts caressed like lightning
The lipstick into your mouth corners.

Trim conductors of your expertise,
Cavorting at your typewriter,
Possessed by infant spirit, puckish,
Who, whatever they did, danced or mimed it
In a weightless largesse of espressivo.
I remember your fingers. And your daughter's
Fingers remember your fingers
In everything they do.
Her fingers obey and honour your fingers.
The Lares and Penates of our house.

From GABRIEL GARCÍA MÁRQUEZ, *Living to Tell the Tale* (2003) translated by Edith Grossman

*Life is not what one lived, but what one remembers
and how one remembers it in order to recount it . . .*

On the day I went with my mother to sell the house, I remembered
everything that had made an impression on my childhood but was
not certain what came earlier and what came later, or what any of
it signified in my life. I was not really aware that in the midst of
the false splendor of the banana company, my parents' marriage
was already inscribed in the process that would put the final touches

on the decadence of Aracataca. Once I began to remember, I heard
– first with a good deal of discretion and then in a loud, alarmed
voice – the fateful sentence repeated: 'They say the company's
leaving.' But either nobody believed it, or nobody dared think of
the devastation it would bring.

My mother's version had such meagre numbers and a setting so
abject for the imposing drama I had imagined that it caused a sense
of frustration in me. Later, I spoke with survivors and witnesses
and searched through newspaper archives and official documents,
and I realized that the truth did not lie anywhere. Conformists said,
in effect, that there had been no deaths. Those at the other extreme
affirmed without a quaver in their voices that there had been more
than a hundred, that they had been seen bleeding to death on the
square, and that they were carried away in a freight train to be
tossed into the ocean like rejected bananas. And so my version was
lost forever at some improbable point between the two extremes.
But it was so persistent that in one of my novels I referred to the
massacre with all the precision and horror that I had brought for
years to its incubation in my imagination. This was why I kept the
number of the dead at three thousand, in order to preserve the epic
proportions of the drama, and in the end real life did me justice:
not long ago, on one of the anniversaries of the tragedy, the
speaker of the moment in the Senate asked for a minute of silence
in memory of the three thousand anonymous martyrs sacrificed by
the forces of law and order.

The massacre of the banana workers was the culmination of others
that had occurred earlier, but with the added argument that the leaders
were marked as Communists, and perhaps they were. I happened to
meet the most prominent and persecuted of them, Eduardo Mahecha,
in the Modelo Prison in Barranquilla at about the time I went with my
mother to sell the house, and I maintained a warm friendship with him
after I introduced myself as the grandson of Nicolás Márquez. It was
he who revealed to me that my grandfather was not neutral but had
been a mediator in the 1928 strike, and he considered him a just man.
So that he rounded out the idea I always had of the massacre, and I
formed a more objective conception of the social conflict. The only
discrepancy among everyone's memories concerned the number of dead,
which in any event will not be the only unknown quantity in our history.

So many contradictory versions have been the cause of my false
memories. The most persistent is of my standing in the doorway of the

house with a Prussian helmet and a little toy rifle, watching the battalion of perspiring Cachacos marching past under the almond trees. One of the commanding officers in parade uniform greeted me as he passed:

'Hello, Captain Gabi.'

The memory is clear, but there is no possibility that it is true. The uniform, the helmet, and the toy rifle coexisted, but some two years after the strike and when there no longer were military forces in Cataca. Multiple incidents like this one gave me a bad name in the house for having intrauterine memories and premonitory dreams.

From HILARY MANTEL, *Giving Up the Ghost* (2003)

We are taught to be chary of early memories. Sometimes psychologists fake photographs in which a picture of their subject, in his or her childhood, appears in an unfamiliar setting, in places or with people who, in real life they have never seen. The subjects are amazed at first but then – in proportion to their anxiety to please – they oblige by producing a 'memory' to cover the experience that they have never actually had. I don't know what this shows, except that some psychologists have persuasive personalities, that some subjects are imaginative, and that we are all told to trust the evidence of our senses, and we do it: we trust the objective fact of the photograph, not our subjective bewilderment. It's a trick, it isn't science; it's about our present, not about our past. Though my early memories are patchy, I think they are not, or not entirely, a confabulation, and I believe this because of their overwhelming sensory power; they come complete, not like the groping, generalised formulations of the subjects fooled by the photograph. As I say 'I tasted,' I taste, and as I say 'I heard,' I hear: I am not talking about a Proustian moment, but a Proustian cine-film. Anyone can run these ancient newsreels, with a bit of preparation, a bit of practice; maybe it comes easier to writers than to many people, but I wouldn't be sure about that. I wouldn't agree either that it doesn't matter what you remember, but only what you think you remember. I have an investment in accuracy; I would never say, 'it doesn't matter, it's history now.' I know, on the other hand, that a small child has a strange sense of time, where a year seems a decade, and everyone over the age of ten seems grown-up and of an equal age, so although I feel sure of what happened, I am less sure of the sequence and the dateline. I know, too, that once a family has acquired a habit of secrecy, memories begin to distort, because its members confabulate to cover the gaps in the facts; you have to make some sort of sense of what's going on around you, so you cobble together a narrative as best you can. You add to it, and reason about it, and the distortions breed distortions.

Still, I think people can remember: a face, a perfume: one true thing or two. Doctors used to say babies didn't feel pain; we know they were wrong. We are born with our sensibilities; perhaps we are conceived that way. Part of our difficulty in trusting ourselves is that in talking of memory we are inclined to use geological metaphors. We talk about buried parts of our past and assume the most distant in time are the hardest to reach: that one has to prospect for them with the help of a hypnotist, or psychotherapist. I don't think memory is like that: rather that it is like St Augustine's 'spreading limitless room'. Or a great plain, a steppe, where all the memories are laid side by side, at the same depth, like seeds under the soil.

HILARY MANTEL, 'Father Figured'

Since my memoir appeared, some people have tried to persuade me that early memories are not authentic, that they cannot be; that they are fictions, only dimly related to the truth. I don't know why people want to believe this – perhaps they find it comforting, as it allows them to scuttle away from confrontation with the facts of the gruesome abuse visited on some babies and young children. They prefer to think of children as blank slates, with nothing much written on them before they reach 'the age of reason'.

But I believe strongly in the power and persistence of memory. Disagreement in accounts of family events is often due to 'point of view' – which, as every storyteller knows, is vital to what is reported. Because you recall things differently from your sibling, it doesn't mean either of you is wrong. Freud, with his passion for archaeology, influenced the way we think of memories, we imagine we have to dig for them. My instinct is that this is not true. In our brains, past and present co-exist; they occupy, as it were, adjoining rooms, but there are some rooms we never enter. We seem to have lost the keys; but they can be retrieved. If you say to someone 'Tell me five things about you when you were five years old,' then from many you will elicit a few bald and fumbling facts. But if you ask them, 'What did you have to eat when you were five?' the effect, after a moment, is quite different. The adult slips away and the child appears, wide-eyed and gleeful, reporting back to you with sensual precision.

Daily Telegraph (23 April 2005)

From BRIAN DILLON, *In the Dark Room* (2005)

The childhood house, we might say, is a machine for making memories. But the conceit, we must admit, is too crude; for how can we separate what we remember from the space which (to put it again too simply) encloses it? In his classic study of domestic space and imagination, *The Poetics of Space*, the philosopher Gaston Bachelard essays an anatomy of our first home, its organs and members. The house works specifically on our bodies: making them accord with its own interior geometry, encouraging us to move around in it in ways that will stay with us for a lifetime. We remember the house, certainly, but it might be more accurate to say that the house marks us physically:

> But over and beyond our memories, the house we were born in is physically inscribed in us. It is a group of organic habits. After twenty years, in spite of all the other anonymous stairways, we would recapture the reflexes of the 'first stairway', we would not stumble on that rather high step. The house's entire being would open up, faithful to our own being. We would push the door that creaks with the same gesture, we would find our way in the dark to the distant attic. The feel of the tiniest latch has remained in our hands.

Our bodies become used, says Bachelard, to certain spaces. He composes an index of the most meaningful: those secret places in which a child's imagination hides, lost in wonder at the 'intimate immensity' of the house, which is both a whole universe and the tiniest sort of dwelling, a shell in which our earliest reveries take shape. In the furrows and expanses of the house, we uncover for the first time the surfaces on which memory and imagination can be set in motion, safely sliding from room to room, from one plane to another in imitation of thoughts and dreams which will one day occupy much larger and unsettling spaces. The house responds to our most original (and, for Bachelard, universal) urge for a place from which to think, to imagine a cosmos that orbits our intimate nook: 'this house that "clings" to its inhabitant and becomes the cell of a body with its walls close together'. To remember such a place, says Bachelard, is to reconnect with our most solitary sense of ourselves. It is not only the place itself that stays with us, but a capacity for reflection which is forever bound up with the way we moved within it: 'the places in which we have experienced daydreaming reconstitute themselves in a new daydream, and it is because our memories of former dwelling-places are relived as daydreams that these dwelling-places of the past remain in us for all time'.

But the house persists, of course, as something lost, as the image of an intimacy to which we can never return. For all Bachelard's enraptured descriptions of the spaces of childhood – the corners, doorways, cabinets and drawers in which the child finds a paradoxically open field in which to exercise his sense of the imaginative vastness of things – in the end we are banished from this idyllic enclosure and discover ourselves adrift, still tied to its centrifugal centre by the threads of recollection. It is not only a matter of nostalgia, of the longing to return. The desire for home, writes Bachelard, is an urge to fulfil its lost promise:

> why were we so quickly sated with the happiness of living in the old house? Why did we not prolong those fleeting hours? In that reality something more than reality was lacking. We did not dream enough in that house. And since it must be recaptured by means of daydreams, liaison is hard to establish. Our memories are encumbered by facts. Beyond the recollections we continually hark back to, we should like to relive our suppressed impressions and the dreams that made us believe in happiness.

The very fact that the house has protected our most unworldly sense of ourselves is what ensures that it now seems utterly lost.

From NICHOLAS HARBERD, *Seed to Seed* (2006)

Saturday 24th January
We went to the Theatre Royal to see *The Play What I Wrote*. It was fun to see these representations of Morecambe and Wise, comedians who had brought such delight in my childhood. Moving to be part of an audience experiencing collective stirrings of memory. Remembered catch-phrases and actions that meant so much thirty years ago. All re-formed now in the telling, making a new thing from the old.

This is the way to arrive at a new direction. By seeing things already seen in a new way, making predictions of unseen things, testing them. But how to do it in reality?

From ERIC R. KANDEL, *In Search of Memory* (2007)

When I first began to study the biological basis of memory, I focused on the memory storage that ensues from the three simplest forms of learning: habituation, sensitization, and classical conditioning. I found that when a simple motor behavior is modified by learning, those modifications directly affect the neural circuit responsible for the behavior, altering the strength of pre-existing connections. Once stored in the neural circuit, that memory can be recalled immediately.

This finding gave us our first insight into the biology of implicit memory, a form of memory that is not recalled consciously. Implicit memory is responsible not only for simple perceptual and motor skills but also, in principle, for the pirouettes of Margot Fonteyn, the trumpeting technique of Wynton Marsalis, the accurate ground strokes of André Agassi, and the leg movements of an adolescent riding a bicycle. Implicit memory guides us through well-established routines that are not consciously controlled.

The more complex memory that had inspired me initially – the explicit memory for people, objects, and places – is consciously recalled and can typically be expressed in images or words. Explicit memory is far more sophisticated than the simple reflex I had studied in *Aplysia*. It depends on the elaborate neural circuitry of the hippocampus and the medial temporal lobe, and it has many more possible storage sites.

Explicit memory is highly individual. Some people live with such memories all the time. Virginia Woolf falls into this category. Her memories of childhood were always at the edge of her consciousness, ready to be summoned up and incorporated into everyday moments, and she had an exquisite ability to describe the details of her recalled experiences. Thus, years after the death of her mother, Woolf's memory of her was still fresh:

> ... there she was, in the very center of that great Cathedral space which was childhood; there she was from the very first. My first memory is of her lap ... Then I see her in her white dressing gown on the balcony ... It is perfectly true that she obsessed me in spite of the fact that she died when I was thirteen, until I was forty-four.
> ... these scenes ... why do they survive undamaged year after year unless they are made of something comparatively permanent?

Other people call up their past life only occasionally. Periodically, I think back and recall the two police officers coming to our apartment and ordering us to leave on the day of Kristallnacht. When this memory enters my consciousness, I can once again see and feel their presence. I can visualize the worried expression on my mother's face, feel the anxiety in my body, and perceive the confidence in my brother's actions while retrieving his coin and stamp collections. Once I place these memories in the context of the spatial layout of our small apartment, the remaining details emerge in my mind with surprising clarity.

Remembering such details of an event is like recalling a dream or watching a movie in which we play a part. We can even recall past emotional states, though often in a much simplified form. To this day I remember some of the emotional context of my romantic encounter with our housekeeper Mitzi.

As Tennessee Williams wrote in *The Milk Train Doesn't Stop Here Anymore*, describing what we now call explicit memory, 'Has it ever struck you . . . that life is all memory, except for the one present moment that goes by you so quickly you hardly catch it going? It's really all memory . . . except for each passing moment.'

For all of us, explicit memory makes it possible to leap across space and time and conjure up events and emotional states that have vanished into the past yet somehow continue to live on in our minds. But recalling a memory episodically – no matter how important the memory – is not like simply turning to a photograph in an album. Recall of memory is a creative process. What the brain stores is thought to be only a core memory. Upon recall, this core memory is then elaborated upon and reconstructed, with subtractions, additions, elaborations, and distortions. What biological processes enable me to review my own history with such emotional vividness?

The Idea of Memory

PLATO, *Theaetetus* (360 BC), translated by
Benjamin Jowett (1892)

Socrates.   I would have you imagine, then, that there exists in
the mind of man a block of wax, which is of different
sizes in different men; harder, moister, and having more
or less of purity in one than another, and in some of
an intermediate quality.

Theaetetus.   I see.

Soc.   Let us say that this tablet is a gift of Memory, the
mother of the Muses; and that when we wish to
remember anything which we have seen, or heard, or
thought in our own minds, we hold the wax to the
perceptions and thoughts, and in that material receive
the impression of them as from the seal of a ring; and
that we remember and know what is imprinted as long
as the image lasts; but when the image is effaced, or
cannot be taken, then we forget and do not know.

Theaet.   Very good. . . .

Soc.   I knowing Theodorus, and remembering in my own
mind what sort of person he is, and also what sort of
person Theaetetus is, at one time see them, and at
another time do not see them, and sometimes I touch
them, and at another time not, or at one time I may
hear them or perceive them in some other way, and
at another time not perceive them, but still I remember
them, and know them in my own mind.

Theaet.   Very true. . . .

Soc.   The only possibility of erroneous opinion is, when
knowing you and Theodorus, and having on the waxen
block the impression of both of you given as by a seal,
but seeing you imperfectly and at a distance, I try to
assign the right impression of memory to the right

visual impression, and to fit this into its own print: if I succeed, recognition will take place; but if I fail and transpose them, putting the foot into the wrong shoe – that is to say, putting the vision of either of you on to the wrong impression, or if my mind, like the sight in a mirror, which is transferred from right to left, err by reason of some similar affection, then 'heterodoxy' and false opinion ensues.

Theaet. Yes, Socrates, you have described the nature of opinion with wonderful exactness. . . .

Soc. When, therefore, perception is present to one of the seals or impressions but not to the other, and the mind fits the seal of the absent perception on the one which is present, in any case of this sort the mind is deceived; in a word, if our view is sound, there can be no error or deception about things which a man does not know and has never perceived, but only in things which are known and perceived; in these alone opinion turns and twists about, and becomes alternately true and false; – true when the seals and impressions of sense meet straight and opposite – false when they go awry and are crooked.

Theaet. And is not that, Socrates, nobly said?

Soc. Nobly! Yes but wait a little and hear the explanation, and then you will say so with more reason; for to think truly is noble and to be deceived is base.

Theaet. Undoubtedly.

Soc. And the origin of truth and error is as follows: – When the wax in the soul of any one is deep and abundant and smooth and perfectly tempered, then the impressions which pass through the senses and sink into the heart of the soul . . . ; these, I say, being pure and clear, and having a sufficient depth of wax, are also lasting, and minds, such as these, easily learn and easily retain, and are not liable to confusion, but have true thoughts, for they have plenty of room, and having clear impressions of things, as we term them, quickly distribute them into their proper places on the block. And such men are called wise. Do you agree?

Theaet. Entirely.

Soc.   But when the heart of any one is shaggy ... or muddy and of impure wax, or very soft, or very hard, then there is a corresponding defect in the mind – the soft are good at learning, but apt to forget; and the hard are the reverse; the shaggy and rugged and gritty, or those who have an admixture of earth or dung in their composition, have the impressions indistinct, as also the hard, for there is no depth in them; and the soft too are indistinct, for their impressions are easily confused and effaced. Yet greater is the indistinctness when they are all jostled together in a little soul, which has no room. These are the natures which have false opinion; for when they see or hear or think of anything, they are slow in assigning the right objects to the right impressions – in their stupidity they confuse them, and are apt to see and hear and think amiss – and such men are said to be deceived in their knowledge of objects, and ignorant.

From PLATO, *Meno* (*c.*382 BC), translated by Benjamin Jowett (1892)

So the soul is immortal and has been many times reborn; and since it has seen all things, both in this world and in the other, there is nothing it has not learnt. No wonder, then, that it can recover the memory of what it has formerly known concerning virtue or any other matter. All Nature is akin and the soul has learnt all things; so there is nothing to prevent one who has recollected – learnt, as we call it – one single thing, from discovering all the rest for himself, if he is resolute and unwearying in the search; for seeking or learning is nothing but recollection.

From ARISTOTLE, *On Memory and Recollection* (*c.*345 BC), translated by W.S. Hett (1936)

It is obvious, then, that memory belongs to that part of the soul to which imagination belongs; all things which are imaginable are essentially objects of memory, and those which necessarily involve imagination are objects of memory only incidentally. The question might be asked how one can remember something which is not present, since it is only the affection that is present, and the fact is not. For it is obvious that one must consider the affection which is produced by sensation in the soul, and in that part of the body which contains the soul – the affection, the lasting state of which we call memory – as a kind of picture; for the stimulus produced impresses a sort of likeness of the percept, just as when men seal with signet rings. Hence in some people, through disability or age, memory does not occur even under a strong stimulus, as though the stimulus or seal were applied to running water; while in others owing to detrition like that of old walls in buildings, or to the hardness of the receiving surface, the impression does not penetrate. For this reason the very young and the old have poor memories; they are in a state of flux, the young because of their growth, the old because of their decay. For a similar reason neither the very quick nor the very slow appear to have good memories; the former are moister than they should be, and the latter harder; with the former the picture does not remain in the soul, with the latter it makes no impression.

Now if memory really occurs in this way, is what one remembers the present affection, or the original from which it arose? If the former, then we could not remember anything in its absence; if the latter, how can we, by perceiving the affection, remember the absent fact which we do not perceive? If there is in us something like an impression or picture, why should the perception of just this be memory of something else and not of itself? For when one exercises his memory this affection is what he considers and perceives. How, then, does he remember what is not present? This would imply that one can also see and hear what is not present. But surely in a sense this can and does occur. Just as the picture painted on the panel is at once a picture and a portrait, and though one and the same, is both, yet the essence of the two is not the same, and it is possible to think of it both as a picture and as a portrait, so in the same way we must regard the mental picture within us both as an object of contemplation in itself and as a mental picture of something else. In so far as we consider it in itself, it is an object of contemplation or a mental picture, but in so far as we consider it in relation to something else, e.g., as a likeness, it is also an aid to memory. Hence when the stimulus of it is operative, if the soul perceives the impression as independent, it appears to occur as a thought, or a mental picture; but if it is considered in relation to something else, it is as though one contemplated a figure in a picture as a portrait, e.g., of Coriscus, although he has not just seen Coriscus. As in this case the affection caused by the contemplation differs from that which is caused when one contemplates the object merely as a painted picture, so in the soul the one object appears as a mere thought, but the other, being (as in the former case) a likeness, is an aid to memory. And for this reason sometimes we do not know, when such stimuli occur in our soul from an earlier sensation, whether the phenomenon is due to sensation, and we are in doubt whether it is memory or not. But sometimes it happens that we reflect and remember that we have heard or seen this something before. Now this occurs whenever we first think of it as itself, and then change and think of it as referring to something else. The opposite also occurs, as happened to Antipheron of Oreus, and other lunatics; for they spoke of their mental pictures as if they had actually taken place, and as if they actually remembered them. This happens when one regards as a likeness what is not a likeness. Memorising preserves the memory of something by constant reminding. This is nothing but the repeated contemplation of an object as a likeness, and not independently.

From SENECA, *Letters to Lucilius*, (1st century BC), translated by Robin Campbell (1969)

It is one thing . . . to remember, another to know. To remember is to safeguard something entrusted to your memory, whereas to know, by contrast, is actually to make each item your own, and not to be dependent on some original and be constantly looking to see what the master said.

From PLUTARCH, 'Cato the Younger' (75 AD), translated by John Dryden (1683)

When he began to learn, he proved dull, and slow to apprehend, but of what he once received his memory was remarkably tenacious. And such in fact we find generally to be the course of nature; men of fine genius are readily reminded of things, but those who receive with most pains and difficulty, remember best; every new thing they learn, being, as it were, burnt and branded in on their minds.

From PLOTINUS, *Fourth Ennead*, (3rd century AD), translated by Stephen McKenna (1930)

A memory has to do with something brought into ken from without, something learned or something experienced; the Memory-Principle, therefore, cannot belong to such beings as are immune from experience and from time.

No memory, therefore, can be ascribed to any divine being, or to the Authentic-Existent or the Intellectual-Principle; these are intangibly immune; time does not approach them; they possess eternity, centred around Being; they know nothing of past and sequent; all is an unbroken state of identity, not receptive of change.

From ST AUGUSTINE, *Confessions*, Book X
(c.AD 400), translated by William Watts (1633)

VIII: I will soar therefore beyond this faculty of my nature, still rising by degrees unto him who hath made both me and that nature. And I come into these fields and spacious palaces of my memory, where the treasures of innumerable forms brought into it from these things that have been perceived by the senses be hoarded up. There is laid up whatsoever besides we think, either by way of enlarging or diminishing, or any other ways varying of those things which the sense hath come at: yea, and if there be anything recommended to it and there laid up, which forgetfulness hath not swallowed up and buried. To this treasury whenever I have recourse, I demand to have anything brought forth whatsoever I will: thereupon some things come out presently, and others must be longer enquired after, which are fetched, as it were, out of some more secret receptacles: other things rush out in troops; and while a quite contrary thing is desired and required, they start forth, as who should say: Lest peradventure it should be we that are called for. These I drive away with the hand of my heart from the face of my remembrance; until that at last be discovered which I desire, appearing in sight out of its hidden cells. Other things are supplied more easily and without disorder, just as they are desired: former notions giving way to the following, by which giving way are they laid up again, to be forthcoming whenever I will have them. Which takes place all together, whenas I repeat anything by heart.

Where are all things distinctly and under general heads preserved, according to the several gates that each notion hath been brought in at? As (for example) light and all colours and forms of bodies brought in by the eyes: and by the ears all sorts of sounds: and all smells by the nostrils; all tastes by the gate of the mouth: and by the sense which belongs to the whole body, is brought in whatsoever is hard or soft: whatsoever is hot or cold; whatsoever is smooth or rugged, heavy or light, in respect of the body either outwardly or inwardly: all these doth that great receipt of the memory receive in her many secret and inexpressible windings, to be forthcoming, and to be called for again, whenas need so requireth, each entering in by his own port, and there lain up in it. And yet do not the things themselves enter the memory; only the images of the things perceived by the senses are ready there at hand, whenever the thoughts will recall them. Which images who can tell how they came to be formed, notwithstanding it plainly appears by which of the senses each hath been fetched in and locked up? For even whilst I dwell in the darkness and silence, yet into my memory can I draw colours, if I please, and can discern betwixt black and white, and what others I desire; nor yet do sounds break in and disturb that notion drawn in by mine eyes, which I am not considering upon: seeing these sounds be in the memory too, and laid up as it were apart by themselves. For I can call for them if I please, and they present themselves to me at an instant; and though my tongue be quiet, and my throat silent, yet can I sing as much as I will. Nor do the images of those colours which notwithstanding be then there, now encroach and interrupt me, when another piece of treasure is called for which came in by the ears. And thus all other things brought in and laid up by other of the senses, do I call to remembrance at my pleasure. Yea, I discern the breath of lilies from that of violets, though at the instant I smell nothing: and I prefer honey before sweet wine, smooth before rough; though at that time I neither taste, nor handle, but remember only.

All this do I within, in that huge court of my memory. For there have I in a readiness the heaven, the earth, the sea, and whatever I could perceive in them, besides those which I have forgotten.

Great is this force of memory, excessive great, O my God; a large and an infinite roomthiness: who can plummet the bottom of it? Yet is this a faculty of mine, and belongs unto my nature: nor can I myself comprehend all that I am. Therefore is the mind too strait to contain itself: so where could that be which cannot contain itself? Is it without itself and not within? How then doth it not contain itself? A wonderful admiration surprises me, and an astonishment seizes me upon this. And men go abroad to wonder at the heights of mountains, the lofty billows of the sea, the long courses of rivers, the vast compass of the ocean, and the circular motions of the stars, and yet pass themselves by, nor wonder that while I spake of all these things I did not then see them with mine eyes; yet could I not have spoken of them, unless those mountains, and billows, and rivers, and stars which I have seen, and that ocean which I believed to be, I saw inwardly in my memory, yea, with such vast spaces between, as if I verily saw them abroad. Yet did

I not swallow them into me by seeing, whenas with mine eyes I beheld them. Nor are the things themselves not within me, but the images of them only. And I distinctly know by what sense of the body each of these took impression in me . . .

XVII: Great is this power of memory; a thing, O my God, to be amazed at, a very profound and infinite multiplicity: and this thing is the mind, and this thing am I. What am I therefore, O my God? What kind of nature am I? A life various and full of changes, yea exceedingly immense. Behold, in those innumerable fields, and dens, and caves of my memory, innumerably full of innumerable kinds of things, brought in, first, either by the images, as all bodies are: secondly, or by the presence of the things themselves, as the arts are: thirdly, or by certain notions and impressions, as the affections of the mind are, – which even then when the mind doth suffer, yet doth the memory retain, since whatsoever is in the mind, is also in the memory: – through all these do I run and flit about, on this side, and on that side, mining into them so far as ever I am able, but can find no bottom. So great is the force of memory, so great is the force of life, even in man living as mortal. What am I now to do, O thou my true Life, my God? I will pass even beyond this faculty of mine which is called memory: yea, I will pass beyond it, that I may approach unto thee, O sweet Light. What sayest thou to me now? See, I am now mounting up by the steps of my soul towards thee who dwellest above me. Yea, I will pass beyond this faculty of mine which is called memory, desirous to touch thee, whence thou mayest be touched; and to cleave fast unto thee, whence one may cleave to thee. For even the beasts and birds have memory; else could they never find their dens and nests again, nor those many other things which they are used unto: nor indeed could they ever enure themselves unto anything, but by their memory. I will pass beyond my memory, therefore, that I may arrive at him who hath separated me from the four-footed beasts and made me wiser than the fowls of the air: yea, I will soar beyond mine own memory, that I may find thee – where, O thou truly Good, and thou secure Sweetness? where shall I be able to find thee? If I now find thee not by my memory, then am I unmindful of thee: and how shall I find thee, if I do not remember thee? . . .

XXV: But whereabouts in my memory is thy residence, O Lord?

Whereabouts there abidest thou? What kind of lodging hast thou there framed for thyself? What manner of shrine hast thou builded for thyself? Thou hast afforded this honour unto my memory, as to reside in it; but in what quarter of it, that am I now considering upon. For I have already passed beyond such parts of it as are common to me with the beasts, whilst I called thee to mind (for as much as I found not thee there amongst the images of corporeal things) and I proceeded to these parts of it, whither I had committed the affections of my mind: nor could I find thee there. Yea, I passed further into it, even to the very seat of my mind itself (which is there in my memory, as appears by the mind's remembering of itself), neither wert thou there: for that as thou art not either any corporeal image, no more art thou any affection of a living man; like as when we rejoice, condole, desire, fear, remember, forget, or whatsoever else we do of the like kind; no, not yet art thou the mind itself, because thou art the Lord God of the mind; and all these are changed, whereas thou remainest unchangeable over all, who yet vouchsafest to dwell in my memory, ever since that first time that I learnt to know thee. But why seek I now in what particular place of my memory thou dwellest, as if there were any places at all in it? Sure I am, that in it thou dwellest: even for this reason, that I have preserved the memory of thee since the time that I first learnt thee, and for that I find thee in it, whensoever I call thee to remembrance.

From MICHEL DE MONTAIGNE, *Essays* (1580), translated by John Florio (1603)

Of Lyers

There is no man living, whom it may lesse beseeme to speake of memorie, than my selfe, for to say truth, I have none at all: and am fully perswaded that no mans can be so weake and forgetfull as mine. All other parts are in me common and vile, but touching memorie, I think to carrie the prise from all other, that have it weakest, nay and to gaine the reputation of it, besides the naturall want I endure (for truely considering the necessities of it, *Plato* hath reason to name it *A great and mighty Goddesse*). In my countrie, if a man will imply that one hath no sense, he will say, such a one hath no memorie: and when I complaine of mine, they reprove me, and will not beleeve me, as if I accused my selfe to be mad and senselesse. They make no difference betweene memorie and wit; which is an empairing of my market: But they doe me wrong, for contrariwise it is commonly seene by experience, that excellent memories do rather accompany weake judgements ... For the Magazin of Memorie is peradventure more stored with matter, than is the store-house of Invention. Had it held out with me, I had ere this wearied all my friends with pratling: the subjects rouzing the meane facultie I have to manage and imploy them, strengthning and wresting my discourses. It is pitie; I have assayed by the trial of some of my private friends: according as their memory hath ministred them a whole and perfect matter, who recoile their narration so farre-backe, and stuff it with so many vaine circumstances, that if the story bee good, they smoother the goodnesse of it; if bad, you must needs either curse the good fortune of their memorie, or blame the misfortune of their judgement. And it is no easie matter, being in the midst of the cariere of a discourse, to stop cunningly, to make a sudden period, and to cut it off. And there is nothing whereby the cleane strength of a horse is more knowne, than to make a readie and cleane stop. Among the skilfull I see some, that strive, but cannot stay their race. Whilest they labour to finde the point to stop their course, they stagger and falter, as men that faint through weaknesse. Above all, old men are dangerous, who have onely the memorie of things past left them, and have lost the remembrance of their repetitions.

From ROBERT BURTON, *The Anatomy of Melancholy* (1621)

Memory lays up all the species which the senses have brought in, and records them as a good *register*, that they may be forth-coming when they are called for by *phantasy* and *reason*.

From THOMAS HOBBES, *Leviathan*, I, ii (1651)

From whence it followeth, that the longer the time is, after the sight, or Sense of any object, the weaker is the Imagination. For the continuall change of mans body, destroyes in time the parts which in sense were moved: So that distance of time, and of place, hath one and the same effect in us. For as at a great distance of place, that which wee look at, appears dimme, and without distinction of the smaller parts; and as Voyces grow weak, and inarticulate: so also after great distance of time, our imagination of the Past is weak; and wee lose (for example) many particular Circumstances. This *decaying sense*, when wee would express the thing it self, (I mean *fancy* it selfe,) wee call *Imagination*, as I said before: But when we would express the *decay*, and signifie that the Sense is fading, old, and past, it is called *Memory*. So that *Imagination* and *Memory*, are but one thing, which for divers considerations hath divers names.

From SIR THOMAS BROWNE, *Hydrotaphia* (1658)

Darknesse and light divide the course of time, and oblivion shares with memory, a great part even of our living beings; we slightly remember our felicities, and the smartest stroaks of affliction leave but short smart upon us . . . To be ignorant of evils to come, and forgetful of evils past, is merciful provision in nature, whereby we digest the mixture of our few and evil dayes, and, our delivered senses not relapsing into cutting remembrances, our sorrows are not kept raw by the edge of repetitions. A great part of Antiquity contented their hopes of subsistency with a transmigration of their souls: a good way to continue their memories . . .

From JOHN LOCKE, *An Essay Concerning Human Understanding* (1690)

Suppose I wholly lose the memory of some parts of my life, beyond a possibility of retrieving them, so that perhaps I shall never be conscious of them again; yet am I not the same person that did those actions, had those thoughts that I once was conscious of, though I have now forgot them? To which I answer, that we must here take notice what the word *I* is applied to; which, in this case, is the *man* only. And the same man being presumed to be the same person, *I* is easily here supposed to stand also for the same person. But if it be possible for the same man to have distinct incommunicable consciousness at different times, it is past doubt the same man would at different times make different persons; which, we see, is the sense of mankind in the solemnest declaration of their opinions, human laws not punishing the mad man for the sober man's actions, nor the sober man for what the mad man did, – thereby making them two persons: which is somewhat explained by our way of speaking in English when we say such an one is 'not himself,' or is 'beside himself'; in which phrases it is insinuated, as if those who now, or at least first used them, thought that self was changed; the self-same person was no longer in that man.

From BARUCH SPINOZA, *Ethics* (1677)

Memory . . . is nothing else than a certain concatenation of ideas, involving the nature of things which are outside the human body, a concatenation which corresponds in the mind to the order and concatenations of the affections of the human body. I say, firstly, that it is a concatenation of those ideas only which involve the nature of things which are outside the human body, and not of those ideas which explain the nature of those things, for there are in truth ideas of the affections of the human body, which involve its nature as well as the nature of external bodies. I say, in the second place, that this concatenation takes place according to the order and concatenation of the affections of the human body, that I may distinguish it from the concatenation of ideas which takes place according to the order of the intellect, and enables the mind to perceive things through their first causes, and is the same in all men. Hence we can clearly understand how it is that the mind from the thought of one thing at once turns to the thought of another thing which is not in any way like the first ... In this manner each person will turn from one thought to another according to the manner in which the habit of each has arranged the images of things in the body. The soldier, for instance, if he sees the footsteps of a horse in the sand, will immediately turn from the thought of a horse to the thought of a horseman, and so to the thought of war. The countryman, on the other hand, from the thought of a horse will turn to the thought of his plough, his field, etc.; and thus each person will turn from one thought to this or that thought, according to the manner in which he has been accustomed to connect and bind together the images of things in his mind.

From DAVID HUME, *A Treatise on Human Nature* (1739)

A painter, who intended to represent a passion or emotion of any kind, wou'd endeavour to get a sight of a person actuated by a like emotion, in order to enliven his ideas, and give them a force and vivacity superior to what is found in those, which are mere fictions of the imagination. The more recent this memory is, the clearer the idea; and when after a long interval he would return to the contemplation of his object, he always finds its idea to be much decay'd, if not wholly obliterated. We are frequently in doubt concerning the ideas of the memory, as they become very weak and feeble; and are at a loss to determine whether any image proceeds from the fancy or the memory, when it is not drawn in such lively colours as distinguish that latter faculty. I think, I remember such an event, says one; but am not sure. A long tract of time has almost worn it out of my memory, and leaves me uncertain whether or not it be the pure offspring of my fancy.

And as an idea of the memory, by losing its force and vivacity, may degenerate to such a degree, as to be taken for an idea of the imagination; so on the other hand an idea of the imagination may acquire such a force and vivacity as to pass for an idea of the memory, and counterfeit its effects on the belief and judgment. This is noted in the case of liars; who by the frequent repetition of their lies, come at last to believe and remember them, as realities; custom and habit having in this case, as in many others, the same influence on the mind as nature, and infixing the idea with equal force and vigour.

Thus it appears, that the *belief* or *assent*, which always attends the memory and senses, is nothing but the vivacity of those perceptions they present; and that this alone distinguishes them from the imagination. To believe is in this case to feel an immediate impression of the senses, or a repetition of that impression in the memory. 'Tis merely the force and liveliness of the perception, which constitutes the first act of the judgment, and lays the foundation of that reasoning, which we build upon it, when we trace the relation of cause and effect.

From SAMUEL TAYLOR COLERIDGE, *Biographia Literaria* (1817)

The IMAGINATION then, I consider either as primary, or secondary. The primary IMAGINATION I hold to be the living Power and prime Agent of all human Perception, and as a repetition in the finite mind of the eternal act of creation in the infinite I AM. The secondary Imagination I consider as an echo of the former, co-existing with the conscious will, yet still as identical with the primary in the kind of its agency, and differing only in degree, and in the mode of operation. It dissolves, diffuses, dissipates, in order to recreate; or where this process is rendered impossible, yet still at all events it struggles to idealise and unify. It is essentially vital, even as all objects (as objects) are essentially fixed and dead.

FANCY, on the contrary, has no other counters to play with, but fixities and definites. The Fancy is indeed no other than a mode of Memory emancipated from the order of time and space; while it is blended with, and modified by that empirical phenomenon of the will, which we express by the word CHOICE. But equally with the ordinary memory the Fancy must receive all its materials ready made from the law of association.

From JAMES MILL, *Analysis of the Phenomena of the Human Mind* (1829)

There is a state of mind familiar to all men, in which we are said to remember. In this state it is certain we have not in the mind the idea which we are trying to have in it. How is it, then, that we proceed in the course of our endeavour, to procure its introduction into the mind? If we have not the idea itself, we have certain ideas connected with it. We run over those ideas, one after another, in hopes that some one of them will suggest the idea we are in quest of; and if any one of them does, it is always one so connected with it as to call it up in the way of association. I meet an old acquaintance, whose name I do not remember, and wish to recollect. I run over a number of names, in hopes that some of them may be associated with the idea of the individual. I think of all the circumstances in which I have seen him engaged; the time when I knew him, the persons along with whom I knew him, the things he did, or the things he suffered; and if I chance upon any idea with which the name is associated, then immediately I have the recollection; if not, my pursuit of it is vain. There is another set of cases, very familiar, but affording very important evidence on the subject. It frequently happens that there are matters which we desire not to forget. What is the contrivance to which we have recourse for preserving the memory – that is, for making sure that it will be called into existence, when it is our wish that it should? All men invariably employ the same expedient. They endeavour to form an association between the idea of the thing to be remembered, and some sensation, or some idea, which they know beforehand will occur at or near the time when they wish the remembrance to be in their minds. If this association is formed, and the association or idea with which it has been formed occurs, the sensation, or idea, calls up the remembrance; and the object of him who formed the association is attained. To use a vulgar instance: a man receives a commission from his friend, and, that he may not forget it, ties a knot in his handkerchief. How is this fact to be explained? First of all, the idea of the commission is associated with the making of the knot. Next, the handkerchief is a thing which it is known beforehand will be frequently seen, and of course at no great distance of time from the occasion on which the memory is desired. The handkerchief being seen, the knot is seen, and this sensation recalls the idea of the commission, between which and itself the association had been purposely formed.

From JOHN STUART MILL, Letter to Dr W.G. Ward (28 November 1859)

[Remembering, trusting to memory, and judging that memory is to be trusted] seem to me to be all three the same act, just as when I press my hand against an object – feeling resistance, trusting the feeling, & judging that it is to be trusted are all one.* We cannot remember what which did not happen; no more can we see or feel what *does* not happen. When I feel so & so, I cannot doubt that I *do* feel so & so, & when I remember to have felt so & so I cannot doubt that I *did* feel so & so. Memory I take to be the present consciousness of a past sensation. It is strange that such consciousness can exist, but the facts denoted by *was*, *is* and *is to come*, are perhaps the most mysterious part of our mysterious existence, as is strikingly expressed in the well-known saying of St Augustine.[1]

From RALPH WALDO EMERSON, *Natural History of the Intellect and Other Papers* (Written 1857, published 1894)

Memory is a primary and fundamental faculty, without which none other can work; the cement, the bitumen, the matrix in which the other faculties are imbedded; or it is the thread on which the beads

---

* Mill is arguing against distinctions made in W.G. Ward's chapter on 'Certitude' in *On Nature and Grace* (1860).

[1.] Probably the famous passage beginning '*Quid est ergo tempus*' from St. Augustine's *Confessions*, Book XI. As translated by William Watts (1912) this passage runs, in part, 'What is time then? If nobody asks me, I know, but if I were desirous to explain it to one that should ask me, plainly I know not . . . If nothing were passing, there would be no past time; and if nothing were coming, there should be no time to come; and if nothing were, there should now be no present time . . . '.

of man are strung, making the personal identity which is necessary to moral action. Without it all life and thought were an unrelated succession. As gravity holds matter from flying off into space, so memory gives stability to knowledge; it is the cohesion which keeps things from falling into a lump, or flowing in waves.

We like longevity, we like signs of riches and extent of nature in an individual. And most of all we like a great memory. The lowest life remembers. The sparrow, the ant, the worm, have the same memory as we. If you bar their path, or offer them somewhat disagreeable to their senses, they make one or two trials, and then once for all avoid it.

Every machine must be perfect of its sort. It is essential to a locomotive that it can reverse its movement, and run backward and forward with equal celerity. The builder of the mind found it not less needful that it should have retroaction, and command its past act and deed. Perception, though it were immense and could pierce through the universe, was not sufficient . . .

The Past has a new value every moment to the active mind, through the incessant purification and better method of its memory. Once it joined its facts by color and form and sensuous relations. Some fact that had a childish significance to your childhood and was a type in the nursery, when riper intelligence recalls it means more and serves you better as an illustration; and perhaps in your age has new meaning. What was an isolated, unrelated belief or conjecture, our later experience instructs us how to place in just connection with other views which confirm and expand it. The old whim or perception was an augury of a broader insight, at which we arrive later with securer conviction. This is the companion, this the tutor, the poet, the library, with which you travel . . .

As every creature is furnished with teeth to seize and eat, and with stomach to digest its food, so the memory is furnished with a perfect apparatus. There is no book like the memory, none with such a good index, and that of every kind, alphabetic, systematic, arranged by names of persons, by colors, tastes, smells, shapes, likeness, unlikeness, by all sorts of mysterious hooks and eyes to catch and hold, and contrivances for giving a hint.

The memory collects and re-collects. We figure it as if the mind were a kind of looking-glass, which being carried through the street of time receives on its clear plate every image that passes; only with this difference that our plate is iodized so that every image sinks into it, and is held there. But in addition to this property it has one more, this, namely, that of all the million images that are imprinted, the very one we want reappears in the centre of the plate in the moment when we want it.

We can tell much about it, but you must not ask us what it is. On seeing a face I am aware that I have seen it before, or that I have not seen it before. On hearing a fact told I am aware that I knew it already. You say the first words of the old song, and I finish the line and the stanza. But where I have them, or what becomes of them when I am not thinking of them for months and years, that they should lie so still, as if they did not exist, and yet so nigh that they come on the instant when they are called for, never any man was so sharp-sighted, or could turn himself inside out quick enough to find.

'Tis because of the believed incompatibility of the affirmative and advancing attitude of the mind with tenacious acts of recollection that people are often reproached with living in their memory. Late in life we live by memory, and in our solstices or periods of stagnation; as the starved camel in the desert lives on his humps. Memory was called by the schoolmen *vespertina cognitio*, evening knowledge, in distinction from the command of the future which we have by the knowledge of causes, and which they called *matutina cognitio*, or morning knowledge . . .

The damages of forgetting are more than compensated by the large values which new thoughts and knowledge give to what we already know. If new impressions sometimes efface old ones, yet we steadily gain insight; and because all nature has one law and meaning, – part corresponding to part, – all we have known aids us continually to the knowledge of the rest of nature. Thus, all the facts in this chest of memory are property at interest. And who shall set a boundary to this mounting value? Shall we not on higher stages of being remember our early history better? . . .

We learn early that there is great disparity of value between our experiences; some thoughts perish in the using. Some days are bright with thought and sentiment, and we live a year in a day. Yet these best days are not always those which memory can retain. This water once spilled cannot be gathered. There are more inventions in the thoughts of one happy day than ages could execute, and I suppose I speak the sense of most thoughtful men when I say, I would rather have a perfect recollection of all I have thought and felt in a day or a week of high activity than read all the books that have been published in a century.

The memory is one of the compensations which Nature grants to those who have used their days well; when age and calamity have bereaved them of their limbs or organs, then they retreat on mental faculty and concentrate on that. The poet, the philosopher, lamed, old, blind, sick, yet disputing the ground inch by inch against fortune, finds a strength against the wrecks and decays sometimes more invulnerable than the heyday of youth and talent . . .

The memory has a fine art of sifting out the pain and keeping all the joy. The spring days when the bluebird arrives have usually only few hours of fine temperature, are sour and unlovely; but when late in autumn we hear rarely a bluebird's notes they are sweet by reminding us of the spring. Well, it is so with other tricks of memory. Of the most romantic fact the memory is more romantic; and this power of sinking the pain of any experience and of recalling the saddest with tranquillity, and even with a wise pleasure, is familiar. The memory is as the affection. Sampson Reed says, 'The true way to store the memory is to develop the affections.' A *souvenir* is a token of love. *Remember me* means, Do not cease to love me. We remember those things which we love and those things which we hate. The memory of all men is robust on the subject of a debt due to them, or of an insult inflicted on them. 'They can remember,' as Johnson said, 'who kicked them last.' . . .

Memory is a presumption of a possession of the future. Now we are halves, we see the past but not the future, but in that day will the hemisphere complete itself and foresight be as perfect as aftersight.

From DAVID SHENK, *The Forgetting* (2003)

On November 12, 1879, two years after he never quite heard, never quite understood, and then entirely forgot Mark Twain's tale of the three famous tramps, Ralph Waldo Emerson, age seventy-six, gave a lecture at the home of Harvard Divinity School professor C.C. Everett. Though Emerson's dementia had steadily progressed over the decade, and he had not written an original lecture in four years, he still occasionally read aloud from old works.

On this particular night, the aging Transcendentalist made a sharply ironic choice of material. Of all things, he read from his twenty-two-year-old essay, 'Memory'. 'Without it,' Emerson intoned, 'all life and thought were an unrelated succession. As gravity holds matter from flying off into space, so memory gives stability to knowledge; it is the cohesion which keeps things from falling into a lump or flowing in waves . . .

'Memory performs the impossible for man by the strength of his divine arms; holds together past and present, beholding both, existing in both, abides in the flowing, and gives continuity and dignity to human life. It holds us to our family, to our friends. Hereby a home is possible; hereby only a new fact has value.'

How poignant, and how awful, that as Emerson read aloud these evocative words, his own memory was broken. Much like H.M., he could form no new memories at all. His life from moment to moment *was* an unrelated succession. There was no more continuity except that provided for him by friends and family. At this particular reading, his daughter and caregiver Ellen stood by as a sort of Seeing Eye memory guide. He continually looked up at her to be sure he did not repeat words or sentences.

This was not just an exercise in caution. Without her help, Emerson had recently lost his place many times in lectures, skipped or repeated sentences, and even reread entire pages over again without noticing. In at least one public reading, he had stopped suddenly in the middle of his material and stood silently at the lectern, oblivious. 'His words are either not all written or not well remembered,' ran a typically disappointed review of these years from the *New Brunswick Daily Times*. '. . . He shows a want of fluency in language, and frequently descends to a tone even fainter than the conversational, and a manner unpleasantly hesitant.'

We will never know for sure, of course, whether Emerson was beset with what we now call 'Alzheimer's disease'. No one bothered to look at the folds of his brain after he died, and if they had they would not have been able to discern anything as detailed as plaques and tangles. Alois Alzheimer was, at the time of Emerson's decline, still a raucous Bavarian youth. Franz Nissl had not yet invented his important tissue stains. Emil Kraepelin had not proposed his radical ideas about autotoxins and organic brain diseases.

From HIPPOLYTE TAINE, *On Intelligence* (1870)

I meet casually in the street a person whose appearance I am acquainted with, and say to myself at once that I have seen him before. Instantly the figure recedes into the past, and wavers about there vaguely, without at once fixing itself in any spot. It persists in me for some time, and surrounds itself with new details. 'When I saw him he was bare-headed, with a working-jacket on, painting in a studio; he is so-and-so, of such-and-such a street. But when was it? It was not yesterday, nor this week, nor recently. I have it: he told me that he was waiting for the first leaves to come out to go into the country. It was before the spring. But at what exact date? I saw, the same day, people carrying branches in the streets and omnibuses: it was Palm Sunday!' Observe the travels of the internal figure, its various shiftings to front and rear along the line of the past; each of these mental sentences has been a swing of the balance. When confronted with the present sensation and with the latent swarm of indistinct images which repeat our recent life, the figure first recoiled suddenly to an indeterminate distance. Then, completed by precise details, and confronted with all the shortened images by which we sum up the proceedings of a day or a week, it again receded beyond the present day, beyond yesterday, the day before, the week, still farther, beyond the ill-defined mass consti-tuted by our recent recollections. Then something said by the painter was recalled, and it at once receded again beyond an almost precise limit, which is marked by the image of the green leaves and denoted by the word spring. A moment afterwards, thanks to a new detail, the recollection of the branches, it has shifted again, but forward this time, not backward; and, by a reference to the calendar, is situ-ated at a precise point, a week further back than Easter, and five weeks nearer than the carnival, by the double effect of the contrary impulsions, pushing it, one forward and the other backward, and which are, at a particular moment, annulled by one another.

From HENRI BERGSON, *Matter and Memory* (1896), translated by Nancy Margaret Paul and W. Scott Palmer (1911)

If matter, so far as extended in space, is to be defined (as I believe it must) as a present which is always beginning again, inversely, our present is the very materiality of our existence, that is to say, a system of sensations and movements, and nothing else. And this system is determined, unique for each moment of duration, just because sensations and movements occupy space, and because there cannot be in the same place several things at the same time. – Whence comes it that it has been possible to misunderstand so simple, so evident a truth, one which is, moreover, the very idea of common sense?

The reason lies simply in the fact that philosophers insist on regarding the difference between actual sensations and pure memory as a mere difference in degree, and not in kind. In our view the difference is radical. My actual sensations occupy definite portions of the surface of my body; pure memory, on the other hand, interests no part of my body. No doubt, it will beget sensations as it materialises; but at that very moment it will cease to be a memory and pass into the state of a present thing, something actually lived; and I shall only restore to it its character of memory by carrying myself back to the process by which I called it up, as it was virtual, from the depths of my past. It is just because I made it active that it has become actual, that is to say, a sensation capable of provoking movements. But most psychologists see in pure memory only a weakened perception, an assembly of nascent sensations. Having thus effaced, to begin with, all difference in kind between sensation and memory, they are led by the logic of their hypothesis to materialise memory and to idealise sensation. They perceive memory only in the form of an image; that is to say, already embodied in nascent sensations. Having thus attributed to it that which is essential to sensation, and refusing to see in the ideality of memory something distinct, something contrasted with sensation itself, they are forced, when they come back to pure sensation, to leave to it that ideality with which they have thus implicitly endowed nascent sensations. For if the past, which by hypothesis is no longer active, can subsist in the form of a weak sensation, there must be sensations that are powerless. If pure memory, which by hypothesis interests no definite part of the body, is a nascent sensation, then sensation is not essentially localised in any point of the body. Hence the illusion that consists in regarding sensation as an ethereal and unextended state which acquires extension and consolidates in the body by mere accident: an illusion which vitiates profoundly, as we have seen, the theory of external perception, and raises a great number of the questions at issue between the various metaphysics of matter. We must make up our minds to it: sensation is, in its essence, extended and localised; it is a source of movement; – pure memory, being inextensive and powerless, does not in any degree share the nature of sensation.

From R.G. COLLINGWOOD, *Speculum Mentis, or the Map of Knowledge* (1924)

A mind which knows its own change is by that very knowledge lifted above change. History, and the same is true of memory . . . is the mind's triumph over time. In the . . . process of thought, the past lives in the present, not as a mere 'trace' or effect of itself on the physical organism, but as the object of the mind's historical knowledge of itself in an eternal present.

From BERTRAND RUSSELL, *Human Knowledge, its Scopes and Limits* (1948)

Memory is the purest example of mirror knowledge. When I remember a piece of music or a friend's face, my state of mind resembles, though with a difference, what it was when I heard the music or saw the face. If I have sufficient skill, I can play the music or paint the face from memory, and then compare my playing or painting with the original, or rather with something which I have reason to believe closely similar to the original. But we trust our memory, up to a point, even if it does not pass this test. If our friend appears with a black eye, we say, 'How did you get that injury?' not 'I had forgotten that you had a black eye.' The tests of memory, as we have already had occasion to notice, are only confirmations; a considerable degree of credibility attaches to a memory on its own account, particularly if it is vivid and recent.

A memory is accurate, not in proportion to the help it gives in handling present and future facts, but in proportion to its resemblance to a past fact. When Herbert Spencer, after fifty years, saw again the lady he had loved as a young man, whom he had imagined still young, it was the very accuracy of his memory which incapacitated him from handling the present fact. In regard to memory, the definition of 'truth', and therefore of 'knowledge', lies in the resemblance of present imagining to past sensible experience. Capacity for handling present and future facts may be confirmatory in certain circumstances, but can never *define* what we mean when we say that a certain memory is 'knowledge'.

From LUDWIG WITTGENSTEIN, *Philosophical Investigations* (1953)

William James, in order to shew that thought is possible without speech, quotes the recollection of a deaf-mute, Mr Ballard, who wrote that in his early youth, even before he could speak, he had had thoughts about God and the world. – What can he have meant? – Ballard writes: 'It was during those delightful rides, some two or three years before my initiation into the rudiments of written language, that I began to ask myself the question: how came the world into being?' – Are you sure – one would like to ask – that this is the correct translation of your wordless thought into words? And why does this question – which otherwise seems not to exist – raise its head here? Do I want to say that the writer's memory deceives him? – I don't even know if I should say *that*. These recollections are a queer memory phenomenon, – and I do not know what conclusions one can draw from them about the past of the man who recounts them.

The words with which I express my memory are my memory-reaction.

From OWEN BARFIELD, *History in English Words* (1962)

Evoking history from words is like looking back at our own past through memory: we see it, as it were, from within. Something has stimulated the memory – a smell, a taste, or a fragment of melody – and an inner light is kindled, but we cannot tell how far that light will throw its beams. Language, like the memory, is not an automatic diary: and it selects incidents for preservation, not so much according to their intrinsic significance as according to the impression they happen to have made upon the national consciousness.

From MARY WARNOCK, *Memory* (1987)

The peculiar value we attach to discursive memory, the recollection of what things were like, seems to derive from its connection with imagination in the developing story of a life.

From PAUL RICOEUR, *Memory, History, Forgetting* (2000), translated by Bridget Patterson

In the context of education – only one part of the *paidea*, as we will soon see – recitation was for a long time the preferred method of instruction, controlled by teachers through texts considered to be, if not the founders of taught culture, at least as prestigious in the sense of texts accepted as having authority. For in the end it is all about authority, or what can more exactly be termed an enunciative authority, to differentiate it from institutional authority. This meaning has connotations in the most fundamental sense with a political concept to do with the establishment of social ties. It is impossible to conceive of a society whose horizontal axis of living together does not intersect with the vertical axis of the authority of the Ancients, as in the old adage quoted by Hannah Arendt: '*potestas in populo, auctoritas in senatu.*'* The supremely political

---

* Power within the people, authority in the Senate.

issue is knowing who the 'senate' is, who the 'Ancients' are, and where their authority comes from. Education has evolved without addressing this problem, apparently protected from facing a challenge in terms of its legitimacy. Whatever this enigma of authority may in fact be – at the heart of what Rousseau called the 'labyrinth of politics' – every society is responsible for the transgenerational transfer of what it holds to be its cultural knowledge. For each generation, acquiring this knowledge saves it the exhausting effort of re-learning everything from scratch every time, as suggested earlier. So in Christian societies people have been learning to recite the catechism for a long time. It is how the rules of writing correctly have been learned – ah! dictation! – , as well as those of grammar and arithmetic. And it is in the same way again that we learn the rudiments of a dead language or a foreign one – ah! Greek and Latin declensions and conjugations! As young children we memorised nursery rhymes and songs; then fables and poems; in this respect have we not moved too far away from the battle against learning by heart? Happy the person who can still, like Jorge Semprun, murmur to a dying man – Maurice Halbwachs,* alas! – Baudelaire's lines: 'O death, old captain, it is time, let us lift anchor . . . our hearts that are known to you are filled with radiance . . .' But learning by heart is not exclusive only to an old-fashioned school. A good many professionals – doctors, lawyers, scientists, engineers, teachers, etc – have recourse throughout their lives to an extensive memorisation of knowledge based on dossiers, lists of items and rules, and stand ready to put them into practice at the right moment. They are all expected to have trained memories.

That's not all: neither the pedagogical nor professional use of memorising can exhaust the treasure-trove of methods of learning ratified by a recitation without mistakes or hesitation. It is important to remember at this point all the arts which Henri Gouhier put under the generic heading of binary arts – dance, theatre, music – where the execution is distinct from the work written in a book, a score, or some sort of inscription. These arts require from their practitioners a laborious training of memory, relying on dogged and patient repetition until they can achieve a performance at once faithful and innovative, in which the preliminary

---

* Maurice Halbwachs (1887–1945). He wrote extensively on public and collective memory.

work can be forgotten in the presence of what appears to be a spontaneous improvisation. How can we fail to admire these dancers, actors and musicians who have sometimes mentally recorded fabulous repertoires which they 'execute' for our pleasure? They are real athletes of memory. They may provide the only unarguable evidence of its use without abuse, obedience to the demands of their work inspiring them with a humility capable of tempering their rightful pride in the feat they have accomplished.

From JEAN-PIERRE CHANGEUX and PAUL RICOEUR, *What Makes Us Think?* 2000, translated by M.B. DeBevoise (2000)

Ricoeur: The case of memory is particularly favorable to the continuation of our discussion. Phenomenology and the neurosciences are in agreement, in fact, with regard to description while diverging with regard to interpretation. Let us consider the problem of description for a moment. It is not by chance that you cited William James in connection with the distribution between immediate memory, understood as working memory, and indirect, or long-term, memory. In Husserl's *Phenomenology of Internal Time Consciousness*, one finds a comparable distinction expressed in the vocabulary of 'retention' and 'remembrance.' In the case of retention, the recent past, which has 'just' occurred, 'still' remains present to consciousness, whereas the distant past no longer plays a role in the present that James calls 'specious' and you call 'apparent'; it is reached through an interval of time by stepping backward into a time other than the present described as 'no longer being,' which is to say 'having been.' You observe that the sense of the unity and continuity of conscious experience depends on working memory – the whole of the duration, I would add, being put together by means of a series of retentions of retentions.

Moving from this observation to consider the question of memory traces, phenomenology may be seen to operate on the plane both of description and interpretation. The descriptive aspect can be examined with the aid of several new pairs of contrasted terms. First there is the distinction introduced by Bergson between 'habit memory' [*mémoire-habitude*] and 'pure memory' [*mémoire-souvenir*]. For it is one thing to execute a familiar task, for example to recite a text learned by heart; it is another to recall learning to execute such a task. The latter form of memory concerns a singular, nonrepeatable event that occurred once in the past. The relation to time, which I will come back to in a moment, is different in the case of each term of the contrasted pair: in the case of habit memory, the past is acted out and incorporated in the present without distance; in the case of pure memory, the anteriority or priorness of the remembered event stands out, whereas in habit memory it does not. This distinction concerning the relation to time is important for dissociating memory and learning, as against the tendency of the biology of memory to treat the two phenomena as continuous – to remember and to memorize are distinct phenomena.

Another pair of terms concerns the relation between spontaneous recollection and more or less labored recall: one pole is represented by Proust's involuntary memory; the other by an effort of memory, which is a type of intellectual effort and which reduces neither to the association of empiricist tradition nor to calculation. This effort involves what Bergson and Merleau-Ponty call a 'dynamic schema' capable of directing memory searches by discarding inappropriate candidates and recognizing the 'right' memory. The phenomenon of recognition is itself very interesting, in the sense that the remembered past and the present moment of recall overlap without being identical: the past is not known, but re-known, as it were – recognized.

A third remarkable pair involves remembering as memory of oneself and, at the same time, as memory of something other than oneself. One may speak here of a polarity between reflexivity and worldliness: on the one hand, as the pronominal form of the French verb 'to remember' [*se souvenir*] suggests, it is of *oneself* that one remembers; on the other hand, the specific intentionality of memory carries it toward events that are said to have happened, to have occurred. Events occur in the world and are linked to places – the places of memory [*lieux de mémoire*] famously analyzed by Pierre Nora. In the case of the most memorable events, these places are 'marked' by collective memory, as a result of which the events linked to them are made memorable; they are inscribed in geographical space just as commemorable events are inscribed in historical time – that is, in the world around us. The connection between reflexivity and worldliness is established by bodily memory, which may itself be immediate or deferred, acted out or represented: it is a self of flesh and blood that we remember, with its moments of pleasure and suffering, its states, its actions, its feelings – which in their turn are situated in an environment, and particularly in places where we have been present with others and which we jointly remember.

Changeux: So far, I agree. The implementation of such a dynamic schema of memory recall by trial and error in terms of a neuronal network seems to me entirely possible and relevant. We will come back to this.

Ricoeur: A final point regarding description: neurobiologists insist on the distinct and derivative character of 'declarative' memory, which is structured by language – mainly by narrative. I wonder whether it is possible to escape the connection between memory and language; the link seems so close that, in the case of problems related to a lesion or other dysfunctions, one can hardly do without the accounts of the subjects themselves. Nonetheless, this is a question that Husserl posed in the unpublished writings: does the prenarrative level rise above muteness? Can one join Dilthey, then, in speaking of the 'cohesion of life' – and therefore of the coherence that life creates with itself – underlying the narrative coherence of personal accounts? For the moment I leave the question open.

Your reference to time, in introducing the problem of memory, leads me now from description to interpretation. The question of memory traces is unavoidable to the extent that the notion of time involves reference to something absent. Plato was the first, to my knowledge, to have formulated the essential paradox: memory, he says in the *Theaetetus*, expresses the presence of something absent. But whereas, for the imagination, the absent is *unreal* (as Sartre emphasized in *The Imaginary*), for memory the absent is *prior*, marked by the adverb 'previously.' Prior to what? To the memory that we now have of it, to the account that we now give of it. Of course, memory and imagination constantly interact, in the form of fantasy, among other things; also owing to the tendency to display our memories in images, as on a screen. This doesn't prevent us from expecting our memories to be trustworthy, and our memory faithful to what has actually taken place – we do not demand this of the imagination, which is permitted to dream. As untrustworthy as memory may be, it is all we have to assure ourselves that something previously took place. The past is therefore absent from our accounts in a specific way. Neuroscience introduces the notion of a trace in order to account for exactly this presence of something absent. Preservation, storage, mobilization at the moment of recall – the competence of objective science with regard to these material operations is indisputable.

For my part, I have no trouble integrating your notions of cortical geography and neuronal inscription with the notion of a basic substrate, understood as an indispensable condition. Besides, in the case of dysfunctions, whether due to lesions or something else, knowledge of these neural mechanisms comes to be altogether naturally incorporated with the experience of one's own body, in the form of therapeutic intervention aimed at adapting behavior to a 'catastrophic' situation, to use Goldstein's term once again. But the use of such knowledge as a practical matter seems to me more problematic, indeed irrelevant, in the case of felicitous memory – even though the forgetting against which we struggle serves to remind us that such memory is not absolutely felicitous, or fully functioning, since forgetting oscillates between the complete erasure of memories and the blocking of memories that are available but inaccessible. In this regard, psychoanalysis is inclined to suppose that we forget less than we fear we do and that with effort – Freud's famous 'effort to remember' – we can recover and reincorporate whole pieces of memory in a more readable and more acceptable personal history.

Changeux: You mention forgetting. Two psychologists, Hermann Ebbinghaus at the end of the nineteenth century and F. C. Bartlett in the 1930s, were the first to quantitatively analyze the development of memory traces. They measured the rate of forgetting through quantitative and qualitative evaluation of conscious recall. The first method makes use of meaningless syllables; the second, by contrast, of meaningful stories. In both cases the trace undergoes a rapid decline within an hour; then a slow process of forgetting over a period of days, weeks, even months. The trace becomes fragmented. Separate elements disappear, others persist. The recall after several months of a complex story displays modifications, omissions, changes in the order of events and alteration of the details. Recalling a memory trace involves, in Bartlett's phrase, 'an effort to understand' – a *reconstruction* based on preexisting schemas and on what has been retained. The agreement with Merleau-Ponty's theses, and even with Freud's 'effort to remember,' is clear. Nonetheless, to create meaning in the course of restoring memories also risks changing them, falsifying them – quite innocently, of course.

In a pathological context, there are 'source' amnesias, often due to age, where the patient can no longer remember when, where, or how a memory was acquired. Recollection in the case of other amnesias is associated with a curious sort of speech containing obviously false, contradictory, bizarre, and in any case improbable information. These fantastic confabulations, typically the result of frontal lobe lesion, are the result of inadequate reconstructions, errors of evaluation in the recollection of memories, and a failure to properly situate them in the context of one's personal history.

In normal subjects, memory *distortions* and implantations of *false* memories frequently occur. Their experimental implementation is simple. One presents the subject with a series of slides depicting a complex event and then reads him an account of the event containing deliberate misinformation; after several other tests, he is finally given a memory test. The result is obvious: not only is a very high proportion of false memories introduced during the misinformation stage, but the subject unhesitatingly believes them. The implantation of false memories in adults, as in children, can have serious consequences. In the United States recently there has been a sort of epidemic of cases of 'resurrected' memories involving persons, sometimes undergoing psychotherapy, who think they have recovered long-forgotten memories of childhood mistreatment (most commonly sexual or other violent abuse). Illusory memories can thus be created in vulnerable patients, leading them to invent a false autobiography.

The Art of Memory

From CICERO, *De Oratore* (55 BC), translated
by F. B. Calvert (1878)

I am not, like Themistocles, of so retentive a genius as to prefer
the art of forgetfulness to that of memory; on the contrary, I am
grateful to Simonides of Ceos, the reputed originator of the system
of artificial memory. It is related that on one occasion, when he
was supping with Scopas at Crannon, in Thessaly, and engaged in
reciting some verses which he had composed in honour of that very
prosperous and noble personage, he introduced, by way of embel-
lishment, much poetical allusion to Castor and Pollux. At the
conclusion, Scopas told him, in rather too sordid a spirit, that only
half the stipulated sum should be paid him for his poem, for the
other moiety, he might look, if he chose, to the Tyndaridae, who
had engrossed full half of the eulogy. Shortly after, a message was
said to have been brought to Simonides, that he was wanted at the
door, where two young men were eagerly inquiring for him; he
immediately rose and went out, but saw nobody. In the short interval
of his absence, however, the hall where Scopas was banqueting
with his friends fell in, crushing him and the whole party to death,
and burying them in the ruins. When the mangled remains could
not by any means be identified by their friends, who came to recover
the bodies, Simonides had so distinct a recollection of the exact
spot occupied by each individual that he was able to give satisfactory directions for their interment. Taking a hint from this occurrence, he is said to have discovered that order was the luminous
guide to memory, and that those, therefore, who wish to cultivate
this faculty should have places portioned off in the mind, fixing in
these several compartments certain images to represent the ideas
they wished to remember; thus the order of places would preserve
the order of ideas, and the symbols would suggest the ideas themselves – the places standing for the wax and the images for the
letters.

But a verbal memory, which is not so necessary for us, must be distinguished by a greater variety of symbols: there are many words connecting, like joints, the different members of language which cannot be represented by any corresponding images; for these certain arbitrary symbols must be invented to be always used in their stead. But the memory of things is properly the memory of the orator, and this we may attain by the creation of distinct and aptly arranged images, so that the signs shall suggest the sentences and the compartments their regular succession. Nor is there any foundation for the objection of the indolent, that the memory is likely to be oppressed with the load of images, and that ideas easily retained by the natural memory are only rendered the more obscure by this artificial process; for I remember having seen two remarkable men with memories of almost superhuman tenacity, viz., Charmadas at Athens, and Scepsius Metrodorus in Asia, the latter of whom is said to be still living, by each of whom I was assured that he could inscribe in the different compartments of his mind whatever he wished to remember as easily as he could trace the letters in wax. Though memory, therefore, cannot be wrought out of the mind unless implanted there by nature, if latent it certainly may be elicited.

From ANON, *Rhetorica ad Herennium*
(1st century BC), translated by Harry Caplan (1954)

Now let me turn to the treasure-house of the ideas supplied by Invention, to the guardian of all the parts of rhetoric, the Memory.

The question whether memory has some artificial quality, or comes entirely from nature, we shall have another, more favourable, opportunity to discuss. At present I shall accept as proved that in this matter art and method are of great importance, and shall treat the subject accordingly. For my part, I am satisfied that there is an art of memory – the grounds of my belief I shall explain elsewhere. For the present I shall disclose what sort of thing memory is.

There are, then, two kinds of memory: one is natural, and the other the product of art. The natural memory is that memory which is imbedded in our minds, born simultaneously with thought. The artificial memory is that memory which is strengthened by a kind of training and system of discipline. But just as in everything else the merit of natural excellence often rivals acquired learning, and art, in its turn, reinforces and develops the natural advantages, so does it happen in this instance. The natural memory, if a person is endowed with an exceptional one, is often like this artificial memory, and this artificial memory, in its turn, retains and develops the natural advantages by a method of discipline. Thus the natural memory must be strengthened by discipline so as to become exceptional, and, on the other hand, this memory provided by discipline requires natural ability. It is neither more nor less true in this instance than in the other arts that science thrives by the aid of innate ability, and nature by the aid of the rules of art. The training here offered will therefore also be useful to those who by nature have a good memory, as you will yourself soon come to understand. But even if these, relying on their natural talent, did not need our help, we should still be justified in wishing to aid the well-endowed. Now I shall discuss the artificial memory.

The artificial memory includes backgrounds and images. By backgrounds I mean such scenes as are naturally or artificially set off on a small scale, complete and conspicuous, so that we can grasp and embrace them easily by the natural memory – for example, a house, an intercolumnar space, a recess, an arch, or the like. An image is, as it were, a figure, mark, or portrait of the object we wish to remember; for example, if we wish to recall a horse, a lion, or an eagle, we must place its image in a definite background. Now I shall show what kind of backgrounds we should invent and how we should discover the images and set them therein.

Those who know the letters of the alphabet can thereby write out what is dictated to them and read aloud what they have written. Likewise, those who have learned mnemonics can set in backgrounds what they have heard, and from these backgrounds deliver it by memory. For the backgrounds are very much like wax tablets or papyrus, the images like the letters, the arrangement and disposition of the images like the script, and the delivery is like the reading. We should therefore, if we desire to memorise a large number of items, equip ourselves with a large number of backgrounds, so that in these we may set a large number of images. I likewise think it obligatory to have these backgrounds in a series, so that we may never by confusion in their order be prevented from following the images – proceeding from any background we wish, whatsoever its place in the series, and whether we go forwards or backwards – nor from delivering orally what has been committed to the backgrounds.

For example, if we should see a great number of our acquaintance standing in a certain order, it would not make any difference to us whether we should tell their names beginning with the person standing at the head of the line or at the foot or in the middle. So with respect to the backgrounds. If these have been arranged in order, the result will be that, reminded by the images, we can repeat orally what we have committed to the backgrounds, proceeding in either direction from any background we please. That is why it also seems best to arrange the backgrounds in a series.

We shall need to study with special care the backgrounds we have adopted so that they may cling lastingly in our memory, for the images, like letters, are effaced when we make no use of them, but the backgrounds, like wax tablets, should abide. And that we may by no chance err in the number of backgrounds, each fifth background should be marked. For example, if in the fifth we should set a golden hand, and in the tenth some acquaintance whose first name is Decimus, it will then be easy to station like marks in each successive fifth background.

Again, it will be more advantageous to obtain backgrounds in a deserted than in a populous region, because the crowding and passing to and fro of people confuse and weaken the impress of the images, while solitude keeps their outlines sharp. Further, backgrounds differing in form and nature must be secured, so that, thus distinguished, they may be clearly visible; for if a person has adopted many intercolumnar spaces, their resemblance to one another will so confuse him that he will no longer know what he has set in each background. And these backgrounds ought to be of moderate size and medium extent, for when excessively large they render the images vague, and when too small often seem incapable of receiving an arrangement of images. Then the backgrounds ought to be neither too bright nor too dim, so that the shadows may not obscure the images nor the lustre make them glitter. I believe that the intervals between backgrounds should be of moderate extent, approximately thirty feet; for, like the external eye, so the inner eye of thought is less powerful when you have moved the object of sight too near or too far away.

Although it is easy for a person with a relatively large experience to equip himself with as many and as suitable backgrounds as he may desire, even a person who believes that he finds no store of backgrounds that are good enough, may succeed in fashioning as many such as he wishes. For the imagination can embrace any region whatsoever and in it at will fashion and construct the setting of some background. Hence, if we are not content with our ready-made supply of backgrounds, we may in our imagination create a region for ourselves and obtain a most serviceable distribution of appropriate backgrounds.

On the subject of backgrounds enough has been said; let me now turn to the theory of images.

Since, then, images must resemble objects, we ought ourselves to choose from all objects likenesses for our use. Hence likenesses are bound to be of two kinds, one of subject-matter, the other of words. Likenesses of matter are formed when we enlist images that present a general view of the matter with which we are dealing; likenesses of words are established when the record of each single noun or appellative is kept by an image.

Often we encompass the record of an entire matter by one nota-tion, a single image. For example, the prosecutor has said that the defendant killed a man by poison, has charged that the motive for the crime was an inheritance, and declared that there are many witnesses and accessories to this act. If in order to facilitate our defence we wish to remember this first point, we shall in our first background form an image of the whole matter. We shall picture the man in question as lying ill in bed, if we know his person. If we do not know him, we shall yet take some one to be our invalid, but not a man of the lowest class, so that he may come to mind at once. And we shall place the defendant at the bedside, holding in his right hand a cup, and in his left tablets, and on the fourth finger a ram's testicles.[1] In this way we can record the man who was poisoned, the inheritance, and the witnesses. In like fashion we shall set the other counts of the charge in backgrounds succes-sively following their order, and whenever we wish to remember a point, by properly arranging the patterns of the backgrounds and

---

[1]. According to Macrobius, *Sat.* 7.13.7–8, the anatomists spoke of a nerve which extends from the heart to the fourth finger of the left hand (the *digitus medicinalis*) where it inter-laces into the other nerves of that finger; the finger was therefore ringed, as with a crown. *Testiculi* suggests *testes* (witnesses). Of the scrotum of the ram purses were made; thus the money used for bribing the witnesses may perhaps also be suggested. (*Translator.*)

carefully imprinting the images, we shall easily succeed in calling back to mind what we wish.

When we wish to represent by images the likenesses of words, we shall be undertaking a greater task and exercising our ingenuity the more. This we ought to effect in the following way:

Iam domum itionem reges Atridae parant.

('And now their home-coming the kings, the sons of Atreus, are making ready.')

If we wish to remember this verse, in our first background we should put Domitius, raising hands to heaven while he is lashed by the Marcii Reges – ('And now their home-coming the kings,'); in the second background, Aesopus and Cimber, being dressed as for the roles of Agamemnon and Menelaus in *Iphigenia* – that will represent 'Atridae parant' ('the sons of Atreus, are making ready'). By this method all the words will be represented. But such an arrangement of images succeeds only if we use our notation to stimulate the natural memory, so that we first go over a given verse twice or three times to ourselves and then represent the words by means of images. In this way art will supplement nature. For neither by itself will be strong enough, though we must note that theory and technique are much the more reliable. I should not hesitate to demonstrate this in detail, did I not fear that, once having departed from my plan, I should not so well preserve the clear conciseness of my instruction.

Now, since in normal cases some images are strong and sharp and suitable for awakening recollection, and others so weak and feeble as hardly to succeed in stimulating memory, we must therefore consider the cause of these differences, so that, by knowing the cause, we may know which images to avoid and which to seek.

Now nature herself teaches us what we should do. When we see in everyday life things that are petty, ordinary, and banal, we generally fail to remember them, because the mind is not being stirred by anything novel or marvellous. But if we see or hear something exceptionally base, dishonourable, extraordinary, great, unbelievable, or laughable, that we are likely to remember a long time. Accordingly, things immediate to our eye or ear we commonly forget; incidents of our childhood we often remember best. Nor could this be so for any other reason than that ordinary things easily slip from the memory while the striking and novel stay longer in mind. A sunrise, the sun's course, a sunset, are marvellous to no one because they occur daily. But solar eclipses are a source of wonder because they occur seldom, and indeed are more marvellous than lunar eclipses, because these are more frequent. Thus nature shows that she is not aroused by the common, ordinary event, but is moved by a new or striking occurrence. Let art, then, imitate nature, find what she desires, and follow as she directs. For in invention nature is never last, education never first; rather the beginnings of things arise from natural talent, and the ends are reached by discipline.

We ought, then, to set up images of a kind that can adhere longest in the memory. And we shall do so if we establish likenesses as striking as possible; if we set up images that are not many or vague, but doing something; if we assign to them exceptional beauty or singular ugliness; if we dress some of them with crowns or purple cloaks, for example, so that the likeness may be more distinct to us; or if we somehow disfigure them, as by introducing one stained with blood or soiled with mud or smeared with red paint, so that its form is more striking, or by assigning certain comic effects to our images, for that, too, will ensure our remembering them more readily. The things we easily remember when they are real we likewise remember without difficulty when they are figments, if they have been carefully delineated. But this will be essential – again and again to run over rapidly in the mind all the original backgrounds in order to refresh the images.

From ABU ALI AHMAD IBN MUHAMMAD MISKAWAYH, an account of Abu'l-Fadl Ibn al-'Amid (11th century)

The talents and virtues which this man displayed were of a sort that made him outshine his contemporaries that the enemy could not resist or the envious fail to acknowledge. No one ever rivalled his combination of qualities. He was like the sun which is hidden from no one, or the sea 'about which one may talk without restraint'. He is the only person whom I ever saw 'whose presence outdid his report'. For example: he was the best clerk of his time, and possessed the greatest number of professional attainments, command of the Arabic language with its rarities, familiarity with grammar and prosody, felicity in etymology and metaphor, retention by memory of pre-Islamic and Islamic collections of poems. I was once told the following by the late Abu'l-Hasan 'Ali ibn Qasim: I used, he said, to recite to my father Abu'l-Qasim difficult poems out of the ancient collections, because the Chief Ustadh was in the habit of asking him to recite them when he saw him, and on such occasions the Ustadh would regularly criticise some mistake in the reading or vocalisation such as had escaped us. This annoyed me and I wanted him to master a poem which the Chief Ustadh would not know or at least be unable to criticise anywhere. I was unable to compass this until I got hold of the Diwan of Kumait, a very copious bard, and selected three of his difficult odes which I fancied the Chief Ustadh had not come across. I helped my father to commit these to memory, and took pains to present myself at the same time. When the eye of the Chief Ustadh lighted on him, he said: Come, Abu'l-Qasim, recite me something that you have learned since my time. – My father commenced his recitation, but as he was proceeding with one of these poems, the Chief Ustadh said to him: Stop, you have omitted a number of verses out of this ode. He then recited them himself; I felt more ashamed than ever before. He then asked my father for some more, and he recited the next ode, and made as before some omissions, which the Ustadh also corrected. My informant concluded: Then I became conscious that the man was an inexhaustible, unfathomable sea. – This is what I was told by this person who was a learned clerk.

As for what I witnessed myself during the time of my association with him for seven years day and night, I may say that no poem was ever recited to him but he knew its author's collection by heart, no ancient or modern poem by anyone deserving to have his verses committed to memory ever came to him as a novelty, and I have heard him recite whole collections of odes by unknown persons such as I was surprised that he should take the trouble to learn. Indeed I once addressed a question to him on the subject. Ustadh, I said, how can you devote your time to acquiring the verse of this person? – He replied: You seem to suppose that it costs me trouble to learn a thing like this by heart. Why, it impresses itself on my memory if I casually hear it once. – He was speaking the truth, for I used to recite to him verses of my own to the number of thirty or forty, and he would repeat them to me afterwards as a sign of approval. Sometimes he would ask me about them and desire me to recite some of them, and I could not repeat three successive lines straight off without his prompting. Several times he told me that in his young days he used to bet his comrades and the scholars with whom he associated that he would commit to memory a thousand lines in one day: and he was far too earnest and dignified a man to exaggerate. I asked him how he managed it. He replied: I made it a condition that if I were required to learn by heart a thousand verses of poetry which I had not previously heard in one day, it must then be written out, and I would then commit to memory twenty or thirty lines at a time, which I would repeat and so have done with them. What, I asked, do you mean by 'having done with them'? He replied: I would not require to repeat them again after that. He went on: I used to recite them once or twice, and then return the paper, to engage upon another, and so get through the whole on one day.

From THOMAS BRADWARDINE, 'On Acquiring a Trained Memory' (14th century), translated by Mary Carruthers and Jan M. Ziolkowski (2002)

Things to be remembered are of two sorts, some sensory and some abstract. Of the sensory things, some are visual and some not. Of those visible some are overly large, some overly small, and others average. I will speak in the first place about those that are average. Suppose that someone must memorise the twelve signs of the Zodiac, that is the Ram, the Bull, etc. So he might, if he wished to, make for himself in the front of the first location a very white ram standing up and rearing on his hind feet, with golden horns. And he might put a very red bull to the right of the ram, kicking the ram with his rear feet; standing erect, the ram with his right foot might kick the bull in his large and super-swollen testicles, causing a copious effusion of blood. And by means of the testicles one will recall that it is a bull, not a castrated ox or a cow.

In a similar manner, a woman may be placed before the bull as though labouring in birth, and in her uterus as if ripped open from her breast may be figured coming forth two most beautiful twins, playing with a horrible, intensely red crab, which holds captive the hand of one of the little ones and thus compels him to weeping and such outward signs, the remaining child wondering yet nonetheless touching the crab in a childish way. Or the two twins might be placed there being born not of a woman but from the bull in a miraculous manner, so that the principle of economy of material may be observed. To the left of the ram a dreadful lion might be placed, who with open mouth and rearing on its legs attacks a virgin, beautifully adorned, tearing her garments. With its left foot the ram might inflict a wound to the lion's head. The virgin might hold in her right hand the scales, for which might be fashioned a balance-beam of silver with a cord of red silk, and weights of gold; on her left may be placed a scorpion horribly stinging her so that her whole arm is swollen; and also she could strive to balance the scorpion in the aforementioned scales.

Then in the front of the second location might be placed an archer with suitable equipment, holding an astounding bow fully extended, in which might be an even more astounding arrow, and he could strive to shoot arrows at a goat standing erect slightly farther back in the same location, remarkably hairy and shaggy, having a weird-looking horn and a golden, luxuriant beard. And he might hold in his right foot a most remarkable jug full of water, in his left foot unusual fishes, onto which he pours crystal-clear water from the water-vessel. And if it should be necessary to remember more things, one may place their images in the following locations in a similar manner. Having done so, the person remembering, is able to recite these things in whatever order he may want, forward or backward.

If however you wish to recall things of extreme size, whether large or small, of the sort such as the world, an army, a city, a millet seed, an iota, or the smallest of worms, one makes average-sized images of them, perhaps of the sort that are depicted by manuscript decorators, or one can acquire the memory of such things through another thing that is opposite, similar, or in some other way analogous to them. If you want to recall sensory phenomena that are not visible, as for instance sweetness, place someone feeding himself with something sweet, like sugar, honey, milk, or happily tasting something else of this sort. But for bitterness, place someone feeding himself on something bitter and immediately vomiting it up in a disgusting manner. For foulness, place something smelling bad in the presence of someone else, who pinches his nostrils with one hand as though against the bad odour and with the other gestures contemptuously toward this thing. For things entirely abstract, such as are God, an angel, infinite space, and such matters, place an image as the painters make it, or you can secure its recollection by means of something that is contrary to it, similar, or analogous in another manner.

From FRANCIS BACON, *The Advancement of Learning* (1605)

For the other principal part of the custody of knowledge, which is Memory, I find that faculty in my judgment weakly enquired of. An art there is extant of it; but it seemeth to me that there are better precepts than that art, and better practices of that art than those received. It is certain the art (as it is) may be raised to points of ostentation prodigious: but in use (as it is now managed) it is barren; not burdensome nor dangerous to natural memory, as is imagined, but barren; that is not dexterous to be applied to the serious use of business and occasions. And therefore I make no more estimation of repeating a great number of names or words upon once hearing, or the pouring forth of a number of verses or rhymes *ex tempore*, or the making of a satirical simile of every thing, or the turning of every thing to a jest, or the falsifying or contradicting of every thing by cavil, or the like, (whereof in the faculties of the mind there is great copie, and such as by device and practice may be exalted to an extreme degree of wonder,) than I do of the tricks of tumblers, funambuloes, baladines; the one being the same in the mind that the other is in the body; matters of strangeness without worthiness.

This art of Memory is but built upon two intentions; the one Prenotion, the other Emblem. Prenotion dischargeth the indefinite seeking of that we would remember, and directeth us to seek in a narrow compass; that is, somewhat that hath congruity with our place of memory. Emblem reduceth conceits intellectual to images sensible, which strike the memory more; out of which axioms may be drawn much better practice than that in use; and besides which axioms, there are divers moe touching help of memory, not inferior to them. But I did in the beginning distinguish, not to report those things deficient, which are but only ill managed.

From JOHN AUBREY, *Brief Lives* (c.1690)

Thomas Fuller was of a middle stature; strong sett; curled haire; a very working head, in so much that, walking and meditating before dinner, he would eate-up a penny loafe, not knowing that he did it. His naturall memorie was very great, to which he added the Art of Memorie: he would repeat to you forwards and backwards all the signes from Ludgate to Charing-crosse.

From RUDYARD KIPLING, *Kim* (1901)

'Play the Play of the Jewels against him. I will keep tally.'

The child dried his tears at once, and dashed to the back of the shop, whence he returned with a copper tray.

'Give me!' he said to Lurgan Sahib. 'Let them come from thy hand, for he may say that I knew them before.'

'Gently – gently,' the man replied, and from a drawer under the table dealt a half-handful of clattering trifles into the tray.

'Now,' said the child, waving an old newspaper. 'Look on them as long as thou wilt, stranger. Count and, if need be, handle. One look is enough for *me*.' He turned his back proudly.

'But what is the game?'

'When thou hast counted and handled and art sure that thou canst remember them all, I cover them with this paper, and thou must tell over the tally to Lurgan Sahib. *I* will write mine.'

'Oah!' The instinct of competition waked in his breast. He bent over the tray. There were but fifteen stones on it. 'That is easy,' he said after a minute. The child slipped the paper over the winking jewels and scribbled in a native account-book.

'There are under that paper five blue stones – one big, one smaller, and three small,' said Kim, all in haste. 'There are four green stones, and one with a hole in it; there is one yellow stone that I can see through, and one like a pipe-stem. There are two red stones, and – and – I made the count fifteen, but two I have forgotten. No! Give me time. One was of ivory, little and brownish; and – and – give me time . . .'

'One – two' – Lurgan Sahib counted him out up to ten. Kim shook his head.

'Hear my count!' the child burst in, trilling with laughter. 'First, are two flawed sapphires – one of two ruttees and one of four as I should judge. The four-ruttee sapphire is chipped at the edge. There is one Turkestan turquoise, plain with black veins, and there are two inscribed – one with a Name of God in gilt, and the other being cracked across, for it came out of an old ring, I cannot read. We have now all five blue stones. Four flawed emeralds there are, but one is drilled in two places, and one is a little carven –'

'Their weights?' said Lurgan Sahib impassively.

'Three – five – five – and four ruttees as I judge it. There is one piece of old greenish pipe amber, and a cut topaz from Europe. There is one ruby of Burma, of two ruttees, without a flaw, and there is a balas-ruby, flawed, of two ruttees. There is a carved ivory from China representing a rat sucking an egg; and there is last – ah ha! – a ball of crystal as big as a bean set on a gold leaf.'

He clapped his hands at the close.

'He is thy master,' said Lurgan Sahib, smiling.

'Huh! He knew the names of the stones,' said Kim, flushing. 'Try again! With common things such as he and I both know.'

They heaped the tray again with odds and ends gathered from the shop, and even the kitchen, and every time the child won, till Kim marvelled.

'Bind my eyes – let me feel once with my fingers, and even *then* I will leave thee opened-eyed behind,' he challenged.

Kim stamped with vexation when the lad made his boast good.

'If it were men – or horses,' he said, 'I could do better. This playing with tweezers and knives and scissors is too little.'

'Learn first – teach later,' said Lurgan Sahib. 'Is he thy master?'

'Truly. But how is it done?'

'By doing it many times over till it is done perfectly – for it is worth doing.'

The Hindu boy, in highest feather, actually patted Kim on the back.

'Do not despair,' he said. 'I myself will teach thee.'

From STEFAN ZWEIG, 'Buchmendel' (1929), translated by Eden and Cedar Paul (2004)

The more I endeavoured to grasp this lost memory, the more obstinately did it elude me; a sort of jellyfish glistening in the abysses of consciousness, slippery and unseizable. Vainly did I scrutinise every object within the range of vision. Certainly when I had been here before the counter had had neither marble top nor cash-register, the walls had not been panelled with imitation rosewood; these must be recent acquisitions. Yet I had indubitably been here, more than twenty years back. Within these four walls, as firmly fixed as a nail driven up to the head in a tree, there clung a part of my ego, long since overgrown. Vainly I explored, not only the room, but my own inner man, to grapple the lost links. Curse it all, I could not plumb the depths!

It will be seen that I was becoming vexed, as one is always out of humour when one's grip slips in this way, and reveals the inadequacy, the imperfections, of one's spiritual powers. Yet I still hoped to recover the clue. A slender thread would suffice, for my memory is of a peculiar type, both good and bad; on the one hand stubbornly untrustworthy, and on the other incredibly dependable. It swallows the most important details, whether in concrete happenings or in faces, and no voluntary exertion will induce it to regurgitate them from the gulf. Yet the most trifling indication – a picture postcard, the address on an envelope, a newspaper cutting – will suffice to hook up what is wanted as an angler who has made a strike and successfully imbedded his hook reels in a lively, struggling, and reluctant fish. Then I can recall the features of a man seen once only, the shape of his mouth and the gap to the left where he had an upper eye-tooth knocked out, the falsetto tone of his laugh, and the twitching of the moustache when he chooses to be merry, the entire change of expression which hilarity effects in him. Not only do these physical traits rise before my mind's eye, but I remember, years afterwards, every word the man said to me, and the tenor of my replies. But if I am to see and feel the past thus vividly, there must be some material link to start the current of associations. My memory will not work satisfactorily on the abstract plane.

I closed my eyes to think more strenuously, in the attempt to forge the hook which would catch my fish. In vain! In vain! There was no hook, or the fish would not bite. So fierce waxed my irritation with the inefficient and mulish thinking apparatus between my temples that I could have struck myself a violent blow on the forehead, much as an irascible man will shake and kick a penny-in-the-slot machine which, when he has inserted his coin, refuses to render him his due.

So exasperated did I become at my failure, that I could no longer sit quiet, but rose to prowl about the room. The instant I moved, the glow of awakening memory began. To the right of the cash-register, I recalled, there must be a doorway leading into a window-less room, where the only light was artificial. Yes, the place actually existed. The decorative scheme was different, but the proportions were unchanged. A square box of a place, behind the bar – the card-room. My nerves thrilled as I contemplated the furniture, for I was on the track, I had found the clue, and soon I should know all. There were two small billiard-tables, looking like silent ponds covered with green scum. In the corners, card-tables, at one of which two bearded men of professorial type were playing chess. Beside the iron stove, close to a door labelled 'Telephone', was another small table. In a flash, I had it! That was Mendel's place, Jacob Mendel's. That was where Mendel used to hang out. Buchmendel. I was in the *Café Gluck!* . . .

A senior student introduced me to him. I was studying the life and doings of a man who is even today too little known, Mesmer the magnetiser. My researches were bearing scant fruit, for the books I could lay my hands on conveyed sparse information, and when I applied to the university librarian for help he told me, uncivilly, that it was not his business to hunt up references for a freshman. Then my college friend suggested taking me to Mendel.

'He knows everything about books, and will tell you where to find the information you want. The ablest man in Vienna, and an original to boot. The man is a saurian of the book world, an antediluvian survivor of an extinct species.'

We went, therefore, to the *Café Gluck*, and found Buchmendel in his usual place, bespectacled, bearded, wearing a rusty black suit, and rocking as I have described. He did not notice our intrusion, but went on reading, looking like a nodding mandarin. On a hook behind him hung his ragged black overcoat, the pockets of which bulged with manuscripts, catalogues and books. My friend coughed loudly, to attract his attention, but Mendel ignored the sign. At length Schmidt rapped on the table-top, as if knocking at a door, and at this Mendel glanced up, mechanically pushed his spectacles on to his forehead, and from beneath his thick and untidy ashen grey brows there glared at us two dark, alert little eyes. My friend introduced me, and I explained my quandary, being careful (as Schmidt had advised) to express great annoyance at the librarian's unwillingness to assist me. Mendel leaned back, laughed scornfully, and answered with a strong Galician accent:

'Unwillingness, you think? Incompetence, that's what's the matter with him. He's a jackass, I've known him (for my sins) twenty years at least, and he's learned nothing in the whole of that time. Pocket their wages – that's all such fellows can do. They should be mending the road, instead of sitting over books.'

This outburst served to break the ice, and with a friendly wave of the hand the bookworm invited me to sit down at his table. I reiterated my object in consulting him; to get a list of all the early works on animal magnetism, and of contemporary and subsequent books and pamphlets for and against Mesmer. When I had said my say, Mendel closed his left eye for an instant, as if excluding a grain of dust. This was, with him, a sign of concentrated attention. Then, as though reading from an invisible catalogue, he reeled out the names of two or three dozen titles, giving in each case place and date of publication and approximate price. I was amazed, though Schmidt had warned me what to expect. His vanity was tickled by my surprise, for he went on to strum the keyboard of his marvellous memory, and to produce the most astounding bibliographical marginal notes. Did I want to know about sleep-walkers, Perkins's metallic tractors, early experiments in hypnotism, Braid, Gassner, attempts to conjure up the devil, Christian Science, theosophy, Madame Blavatsky? In connection with each item there was a hailstorm of book-names, dates, and appropriate details. I was beginning to understand that Jacob Mendel was a living lexicon, something like the general catalogue of the British Museum Reading Room, but able to walk about on two legs. I stared dumbfounded at this bibliographical phenomenon, which masqueraded in the sordid and rather unclean appearance of a Galician second-hand book dealer, who, after rattling off some eighty titles (with assumed indifference, but really with the satisfaction of one who plays an unexpected trump), proceeded to wipe his spectacles with a hand-kerchief which might long before have been white.

Hoping to conceal my astonishment, I inquired:

'Which among these works do you think you could get for me without too much trouble?'

'Oh, I'll have a look round,' he answered. 'Come here tomorrow and I shall certainly have some of them. As for the others, it's only a question of time, and of knowing where to look.'

'I'm greatly obliged to you,' I said; and; then, wishing to be civil, moved in haste, proposing to give him a list of the books I wanted. Schmidt nudged me warningly, but too late. Mendel had already flashed a look at me – such a look, at once triumphant and affronted, scornful and overwhelmingly superior – the royal look with which Macbeth answers Macduff when summoned to yield without a blow. He laughed curtly. His Adam's apple moved excitedly. Obviously he had gulped down a choleric, an insulting epithet.

Indeed he had good reason to be angry. Only a stranger, an ignoramus, could have proposed to give him, Jacob Mendel, a memorandum, as if he had been a bookseller's assistant or an under-ling in a public library. Not until I knew him better did I fully understand how much my would-be politeness must have galled this aberrant genius – for the man had, and knew himself to have, a titanic memory, wherein, behind a dirty and undistinguished-looking forehead, was indelibly recorded a picture of the title-page of every book that had been printed. No matter whether it had issued from the press yesterday or hundreds of years ago, he knew its place of publication, its author's name, and its price. From his mind, as if from the printed page, he could read off the contents, could reproduce the illustrations; could visualise, not only what he had actually held in his hands, but also what he had glanced at in a bookseller's window; could see it with the same vividness as an artist sees the creations of fancy which he has not yet reproduced upon canvas. When a book was offered for six marks by a Regensburg dealer, he could remember that, two years before, a copy of the same work had changed hands for four crowns at a Viennese auction, and he recalled the name of the purchaser. In a word, Jacob Mendel never forgot a title or a figure; he knew every plant, every animal, every star, in the continually revolving and incessantly changing cosmos of the book-universe. In each literary specialty, he knew more than the specialists; he knew the contents of the libraries better than the librarians; he knew the book-lists of most publishers better than the heads of the firms concerned – though he had nothing to guide him except the magical powers of his inexplicable but invariably accurate memory.

True, this memory owed its infallibility to the man's limitations, to his extraordinary power of concentration. Apart from books, he knew nothing of the world. The phenomena of existence did not begin to become real for him until they had been set in type, arranged upon a composing stick, collected and, so to say, sterilised in a book. Nor did he read books for their meaning, to extract their spiritual or narrative substance.

What aroused his passionate interest, what fixed his attention, was the name, the price, the format, the title-page. Though in the last analysis unproductive and uncreative, this specifically antiquarian memory of Jacob Mendel, since it was not a printed book-catalogue but was stamped upon the grey matter of a mammalian brain, was, in its unique perfection, no less remarkable a phenomenon than Napoleon's gift for physiognomy, Mezzofanti's talent for languages, Lasker's skill at chess-openings, Busoni's musical genius. Given a public position as teacher, this man with so marvellous a brain might have taught thousands and hundreds of thousands of students, have trained others to become men of great learning and of incalculable value to those communal treasure-houses we call libraries. But to him, a man of no account, a Galician Jew, a book-dealer whose only training had been received in a Talmudic school, this upper world of culture was a fenced precinct he could never enter; and his amazing faculties could only find application at the marble-topped table in the inner room of the *Café Gluck*. When, some day, there arises a great psychologist who shall classify the types of that magical power we term memory, as effectively as Buffon classified the genus and species of animals, a man competent to give a detailed description of all the varieties, he will have to find a pigeon-hole for Jacob Mendel, forgotten master of the lore of book-prices and book-titles, the ambulatory catalogue alike of incunabula and the modern commonplace.

From JORGE LUIS BORGES, 'Funes the Memorious' (1944), translated by James E. Irby (1964)

I remember him (I have no right to utter this sacred verb, only one man on earth had that right and he is dead) with a dark passion flower in his hand, seeing it as no one has ever seen it, though he might look at it from the twilight of dawn till that of evening, a whole lifetime. I remember him, with his face taciturn and Indian-like and singularly *remote*, behind the cigarette. I remember (I think) his angular, leather-braiding hands. I remember near those hands a maté gourd bearing the Uruguayan coat of arms; I remember a yellow screen with a vague lake landscape in the window of his house. I clearly remember his voice: the slow, resentful, nasal voice of the old-time dweller of the suburbs, without the Italian sibilants we have today. I never saw him more than three times; the last was in 1887. . . . I find it very satisfactory that all those who knew him should write about him; my testimony will perhaps be the shortest and no doubt the poorest, but not the most impartial in the volume you will edit. My deplorable status as an Argentine will prevent me from indulging in a dithyramb, an obligatory genre in Uruguay whenever the subject is an Uruguayan. *Highbrow, city slicker, dude*: Funes never spoke these injurious words, but I am sufficiently certain I represented for him those misfortunes. Pedro Leandro Ipuche has written that Funes was a precursor of the supermen, 'a vernacular and rustic Zarathustra'; I shall not debate the point, but one should not forget that he was also a kid from Fray Bentos, with certain incurable limitations.

My first memory of Funes is very perspicuous. I can see him on an afternoon in March or February of the year 1884. My father, that year, had taken me to spend the summer in Fray Bentos. I was returning from the San Francisco ranch with my cousin Bernardo Haedo. We were singing as we rode along and being on horseback was not the only circumstance determining my happiness. After a sultry day, an enormous slate-coloured storm had hidden the sky. It was urged on by a southern wind, the trees were already going wild; I was afraid (I was hopeful) that the elemental rain would take us by surprise in the open. We were running a kind of race with the storm. We entered an alleyway that sank down between two very high brick sidewalks. It had suddenly got dark: I heard some rapid and almost secret footsteps up above; I raised my eyes and saw a boy running along the narrow and broken path as if it were a narrow and broken wall. I remember his baggy gaucho trousers, his rope-soled shoes, I remember the cigarette in his hard face, against the now limitless storm cloud. Bernardo cried to him unexpectedly: 'What time is it, Ireneo?' Without consulting the sky, without stopping, he replied: 'It's four minutes to eight, young Bernardo Juan Francisco.' His voice was shrill, mocking.

I am so unperceptive that the dialogue I have just related would not have attracted my attention had it not been stressed by my cousin, who (I believe) was prompted by a certain local pride and the desire to show that he was indifferent to the other's tripartite reply.

He told me the fellow in the alleyway was one Ireneo Funes, known for certain peculiarities such as avoiding contact with people and always knowing what time it was, like a clock. He added that he was the son of the ironing woman in town, María Clementina Funes, and that some people said his father was a doctor at the meat packers, an Englishman by the name of O'Connor, and others that he was a horse tamer or scout from the Salto district. He lived with his mother, around the corner from the Laureles house.

During the years eighty-five and eighty-six we spent the summer in Montevideo. In eighty-seven I returned to Fray Bentos. I asked, as was natural, about all my acquaintances and, finally, about the 'chronometrical' Funes. I was told he had been thrown by a half-tamed horse on the San Francisco ranch and was left hopelessly paralysed. I remember the sensation of uneasy magic the news produced in me: the only time I had seen him, we were returning from San Francisco on horseback and he was running along a high place; this fact, told me by my cousin Bernardo, had much of the quality of a dream made up of previous elements. I was told he never moved from his cot, with his eyes fixed on the fig tree in the back or on a spider web. In the afternoons, he would let himself be brought out to the window. He carried his pride to the point of acting as if the blow that had felled him were beneficial ... Twice I saw him behind the iron grating of the window, which harshly emphasised his condition as a perpetual prisoner: once, motionless, with his eyes closed; another time, again motionless, absorbed in the contemplation of a fragrant sprig of santonica.

Not without a certain vaingloriousness, I had begun at that time my methodical study of Latin. My valise contained the *De viris illustribus* of Lhomond, Quicherat's *Thesaurus*, the commentaries of Julius Caesar and an odd volume of Pliny's *Naturalis historia*, which then exceeded (and still exceeds) my moderate virtues as a Latinist. Everything becomes public in a small town; Ireneo, in his house on the outskirts, did not take long to learn of the arrival of these anomalous books. He sent me a flowery and ceremonious letter in which he recalled our encounter, unfortunately brief, 'on the seventh day of February of the year 1884', praised the glorious services my uncle Gregorio Haedo, deceased that same year, 'had rendered to our two nations in the valiant battle of Ituzaingó' and requested the loan of any one of my volumes, accompanied by a dictionary 'for the proper intelligence of the original text, for I am as yet ignorant of Latin'. He promised to return them to me in good condition, almost immediately. His handwriting was perfect, very sharply outlined; his orthography, of the type favoured by Andrés Bello: *i* for *y*, *j* for *g*. At first I naturally feared a joke. My cousins assured me that was not the case, that these were peculiarities of Ireneo. I did not know whether to attribute to insolence, ignorance or stupidity the idea that the arduous Latin tongue should require no other instrument than a dictionary: to disillusion him fully, I sent him the *Gradus ad Parnassum* of Quicherat and the work by Pliny.

On the fourteenth of February, I received a telegram from Buenos Aires saying I should return immediately, because my father was 'not at all well'. May God forgive me; the prestige of being the recipient of an urgent telegram, the desire to communicate to all Fray Bentos the contradiction between the negative form of the message and the peremptory adverb, the temptation to dramatise my suffering, affecting a virile stoicism, perhaps distracted me from all possibility of real sorrow. When I packed my valise, I noticed the *Gradus* and the first volume of the *Naturalis historia* were missing. The *Saturn* was sailing the next day, in the morning; that night, after supper, I headed towards Funes's house. I was astonished to find the evening no less oppressive than the day had been.

At the respectable little house, Funes's mother opened the door for me.

She told me Ireneo was in the back room and I should not be surprised to find him in the dark, because he knew how to pass the idle hours without lighting the candle. I crossed the tile patio, the little passageway; I reached the second patio. There was a grape arbour; the darkness seemed complete to me. I suddenly heard Ireneo's high-pitched, mocking voice. His voice was speaking in Latin; his voice (which came from the darkness) was articulating with morose delight a speech or prayer or incantation. The Roman syllables resounded in the earthen patio: my fear took them to be indecipherable, interminable; afterwards, in the enormous dialogue of that night, I learned they formed the first paragraph of the twenty-fourth chapter of the seventh book of the *Naturalis historia*. The subject of that chapter is memory; the last words were *ut nihil non iisdem verbis redderetur auditum*.

Without the slightest change of voice, Ireneo told me to come in. He was on his cot, smoking. It seems to me I did not see his face until dawn: I believe I recall the intermittent glow of his cigarette. The room smelled vaguely of dampness. I sat down; I repeated the story about the telegram and my father's illness.

I now arrive at the most difficult point in my story. This story (it is well the reader knows it by now) has no other plot than that dialogue which took place half a century ago. I shall not try to reproduce the words, which are now irrecoverable. I prefer to summarize with veracity the many things Ireneo told me. The indirect style is remote and weak: I know I am sacrificing the efficacy of my narrative; my readers should imagine for themselves the hesitant periods which overwhelmed me that night.

Ireneo began by enumerating, in Latin and in Spanish, the cases of prodigious memory recorded in the *Naturalis historia*: Cyrus, king of the Persians, who could call every soldier in his armies by name; Mithridates Eupator, who administered the law in the twenty-two languages of his empire; Simonides, inventor of the science of mnemonics; Metrodorus, who practised the art of faithfully repeating what he had heard only once. In obvious good faith, Ireneo was amazed that such cases be considered amazing. He told me that before that rainy afternoon when the blue-grey horse threw him, he had been what all humans are: blind, deaf, addle-brained, absent-minded. (I tried to remind him of his exact perception of time, his memory for proper names; he paid no attention to me.) For nineteen years he had lived as one in a dream: he looked without seeing, listened without hearing, forgetting everything, almost everything. When he fell, he became unconscious; when he came to, the present was almost intolerable in its richness and sharpness, as were his most distant and trivial memories. Somewhat later he learned that he was paralysed. The fact scarcely interested him. He reasoned (he felt) that his immobility was a minimum price to pay. Now his perception and his memory were infallible.

We, at one glance, can perceive three glasses on a table; Funes, all the leaves and tendrils and fruit that make up a grape vine. He knew by heart the forms of the southern clouds at dawn on 30 April 1882, and could compare them in his memory with the mottled streaks on a book in Spanish binding he had only seen once and with the outlines of the foam raised by an oar in the Río Negro the night before the Quebracho uprising. These memories were not simple ones; each visual image was linked to muscular sensations, thermal sensations, etc. He could reconstruct all his dreams, all his half-dreams. Two or three times he had reconstructed a whole day; he never hesitated, but each reconstruction had required a whole day. He told me: 'I alone have more memories than all mankind has probably had since the world has been the world.' And again: 'My dreams are like you people's waking hours.' And again, towards dawn: 'My memory, sir, is like a garbage heap.' A circle drawn on a blackboard, a right triangle, lozenge – all these are forms we can fully and intuitively grasp; Ireneo could do the same with the stormy mane of a pony, with a herd of cattle on a hill, with the changing fire and its innumerable ashes, with the many faces of a dead man throughout a long wake. I don't know how many stars he could see in the sky.

.These things he told me; neither then nor later have I ever placed them in doubt. In those days there were no cinemas or phonographs; nevertheless, it is odd and even incredible that no one ever performed an experiment with Funes. The truth is that we live out our lives putting off all that can be put off; perhaps we all know deep down that we are immortal and that sooner or later all men will do and know all things.

Out of the darkness, Funes's voice went on talking to me.

He told me that in 1886 he had invented an original system of numbering and that in a very few days he had gone beyond the twenty-four-thousand mark. He had not written it down, since anything he thought of once would never be lost to him. His first stimulus was, I think, his discomfort at the fact that the famous thirty-three gauchos of Uruguayan history should require two signs and two words, in place of a single word and a single sign. He then applied this absurd principle to the other numbers. In place of seven thousand thirteen, he would say (for example) *Máximo Pérez*; in place of seven thousand fourteen, *The Railroad*; other numbers were *Luis Melián Lafinur, Olimar, sulphur, the reins, the whale, the gas, the cauldron, Napoleon, Agustín de Vedia*. In place of five hundred, he would say *nine*. Each word had a particular sign, a kind of mark; the last in the series were very complicated . . . I tried to explain to him that his rhapsody of incoherent terms was precisely the opposite of a system of numbers. I told him that saying 365 meant saying three hundreds, six tens, five ones, an analysis which is not found in the 'numbers' *The Negro Timoteo* or *meat blanket*. Funes did not understand me or refused to understand me.

Locke, in the seventeenth century, postulated (and rejected) an impossible language in which each individual thing, each stone, each bird and each branch, would have its own name; Funes once projected an analogous language, but discarded it because it seemed too general to him, too ambiguous. In fact, Funes remembered not only every leaf of every tree of every wood, but also every one of the times he had perceived or imagined it. He decided to reduce each of his past days to some seventy thousand memories, which would then be defined by means of ciphers. He was dissuaded from this by two considerations: his awareness that the task was interminable, his awareness that it was useless. He thought that by the hour of his death he would not even have finished classifying all the memories of his childhood.

The two projects I have indicated (an infinite vocabulary for the natural series of numbers, a useless mental catalogue of all the images of his memory) are senseless, but they betray a certain stammering grandeur. They permit us to glimpse or infer the nature of Funes's vertiginous world. He was, let us not forget, almost incapable of ideas of a general, Platonic sort. Not only was it difficult for him to comprehend that the generic symbol *dog* embraces so many unlike individuals of diverse size and form; it bothered him that the dog at three fourteen (seen from the side) should have the same name as the dog at three fifteen (seen from the front). His own face in the mirror, his own hands, surprised him every time he saw them. Swift relates that the emperor of Lilliput could discern the movement of the minute hand; Funes could continuously discern the tranquil advances of corruption, of decay, of fatigue. He could note the progress of death, of dampness. He was the solitary and lucid spectator of a multiform, instantaneous and almost intolerably precise world. Babylon, London and New York have overwhelmed with their ferocious splendour the imaginations of men; no one, in their populous towers or their urgent avenues, has felt the heat and pressure of a reality as indefatigable as that which day and night converged upon the hapless Ireneo, in his poor South American suburb. It was very difficult for him to sleep. To sleep is to turn one's mind from the world; Funes, lying on his back on his cot in the shadows, could imagine every crevice and every moulding in the sharply defined houses surrounding him. (I repeat that the least important of his memories was more minute and more vivid than our perception of physical pleasure or physical torment.) Towards the east, along a stretch not yet divided into blocks, there were new houses, unknown to Funes. He imagined them to be black, compact, made of homogeneous darkness; in that direction he would turn his face in order to sleep. He would also imagine himself at the bottom of the river, rocked and annihilated by the current.

With no effort, he had learned English, French, Portuguese and Latin. I suspect, however, that he was not very capable of thought. To think is to forget differences, generalise, make abstractions. In the teeming world of Funes, there were only details, almost immediate in their presence.

The wary light of dawn entered the earthen patio.

Then I saw the face belonging to the voice that had spoken all night long. Ireneo was nineteen years old; he had been born in 1868; he seemed to me as monumental as bronze, more ancient than Egypt, older than the prophecies and the pyramids. I thought that each of my words (that each of my movements) would persist in his implacable memory; I was benumbed by the fear of multiplying useless gestures.

Ireneo Funes died in 1889, of congestion of the lungs.

FRANCES A. YATES'S discussion in *The Art of Memory* (1966) of the Theatre Memory System of Robert Fludd (1574–1637)

The chapter on 'the science of spiritual memorising which is vulgarly called *Ars Memoriae*'[1] is introduced by a picture illustrating this science. We see a man with a large 'eye of imagination' in the fore part of his head; and beside him five memory *loci* containing memory images. Five is Fludd's favourite number for a group of memory places, as will appear later, and the diagram also illustrates his principle of having one main image in a memory room. The main image is an obelisk; the others are the Tower of Babel, Tobias and the Angel, a ship, and the Last Judgement with the damned entering the mouth of Hell – an interesting relic in this very late Renaissance system of the medieval virtue of remembering Hell by the artificial memory. These five images are nowhere explained or referred to in the following text. I do not know whether they are intended to be read allegorically – the obelisk as an Egyptian symbol referring to the 'inner writing' of the art which will overcome the confusions of Babel and conduct its user under angelic guidance to religious safety. This may be over-fanciful, and in the absence of any explanation by Fludd it is better to leave them unexplained.

After some of the usual definitions of artificial memory, Fludd devoted a chapter to explaining the distinction which he makes

---

[1.] Robert Fludd, *Utriusque Cosmi Historia* (1617–21), II, section 2, pp. 48ff.

between two different types of art, which he calls respectively
the 'round art [*ars rotunda*]', and the 'square art [*ars quadrata*]'.

> For the complete perfection of the art of memory the fantasy is oper-
> ated in two ways. The first way is through *ideas*, which are forms
> separated from corporeal things, such as spirits, shadows [*umbrae*],
> souls and so on, also angels, which we chiefly use in our *ars rotunda*.
> We do not use this word 'ideas' in the same way that Plato does,
> who is accustomed to use it of the mind of God, but for anything
> which is not composed of the four elements, that is to say for things
> spiritual and simple conceived in the imagination; for example angels,
> demons, the effigies of stars, the images of gods and goddesses to
> whom celestial powers are attributed and which partake more of a
> spiritual than of a corporeal nature; similarly virtues and vices
> conceived in the imagination and made into shadows, which were
> also to be held as demons.

The 'round art', then, uses magicised or talismanic images, effi-
gies of the stars; 'statues' of gods and goddesses animated with
celestial influences; images of virtues and vices, as in the old
medieval art, but now thought of as containing 'demonic' or
magical power. Fludd is working at a classification of images into
potent and less potent such as was [Giordano] Bruno's constant
preoccupation.

The 'square art' uses images of corporeal things, of men, of
animals, of inanimate objects. When its images are of men or of
animals, these are active, engaged in action of some kind. The
'square art' sounds like the ordinary art of memory, using the
active images of *Ad Herennium* and perhaps 'square' because
using buildings or rooms as places. These two arts, the round
and the square, are the only two possible arts of memory, states
Fludd.

> Memory can only be artificially improved, either by medicaments,
> or by the operation of the fantasy towards *ideas* in the round art,
> or through images of corporeal things in the square art.

The practice of the round art, though it is quite different from the
art with the 'ring of Solomon' of which Fludd heard rumours at

Toulouse (and which must have been blackly magical), demands nevertheless, he says, the assistance of demons (in the sense of daemonic powers not of demons in Hell) or the metaphysical influence of the Holy Spirit. And it is necessary that 'the fantasy should concur in the metaphysical act'.[2]

Many people, continues Fludd, prefer the square art because it is easier, but the round art is infinitely the superior of the two. For the round art is 'natural' using 'natural' places and is naturally adapted to the microcosm. Whereas the square art is 'artificial' using artificially made up places and images.

Fludd then devotes a whole, fairly long chapter, to a polemic against the use of 'fictitious places' in the square art. To understand this we must remind ourselves of the age-long distinction, stemming from *Ad Herennium* and the other classical sources, between 'real' and 'fictitious' memory places. 'Real' places are real buildings of any kind used for forming places in the normal way in the mnemotechnic. 'Fictitious' places are imaginary buildings or imaginary places of any kind which the author of *Ad Herennium* said might be invented if not enough real places were available. The distinction between 'real' and 'fictitious' places went on for ever in the memory treatises with much elaborate glossing on these themes. Fludd is very much against the use of 'fictitious' buildings in the square art. These confuse memory and add to its task. One must always use real places in real buildings. 'Some who are versed in this art wish to place their square art in palaces fabricated or erected by invention of the imagination; that this opinion is inconvenient we will now briefly explain.' So opens the chapter against the use of fictitious places in the square art. It is an important chapter for, if true to these strongly held views against fictitious places, the buildings which Fludd will use in his memory system will be 'real' buildings.

Having laid down his distinction between the *ars rotunda* and the

---

2. The extremely magical art of memory of which Fludd has heard at Toulouse sounds like the *ars notoria*. Fludd might possibly be referring to Jean Belot who had been publishing in France earlier in the century works on chiromancy, physiognomy, and the art of memory. Belot's highly magical artificial memory, in which he mentions Lull, Agrippa, and Bruno, is reprinted in the edition of his *Oeuvres* (Lyons, 1654), pp. 329 ff. The art of memory by R. Saunders (*Physiognomie and Chiromancie . . . whereunto is added the Art of Memory*, 1653, 1671) is based on that of Belot and repeats his mention of Bruno. Saunders dedicated his book to Elias Ashmole.

ars quadrata and the different kinds of images to be used in each, and having made clear his view that the *ars quadrata* must always use real buildings, Fludd now arrives at the exposition of his memory system. This is a combination of the round and the square. Based on the round heavens, the zodiac and the spheres of the planets, it uses, in combination with these, buildings which are to be placed in the heavens, buildings containing places with memory images on them which will be, as it were, astrally activated by being organically related to the stars. We have met this kind of thing before. In fact the idea is exactly the same as that in Bruno's *Images*, where he used sets of *atria* or rooms, cubicles, and 'fields', crammed with images, and activated by being organically affiliated to his 'round' art, the images in which were gods and goddesses to whom celestial influences were attributed. Bruno had also laid down the distinction between what Fludd calls the 'round' and the 'square' arts in his *Seals* published in England thirty-six years before Fludd's work.

The striking and exciting feature of Fludd's memory system is that the memory buildings which are to be places in the heavens in this new combination of the round and the square arts, are what he calls 'theatres'. And by this word 'theatre' he does not mean what we should call a theatre, a building consisting of a stage and an auditorium. He means a stage. The truth of this statement that the 'theatre' which Fludd illustrates is really a stage, will be amply proved later. It will, however, be useful to state it here in advance before starting on the memory system.

The 'common place' of the *ars rotunda*, states Fludd, is 'the ethereal part of the world, that is the celestial orbs numbered from the eighth sphere and ending in the sphere of the moon'. This statement is illustrated by a diagram showing the eighth sphere, or zodiac, marked with the signs of the zodiac, and enclosing seven circles representing the spheres of the planets, and a circle representing the sphere of the elements at the centre. This represents, says Fludd, a 'natural' order of memory places based on the zodiac, and also a temporal order through the movement of the spheres in relation to time.[3]

3. If this, the basic diagram for the *ars rotunda*, is compared with the design on the title-page of the first volume of the *Utriusque Cosmi . . . Historia*, we see there the temporal revolution visually depicted through the rope wound round macrocosm and microcosm which Time is pulling. We can also understand by comparison with this picture, in which the microcosm is represented within the macrocosm, why the 'round' art of memory is the 'natural' one for the microcosm.

On either side of the sign Aries, two small buildings are shown. They are tiny 'theatres', or stages. These two 'theatres', in this actual form with two doors at the back of the stage, are never illustrated again nor referred to in the text. An occult memory system always has many unexplained lacunae and I do not understand why Fludd never afterwards mentions these two 'theatres'. I can only suppose that they are placed here on the cosmic diagram as a kind of advance statement of the principle of this memory system, which will use 'theatres', buildings containing memory *loci* after the manner of the *ars quadrata*, but placed on the great common place of the *ars rotunda*, that is placed in the zodiac.

Exactly facing the diagram of the heavens, on the next page of the book, there is an engraving of a 'theatre'. The diagram of the heavens and the picture of the 'theatre' are placed on opposite pages in such a manner that, when the book is closed, the heavens cover the theatre. This theatre, as already stated, is not a complete theatre but a stage. The wall facing us, as we gaze at it, is its *frons scaenae*, containing five entrances, as in the classical *frons scaenae*. This is, however, not a classical stage. It is an Elizabethan or Jacobean multi-level stage. Three of the entrances are on ground level; two are arches, but the central one can be closed by heavy hinged doors which are shown half open. The other two entrances are on an upper level; they open on to a battlemented terrace. In the centre, as a very noticeable feature of this stage, there is a kind of bay window, or an upper chamber or room.

This picture of a 'theatre' or stage is introduced by Fludd with the following words:

> I call a theatre [a place in which] all actions of words, of sentences, of particulars of a speech or of subjects are shown, *as in a public theatre in which comedies and tragedies are acted.*

Fludd is going to use this theatre as a memory place system for memory for words and memory for things. But the theatre itself is like 'a public theatre in which comedies and tragedies are acted'. Those great wooden theatres in which the works of Shakespeare and others were played were technically known as 'public theatres'. In view of Fludd's strong convictions about the undesirability of using 'fictitious places' in memory, can we assume that this is a real stage in a public theatre which he is showing us?

The chapter containing the illustration of the theatre is headed 'The description of the eastern and western theatres' and it appears that there are to be two of these theatres, the one 'eastern' and the other 'western', identical in plan but different in colour. The eastern theatre is to be light, bright and shining, since it will hold actions belonging to the day. The western theatre will be dark, black and obscure, belonging to the night. Both are to be placed in the heavens, and refer, presumably, to the day and night 'houses' of the planets. Is there to be an eastern and a western theatre for each of the signs of the zodiac? Are they to be placed as we see those two little stages on each side of Aries on the plan, but not only with one sign but all round the heavens? I rather think so. But we are in the realms of occult memory and it is not easy to follow how these theatres in the heavens are supposed to work.

The closest comparison for this system is Bruno's system in *Images* in which elaborate arrangements of memory rooms containing places for memory images (as in what Fludd calls the 'square' art) are affiliated to a 'round' or celestial system. Similarly (or so I believe) Fludd's 'theatres' are memory rooms which are to be affiliated to the round heavens by being placed in the zodiac. If he intends that two such 'theatres' are to be placed with each sign, then the 'theatre' which he illustrates would be one of twenty-four identical memory rooms. The 'eastern' and 'western' or day and night theatres introduce time into a system which is attached to the revolution of the heavens. It is of course a highly occult or magical system, based on belief in the macrocosm–microcosm relationship.

On the bay window of the 'theatre' are inscribed the words THEATRUM ORBI. Since Fludd and the highly educated engraver certainly knew Latin it seems difficult to believe that this can be a mistake for THEATRUM ORBIS. I suggest therefore (though with diffidence) that the dative case is intentional and that the inscription means, not that this is a 'theatre of the World' but one of the 'theatres' or stages to be placed with or in the world, that is in the heavens shown on the opposite page.

'Each of the theatres will have five doors distinct from one another and about equidistant, the use of which we will explain later,' says Fludd. Thus the five doors or entrances seen in the picture of the 'theatre' are confirmed by the text which states that the theatres have five doors. There is agreement between picture and text about this. The use of the five doors in the theatres which Fludd explains later is that they are to serve as five memory *loci*, which stand in a relationship with five columns to which they are said to be opposite. The bases of these five columns are shown in the foreground of the picture of the 'theatre'. One is round, the next square, the central one is hexagonal, and then come another square one and another round one. 'There are to be feigned five columns, distinguished from one another by shape and colour. The shapes of the two at each extremity are circular and round; the middle column will have the figure of a hexagon; and the intermediary ones will be square.'⁴ Here again the picture corresponds with the text, for the picture shows the bases of columns of these shapes and arranged in this order.

These columns, continues Fludd, are of different colours, corresponding to 'the colours of the doors of the theatres opposite to them'. These doors are to be used as five memory *loci* and are to be distinguished from one another by being remembered as different in colour. The first door will be white, the second red, the third green, the fourth blue, and the fifth black. The correspondence between the doors and the columns is perhaps indicated in the picture of the 'theatre' by the geometrical forms shown on the battlemented terrace. I do not understand how these correspondences are supposed to work in detail, though it is clear that the main central door on ground level would correspond to the main central column in the shape of a hexagon, and the other four doors to the four circular and square columns.

With this set of ten places, five doors and five columns, in all the 'theatres', Fludd is proposing to remember things and words in his magical memory system. Though he does not

---

4. 'His pratis oppositae fingantur quinque columnae, quae itidem debent figura & colore distingui; Figura enim duarum extremarum erit circularis & rotunda, mediae autem columna habebit figuram hexagoneam, & quae his intermedia sunt quadratam possidebunt figuram' (*ibid.*, p. 63). Though he speaks of 'fields' [*prata*] here, he is thinking of the five doors as memory fields or places.

mention the rules of *Ad Herennium* in connection with the doors and the columns he certainly has these in mind. The doors are spaced to form suitable memory places. The columns are of different shapes so that they may not be too much alike and confuse the memory. The notion of remembering memory *loci* as of different colours as an additional help for distinguishing between them is not in *Ad Herennium* but is often advised in the memory treatises.

The system works through being hitched to the stars, or rather to the 'principle ideas' as Fludd calls them in a chapter on the relation of the planets to the signs of the zodiac. This chapter gives the celestial basis of the system; and it is immediately followed by the chapter on the five doors and five columns in the memory theatres. The heavens work together with the theatres, and the theatres are in the heavens. The 'round' and the 'square' art are united to from a memory 'Seal', or an occult memory system of extreme complexity. Fludd never uses the word 'Seal', but his memory system is undoubtedly of a Brunian type.

From A.R. LURIA, *The Mind of a Mnemonist* (1968), translated by Lynn Solotaroff

It was only natural, then, that the *visual quality of his recall* was fundamental to his capacity for remembering words. For when he heard or read a word it was at once converted into a visual image corresponding with the object the word signified for him. Once he formed an image, which was always of a particularly vivid nature, it stabilised itself in his memory, and though it might vanish for a time when his attention was taken up with something else, it would manifest itself once again whenever he returned to the situation in which the word had first come up. As he described it:

> When I hear the word *green*, a green flowerpot appears; with the word *red* I see a man in a red shirt coming toward me; as for *blue*, this means an image of someone waving a small blue flag from a window ... Even numbers remind me of images. Take the number 1. This is a proud, well-built man; 2 is a high-spirited woman; 3 a

gloomy person (why, I don't know); 6 a man with a swollen foot; 7 a man with a mustache; 8 a very stout woman – a sack within a sack. As for the number 87, what I see is a fat woman and a man twirling his mustache. (Record of September 1936)

One can easily see that the images produced by numbers and words represent a fusion of graphic ideas and synesthetic reactions. If S. heard a word he was familiar with, the image would be sufficient to screen off any synesthetic reactions; but if he had to deal with an unfamiliar word, which did not evoke an image, he would remember it 'in terms of lines.' In other words, the sounds of the word were transformed into colored splotches, lines, or splashes. Thus, even with an unfamiliar word, he still registered some visual impression which he associated with it but which was related to the phonetic qualities of the word rather than to its meaning.

When S. read through a long series of words, each word would elicit a graphic image. And since the series was fairly long, he had to find some way of distributing these images of his in a mental row or sequence. Most often (and this habit persisted throughout his life), he would 'distribute' them along some roadway or street he visualised in his mind. Sometimes this was a street in his home town, which would also include the yard attached to the house he had lived in as a child and which he recalled vividly. On the other hand, he might also select a street in Moscow. Frequently he would take a mental walk along that street – Gorky Street in Moscow – beginning at Mayakovsky Square, and slowly make his way down, 'distributing' his images at houses, gates, and store windows. At times, without realising how it had happened, he would suddenly find himself back in his home town (Torzhok), where he would wind up his trip in the house he had lived in as a child. The setting he chose for his 'mental walks' approximates that of dreams, the difference being that the setting in his walks would immediately vanish once his attention was distracted but would reappear just as suddenly when he was obliged to recall a series he had 'recorded' this way.

This technique of converting a series of words into a series of graphic images explains why S. could so readily reproduce a series from start to finish or in reverse order; how he could rapidly name the word that preceded or followed one I'd select from the series.

To do this, he would simply begin his walk, either from the beginning or from the end of the street, find the image of the object I had named, and 'take a look at' whatever happened to be situated on either side of it. S.'s visual patterns of memory differed from the more commonplace type of figurative memory by virtue of the fact that his images were exceptionally vivid and stable; he was also able to 'turn away' from them, as it were, and 'return' to them whenever it was necessary.

It was this technique of recalling material graphically that explained why S. always insisted a series be read clearly and distinctly, that the words not be read off too quickly. For he needed some time, however slight, to convert the words into images. If the words were read too quickly, without sufficient pause between them, his images would tend to coalesce into a kind of chaos or 'noise' through which he had difficulty in discerning anything.

In effect, the astonishing clarity and tenacity of his images, the fact that he could retain them for years and call them up when occasion demanded it, made it possible for him to recall an unlimited number of words and to retain these indefinitely. Nonetheless, his method of 'recording' also had certain drawbacks.

Once we were convinced that the capacity of S.'s memory was virtually unlimited, that he did not have to 'memorise' the data presented but merely had to 'register an impression,' which he could 'read' on a much later date . . . we naturally lost interest in trying to 'measure' his memory capacity. Instead, we concentrated on precisely the reverse issue: was it possible for him to forget? We tried to establish the instances in which S. had omitted a word from a series.

Indeed, not only were such instances to be found, but they were fairly frequent. Yet how was one to explain forgetting in a man whose memory seemed inexhaustible? How explain that sometimes there were instances in which S. *omitted* some elements in his recall but scarcely ever *reproduced material inaccurately* (by substituting a synonym or a word closely associated in meaning with the one he'd been given)?

The experiments immediately turned up answers to both questions. S. did not 'forget' words he'd been given; what happened was that he omitted these as he 'read off' a series. And in each case there was a simple explanation for the omissions. If S. had placed a particular image in a spot where it would be difficult for him to 'discern' – if he, for example, had placed it in an area that was poorly lit or in a spot where he would have trouble distinguishing the object from the background against which it had been set – he would omit this image when he 'read off' the series he had distributed along his mental route. He would simply walk on 'without noticing' the particular item, as he explained.

These omissions (and they were quite frequent in the early period of our observation, when S.'s technique of recall had not developed to its fullest) clearly were not *defects of memory* but were, in fact, *defects of perception*. They could not be explained in terms of established ideas on the neuro-dynamics of memory traces (retroactive and proactive inhibition, extinction of traces, etc.) but rather by certain factors that influence perception (clarity, contrast, the ability to isolate a figure from its background, the degree of lighting available, etc.). His errors could not be explained, then, in terms of the psychology of memory but had to do with the psychological factors that govern perception.

Excerpts from the numerous reports taken on our sessions with S. will serve to illustrate this point. When, for example, S. reproduced a long series of words, he omitted the word *pencil*; on another occasion he skipped *egg*; in a third series it was the word *banner*, and in a fourth, *blimp*. Finally, S. omitted from another series the word *shuttle*, which he was not familiar with. The following is his explanation of how this happened:

> I put the image of the *pencil* near a fence . . . the one down the street, you know. But what happened was that the image fused with that of the fence and I walked right on past without noticing it. The same thing happened with the word *egg*. I had put it up against a white wall and it blended in with the background. How could I possibly spot a white egg up against a white wall? Now take the word *blimp*. That's something gray, so it blended in with the gray of the pavement . . . *Banner*, of course, means the Red Banner. But, you know, the building which houses the Moscow City Soviet of Workers' Deputies is also red, and since I'd put the banner close to one of the walls of the building I just walked on without seeing it . . . Then there's the word *putamen*, I don't know what this means, but it's such a dark word that I couldn't see it . . . and, besides, the street lamp was quite a distance away. (Record of December 1932)

From MARY J. CARRUTHERS, *The Book of Memory: A Study of Memory in Medieval Culture* (1992)

A remarkably fierce animal suddenly looms into a Biblical *interpretatio* by the Dominican scholar, Hugh of St Cher, which may help to shed light on how the *voces animantium* could be used for organising material in the memory. It occurs in his comment on the phrase 'in medio umbrae mortis,' Ps. 22: 4. 'Et nota,' he says in a phrase which, I have already suggested, is both an invitation to remember (in reading) and a trigger for recollection (in composing), 'quod inter omnes peccatores, detractores proprie dicuntur umbrae mortis,' 'among all sinners detractors are most fittingly called shadows of death.' For death indeed spares no one but carries off everyone equally; likewise detractors detract everything. Wherefore, a detractor is signified by a bear (*ursus*). A bear has a great big voracious mouth, just like a backbiter or detractor. And it has three rows of teeth, which Hugh of St Cher proceeds to moralise in terms of a backbiter's nasty characteristics.

Where did the bear come from? Judson Allen, who carefully studied this matter, says that Hugh's comment is found in no other Psalter gloss; it is his own. Hugh of St Cher cites the most famous bear in Scripture, the one with all the teeth in Daniel's dream (Dan. 7: 5). This text supplies the details of the image: 'tres ordines erant in ore ejus, et in dentibus ejus,' 'three rows were in his mouth, and in the teeth' (the King James Version so differs from the Vulgate that I have translated the Latin directly).

The bear has a wide, devouring mouth, as does death, as do backbiters – the 'moralising,' hermeneutic connections are reasonable enough. And the connection of death with biting is clear, basically by means of the homophony of Latin *mors*, 'death,' and *morsus*, 'bite.' Furthermore, though Latin *detractor* has no homophonic or etymological connection to *mors* or *morsus*, the late Latin participle *mordentem*, from *mordere* 'to bite' and, by a metaphorical extension, 'to make a caustic comment,' clearly connects to 'detractors' in meaning, and to 'death,' 'biting,' and 'teeth' in sound. The Old French word, *mordant*, 'bitter speaking,' would have been familiar to Hugh for he was French; he may well also have known the word *backbiter* from English students at Paris. Such a mnemonically useful tissue of homophonies accords with John of Garland's advice regarding the use of the sounds of all kinds of languages to help fix etymologies and interpretations in the memory. But none of these words requires a bear.

I suspect that the reason why a bear entered Hugh of St Cher's compositional memory is because the word *ursus*, like *umbra*, starts with a U. *Ursus*, together with its *voces* – the most vivid of which is its big mouth, according to Isidore, who derives *ursus* from *os*, 'mouth' – and texts relevant to it, such as this obvious one from Daniel, would be stored in Hugh's memory under 'U', helping to mark etymologies, distinctions, and interpretations of words and texts which also start with 'U'. And so, when composing his *distinctio* on *umbra*, the U-animal comes to mind, and it has characteristics (*voces*) which, happily, can this time be pressed into service of the point he wishes to make. In other words, what first led Hugh to a bear was not its hermeneutical aptness, but the simple fact that *ursus* and *umbra* have the same initial letter. *Ursus* leads to its etymology in *os*, *oris*; hence 'teeth,' and the happy homophony of *mors* and *morsus* that I sketched out earlier. So the bear's appearance in the written text is a vestige of Hugh's mental organisational scheme. That it also serves his interpretation is, of course, why that connection is preserved in the final composition.

From ROBERT IRWIN, *Night and Horses and the Desert* (1999)

Ibn Khaldun, having noted that poetry rather than the Qur'an was used to teach Arabic in Andalusia, went on to urge poets to train themselves in their art by memorising the poems of their great predecessors, especially those included in al-Isfahani's anthology, the *Kitab al-Aghani*. Ibn Khaldun believed that one was what one had committed to memory; the better the quality of what had been memorised, the better it was for one's soul. For Ibn Khaldun and his contemporaries, rote-learning was a source of creativity rather than a dreary alternative to it. The impromptu quotation of apposite verses or maxims (so greatly esteemed by those who attended literary soirées) was only made possible by a well-stocked memory. Similarly the ability of poets to extemporise within traditional forms depended in the first instance on memory.

Riwaya, which in modern Arabic means 'story', originally referred to the act of memorisation and transmission. The written word was seen as an accessory, a kind of *aide-mémoire* for people who preferred to rely on memorisation and oral transmission. Often manuscripts were copied with the sole aim of committing to memory what was being copied. Reading aloud also helped to fix a book in the memory. Incidentally, reading silently in private was commonly disapproved of. One should read aloud with a master and by so doing insert oneself in a chain of authoritative transmission. Medieval literature was a continuous buzz.

Repetition was crucial to memorisation. According to one twelfth-century scholar, 'If you do not repeat something fifty times, it will not remain firmly embedded in the mind.' Treatises on technical and practical subjects, such as law, warfare, gardening or the rules of chess, were commonly put into verse or rhymed prose in order to assist in their memorisation. Men worried ceaselessly about how to improve their memory. Honey, toothpicks and twenty-one raisins a day were held to be good for the memory, whereas coriander and aubergine were supposed to be bad. Ibn Jama'a, a thirteenth-century scholar, held that reading inscriptions on tombs, walking between camels haltered in a line, or flicking away lice, all interfered with memory.

From DANIEL ARASSE, *Anselm Kiefer* (2001), translated by Mary Whittall (2006)

His highly specific artistic practice is one of the sources of the overdetermination that characterises Kiefer's work. It also explains what is unique about Kiefer in the midst of the collective work of memory that informed German art and culture in the 1960s and 1970s. What Kiefer does is not so much a work *of* memory as a work *on* memory. While the former would attempt to recall and bring order to memories and so make it impossible to forget, the questions Kiefer was asking during the 1970s were of a subtly different nature. Firstly, *what* to remember? What recollections and ideas should be allowed into our memories? For a German who was born in 1945 and reached the age of twenty-three in 1968, this primarily means how should he recall and represent Nazism, and the relationship to the more distant German past that it claimed to possess? Secondly, *how* to remember? The second question is about form, but for that very reason it is crucial, particularly for a young German artist whose memory is without 'recollections', because he has no personal memories of the Nazi years (unlike Beuys, notoriously), and because the only 'memory' of it he can have is one built out of pre-existing documents, whether in the form of words (spoken or written) or of visual images. Kiefer proceeds as if he were constructing memories of (and with) things that he himself cannot remember. He appropriates objects, texts and images – the only 'recollections' available to him – and integrates them into other settings, which he then uses to create works that eventually come to constitute a personal memory of the Third Reich and his own German heritage.

The issue of the quantity and accuracy of the photographic documents he borrowed from Third Reich propaganda and other publications to use as the basis of his own representations will be deferred until later. As a starting point, one object should provide sufficient evidence of the complexity and concerns of his art: the zinc bath, which over the years has played a major role in many works on very different themes. In 1969 we encounter it in the books *Heroic Symbols* and *To Genet*. We find it again in 1975, in the books and pictures devoted to *Operation Sea Lion*; in 1978, in the book *Hoffmann von Fallersleben on Heligoland*; and in 1980, in the book *Alaric's Tomb*. It reappears in *Tutein's Tomb* (1981–83), and finally in the picture *The Red Sea* (1984–85). Over those fifteen years, Kiefer put this apparently incongruous object to some very different uses. Bathtubs had already been put to artistic use before Kiefer turned to them: in 1960, Beuys had made a 'wounded' bath the subject of a work which turned out to be particularly prophetic of his future art, and in 1969, with *Bathtub for 'Ludwig van'*, a zinc bath filled with sixteen busts of Beethoven made of white sugar, brown chocolate and lard, Dieter Roth visually expounded (and denounced) the cult of the German composer which had turned him into an edible piece of kitsch. But when Kiefer made a bathtub one of his personal motifs, it was for different reasons. As he himself has said, he found it interesting because it was a 'souvenir' of the Third Reich: during the 1930s the National Socialist party had issued a bathtub of that type to every household to ensure the daily cleanliness of the German people, and the tub Kiefer used was one he had found in the attic of his grandmother's house, where he lived until 1951. From the very beginning, his use of this 'souvenir' differed both from Roth's and from Beuys's. The bathtub went back to childhood in Beuys's case as well, but he used it allegorically to evoke the trauma of birth. To Kiefer it recalls Nazism and, very specifically in the case of *Operation Sea Lion*, the plans for the invasion of Great Britain which, as military legend has it, Hitler's generals discussed by using model boats in bathtubs. The Nazi bathtub, inherited from his grandmother, became a personal souvenir, and part of the process of constructing a memory of Nazism and its practices – as is implicit in the note written in French on page 6 of the book *To Genet*: 'Attempt to walk on the water in my bathtub in the studio' . . .

At this juncture we need to visit a distant past. Among the many *artes memoriae* known since antiquity, there is one that deserves particular attention, one that was known over a very wide area and has long been connected with the visual arts. The *Ad Herennium*, a text wrongly attributed to Cicero, describes a technique intended primarily for orators. In order to memorise a speech, an orator should think of a building (preferably one he knows well), select a certain number of precise places (*loci*) in it, in a predetermined order, and position images (*imagines*) within them. The images should be as striking and unusual as he can make them, and he must be able to associate them with the ideas and arguments of his discourse. When he makes his speech, all he has to do is move through the building in his mind and find each argument in its proper place. Clearly (and this is the key point for our purposes) the choice and order of the *loci* are crucial: they must remain fixed while the images deposited in them can (and should) change according to the speech being made and the arguments that need to be memorised.

From an historical point of view, a comparison of the techniques of *artes memoriae* with Anselm Kiefer's artistic practice would be arbitrary. All the same, the correlation does cast some light on the unusual methods involved in the work on memory he undertook in the 1970s and 1980s. During those two decades, Kiefer seems to be progressively constructing a Memory Theatre from his work, and using it to interiorise and structure the passed-on 'memories' of a German past he knew only at second hand.

Memory and Science

From ARISTOTLE, *History of Animals* (4th century BC), translated by W.D. Ross (1928)

Many animals have memory, and are capable of instruction; but no other creature except man can recall the past at will.

From WILLIAM HARVEY, *Animal Generation* (1651)

The things perceived by sense remain in some animals; in others they do not remain. Those in whom they do not remain, however, have either no knowledge at all, or at least none beyond the simple perception of the things which do not remain; others, again, when they perceive, retain a certain something in their soul. Now, as there are many animals of this description, there is already a distinction between one animal and another; and to this extent, that in some there is reason from the memory of things; and in others there is none. Memory, therefore, as is said, follows from sense; but from repeated recollection of the same thing springs experience (for repeated acts of memory constitute a single experience) . . .

Wherefore . . . there is no perfect knowledge which can be entitled ours, that is innate; none but what has been obtained from experience, or derived in some way from our senses; all knowledge, at all events, is examined by these, approved by them, and finally presents itself to us firmly grounded upon some preexisting knowledge which we possessed: because without memory there is no experience, which is nothing else than reiterated memory; in like manner memory cannot exist without endurance of the things perceived, and the thing perceived cannot remain where it has never been.

From FRANCIS GALTON, 'Psychometric Experiments', in *Inquiries into Human Faculty* (1883)

When we attempt to trace the first steps in each operation of our minds, we are usually balked by the difficulty of keeping watch, without embarrassing the freedom of its action. The difficulty is much more than the common and well-known one of attending to two things at once. It is especially due to the fact that the elementary operations of the mind are exceedingly faint and evanescent, and that it requires the utmost painstaking to watch them properly. It would seem impossible to give the required attention to the processes of thought, and yet to think as freely as if the mind had been in no way preoccupied. The peculiarity of the experiments I am about to describe is that I have succeeded in evading this difficulty. My method consists in allowing the mind to play freely for a very brief period, until a couple or so of ideas have passed through it, and then, while the traces or echoes of those ideas are still lingering in the brain, to turn the attention upon them with a sudden and complete awakening; to arrest, to scrutinise them, and to record their exact appearance. Afterwards I collate the records at leisure, and discuss them, and draw conclusions. It must be understood that the second of the two ideas was never derived from the first, but always directly from the original object. This was ensured by absolutely withstanding all temptation to reverie. I do not mean that the first idea was of necessity a simple elementary thought; sometimes it was a glance down a familiar line of associations, sometimes it was a well-remembered mental attitude or mode of feeling, but I mean that it was never so far indulged in as to displace the object that had suggested it from being the primary topic of attention.

I must add, that I found the experiments to be extremely trying and irksome, and that it required much resolution to go through with them, using the scrupulous care they demanded. Nevertheless the results well repaid the trouble. They gave me an interesting and unexpected view of the number of the operations of the mind, and of the obscure depths in which they took place, of which I had been little conscious before. The general impression they have left upon me is like that which many of us have experienced when the basement of our house happens to be under thorough sanitary repairs, and we realise for the first time the complex system of drains and gas and water pipes, flues, bell-wires, and so forth, upon which our comfort depends, but which are usually hidden out of sight, and with whose existence, so long as they acted well, we had never troubled ourselves.

The first experiments I made were imperfect, but sufficient to inspire me with keen interest in the matter, and suggested the form of procedure that I have already partly described. My first experiments were these. On several occasions, but notably on one when I felt myself unusually capable of the kind of effort required, I walked leisurely along Pall Mall, a distance of 450 yards, during which time I scrutinised with attention every successive object that caught my eyes, and I allowed my attention to rest on it until one or two thoughts had arisen through direct association with that object; then I took very brief mental note of them, and passed on to the next object. I never allowed my mind to ramble. The number of objects viewed was, I think, about 300, for I had subsequently repeated the same walk under similar conditions and endeavoured to estimate their number, with that result. It was impossible for me to recall in other than the vaguest way the numerous ideas that had passed through my mind; but of this, at least, I am sure, that samples of my whole life had passed before me, that many bygone incidents, which I never suspected to have formed part of my stock of thoughts, had been glanced at as objects too familiar to awaken the attention. I saw at once that the brain was vastly more active than I had previously believed it to be, and I was perfectly amazed at the unexpected width of the field of its everyday operations. After an interval of some days, during which I kept my mind from dwelling on my first experiences, in order that it might retain as much freshness as possible for a second experiment, I repeated the walk, and was struck just as much as before by the variety of the ideas that presented themselves, and the number of events to which they referred, about which I had never consciously occupied myself of late years. But my admiration at the activity of the mind was seriously diminished by another observation which I then made, namely, that there had been a very great deal of repetition of thought. The actors in my mental stage were indeed very numerous, but by no means so numerous as I had imagined. They now seemed to be something like the actors in theatres where large processions are represented, who march off one side of the stage, and, going round by the back, come on again at the other. I accordingly cast around for means of laying hold of these fleeting thoughts, and, submitting them to statistical analysis, to find out more about their tendency to repetition and other matters, and the method I finally adopted was the one already mentioned. I selected a list of suitable words, and wrote them on different small sheets of paper. Taking care to dismiss them from my thoughts when not engaged upon them, and allowing some days to elapse before I began to use them I laid one of these sheets with all due precautions under a book, but not wholly covered by it, so that when I leaned forward I could see one of the words, being previously quite ignorant of what the word would be. Also I held a small chronograph, which I started by pressing a spring the moment the word caught my eye, and which stopped of itself the instant I released the spring; and this I did so soon as about a couple of ideas in direct association with the word had arisen in my mind. I found that I could not manage to recollect more than two ideas with the needed precision, at least not in a general way; but sometimes several ideas occurred so nearly together that I was able to record three or even four of them, while sometimes I only managed one. The second ideas were, as I have already said, never derived from the first, but always direct from the word itself, for I kept my attention firmly fixed on the word, and the associated ideas were seen only by a half glance. When the two ideas had occurred, I stopped the chronograph and wrote them down, and the time they occupied. I soon got into the way of doing this in a very methodical and automatic manner, keeping the mind perfectly calm and neutral, but intent and, as it were, at full cock and on hair trigger, before displaying the word. There was no disturbance occasioned by thinking of the forthcoming revulsion of the mind the moment before the chronograph was stopped. My feeling before stopping it was simply that I had delayed long enough, and this in no way interfered with the free action of the mind. I found no trouble in ensuring the complete fairness of the experiment, by using a number of little precautions, hardly necessary to describe, that practice suggested, but it was a most repugnant and laborious work, and it was only by strong self-control that I went through my schedule according to programme. The list of words that I finally secured was 75 in number, though I began with more. I went through them on four separate occasions, under very different circumstances, in England and abroad, and at intervals of about a month. In no case were the associations governed to any degree worth recording, by remembering what had occurred to me on previous occasions, for I found that the process itself had great influence in discharging the memory of what it had just been engaged in, and I, of course, took care between the experiments never to let my thoughts revert to the words. The results seem to me to be as trustworthy as any other statistical series that has been collected with equal care.

On throwing these results into a common statistical hotch-pot, I first examined into the rate at which these associated ideas were formed. It took a total time of 660 seconds to form 505 ideas; that is, at about the rate of 50 in a minute, or 3,000 in an hour. This would be miserably slow work in reverie, or wherever the thought follows the lead of each association that successively presents itself. In the present case, much time was lost in mentally taking the word in, owing to the quiet unobtrusive way in which I found it necessary to bring it into view, so as not to distract the thoughts. Moreover, a substantive standing by itself is usually the equivalent of too abstract an idea for us to conceive properly without delay. Thus it is very difficult to get a quick conception of the word 'carriage', because there are so many different kinds – two-wheeled, four-wheeled, open and closed, and all of them in so many different possible positions, that the mind possibly hesitates amidst an obscure sense of many alternatives that cannot blend together. But limit the idea to say a laudau, and the mental association declares itself more quickly. Say a laudau coming down the street to opposite the door, and an image of many blended laudaus that have done so forms itself without the least hesitation.

Next, I found that my list of 75 words gone over four times, had given rise to 505 ideas and 13 cases of puzzle, in which nothing sufficiently definite to note occurred within the brief maximum period of about four seconds, that I allowed myself to any single trial. Of these 505 only 289 were different. The precise proportions in which the 505 were distributed in quadruplets, triplets, doublets, or singles, is shown in the uppermost lines of Table 1. The same facts are given under another form in the lower lines of the table, which show how the 289 different ideas were distributed in cases of fourfold, treble, double or single occurrences.

TABLE I
Recurrent Associations

Total number of associations	Quadruplets	Occurring in Triplets	Doublets	Singles
505	116	108	114	167
Per cent 100	23	21	23	33
Total number of Different associations	Four times	Occurring Three times	Twice	Once
289	29	36	57	167
Per cent 100	10	12	20	58

I was fully prepared to find much iteration in my ideas but had little expected that out of every 100 words 23 would give rise to exactly the same association in every one of the four trials; 21 to the same association in three out of the four, and so on, the experiments having been purposely conducted under very different conditions of time and local circumstances. This shows much less variety in the mental stock of ideas than I had expected, and makes us feel that the roadways of our minds are worn into very deep ruts. I conclude from the proved number of faint and barely conscious thoughts, and from the proved iteration of them, that the mind is perpetually travelling over familiar ways without our memory retaining any impression of its excursions. Its footsteps are so light and fleeting that it is only by such experiments as I have described that we can learn anything about them. It is apparently always engaged in mumbling over its old stores, and if any one of these is wholly neglected for a while, it is apt to be forgotten, perhaps irrecoverably. It is by no means the keenness of interest and of the attention when first observing an object, that fixes it in the recollection. We pore over the pages of a *Bradshaw*, and study the trains for some particular journey with the greatest interest; but the event passes by, and the hours and other facts which we once so eagerly considered become absolutely forgotten. So in games of whist, and in a large number of similar instances. As I understand it, the subject must have a continued living interest in order to retain an abiding place in the memory. The mind must refer to it frequently, but whether it does so consciously or unconsciously is not perhaps a matter of much importance. Otherwise, as a general rule, the recollection sinks, and appears to be utterly drowned in the waters of Lethe. . . .

[Galton's Table II illustrated the frequency of specific sets of associations. He then returned to a particular group of words, beginning with 'a', which had occurred to him repeatedly.]

I found, after the experiments were over, that the words were divisible into three distinct groups. The first contained 'abbey', 'aborigines', 'abyss', and others that admitted of being presented under some mental image. The second group contained 'abasement', 'abhorrence', 'ablution', etc., which admitted excellently of histrionic representation. The third group contained the more abstract words, such as 'afternoon', 'ability', 'abnormal', which were variously and imperfectly dealt with by my mind. I give the results in the upper part of Table III, and, in order to save trouble, I have reduced them to percentages in the lower lines of the table.

TABLE III
Comparison between the Quality of the Words and that of the Ideas in Immediate Association with them

Number of words in each series		Sense imagery	Histrionic	Purely names of persons	Verbal phrases and quotations	Total
26	'Abbey' series	46	12	32	17	107
20	'Abasement' series	25	26	11	17	79
29	'Afternoon' series	23	27	16	38	104
75						290
	'Abbey' series	43	11	30	16	100
	'Abasement' series	32	33	13	22	100
	'Afternoon' series	22	25	16	37	100

We see from this that the associations of the 'abbey' series are nearly half of them in sense imagery, and these were almost always visual. The names of persons also more frequently occurred in this series than in any other . . . Verbal memories of old date, such as Biblical scraps, family expressions, bits of poetry, and the like, are very numerous, and rise to the thoughts so quickly, whenever anything suggests them, that they commonly outstrip all competitors. Associations connected with the 'abasement' series are strongly characterised by histrionic ideas, and by sense imagery, which to a great degree merges into a histrionic character. Thus the word 'abhorrence' suggested to me, on three out of the four trials, an image of the attitude of Martha in the famous picture of the raising of Lazarus by Sebastian del Piombo in the National Gallery. She stands with averted head, doubly sheltering her face by her hands from even a sidelong view of the opened grave. Now I could not be sure how far I saw the picture as such, in my mental view, or how far I had thrown my own personality into the picture, and was acting it as actors might act a mystery play, by the puppets of my own brain, that were parts of myself. As a matter of fact, I entered it under the heading of sense imagery, but it might very properly have gone to swell the number of the histrionic entries.

The 'afternoon' series suggested a great preponderance of mere catch-words, showing how slowly I was able to realise the meaning of abstractions; the phrases intruded themselves before the thoughts became defined. It occasionally occurred that I puzzled wholly over a word, and made no entry at all; in thirteen cases either this happened, or else after one idea had occurred the second was too confused and obscure to admit of record, and mention of it had to be omitted in the foregoing table. These entries have forcibly shown to me the great imperfection in my generalising powers; and I am sure that most persons would find the same if they made similar trials. Nothing is a surer sign of high intellectual capacity than the power of quickly seizing and easily manipulating ideas of a very abstract nature. Commonly we grasp them very imperfectly, and cling to their skirts with great difficulty.

In comparing the order in which the ideas presented themselves, I find that a decided precedence is assumed by the histrionic ideas, wherever they occur; that verbal associations occur first and with great quickness on many occasions, but on the whole that they are only a little more likely to occur first than second; and that imagery is decidedly more likely to be the second than the first of the associations called up by a word. In short, gesture-language appeals the most quickly to my feelings.

It would be very instructive to print the actual records at length, made by many experimenters, if the records could be clubbed together and thrown into a statistical form; but it would be too absurd to print one's own singly. They lay bare the foundations of a man's thoughts with curious distinctness, and exhibit his mental anatomy with more vividness and truth than he would probably care to publish to the world.

It remains to summarise what has been said in the foregoing memoir. I have desired to show how whole strata of mental operations that have lapsed out of ordinary consciousness, admit of being dragged into light, recorded and treated statistically, and how the obscurity that attends the initial steps of our thoughts can thus be pierced and dissipated. I then showed measurably the rate at which associations spring up, their character, the date of their first formation, their tendency to recurrence, and their relative precedence. Also I gave an instance showing how the phenomenon of a long-forgotten scene, suddenly starting into consciousness, admitted in many cases of being explained. Perhaps the strongest of the impressions left by these experiments regards the multifariousness of the work done by the mind in a state of half-unconsciousness, and the valid reason they afford for believing in the existence of still deeper strata of mental operations sunk wholly below the level of consciousness, which may account for such mental phenomena as cannot otherwise be explained. We gain an insight by these experiments into the marvellous number and nimbleness of our mental associations, and we also learn that they are very far indeed from being infinite in their variety. We find that our working stock of ideas is narrowly limited and that the mind continually recurs to the same instruments in conducting its operations, therefore its tracks necessarily become more defined and its flexibility diminished as age advances.

From I.P. PAVLOV, *Lectures on Conditioned Reflexes* (1927), translated by W. Horsley Gantt (1928)

The general characteristic of living substance consists in this, that it responds with its definite specific activity not only to those external stimulations with which connections have existed from the day of birth, but to many other stimulations, connections with which have developed in the course of the individual's life; or in other words, that the living substance possesses the function of adaptability. . . .

Reflexes are always of two kinds: the constant reflex to a definite stimulus, existing in each animal from the day of birth, and the temporary reflex, formed to the most diverse kinds of stimuli which the organism meets during its life. Concerning the higher animals, for example the dog, to which all our investigations refer, these two sorts of reflexes are applicable to the various parts of the central nervous system. The constant reflexes, those which have always been known as reflexes, are connected with all parts of the central nervous system, even with the cerebral hemispheres. But the hemispheres are especially the seat of formation of temporary connections, of transient relations of the animal to the surrounding world, the organ of conditioned reflexes.

You will know that until recently, until the end of the last century, these provisional relations, the transitory connections of the animal organism with the surroundings, were not even considered physiologically, and they were designated as psychical relations. Recent work has shown, however, that there is no reason whatever to exclude them from the scope of physiological investigation.

From these general statements I now pass over to a series of special facts.

Take some injurious influence, some harmful agent such as fire, which the animal avoids and which burns the animal if he happens within its sphere of action or comes into contact with it. This, of course, is a usual inborn reflex, the work of the lower parts of the central nervous system. But if the animal is guarded by the distance from a red light and the representation of the fire, then this reaction, formed during the life of that animal, will be a temporal connection. This impermanent acquired reflex may be present in one animal, but in another which has not come into contact with fire, it may be entirely absent.

Consider another kind of stimulation, such as the food reflex, i.e. the seizing of food. First of all, this is a constant reflex and children and new-born animals make special movements to take the food into the mouth. But there is also the response seen when the animal runs toward food at a distance on account of some of its aspects, perhaps a sound which is emitted, as, for example, from small animals serving as food for others. This is also a food reflex, but one which is formed during that individual's life with the help of the cerebral hemispheres. It is a temporary reflex which from the practical point of view might be called a signalling reflex. In such a case the stimulus signals the real object, the actual purpose of the simple inborn reflex.

At present, the investigation of these reflexes has gone far. Here is a common example which we constantly see: You give or show to a dog food. A reaction to this food begins: the dog tries to get it, seizes it in his mouth, saliva begins to flow, etc. In order to call out this same motor and secretory reaction, we can substitute for the food any accidental stimulus, whatever we will, as long as it has with the food a connection in time. If you whistle, or ring a bell, or raise the hand, or scratch the dog – whatever you will – and now give the dog food and repeat this several times, then each one of these stimuli will evoke the same food reaction: the animal will strive toward the stimulus, lick his lips, secrete saliva, etc. – there will be the same reflex as before.

Obviously it is highly important for the animal under the circumstances of his life to be physiologically connected thus distantly and variedly with the favourable conditions which are necessary for his existence or with the injurious influences which threaten him. If some danger, for example, is signalled by a sound from a distance, then the animal will have time to save himself, etc. It is clear that the higher adaptability of animals, the most delicate equilibrations with the surrounding medium, are unfailingly connected with this kind of temporarily formed reflex. The two kinds of reflexes we are accustomed to designate by two adjectives: the inborn, constant ones we call unconditioned reflexes, but those which are built up on the inborn reflexes during the individual's life, conditioned reflexes.

From F.C. BARTLETT, *Remembering* (1932)

The general problem was to attempt to carry through a study of ways of perceiving, and of the factors influencing those ways and their results. It soon became evident that this would involve a study of the nature of imaging, for the two processes are commonly found together in a single act of observation, although they are of course to be discriminated . . .

Variety in interpretation tended to increase throughout with increase in the amount of detail presented. The greater the detail the greater is the tendency to pass from what is seen actually to a construction of what is seen only imperfectly, or is not noticed at all. Imaging comes in more and more. The pictures now used were all rather full of detail; the subjects knew that they were expected to make something of them, for they represented concrete scenes, while the fact that the experiments took place in a dark room meant that there was practically nothing beside the presented picture to attract the subject's attention. All this may have tended to increase greatly the part played by acts of imaging.

Perhaps the most striking illustrations of this were given in the different interpretations placed upon a representation of the well-known painting of *Hubert and Arthur* by W. F. Yeames. Every person who was given this picture to describe made of it something different from everybody else. A few illustrations may be given. Repeated observation was always found necessary.

At the first glance one observer said: 'It is a woman in a white apron with a child standing by her knee. She is sitting down and has her legs crossed. She is on the right of the picture as I see it, and the child is looking at her.'

At the second attempt he said that the woman was standing up, and then, during thirteen trials, made few alterations and added very little detail. At trial sixteen he said: 'I had a vague feeling that I have seen it all before somewhere, but I don't know where, and I am not sure what it is.' At the next attempt he spoke of a 'girl', leaning forward and stretching upwards towards her mother, 'well, towards the woman'. Further details were given, and then, at trial twenty-five, he remarked: 'Now I can see. The picture is that of a little girl saying her prayers on the other side of her mother's knee. She is dressed in a nightgown. The length of the nightgown made it look as if she is standing.'

The picture was given thirty-eight times in all, but there was no further change in the general idea of the interpretation, though additional details were given. The subject said that he had seen the picture in somebody's bedroom a long time before, and that when he really made it out to his own satisfaction he had a definite visual image of this picture.

Another observer at first simply saw two figures, but at the third attempt he said: 'Yes, there are two figures. One of them seems to be leaning back a little, and the other is struggling with him, or is about to struggle.' Thereafter the story was one of the development of this idea that two people were wrestling. A 'dark fellow' was made out, and was said to be 'getting the worst of it'. The subject saw the same picture fifty-five times.

A third observer began in much the same way: 'I saw nothing definite, but merely a sort of contrast of black and white. There was something very like a white shape wrestling with a black one.' At the second attempt he got his general setting: 'Evidently it is a room with a black or shaded side to the right, and windows, or else a highly illuminated part, to the left. There was a black figure turning towards a white one. It was like a representation of Othello saying to Desdemona: "Come, fly with me".' There were alterations and many additions of detail, but the subject stuck to his general description throughout fifty-seven different observations.

Yet another observer began very confidently: 'It is the interior of a house. There are three figures. One is tall, the second less tall, the third less tall still. The figures are leaning against a pillar or wall. Probably I am looking at a copy of some old master. It might well be "The Woman Taken in Adultery".' He soon withdrew this, and said that there were two figures only. He thought that the picture was one of Charles the First and Henrietta, and to this view he adhered throughout the remaining observations, though with no great certainty.

From KONRAD LORENZ, *King Solomon's Ring* (1949), translated by Marjorie Kerr Wilson (1952)

In a territory unknown to it, the water-shrew will never run fast except under pressure of extreme fear, and then it will run blindly along, bumping into objects and usually getting caught in a blind alley. But, unless the little animal is severely frightened, it moves, in strange surroundings, only step by step, whiskering right and left all the time and following a path that is anything but straight. Its course is determined by a hundred fortuitous factors when it walks that way for the first time. But, after a few repetitions, it is evident that the shrew recognises the locality in which it finds itself and that it repeats, with the utmost exactitude, the movements which it performed the previous time. At the same time, it is notice-able that the animal moves along much faster whenever it is repeating what it has already learned. When placed on a path which it has already traversed a few times, the shrew starts on its way slowly, carefully whiskering. Suddenly it finds known bearings, and now rushes forward a short distance, repeating exactly every step and turn which it executed on the last occasion. Then, when it comes to a spot where it ceases to know the way by heart, it is reduced to whiskering again and to feeling its way step by step. Soon, another burst of speed follows and the same thing is repeated, bursts of speed alternating with very slow progress. In the begin-ning of this process of learning their way, the shrews move along at an extremely slow average rate and the little bursts of speed are few and far between. But gradually the little laps of the course which have been 'learned by heart' and which can be covered quickly begin to increase in length as well as in number until they fuse and the whole course can be completed in a fast, unbroken rush.

Often, when such a path-habit is almost completely formed, there still remains one particularly difficult place where the shrew always loses its bearings and has to resort to its senses of smell and touch, sniffing and whiskering vigorously to find out where the next reach of its path 'joins on'. Once the shrew is well settled in its path-habits it is as strictly bound to them as a railway engine to its tracks and as unable to deviate from them by even a few centi-metres. If it diverges from its path by so much as an inch, it is forced to stop abruptly, and laboriously regain its bearings. The same behaviour can be caused experimentally by changing some small detail in the customary path of the animal. Any major alter-ation in the habitual path threw the shrews into complete confu-sion. One of their paths ran along the wall adjoining the wooden table opposite to that on which the nest-box was situated. This table was weighted with two stones lying close to the panes of the tank, and the shrews, running along the wall, were accustomed to jump on and off the stones which lay right in their path. If I moved the stones out of the runway, placing both together in the middle of the table, the shrews would jump right up into the air in the place where the stone should have been; they came down with a jarring bump, were obviously disconcerted and started whiskering cautiously right and left, just as they behaved in an unknown environment. And then they did a most interesting thing: they went back the way they had come, carefully feeling their way until they had again got their bearings. Then, facing round again, they tried a second time with a rush and jumped and crashed down exactly as they had done a few seconds before. Only then did they seem to realise that the first fall had not been their own fault but was due to a change in the wonted pathway, and now they proceeded to explore the alteration, cautiously sniffing and be-whiskering the place where the stone ought to have been. This method of going back to the start, and trying again always reminded me of a small boy who, in reciting a poem, gets stuck and begins again at an earlier verse.

From COLIN BLAKEMORE, Mechanics of the Mind (1977)

Penfield hoped to discover in each patient an area in the brain which, upon stimulation, would arouse the same curious mental aura that ushered in the epileptic attacks. That would be the spot to destroy, Penfield argued; and this approach was remarkably successful. But it also gave him the chance to discover the functions of the other parts of the cerebral cortex. Stimulation of the motor cortex caused jerky twitches of the muscles which the patient could not control; excitation of the touch area produced strange sensations felt by the patient in his skin; stimulation of the visual cortex made the patient see flashes of light or swirling coloured forms in his visual field. But when Penfield moved his stimulating electrode to the temporal lobe and the hippocampus itself, the experiences of the patient were not mere fragments of movement or sensation. They were whole episodes of existence, plucked from the patient's previous life. The person would suddenly be transported into the past and would feel himself eavesdropping on a familiar scene.

One of Penfield's patients was a young woman. As the stimulating electrode touched a spot on her temporal lobe she cried out, 'I think I heard a mother calling her little boy somewhere. It seemed to be something that happened years ago . . . in the neighbourhood where I live.' A moment later the same spot was stimulated. 'Yes,' she said, 'I hear the same familiar sounds; it seems to be a woman calling; the same lady.' Then the electrode was moved a little and she said, 'I hear voices. It is late at night, around the carnival somewhere – some sort of travelling circus. I just saw lots of big wagons that they use to haul animals in.'

There can be little doubt that Wilder Penfield's electrodes were arousing activity in the hippocampus, within the temporal lobe, jerking out distant and intimate memories from the patient's stream of consciousness.

Memory, its physical structure, is an unsolved challenge. It is, perhaps, the *central* question, rather like the problem of the structure of DNA, deoxyribonucleic acid, for molecular biology and genetics. But theories about the nature of memory have still not really progressed beyond the stage of description through analogy. Analogy has often been a valuable step in the discussion of biological problems, but it is, of its nature, constrained by the technological development of the time or the level of scientific knowledge in other fields. The restrictive nature of argument by analogy is aptly illustrated by historical models of memory. They are almost all based on the devices used by man himself to store information.

According to Aristotle, sensory impressions entered the head with such force that they left physical inscriptions in the brain, like a scribe engraving on a wax tablet. This idea, that the mind is a *tabula rasa* on which experiences are literally written, was espoused by the Empiricist school of philosophy. 'Let us then suppose the mind to be, as we say, white paper, void of all characters, without any ideas;' wrote John Locke in 1690, 'how comes it to be furnished? Whence comes it by that vast store, which the busy and boundless fancy of man has painted on it with an almost endless variety? . . . To this I answer in one word, from experience.'

Even current models of memory dwell on analogies with existing, artificial methods of storing information. Mental memory has been compared with the electromagnetic polarisation of ferrite rings in the core memory of a computer, and with the 'distributed' image of a hologram – a device that stores a record of a three-dimensional scene by photographing the interference pattern produced by illuminating it with laser light.

Each analogy has a certain attraction because it mirrors some particular special feature of memory. The permanence of lines scratched in a wax tablet or written on paper mimics the durability of real memory. The speed of access to the memory of a computer core is reminiscent of the remarkably rapid way in which neuronal memory can be consulted.

Because the information in a holographic place is 'distributed', a somewhat degraded reconstruction of the entire stored image can still be retrieved even when part of the plate is destroyed. Now the psychologist Karl Lashley, working in the first half of this century, described a similar kind of resistance to local injury in the store of information in the rat's brain. The actual representation of remembered events is almost certainly in the cerebral cortex, but Lashley found that small areas of damage in the rat's cortex simply blurred the animal's ability to perform tasks that it had previously learned. The degree of degradation of memory was roughly proportional to the area of damaged cortex. He concluded that the cerebral hemispheres have a kind of 'mass action' in the remembering process. In the same way, the steady attrition of about 50,000 nerve cells that unavoidably die each day in the cerebral cortex of man does not rob us, piecemeal, of individual elements of memory; it gradually removes the edge from remembered events and stunts the power to capture new ones. Lashley expressed his frustration in failing to track down the physical substance of individual stored remembrances in a famous scientific paper in 1950. 'I sometimes feel,' he wrote, 'in reviewing the evidence on the localization of the memory trace, that the necessary conclusion is that learning just is not possible.'

From J.Z. YOUNG, Programs of the Brain (1978)

All *animal* memories can be considered as stored information for the performance of skills. We only know that an animal has learned by studying its actions. I will not say that this disposes of Gregory's second category, of memory for events.* We humans certainly do have the facility to recall single events that occurred both recently and long ago. Capacity to do this may be one of our unique features and some workers would recognise two categories here, semantic memory, for meanings of words and concepts, and episodic memory for personal experiences. In order to find out what the memory system of the brain is like it is probably wiser to begin by studying the memory for skills rather than events. This, of course, does not mean that the two sorts of memory are unrelated, nor that we must restrict ourselves to animals.

A physical event outside the body provides 'information' only if the nervous system identifies it as a symbol, a sign that something is likely to have a particular relevance for life, which may be good or bad. The smell of food is not eatable, nor do nerve impulses in the olfactory nerve provide calories, but an adult animal or man can learn to go towards those smells that are likely to yield food but to avoid others. What we now want to know is what changes occur in the brain during such adult learning. How do particular patterns of nerve impulses come to have symbolic meaning?

An animal or man will only learn if he tries to do things. A creature that sits still and does nothing cannot learn anything. Put the other way round, this reminds us once again that whatever the memory is, it is certainly a part of an action system. It is not a passive structure nor a picture, nor a model in any literal representational sense. It is particularly important to stress this because, following Bartlett and Craik many people, including myself, have developed the concept that by learning we build a model in the brain. I am using now the concept of programs or hypotheses or plans partly because people are so apt to consider a model as a static thing. We have defined the programs of the brain as plans for action and we are now asking how these are learned. But of course whether we speak of models or programs of plans, they must have a physical basis. Even if human memory records are set up 'in our minds', I think all scientists at least would agree that when we learn there must also be a change in our brains.

Out of all the immense amount of work that has been devoted to memory, there have emerged three types of theory about the

---

* R.L. Gregory (1969), on how so little information controls so much behaviour. *Towards a Theoretical Biology* 2, 236–47. An IUBS Symposium, ed. C.H. Waddington, Ednburgh University Press.

nature of the change that establishes a memory record. There might be (1) a change of standing pattern of activity, or (2) a change of some specific chemical molecules, such as the instructional molecules of RNA or (3) a change in the pathways between neurons within the nervous system. This last is probably the main basis for stable memory records, but all three methods are worth examining.

The brain is continually active and one sign of this is its electrical activities, whether action potentials or slower potential changes such as can be seen in electroencephalograms. Several workers have shown that as an animal learns there are changes in the electrical activity of the brain. The late J. Olds and his colleagues at the California Institute of Technology developed a technique by which after implanting electrodes in the brain of a rat, they could follow the electrical activity of various regions before, during, and after learning a simple task such as pressing a lever to obtain a pellet of food. The whole experiment can be done in two or three days. Changes in electrical activity were found in many parts of the brain. Very interestingly, the earliest signs were in certain regions near the hind end of the brain, including the medial forebrain bundle, which we shall later identify as a possible reward pathway. Changes in the thalamus come later in the learning process, and changes in the cerebral cortex later still.

Unfortunately, we do not yet know how these electrical changes operate to produce the new behaviour of the animal. An early suggestion was that learning sets up cycles of activity in the brain and that these serve to maintain a particular pattern of activity. The importance of self-re-exciting chains of nervous action was first realised, I think, by Alexander Forbes of Harvard in 1922, dealing with the spinal cord, and then by Lorenté de No in 1933 for the control of eye movements. I learned of it from Lorenté during a visit to St Louis in 1936. I then noticed that in the brains of cuttlefishes there are very beautiful self-re-exciting circuits. We found that cuttlefishes show an interesting simple sort of memory. When their prey, say a prawn, disappears out of sight, they will follow it. But they cannot do this if the circuit has been interrupted by a cut. So it may be that the nerve impulses going round the circuit serve as it were to keep the representation of the prawn acting upon the cuttlefish, even when the image is no longer on the retina. This has never been proved to be the explanation of this case, but the circuit arrangement is very striking and there is more evidence for such a mechanism in octopuses.

Many workers have since used the concept of self-re-exciting chains as parts of their theories of memory: D.O. Hebb is often cited as the originator of the concept. It is unlikely that this is the main basis for long-term memory, but such circuits may play an important part in setting up the record. Shocks to the brain received immediately after an event prevent the establishment of a long-term memory record of it. This is a fact that is well attested by those who suffer accidents, and is confirmed by many experiments with electrical shocks given to men or animals. A shock received say one hour later has no such effect on the memory. Footballers questioned immediately after they had been concussed were able to give information about what happened, but half an hour later could remember nothing. There had been no transfer to the long-term store. So the conception has grown up that the record is formed in two stages (perhaps more). In the first or *short-term memory*, the record is maintained by an ongoing activity, perhaps of the cyclic form I have discussed. Thereafter, a process known as consolidation takes place and the record is firmly established. This *long-term memory record* surely must involve some stable physical change, for records of single events can remain for up to 100 years in man. Cyclic activity could not last for a fraction of this time without becoming distorted. Moreover, procedures that must upset activity, or retard or even stop it, such as shock, anaesthesia, or cooling nearly to freezing point, do not disrupt the memory in an animal.

From KONRAD LORENZ, *The Foundations of Ethology*, translated by R. W. Kickert (1982)

Habit formation, in the sense of becoming accustomed to a stimulus configuration to the point of making it *indispensable*, plays a very important part in the formation of social bonds in many different animals, as well as in man. For those animals in which the process is limited to a strictly definable period during ontogeny, as is the first bond formation in humans, it bears a certain resemblance to the process of *imprinting*. One example of the similarity is this: a newly hatched, inexperienced greylag gosling first reacts by 'greeting,' and a little later by following, any moving object which gives, in response to its 'lost piping,' a series of rhythmically repeated sounds within a certain range of pitch. After having 'greeted' in this manner a human being two or three times, the gosling refuses to react in the same way to any other object, its real mother included. The irreversibility of this 'object fixation' – as Freud would call it – is characteristic of imprinting.

One of the great mysteries of imprinting is to be found in the fact that it fixates behavior onto the *species* and not onto the individuality of the object. Once the gosling's following response has been imprinted on humans, the gosling cannot be made to follow a goose, but the human individual fostering it can be exchanged for another without any diminishing of the following response. Also, a gosling hatched by its real mother occasionally changes over to another goose family and remains with that family.

Imprinting of the following response is succeeded by a process of habit or custom formation. During a timespan of roughly twenty hours, the gosling does not reliably recognize its parents as individuals. Interestingly enough, the parents' voices are recognized slightly sooner than are their physical forms. The process of getting to know the parents is demonstrably independent of reward or punishment; if a gosling happens to wander away from its family soon after leaving the nest, it will try to join any strange family with goslings of approximately the same age. If the latter are more than two days old, their parents will take exception to the little stranger and bite it, in a mild and inhibited manner, but still strongly enough to make it utter distress calls and to run away. If one reunites the wayfarer with its own family, it shows that it has definitely not profited by its disagreeable experience; on the contrary, goslings which have once joined a strange family tend to repeat this error. It is as if even a short following in the wake of the 'wrong' parents tends to blur the image of the true ones.

In the process of learning to recognize its parents, the gosling's IRM [innate releasing mechanism], which releases all filial responses, becomes associated with one of the most complex functions of gestalt perception. In ourselves, the analogous faculty of visually recognizing our fellow humans as individuals is largely dependent upon our perception of the configurations of eyes, eyebrows, and nose. It is surprising how effectively the covering of this area impedes recognition; the small, conventional carnival mask is sufficient to do so quite effectively. Curiously enough, it is the same portion of the head which is essential for personal recognition among geese; a sleeping goose with bill and forehead tucked under its wing becomes completely unrecognizable to its fellows and is occasionally bitten by mistake. One of the funniest sequences is that in which a gander, having thus bitten his beloved mate, recoils with astonishment and switches to abject greeting patterns. Fledged, full-grown goslings, temporarily separated from their parents, search for them most assiduously and, while doing so, respond optimistically to any goose that is not positively identifiable because its head is hidden under its wing or under water – as if it could be one of the lost parents, they rush up to it greeting intensely, and start back disappointed when the head of a stranger appears. Hand-reared goslings are perfectly capable of transferring their mechanism of facial recognition to the human foster parents in spite of the enormous differences of body proportions. After a time, and somewhat longer than that taken for parent-reared goslings to learn individual recognition, the filial responses of hand-reared goslings, such as greeting, following and snuggling up, can be released exclusively by the foster mother, no matter how she is dressed. It is the image of the face alone that is relevant, as the following response is in no way diminished if the body of the human, unlike that of a goose, becomes invisible when swimming.

From SEMIR ZEKI, 'Art and the Brain' (1988)

We know a little, but not much, about the brain's stored visual memory system for objects. We know that it must involve a region of the brain known as the inferior convolution of the temporal lobes, because damage here causes severe problems in object recognition. Although very much in their infancy, recent physiological studies have started to give us some insights into the more detailed physiological mechanisms involved. When a monkey, an animal that is close to man, is exposed to different views of objects that it has never encountered before (objects generated on a television screen), recording from single cells in its inferior temporal cortex can show how they respond when these same objects are subsequently shown on the screen again. Most cells respond to one view only, and their response declines as the object is rotated in such a way as to present increasingly less-familiar views. A minority of cells respond to only two views, but only a very small proportion, amounting to less than 1 per cent, respond in a view-invariant manner. Whether they respond to one or more views, the actual size of the stimuli or the precise position in the field of view in which they appear make little difference to the responses of the cell. On the other hand, no cells have ever been found that are responsive to views with which the animal has not been familiarised; hence, exposure to the stimulus is necessary, from which it follows that the cells may be plastic enough to be 'tuned' to one or more views of an object. In summary, many cells, each one responsive to one view only, may be involved during recognition of an object, with the whole group acting as an ensemble. But the presence of that small 1 per cent of cells that respond in a view-invariant manner suggests also that form constancy may be the function of a specialised groups of cells, since 1 per cent represents an enormous number in absolute terms.

When undertaking their work, artists generally are concerned not with philosophical views but rather with achieving desired effects on canvas – by experimenting, by 'sacrificing a thousand apparent truths' and distilling the essence of their visual experience. We are told, for example, that Cézanne's work is 'a painted epistemology' (*Erkenntnis Kritik*), since Cézanne supposedly shared Kant's ideology. But Cézanne, in particular, put paid to all these empty speculations even before they were made when he said that 'les causeries sur l'art sont presque inutiles'. I agree with Kahnweiler when he states, 'J'insiste, en passant, sur le fait qu'aucun de ces peintres . . . n'avait de culture philosophique, et que les rapprochments possibles – avec Locke et Kant surtout – d'une telle attitude leur étaient inconnus, *leur classement étant, d'ailleurs, instinctif plus que raisonné.*' The preoccupation of artists has instead been less exalted and more similar to the physiological experiments described earlier: exposing themselves to as many views of their subject as possible and thus obtaining a brain record from which they can distil on canvas the best combination. If, in executing his work, the artist is indifferent to these polar views – Plato on the one hand, and Hegel and Kant on the other – so should the neurobiologist be, if he accepts my equation of the Platonic

Ideal and the Hegelian Concept with the brain's stored record of what it has seen. Whether art succeeds in presenting the real truth, the essentials, or whether it is the only means of getting to that truth in the face of constantly changing and ephemeral sense data, the opposing views are at least united in suggesting that there is (Hegel) or that there should be (Plato and Schopenhauer) a strong relationship between painting and the search for essentials.

Daedalus, Spring 1988

From NICOLAAS TINBERGEN, *The Study of Instinct* (1989)

'Localised learning.' The student of innate behaviour, accustomed to studying a number of different species and the entire behaviour pattern, is repeatedly confronted with the fact that an animal may learn some things much more readily than others. That is to say, some parts of the pattern, some reactions, may be changed by learning while others seem to be so rigidly fixed that no learning is possible. In other words, there seem to be more or less strictly localised 'dispositions to learn'. Different species are predisposed to learn different parts of the pattern. So far as we know, these differences between species have adaptive significance.

Some instances may illustrate this important fact of localised dispositions.

Herring gulls have a number of innate reactions to the young: they brood them, feed them, and rescue them if attacked by strangers or predators. Interchanging the young of two nests of the same age has very different effects, depending on the age of the young. When they are only a few days old they will be accepted by their 'foster parents'. But if the same test is made when the young are more than 5 days old, they will not be accepted. This means that after a period of about 5 days, during which a parent herring gull is willing to take care of any young of the right age, the parents are conditioned to their own young. They will then neglect or even kill any other young forced upon them. Approximately the same results have been obtained in various species of terns. This learning to 'know' the chicks individually is very remarkable, for the human observer rarely succeeds in distinguishing the young and never reaches the same degree of accuracy as the birds.

The ability of a herring gull to learn its own eggs is, by contrast, amazingly poor. The eggs of different gulls vary a good deal in colour and speckling, in fact they vary much more than the chicks do. Yet even gulls that have eggs of a very distinctive type such as bluish, poorly pigmented eggs, or eggs with exceptionally large or small spots, never show any preference for their own eggs. The innate releasing mechanism of the brooding reactions does not undergo any change by conditioning, so far as the egg itself is concerned. There is, in this respect, a sharp contrast between the reactions to young and those to eggs.

The sexual pattern, again, is readily conditioned. Herring gulls, like a great many other birds, are strictly monogamous, and each bird confines its sexual activities to its own mate once the formation of pairs has taken place. Here again the gull's ability to recognise its mate is far superior to our powers of recognising the gulls. There is proof of the amazing fact that a herring gull instantly recognises its mate (that is, reacts selectively to it amongst a group of other gulls) from a distance of 30 yards. Nor is the herring gull alone in this respect; similar facts are known about jackdaws, geese, terns, and other birds. Recognition is based partially on visual stimuli, partly on voice.

The fact that many species, man included, seem to distinguish individuals of their own species much more readily than individuals of other species is another aspect of the innate basis of learning.

Other instances of localised learning dispositions have been found in the digger wasp, *Philanthus triangulum*. Females of this species have innate releasing mechanisms directing the chain of prey-hunting activities to the hive bee alone, among hundreds of other insect species. There is no indication of a conditioning of the hunting pattern, apart, perhaps, from the development of a certain preference for favourable hunting territories. Each wasp, however, learns, with astonishing rapidity and precision, the locality of each new nest it builds.

From RICHARD DAWKINS, *The Selfish Gene* (1989)

The gene, the DNA molecule, happens to be the replicating entity that prevails on our own planet. There may be others. If there are, provided certain other conditions are met, they will almost inevitably tend to become the basis for an evolutionary process.

But do we have to go to distant worlds to find other kinds of replicator and other, consequent, kinds of evolution? I think that a new kind of replicator has recently emerged on this very planet. It is staring us in the face. It is still in its infancy, still drifting clumsily about in its primeval soup, but already it is achieving evolutionary change at a rate that leaves the old gene panting far behind. The new soup is the soup of human culture. We need a name for the new replicator, a noun that conveys the idea of a unit of cultural transmission, or a unit of *imitation*. 'Mimeme' comes from a suitable Greek root, but I want a monosyllable that sounds a bit like 'gene'. I hope my classicist friends will forgive me if I abbreviate mimeme to *meme*. If it is any consolation, it could alternatively be thought of as being related to 'memory', or to the French word *même*. It should be pronounced to rhyme with 'cream'.

Examples of memes are tunes, ideas, catch-phrases, clothes fashions, ways of making pots or of building arches. Just as genes propagate themselves in the gene pool by leaping from body to body via sperms or eggs, so memes propagate themselves in the meme pool by leaping from brain to brain via a process which, in the broad sense, can be called imitation. If a scientist hears, or reads about, a good idea, he passes it on to his colleagues and students. He mentions it in his articles and his lectures. If the idea catches on, it can be said to propagate itself, spreading from brain to brain. As my colleague N. K. Humphrey neatly summed up an earlier draft of this chapter: '. . . memes should be regarded as living structures, not just metaphorically but technically. When you plant a fertile meme in my mind you literally parasitize my brain, turning it into a vehicle for the meme's propagation in just the way that a virus may parasitize the genetic mechanism of a host cell. And this isn't just a way of talking – the meme for, say, "belief in life after death" is actually realized physically, millions of times over, as a structure in the nervous systems of individual men the world over.'

Consider the idea of God. We do not know how it arose in the meme pool. Probably it originated many times by independent 'mutation'. In any case, it is very old indeed. How does it replicate itself? By the spoken and written word, aided by great music and great art. Why does it have such high survival value? Remember that 'survival value' here does not mean value for a gene in a gene pool, but value for a meme in a meme pool. The question really means: what is it about the idea of a god that gives it its stability and penetrance in the cultural environment? The survival value of the god meme in the meme pool results from its great psychological appeal. It provides a superficially plausible answer to deep and troubling questions about existence. It suggests that injustices in this world may be rectified in the next. The 'everlasting arms' hold out a cushion against our own inadequacies which, like a doctor's placebo, is none the less effective for being imaginary. These are some of the reasons why the idea of God is copied so readily by successive generations of individual brains. God exists, if only in the form of a meme with high survival value, or infective power, in the environment provided by human culture.

Some of my colleagues have suggested to me that this account of the survival value of the god meme begs the question. In the last analysis they wish always to go back to 'biological advantage'. To them it is not good enough to say that the idea of a god has 'great psychological appeal'. They want to know *why* it has great psychological appeal. Psychological appeal means appeal to brains, and brains are shaped by natural selection of genes in gene-pools. They want to find some way in which having a brain like that improves gene survival.

From GEORGE JOHNSON, *In the Palaces of Memory* (1992)

As the digital computer rose to power in the second half of the twentieth century, the localizationist view became dominant. In a computer, memories are stored in very precise locations. Why should it be different in the brain? A number of psychologists were seized by this idea that the mind could be thought of as software running on some sort of biological machine. 'The mind is what the brain does' became their battle cry. While this was a neat way to argue against dualism – the idea that the brain is inhabited by a separate, ethereal mind stuff – the biologists were not very impressed. When it came to memory, the computer metaphor was not much more illuminating than its precedessors. After all, a computer doesn't really remember any more than a video camera sees. In a computer, what passes for memory consists of the 1s and 0s of binary code stored in a bank of transistors, the precursor of the chip, or on a spinning magnetic drum. The computer metaphor was just a fancier version of the video recorder model. Maybe on some level the brain was a kind of computing machine. But nothing explained how it could store such a vast amount of information, not simply recording it but actively arranging and rearranging it into structures, fitting in a new memory among everything else that was already known.

While the computer model of the mind continued to enchant the psychologists, the search for the engram moved to different ground. Inspired by Watson and Crick's discovery of the double helical structure of the DNA, a few biologists began to consider an entirely different storage site, the molecules inside the brain. If a sequence of molecules called nucleotides – the steps in the helical staircase – could encode the genetic information necessary to make a human, why couldn't memories be recorded this way? The alphabet of memory would be the letters *A*, *C*, *T* and *G* – the molecules adenine, cytosine, thymine and guanine that spell the instructions for making enzymes and other proteins, the very substance of life. While it was not at all clear how this four-letter code would spell out a memory, much less a whole childhood experience, the notion of a biological code whose symbols were molecules was hard to resist. How wonderful it would be if evolution had taken the same mechanism used to store a species' genetic memory and adapted it for use in the brain.

For a while it seemed that this might be the metaphor the neuroscientists were seeking. In 1965 a neurobiologist named Allan Jacobson reported that he had trained rats to react to a flashing light by heading for their food dispensers, where they were rewarded with nourishment. Jacobson killed the animals, extracted RNA (an information-carrying molecule similar to DNA) from their brains, and injected it into the stomachs of untrained rats. Then he would test these animals by flashing a light and seeing how they reacted. Sure enough, Jacobson claimed, the rats would tend to head for the food dispenser, as though they had gone through the training sequence. A memory, it seemed, had been taken from the brain of one rat and squirted into another. The engram appeared to be something that could be carried around in a syringe. In other experiments, worms called Planaria were trained to avoid light, then chopped up and fed to other Planaria, which seemed to inherit the trait.

One researcher, Georges Ungar, insisted that memory was encoded not in nucleic acids but in a different molecular alphabet: the sequence of amino acids that make up protein chains. Working in the early 1970s, he used electrical shocks to train rats to avoid darkness. Then he extracted chemicals from their brains. By analyzing this mixture, he found a proteinlike substance (a polypeptide consisting of eight to fifteen amino acids) that seemed to contain the memory of the electrical shock.

Other rats injected with this molecule, or even a synthesized version of it, also tended to avoid the dark. Ungar called the chemical scotophobin – derived from the Greek words for 'fear of the dark' – and claimed to have found similar molecules that carried other memories. A few people imagined the day when pills would replace books. Starving M.B.A. students could sell brain fluid to pharmaceutical companies instead of blood plasma. But most researchers remained skeptical. In all these cases, the evidence was statistical, unconvincing, and impossible to replicate. With Ungar's death in 1977, research into chemical engrams lapsed into obscurity. Now most neuroscientists believe that scotophobin is to psychology what phlogiston is to chemistry – a figment of the imagination.

From DANIEL L. ALKON, Memory's Voice: Deciphering the Mind–Brain Code (1994)

Joseph Farley, working with me at the Marine Biological Laboratory in Woods Hole, provided additional support for the type B cell's memory record by inserting microelectrodes into B cells of living snails that had not been trained with light and rotation. By injecting electrical current shortly after a light flash occurred, he artificially enhanced the B cell responses and thereby mimicked the effect of learning on the type B cells. After allowing the animals to recover, he found that they showed evidence of learning the light-rotation association just as if they had been conditioned with natural stimuli.

We were, therefore, at a storage site. At this site the memory record 'looked like' more signals in response to light. More electrical signals send more synaptic messages to other neurons and therefore store the memory. But what in the neuron makes more electrical signals? We knew that the flow of charged particles through channels in the neuron's wall produced the signals. Perhaps learning regulated channels? Memory-regulated channels would in turn alter the charged particle flow, the signals, and the synaptic messages.

We had to look at the channels. This would require another level of acrobatics with microelectrodes. One microelectrode in the type B neuron would not be enough. I now inserted two or three into the same cell. Inserting each microelectrode without knocking the others out or tearing the cell wall apart proved to be a nerve-racking balancing act. Yet I eventually managed to record this way for hours on end, sometimes with one of the microelectrodes within the wirelike axon, only a millionth of a meter in diameter. The signals recorded by such microelectrode ensembles revealed the flow of charged particles through the channels in the neuron's wall.

Soon after I began measuring particle flow across the neuron wall, or membrane, something peculiar caught my attention. Once activated by the light flash, the flow of certain charged particles, those of a potassium salt, across the membrane could not be entirely reactivated for many seconds afterward. It was as if the potassium flow had a memory of its prior activation. I remember sitting in the dark marveling at the slowness of this recovery (originally observed by John Connor in other neurons) and thinking how different this was from the classic story worked out for electrical signals, which spread down axons at fantastic speeds. Each of these axonal signals, also present in the type B axon, was completed within a few thousandths of a second and ready to be reactivated almost immediately thereafter. Maybe, I thought, the prolonged recovery of the potassium flow was in some way related to the prolonged nature of memory storage. Maybe a recovery lasting many seconds could, during memory acquisition, be extended to many hours, days, and longer. When all was said and done, this would prove to be the case. A permanently altered flow of potassium particles through membrane channels provides a memory record for later recall not only in the snail, but also in mammals.

Now the words *memory record* and *memory trace* took on a new and exciting meaning. A memory record 'looks like' altered molecular channels in neuronal membranes. Channels in a mature neuron's membrane remained changed for weeks after the light occurred together in time with rotation. Nothing comparable had ever been encountered in any fully formed cell known to science. This was not what I or anyone else had expected. Since Helmholtz first measured its speed, Bernstein theorized how it was generated, and Hodgkin and Huxley measured its underlying flow of charged particles, no one imagined that a neuron's electrical signal could remain transformed for days or even weeks. True, the signal developed along with the neuron. But once development is complete, a neuron's signals were thought to be just as constant as those that pace the heart. Yet our observations in the snail's brain and later the rabbit's hippocampus violated our expectations and led us to a new way of thinking about particle flow. Experience could produce long-lasting changes of particle flow. Nature heard nurture's voice in the movements of particles through membrane channels . . .

The potassium channel changes that stored the memory of the light-rotation link in the snail were telling us, then, not to look for an increased number of synapses or greater complexity of branches but for modified membranes distributed throughout systems of neurons that already existed – that had already developed according to genetic blueprints. They were telling us that the neuronal code for memory has its own unique features, quite distinct from codes that allow for development of the neurons themselves. The initial changes during snail and, later, rabbit learning were saying that the cellular expressions of remembered time that are due to an individual animal's experience are different from expressions of evolutionary time that are due to an entire species' experience. And to understand memory, particularly memory as complex as that of humans, these differences would have to be sorted out.

From STEVEN PINKER, *The Language Instinct* (1994)

The most sophisticated estimate [of human vocabulary] comes from the psychologists William Nagy and Richard Anderson. They began with a list of 227,553 different words. Of these, 45,453 were simple roots and stems. Of the remaining 182,100 derivatives and compounds, they estimated that all but 42,080 could be understood in context by someone who knew their components. Thus there were a total of 44,453 + 42,080 = 88,533 listeme words. By sampling from this list and testing the sample, Nagy and Anderson estimated that an average American high school graduate knows 45,000 words – three times as many as Shakespeare managed to use! Actually, this is an underestimate, because proper names, numbers, foreign words, acronyms, and many common undecomposable compounds were excluded. There is no need to follow the rules of Scrabble in estimating vocabulary size; these forms are all listemes, and a person should be given credit for them. If they had been included, the average high school graduate would probably be credited with something like 60,000 words (a tetrabard?), and superior students, because they read more, would probably merit a figure twice as high, an octobard.

Is 60,000 words a lot or a little? It helps to think of how quickly they must have been learned. Word learning generally begins around the age of twelve months. Therefore, high school graduates, who have been at it for about seventeen years, must have been learning an average of ten new words a day continuously since their first birthdays, or about a new word every ninety waking minutes. Using similar techniques, we can estimate that an average six-year-old commands about 13,000 words (notwithstanding those dull, dull *Dick and Jane* reading primers, which were based on ridiculously lowball estimates). A bit of arithmetic shows that preliterate children, who are limited to ambient speech, must be lexical vacuum cleaners, inhaling a new word every two waking hours, day in, day out. Remember that we are talking about listemes, each involving an arbitrary pairing. Think about having to memorize a new batting average or treaty date or phone number every ninety minutes of your waking life since you took your first steps. The brain seems to be reserving an especially capacious storage space and an especially rapid transcribing mechanism for the mental dictionary. Indeed, naturalistic studies by the psychologist Susan Carey have shown that if you casually slip a new color word like *olive* into a conversation with a three-year-old, the child will probably remember something about it five weeks later.

From FRANCIS CRICK, *The Astonishing Hypothesis: The Scientific Search for the Soul* (1994)

What about short-term memory? What is known about that? A memory might be defined as a change in a system, due to experience, that makes some alteration to its subsequent thoughts or behaviour, but this is too broad to be of much value. It would cover fatigue, injury, poisoning, and so on, and would not distinguish between learning and development (early growth). The Israeli neurobiologist Yadin Dudai has produced a more useful and more sophisticated definition. He first describes what he means by an 'internal representation' of the 'world' – that is, of both the external and internal milieu. He defines an internal representation as 'neuronally encoded, structured, versions of the world that could potentially guide behaviour'. This emphasises that, at bottom, we are mainly concerned with how nerve cells (neurons) influence behaviour. 'Learning' is then the creation or modification of such an internal representation, produced by experience. Such changes persist for an appreciable time (sometimes for years), although we shall be interested mainly in memories that last only a very short time.

I shall not be concerned with very simple forms of memory, such as habituation or sensitisation. (Suppose you show a baby the same picture ten times in succession. At first he is interested, but soon he becomes bored with it. This is called 'habituation'.) These processes are classed as 'nonassociative'. They occur even in very lowly animals, such as the sea slug. We shall be more interested in 'associative learning' in which the organism responds to *relations* among stimuli and actions.

It is useful to divide memory into several fairly distinct types, although exactly how they should be described is a matter of controversy. One convenient division is into episodic, categorical, and procedural memory. Episodic memory is a memory of an event, often together with irrelevant details associated with the event. A good example would be remembering where you were when you heard that President Kennedy had been assassinated. An example of a categorical memory would be the meaning of a word, such as 'assassination' or 'dog', whereas the knowledge of how to swim or to drive a car would be classed as procedural memory.

Another method of classification depends on timing: how long it takes to acquire the memory and how long the memory usually lasts. Some memories, especially episodic memories, are classed as 'one-shot' or 'flash-bulb' learning. One remembers them strongly after only a single instance. (Such memories may of course be strengthened by rehearsal – by telling the story over again, not always correctly.) Other types of memory benefit from repeated instances, from which one extracts the general nature of something, such as the meaning of an (undefined) word.

Procedural knowledge, such as driving a car, is often difficult to acquire from a single experience and usually benefits from repeated practice. It often lasts for a remarkably long time. Once you have learned to swim you can swim fairly well even if you haven't swum for many years. A famous pianist said to me, about forgetting a familiar piece of music, 'Muscle memory is the last to go,' meaning by that term playing the piece automatically and without thinking about it.

Memories typically last for different times and are often divided into long-term and short-term memory, although the terms mean different things to different people. 'Long-term' usually means for hours, days, months, or even years. 'Short-term' can cover periods from a fraction of a second to a few minutes or more. Short-term memory is usually labile and of limited capacity.

Consider what happens when you are dreaming. It appears that you cannot put anything into long-term memory (or at least, anything you can explicitly recall) while you are actually dreaming. Your brain holds the dream in some form of short-term memory. When you wake up (which may happen more often than you realise) the long-term memory system switches on. Anything still in short-term memory can then be transferred into long term – that is why you remember, not everything you have dreamt, but the last few minutes of the dream. If, shortly after waking, you are disturbed – by a telephone call, for example – your short-term memory of the dream, being interrupted, may decay and be lost, so that after the telephone call is over you can no longer recall even the last part of your dream.

Recalling a memory, as we all know, is not a straightforward process. Usually some clue is needed to address the memory, and even then the memory may be elusive. Some memories become weak, and need stronger clues to evoke them. Others appear to fade until they are completely lost. A related memory may intrude and block access to the one you want, and so on.

From GERALD M. EDELMAN, 'Building a Picture of the Brain' (2001)

To say, as is commonplace, that memory involves storage raises the question: What is stored? Is it a coded message? When it is 'read out' or recovered, is it unchanged? These questions point to the widespread assumption that what is stored is some kind of representation. This in turn implies that the brain is supposed to be concerned with representations, at least in its cognitive functions. In perception, for example, even before memory occurs, alterations in the brain are supposed to stand for, symbolize, or portray what is experienced. In this view, memory is the more or less permanent laying down of changes that, when appropriately addressed, can recapture a representation – and, if necessary, act on it. In this view, learned acts are themselves the consequences of representations that store definite procedures or codes.

The idea that representational memory occurs in the brain carries with it a huge burden. While it allows an easy analogy to human informational transactions embedded in computers, that analogy poses more problems than it solves. In the case of humans working with computers, semantic operations occurring in the brain, not in the computer, are necessary to make sense of the coded syntactical strings that are stored physically in the computer either in a particular location or in a distributed form. Coherency must be maintained in the code (or error correction is required) and the capacity of the system is quite naturally expressed in terms of storage limits.

Above all, the input to a computer must itself be coded in an unambiguous fashion; it must be syntactically ordered information.

The problem for the brain is that signals from the world do not in general represent a coded input. Instead, they are potentially ambiguous, are context-dependent, are subject to construction, and are not necessarily adorned by prior judgments as to their significance. An animal must categorize these signals for adaptive purposes, whether in perception or in memory, and somehow it must associate this categorization with subsequent experiences of the same kinds of signals. To do this with a coded or replicative storage system would require endless error correction, and a precision at least comparable to and possibly greater than that of computers. There is no evidence, however, that the structure of the brain could support such capabilities directly; neurons do not do floating-point arithmetic. It seems more likely that such mathematical capabilities have arisen in human culture as a consequence of symbolic exchange, linguistic interactions, and the application of logic.

Representation implies symbolic activity. This activity is at the center of our semantic and syntactical skills. It is no wonder that, in thinking about how the brain can repeat a performance, we are tempted to say that the brain represents. The flaws with such an assertion, however, are obvious: there is no precoded message in the signal, no structures capable of high-precision storage of a code, no judge in nature to provide decisions on alternative patterns, and no homunculus in the head to read a message. For these reasons, memory in the brain cannot be representational in the same way as it is in our devices.

What is it then, and how can one conceive of a nonrepresentational memory? In a complex brain, memory results from the selective matching that occurs between ongoing neural activity and signals from the world, the body, and the brain itself. The synaptic alterations that ensue affect the future responses of the brain to similar or different signals. These changes are reflected in the ability to repeat a mental or physical act in time and in a changing context. It is important here to indicate that by the word 'act,' I mean any ordered sequence of brain activities in a domain of perception, action, consciousness, speech, or even in the domain of meaning that in time leads to neural output. I stress time in my definition because it is the ability to recreate an act separated by a certain duration from the original signal set that is characteristic of memory.

And in mentioning a changing context, I pay heed to a key property of memory in the brain: that it is, in some sense, a form of *recategorization* during ongoing experience rather than a precise replication of a previous sequence of events . . .

In this view, there are many hundreds, if not thousands, of separate memory systems in the brain. They range from all of the perceptual systems in different modalities to those systems governing intended or actual movement to those of the language system and speech sound. This gives recognition to the various types of memory tested by experimentalists in the field – procedural, semantic, episodic, and so on – but it does not restrict itself only to these types, which are defined mainly operationally and to some degree biochemically.

While individual memory systems differ, the key general conclusion is that memory itself is a system property. It cannot be equated solely to circuitry, synaptic changes, biochemistry, value constraints, or behavioral dynamics. Instead, it is the dynamic result of the interactions of *all* of these factors within a given system acting to select an output that repeats a performance. The overall characteristics of a particular performance may be similar to a previous performance within some threshold criterion, but the structures underlying any two similar performances can be quite different.

From JOHN MCCRONE, 'Not-so Total Recall', (2003)

Who are you? For most of us, our sense of self relies on a personal history of memories that can be dipped into just as readily as turning the pages of a photo album: the child who broke an arm falling out of a tree, the gawky teenager on a first date, the proud parent. But can your memory really be trusted with something as fundamental as your sense of identity?

Psychologists have long known that our memories are easily embellished. We add imaginary details through wishful thinking or to make a more logical story. More controversially, memory may be falsified through suggestion and manipulative questioning, bringing some eyewitness testimony and 'recovered' memories into doubt. And we all forget things too. But despite these flaws it was always presumed that the core experiences themselves – the memory traces stamped into the fabric of our brain – were permanent. Look in the right place and we could always dig back to what really happened.

But that's simply not so, according to some surprising new research. A memory is anything but static. Resurrecting a memory trace appears to render it completely fluid, as pliable and unstable as the moment it was first formed, and in need of fixing once again into the brain's circuitry. Any meddling with this fixing process could alter the trace – or even erase it completely. Simply retelling a tale may be enough to change that memory for good. Long-term memory is effectively a myth.

What does it mean? Who are we if our personal memories are so volatile that the very act of remembering might allow past experiences to vanish into thin air? How can we trust our minds at all? Well, common sense tells us that our brains aren't that bad at keeping a record of our lives. So maybe what needs changing here is how we think about memory. A memory trace that goes all floppy every time it gets used only seems a disaster if you believe the brain to be something like a computer where data needs to be preserved in fixed form. Fluidity, on the other hand, may be precisely what is required for memory to work as something much more organic – a living network of understanding rather than a dormant warehouse of facts.

The standard story on memory is that the brain first captures a snapshot of each moment. The firing of a particular arrangement of neurons leaves them electrochemically aroused and ready to fire again in the same pattern, primed to recreate the just-happened experience. But this short-term memory trace lasts barely a few seconds and needs to be turned into something more permanent by a complex cascade of brain events. One of the great goals of neuroscience is to unravel the fine detail of this process of memory consolidation.

In the past few years it has become clear that the transient sensitisation of nerve junctions – the synapses connecting neurons together – leads to an almost immediate swelling. The synapses bulk up with more receptors and more neurotransmitters, and become inflamed to make a stronger connection. Then after a few hours, the neurons begin to physically grow, sprouting new and thicker connections to wire in a permanent memory trace. A mass of protein, produced by a range of genes, will be employed to build a remodelled brain circuit.

What makes the process of consolidation so complex is that as well as the neural-level rewiring, the memory trace also migrates. When a memory pattern is fresh, it is stored in specialist memory organs such as the hippocampus, deep within the brain. But over a number of days, weeks or even years, it settles back across the brain and becomes lodged in more general areas. Rather like computer files being transferred from hard disc to back-up tape, old memories eventually get consigned to the vast, wrinkled vaults of the cortex.

Neuroscientists felt this hierarchical filing system was a little long-winded. But it sounded reliable. Once fossilised in some dusty forgotten corner of the brain, a memory trace might become a little harder to retrieve, yet it ought to remain absolutely stable. This was the accepted story until a very simple experiment blew it away.

To study memory consolidation, researchers interfere with steps in the fixing process in order to test their influence on long-term recall. While doing this kind of work, researchers including Karim Nader of McGill University, Montreal, and Joseph Ledoux of New York University noticed something odd. They trained rats to associate an electric shock to their paws with a darkened box. The rats learn that the box is 'nasty' and freeze the next time they are put back. If, a few days after training, the animals were given a drug to stop protein synthesis before being reminded of the conditioning stimulus – the sight of the training box – it made no difference to their ability to remember it. The memory seemed fixed and safely stored. But if the rats had a brief reminder of the stimulus just before the drug was given, then a memory that should have been fixed and stable seemed to be erased.

What did it mean? Nader and LeDoux coined the term reconsolidation, suggesting that the act of recalling something renders it flexible, giving the chance to expand or generalise the original memory trace – a form of reaffirmation. The drug given to the rats prevented this reconsolidation step, somehow leading to the decay of the original memory. The publication of their results in *Nature* caused quite a stir, and no small amount of scepticism.

But in a detailed follow-up published in the journal *Neuron* late last year, they made a more convincing case. Again the rats were put in a box and given an electric shock to their paws, and would freeze the next time they were put in the box. According to traditional consolidation theory, such memories are fixed locally by protein changes in a matter of hours and then safely filed to long-term storage in the cortex after about a month. The team waited a full 45 days to test the rats, by which time the memory trace should have been quite immune to interference.

As expected, the rats that were given no reminders of the original experience showed no memory loss when injected with the protein-blocking drugs – they froze when tested. Likewise the complete destruction of the hippocampus left the memory intact, as it was now resident in the vaults of the cortex.

But if the rats were reminded of the sight of the box just before the drug was injected, the result was precisely the opposite. Now the protein-blocking drug created amnesia. And destroying the hippocampus also erased the fear association. The rats nosed about the box quite unconcerned. At both the synaptic level and the anatomical level, it was as if the consolidated memory had been released and needed to undergo the whole fixing process again if it were to be remembered. Recall had made an established trace shaky.

'The dogma was that once a memory trace has been consolidated, it is permanent,' says Nader. 'But here it was labile – subject to interference in exactly the same way as a brand-new experience.' The old static picture of memory could not be right. 'We were showing memory to be something incredibly dynamic.'

Some researchers, such as James McGaugh and Larry Cahill of the University of California at Irvine, were sceptical. They didn't think this 'reconsolidation' effect would be replicated. Cahill describes the work as 'iffy' and feels a simpler interpretation of the results – such as some kind of suppression mechanism – might still be forthcoming.

But confirmation has been pouring in. 'Reconsolidation has now been demonstrated in all sorts of situations and all sorts of animals – crabs, slugs, chickens,' says Nader. 'This tells me it's a basic feature of the memory system.' He now believes that there's no longer any question about whether the effect exists. Instead he's keen to find out what it means.

For example, does it imply that our memory is always unreliable? Clearly not. But it isn't completely stable either. But even if reconsolidation doesn't yet convince all memory researchers of that fact, there's another reason to suggest instability is inevitable – molecular turnover. The proteins, fats and other complex molecules making up a cell generally last an astonishingly short time, anything from a matter of days down to just a few minutes, and so need constant replacing. Cells are not static creations but fragile things that are continually renewing themselves.

For brain cells – where their shape and synaptic structures determine their function – the issue is all the more acute. The protein filaments that give the cells their internal shape have a half-life of just a few minutes. And the receptor proteins that stud the synapses need replacing every few days. As Joe Tsien, a neurobiologist at Princeton University in New Jersey, says, the brain you have this week is not the one you had last week. Even the DNA needs to be repaired. So if 'you' are essentially a pattern of synaptic connections, a tangled web of memories, then there is a big problem of how this pattern endures. 'I don't know how people ever got this static picture of the brain,' says Tsien. 'A memory trace would have to be a dynamic thing just because of molecular turnover.'

The idea that we enjoy a photographic record of the past is a myth that has also been exploded by experiments such as the eyewitness research of Elizabeth Loftus of the University of California at Irvine. Here, subjects incorporated overheard details about a staged bank robbery or car crash in their own memories of the event. Loftus's work seems clear proof that our memories are fluid creations that can be edited or embroidered.

And the more you think about it, the more such dynamism makes sense. Susan Sara of the Pierre and Marie Curie University in Paris, who found indications of a reconsolidation effect in her own experiments in 1997, says the real problem for the brain is not how well it can preserve the past but how successful it is at integrating new learning with old learning. Memories exist to make sense of the present – to recognise and understand the world – and the brain needs to be able to optimise all its circuits, strengthening or generalising some connections while weakening or erasing others. Reconsolidation may seem a radical and unnecessary step for a brain that just wants to be a dormant warehouse. But, Sara says, if a memory becomes completely plastic every time it is roused, then it can be refiled in a carefully updated way. Active choices can be made about whether to merge the old and the new – or by contrast, to reinforce their separateness.

'It's just an accident that reconsolidation has been demonstrated by erasing memories,' says Sara. This is what is creating the misconception of the shaky trace. It's easier to interfere with the reconsolidation in this way than it is to show the opposite – a memory being strengthened. But Sara and her team hope to show that drugs which arouse the brain will reinforce an activated memory.

The bottom line is that there is no reason to believe that rousing your personal memories is a risky affair, she says. Thinking about the past probably does require a surprisingly drastic change in the state of a memory trace. They may not be simple snapshots of events that are passively read out but constructive and ever changing. However, there is no cause to think the brain does a poor job of reintegrating a memory that has been roused. Our memories may not be an infallible recording device, but frequently recalling a childhood memory seems more likely to reinforce it than erase it.

By the same token, the reconsolidation finding goes a long way to support the claims of psychologists like Loftus, who say that society needs to take better account of the essentially reconstructive nature of human memory. Loftus first demonstrated more than thirty years ago the ease with which the memories of eyewitnesses could be biased. But, she says, it is only recently that advances in DNA testing have brought a spate of wrongful convictions to light, forcing US legal authorities to take the issue more seriously. Loftus has also been at the centre of the false memory syndrome controversy, where the suggestive questioning style of psychotherapists has been blamed for creating imagined incidents of childhood abuse.

'In most avenues of life, it doesn't really matter if you make a few mistakes in your memory,' says Loftus. 'But if somebody's liberty is at stake, or they are going to be involved in a horrible lawsuit of some sort, then very precise memory does matter.' She has been calling for changes in legal and therapeutic interview practices so as to minimise the chances of contaminating the memory of witnesses.

Yet even Loftus confesses to be a little taken aback that neurology might prove the brain to be quite so labile. She often quotes the Uruguayan novelist, Eduardo Galeano, who said: 'Memory is born every day, springing from the past, and set against it.' Now, says Loftus, this may be even truer than anyone ever suspected.

New Scientist (3 May 2003)

From VILAYANUR RAMACHANDRAN, *The Emerging Mind* (2003)

Prosopognosia is very well known but there is another syndrome that is quite rare – the Capgras syndrome. A patient I saw not long ago had been in a car accident, sustaining a head injury, and was in a coma. He came out of the coma after a couple of weeks and was quite intact neurologically when I examined him. But he had one profound delusion – he would look at his mother and say, 'Doctor, this woman looks exactly like my mother but she isn't, she is an impostor.' Why would this happen? Bear in mind that this patient, who I will call David, is completely intact in other respects. He is intelligent, alert, fluent in conversation (at least by American standards) and not emotionally disturbed in any other way.

To understand this disorder, you have to first realise that vision is not a simple process. When you open your eyes in the morning, it's all out there in front of you and so it's easy to assume that vision is effortless and instantaneous. But in fact within each eyeball, all you have is a tiny distorted upside-down image of the world. This excites the photoreceptors in the retina and the messages then go through the optic nerve to the back of your brain, where they are analysed in thirty different visual areas. Only after that do you begin to finally identify what you're looking at. Is it your mother? Is it a snake? Is it a pig? And that process of indentification takes place partly in a small brain region called the fusiform gyrus – the region which is damaged in patients with face blindness or prosopognosia. Finally, once the image is recognised, the message is relayed to a structure called the amygdala, sometimes called the gateway to the limbic system, the emotional core of your brain, which allows you to gauge the emotional significance of what you are looking at. Is this a predator? Is it prey which I can chase? Is it a potential mate? Or is it my departmental chairman I have to worry about, a stranger who is not important to me, or something utterly trivial like a piece of driftwood? What is it?

In David's case, perhaps the fusiform gyrus and all the visual areas are completely normal, so his brain tells him that the woman he sees looks like his mother. But, to put it crudely, the 'wire' that goes from the visual centres to the amygdala, to the emotional centres, is cut by the accident. So he looks at his mother and thinks, 'She looks just like my mother, but if it's my mother why don't I feel anything towards her? No, this can't possibly be my mother, it's some stranger pretending to be my mother.' This is the only interpretation that makes sense to David's brain, given the peculiar disconnection.

How can an outlandish idea like this be tested? My student Bill Hirstein and I in La Jolla, and Haydn Ellis and Andrew Young in England, did some very simple experiments measuring galvanic skin response. We found – sure enough – that in David's brain there was a disconnection between vision and emotion as predicted by our theory. Even more amazing is that when David's mother phones him he instantly recognises her from her voice. There is no delusion. Yet if an hour later his mother were to walk into the room he would tell her that she looked just like his mother but was an impostor. The reason for this anomaly is that a separate pathway leads from the auditory cortex in the superior temporal gyrus to the amygdala, and that pathway perhaps was not cut by the accident. So auditory cognisance remains intact while visual cognisance has disappeared. This is a lovely example of the sort of thing we do: of cognitive neuroscience in action; of how you can take a bizarre, seemingly incomprehensible neurological syndrome – a patient claiming that his mother is an impostor – and then come up with a simple explanation in terms of the known neural pathways in the brain.

From WELLCOME TRUST, 'Magic Memories' (2004)

We seem to hold an internal map of the world in our heads. Understanding how the brain stores such maps could help people whose memory has been damaged by a stroke or other trauma.

In a study that generated considerable media interest (and won her an Ig Nobel Prize), in 2000 Dr Eleanor Maguire scanned the brains of 16 London black-cab drivers, who had spent an average of two years learning 'the Knowledge' – street names and routes in London. The taxi drivers had a larger right hippocampus than control subjects, and the longer they had been on the job the larger their hippocampus was. These findings seem to indicate that the right hippocampus plays an important role in storing spatial memories.

Dr Maguire, a Wellcome Trust Senior Research Fellow at the Wellcome Department of Imaging Neuroscience at University College London, is continuing her investigations into what happens in our brains when we navigate large-scale space. 'When we travel down a route we are familiar with, we often can't see our destination. Instead, we have an image of it in our mind, and a mental map of how to get there. But this mental map is very different from a street map. I'm trying to understand how we create internal three-dimensional representation of space and our position within it.'

She is also interested in another form of memory, linked to spatial memory, which appears to be mediated by the left, rather than the right hippocampus. 'Having created an internal representation of large-scale space, how do we structure episodic memories – particular events and personal experiences that occurred at a specific time and place – within that environment?'

Dr Maguire will be using magnetic resonance imaging (MRI) techniques[1] to establish which neural elements, or brain circuits, are involved in storing and recollecting these two types of memory: spatial and episodic. Results from the MRI scans will be combined with findings from psychological tests to shed light on the cognitive processes that support neural activity in the formation of memory.

Together, she hopes these neural and cognitive findings will provide an integrated, holistic picture of how we understand who and where we are, by locating ourselves in the world and recalling the personal experiences that constitute our recent and distant past.

Measuring someone's brain activity while they navigate large-scale space poses a challenge, since MRI techniques require the subject to lie in a brain scanner. Dr Maguire has therefore developed a series of virtual reality tasks that the subject can carry out, without physically moving, on a screen inside a scanner.[2] The complex, naturalistic nature of these tasks closely mimics 'real-life' situations.

'We ask subjects to find their way around a virtual city using a

[1] In collaboration with the Functional Imaging Laboratory, at the Institute of Neurology, University College London.
[2] In collaboration with the Institute of Cognitive Neuroscience, University College London.

joystick or keypad, and scan their brains while they're doing it, to find out which brain regions are activated,' explains Dr Maguire. 'We vary factors like familiarity by allowing some subjects to practise first; or we get people to take detours or short-cuts or we put a road block in their normal route.' Developing these virtual-reality environments can be done by adapting commercially available video games. 'A lot of video games have good editors and are therefore adaptable. We take out all the shooting and monsters so we're left with the basic environment, which is ideal for our purposes.'

She has adapted the same method of 'in-scanner' testing for tasks involving episodic memory. Unlike recall of facts or object recognition, memories of personal experiences are coloured with emotions and played out in a rich spatial, temporal and social context. To understand how the brain stores and recalls this form of memory, it is important to evoke the 'whole' memory during MRI scanning. One way of doing this is to project a photo of a party or wedding from a family album on to the screen, prompting the subject to recall and re-experience this particular event in their past.

As well as understanding how these memories are structured in 'normal' healthy subjects, Dr Maguire also hopes to find out more about what happens in the brains of people who lose these abilities.

'The ability to find our way around an environment and to remember the events that occur within it – both thought to be mediated by the hippocampus – are fundamental to normal functioning in daily life,' she says. 'Unfortunately, the hippocampus is vulnerable to brain damage by epilepsy, dementia, and anoxia (when the brain is deprived of oxygen), which impacts on both these capacities, leaving patients severely debilitated and dependent on others for day-to-day living.'

The symptoms can be very problematic. 'If spatial cognition is affected, people literally don't know where they are, and if episodic memory is damaged, it can lead to amnesia,' says Dr Maguire. People with amnesia live permanently in the present. Their speech and general intellect tends to remain intact, because remembering facts and general knowledge is not dependent on the hippocampus, but everything is frozen in time: they cannot remember anything that occurs after the damage took place. 'If they do a couple of hours of tests with me, for example, and I leave the room for ten minutes and come back, they can't remember anything about me or what they had been doing. They can't live alone because they can't remember if they turned the gas off or paid their bills. Sometimes, which is very sad, if a spouse dies, they can't remember their loved one is now gone.'

For people suffering from hippocampal damage and associated difficulties with spatial and episodic memory, the question of whether the brain can mend itself and memory be recovered is a pressing one. 'It has long been thought that the adult brain only has a limited amount of plasticity,' says Dr Maguire. 'But findings like those from our study of London cab drivers show that structural changes can occur in healthy human brains. Perhaps in the future we could use that kind of understanding to help people with hippocampal damage.'

Dr Maguire is therefore attempting to characterise the brain's plasticity in more detail by taking a unique lifespan approach to her study of memory. 'We'll be measuring the effects of disease or injury on the brain and memory at all stages of life – from developmental disorders in children to dementia in the elderly – and comparing these with healthy subjects.'[3] As well as examining memories at single points in time, she will also be tracking how people's brains change over short and longer timescales, again comparing diseased or injured brains with healthy brains of the same age. 'If you see a measurable difference in the brain of a particular individual over time, such as growth of their hippocampus, then you know that structural changes have definitely occurred in that particular person's brain. This is different from simply comparing groups of people at one point in time.'

Alongside these projects, Dr Maguire will be conducting further work on black-cab drivers. This time she will be testing retired cabbies to see if the plasticity goes both ways – whether the hippocampus shrinks again when they stop full-time navigation around London. She also wants to establish whether this plasticity is limited to navigation, or whether it is generalisable to other areas of the brain.

Findings from her research will be used to provide benchmarks for assessing the effects of disease or injury on memory, for people of different ages, and could aid development of clinical memory tests for early diagnosis of pathology. 'In the long term, we hope

---

[3.] In collaboration with the National Hospital for Neurology and Neurosurgery.

we'll be able to use this information to develop new kinds of re-habilitation programmes for people with hippocampal damage – but we still have a very long way to go.'

Dr Maguire's study on London black-cab drivers showed distinct structural changes to the brain linked to the memorising of large interconnected spatial environments. She was interested to find out if similar changes accompanied another feat of exceptional memory, those on show at the World Memory Championships, which take place every year in London.

'People entering the World Memory Championships can do amazing things,' she says. 'They can memorise the order of cards in deck after deck of cards, for example. One memory champion passed time waiting in reception prior to his scan by memorising pages from the phone book – pretty well too; I tested him on it.'

Despite their high performance on memory tasks, however, Dr Maguire could find no structural changes. 'I then asked them what strategies they used. Nine out of ten of them used the same strategy: an ancient Greek method, called the method of loci. It's based on navigation: they imagine going down a street they know well, place items at certain positions along the street, then mentally retrace their route to find the items.'

Although this strategy uses spatial memory to boost perform-ance, the amount of large-scale space memorised is small, possibly accounting for the lack of structural changes in the right hippocampus. 'Their brain doesn't have to change to accommo-date a large map of London in their heads as it does for the cab drivers; the memory champions just need to memorise a couple of routes in detail.'

From the *Economist*, 'Sleeping on it' (2000)

When an Arctic ground squirrel hibernates, its body temperature drops below the freezing point of water and the blood-flow through its brain slows to a trickle. Though the squirrel's brain survives, it loses many of the nerve-cell connections that govern how it oper-ates. The brain regenerates itself soon after the animal emerges from its long sleep. Exactly how is a matter of intense research but one group of scientists thinks that part of the explanation lies with a protein associated with Alzheimer's disease. And that raises the hope that the ravages wrought on the human mind by Alzheimer's disease could be as reversible as the winter freeze.

Arctic ground squirrels hibernate for up to seven months of the year, sinking into a torpor from which they periodically rewarm their bodies to 37°C before re-entering the supercooled state. Research has shown that during hibernation these animals lose memories they laid down beforehand and also their ability to form new ones. This loss must be temporary, however, or the animal would become more amnesic with each hibernation.

The brain stores information in neuronal networks. The chemical connections between neurons, called synapses, are thought to be critical to the formation of those networks and hence the laying down of memories. In 2003 a group led by Thomas Arendt of the University of Leipzig in Germany showed that the number of synapses in the hippocampus, a brain structure crucial for learning and memory, falls during hibernation. This is partly because hippocampal neurons lose many of their branching projections, or dendrites, and so provide less opportunity for forming synapses with neighbouring neurons.

All that changes within two or three hours of an animal emerging from hibernation, when a wave of new growth ensures that the number of synapses in the hippocampus soars beyond even prehibernation levels. The next 20 hours see a pruning back of those connections, rather as in the very young human brain. Just as in that developmental process, the new synapses seem to enhance memory only once the pruning has taken place.

Nobody knows what triggers these dramatic morphological changes in the hippocampus during and after hibernation. But Dr Arendt's group has made the startling discovery that hibernating brains accumulate a protein called hyperphosphorylated tau. This protein is known also to accumulate in the neurons that degenerate in the brains of people with Alzheimer's disease. Notably, though by no means exclusively, it accumulates in the hippocampal neurons, where it is associated with the formation of lesions.

There are several competing theories about what causes Alzheimer's disease. One possibility is that the tau protein causes the lesions in the brain. Another is that something else causes the lesions, and the tau protein is the brain's defence against that attack.

Thus, it is possible that the tau protein might not be the problem, but rather a symptom of the problem.

During hibernation, the levels of tau protein in a squirrel's hippocampal cells are directly correlated with the loss of synapses – but not with the appearance of lesions. On emerging from hibernation, the squirrel eliminates the tau protein from its brain. This has led Dr Arendt to suggest that rather than being a part of a disease process, the formation of the tau protein could be a mechanism by which the brain protects itself. He argues that the brain is armed with mechanisms for clearing the tau protein and that the reason it doesn't in people with Alzheimer's disease is because the protein is protecting the neurons.

His stance is contentious. 'As the field stands, viewing pathology as anything other than pathogenic is controversial. Saying it is protective is heretical,' says Mark Smith of Case Western Reserve University in Cleveland, Ohio. He has conducted studies on living neurons which suggest that the tau protein is produced in response to oxidative stress, thus lending support to the protective hypothesis.

Dr Arendt's group is now engaged in discovering exactly how the tau protein can be cleared from the brain. Help for Alzheimer's patients remains uncertain and a very long way off, but spring seems to have come a bit closer.

The Economist (4 February 2000)

ANTONIO DAMASIO, 'The Hidden Gifts of Memory' (updated in 2006 from *The Feeling of What Happens*, 2000)

One of the gifts memory bestows on the human mind is related to an apparent paradox identified by William James in his discussions of consciousness. Here is the paradox: the self in our stream of consciousness appears to change continuously as it moves forward in time; at the same time, we retain a sense that the self remains the same throughout our existence. The solution of the paradox comes from the fact that the seemingly changing self and the seemingly permanent self, although closely related, are not one entity with two irreconcilable aspects but rather two entities. The ever-changing self identified by James is the core self, the sense that is born out of the process of core consciousness. It is not so much that the core self mutates but rather that its existence is transient, ephemeral, that it needs to be remade and reborn continuously. The self that appears to remain the same is the autobiographical self, the sense that is born out of the process of extended consciousness. The autobiographical self appears intransient because it is based on a repository of memories for stable facts in an individual biography. Those facts can be reliably reactivated and thus provide continuity and seeming permanence in our lives.

This arrangement requires the availability of memory. Core consciousness provides us with a core self, but we also need conventional memory to construct an autobiographical self, and we need both core consciousness and working memory to make the auto-biographical self explicit, that is, to display the contents of the autobiographical self in extended consciousness. Creatures with limited memory do not face James's paradox. They inhabit a world one step up from innocence. They probably have the seemingly continuous experience of moments of conscious individuality, but they are neither burdened nor enriched by the memories of a personal past, let alone by memories of an anticipated future.

In my proposal, core consciousness is a central resource produced by a circumscribed mental and neural system. The fact that core consciousness is central does not mean that it depends on one structure. Indeed, a large number of neural structures is necessary for core consciousness to occur. But the complexity of the system, the multiplicity of its components, and the required concertedness of its operation should not make us overlook the following fact: when we consider the anatomical scale of the whole brain, the basic system underlying core consciousness is relatively confined to one set of anatomical sites rather than being widespread throughout the brain. In brief, there are plenty of brain sites not concerned with the making of core consciousness.

The robustness of core consciousness comes from this anatomical and functional centrality, and from the fact that *any content of mind*, whether actively processed in a live interaction or recalled from memory, can coax the core consciousness system into action, provoke it, so to speak, and in so doing generate a pulse of transient core consciousness. Core consciousness is not organised by sensory modality. In other words, there is no 'visual' core consciousness or 'auditory' core consciousness. Rather, core consciousness can be *used* by any sensory system and by the motor system to generate knowledge about any object or movement.

The contents of the autobiographical self are the organised, reactivated memories of fundamental facts from an individual's biography. They are the prime beneficiaries of core consciousness. Whenever an object X provokes a pulse of core consciousness and the core self emerges relative to object X, selected sets of facts from the implicit autobiographical self are also consistently activated as explicit memories and provoke pulses of core consciousness of their own.

At any given moment of our sentient lives, then, we generate pulses of core consciousness for one or a few target objects. But that is not all. We also generate pulses of core consciousness *for a set of accompanying, reactivated autobiographical memories.* Without such autobiographical memories we would have no sense of past or future, there would be no historical continuity to our persons. However, without the narrative of core consciousness, and without the transient core self that is born within it, we would have no knowledge whatsoever of the moment, or of the memorised past, or of the anticipated future plans that we also have committed to memory. Core consciousness is a foundational must. It takes precedence, evolutionarily and individually, over extended consciousness. And yet, without extended consciousness, core consciousness would not have the resonance of past and future. The interlocking of core and extended consciousnesses, of core and autobiographical selves, is complete.

To understand the neuroanatomical foundation of the autobiographical self that I envision we need to outline, however briefly, the theoretical framework with which mental images and brain structures can be brought together. The framework posits an *image space*, the space in which images of all sensory types explicitly occur in mind, and a *dispositional space*, a space filled with records of implicit knowledge on the basis of which images can be constructed in recall, movements can be generated, and the processing of images can be facilitated. Dispositions can hold the memory of an image perceived on some previous occasion and can help reconstruct a similar image from that memory; dispositions can also assist the processing of a currently perceived image – for instance, in terms of the degree of attention accorded to the image and the degree of its subsequent enhancement.

There is a brain counterpart for the image space and a brain counterpart for the dispositional space. Brain structures such as the so-called early cortices of the varied sensory modalities (e.g. vision, audition, touch) support neural patterns that are likely to be the basis for mental images. On the other hand, higher-order cortices and varied neural nuclei beneath the cortical level hold dispositions with which both images and actions can be generated, rather than holding or displaying the explicit patterns manifest in images or actions themselves.

I have proposed that dispositions are held in neuron ensembles which I call *convergence zones*. To the partition of cognition between an image space and a dispositional space, then, corresponds a partition of the brain into (1) neural-pattern maps, activated in the early sensory cortices, in the so-called limbic cortices, and in some subcortical nuclei, and (2) convergence zones, located in the higher-order cortices and in some subcortical nuclei.

The brain forms memories in a highly distributed manner. Take, for instance, the memory of a hammer. There is no single place in our brain where you can hold *the* record for hammer, no single place where you would find an entry with the word *hammer* followed by a neat dictionary definition of what a hammer is. Instead, as current evidence suggests, there are several records in our brain that correspond to different aspects of our past interaction with hammers. Those aspects include the shape of hammers, the typical movement with which we use them, the hand shape and the hand motion required to manipulate a hammer, the result of the action, and the word that designates hammer in whatever many languages we know. These records are dormant, dispositional, and implicit. Dormant, dispositional and implicit are key traits in the nature of memory storage. Memory records exist in dormant and implicit form until they are activated and become explicit; and memory records are dispositional in the sense that to become explicit a certain number of procedures or dispositions must be executed. Dispositional records of memory unfold, as it were. And all of the records related to the hammer of the example are based on separate neural sites located in separate brain regions. The separation is imposed by the design of the brain and by the physical nature of our environment. Appreciating the shape of a hammer visually is different from appreciating its shape by touch; the mental pattern corresponding to our manipulation of the hammer cannot be stored in the same brain region that 'stores' the pattern of its movement as we see it; the former is stored in somatosensory and motor regions, while the latter is stored in visual regions; the phonemes with which we make the word *hammer* cannot be stored in the same place, either, and are housed in auditory and somatomotor regions. The spatial separation of the records poses no problem, as it turns out, because when all the records are made explicit in image form they are exhibited in only a few brain sites and are co-ordinated in time in such a fashion that all the recorded components appear seamlessly integrated.

If I offer you the word *hammer* and ask you to tell me what 'hammer' means, you come up with a workable definition of the thing, without any difficulty, in no time at all. One basis for the definition is the rapid deployment of a number of explicit mental patterns concerning some of the varied aspects of hammer itemised above. Although the memory of separate aspects of our interaction with hammers is kept in separate parts of the brain, in dormant fashion, those different parts are co-ordinated in terms of their circuitries such that the dormant and implicit records can be turned into explicit albeit sketchy images, rapidly and in close temporal proximity. The availability of all those images allows us, in turn, to create a verbal description of the entity and that serves as a base for the definition.

I would like to suggest that the memories for the entities and events that constitute our present autobiography are likely to use the same sort of framework used for the memories we form about any entity or event. What makes those memories special is that they refer to established, invariant facts of our personal histories.

I propose that we store records of our personal experiences in the same distributed manner, in as varied brain regions as are needed to match the variety of our live interactions. Those records are closely co-ordinated by neural connections so that the contents of the records can be recalled and made explicit, as ensembles, rapidly and efficiently.

The critical elements of our autobiography that need to be reliably activated in a nearly permanent fashion are those that correspond to our identity, to our recent experiences, and to the experiences that we anticipate in the future. I propose that those critical elements arise from a continually reactivated network based on convergence zones which are located in the temporal and the frontal higher-order cortices, as well as in subcortical nuclei such as those in the amygdala. The co-ordinated activation of this multisite network is paced by thalamic nuclei, while the holding of the reiterated components for extended periods of time requires the support of prefrontal cortices involved in working memory. In brief, the autobiographical self is a process of co-ordinated activation and display of personal memories, based on a neural network with several sites. The images which represent those memories explicitly are generated and exhibited in several early sensory cortices. Finally, they are held over for as long as they are needed by the process of working memory. They are, in and of themselves, treated as any other objects. They become known to us because they can generate their own pulses of core consciousness.

Another hidden gift of memory opens the way for interpreting our own mental states and, no less importantly, the mental states of others. In the early 1990s I proposed that the brain not only represents, on-line, the states of our body that are associated with emotions and with general physiology but also has the possibility of *simulating* body states that are not actually happening. I outlined this hypothesis, the *as-if-body-loop mechanism* of feeling, at a time in which the evidence for its existence was merely circumstantial. Today the evidence for this curious brain device is abundant and we can begin to take stock of its functional significance and of its connection to autobiographical memory.

First, personal memories of past events have the power to reconstitute in the brain's body-sensing regions (such as the insular cortex) the configuration that our body assumed during a particular kind of emotion in the past. Never mind that the body will not be in that exact state at the moment; the body-sensing regions will behave 'as-if' it were, in a most convenient sleight of simulation. Thus memory helps us reconstitute integrated past experiences by commanding the manufacture of a simulated body state which signifies past feelings. This is a most effective device because it saves time and energy (it takes less time and less energy to concoct an 'as-if' body state than to replicate a real one in the body), and because it saves on storage space as well (provided we memorise the facts of an event we do not need to store records for the accompanying emotions and feelings; we just simulate them).

So far this is all very sensible and very much in keeping with the usual habits of brain evolution, i.e. save and make simple and make quick, whenever possible. What is less expected is the marvellous use to which the as-if-body-loop mechanism can be put. By connecting our body states, as sensed through the somatosensory system, to the visual and auditory counterparts of those body states, we have developed the possibility of connecting the *seen* or *heard* presentations of others to our *own felt body states*. We can achieve this because we can use the as-if-body-loop mechanism to simulate not just our states but also those of others. By means of those simulations we can connect those simulations with the memories which reveal their significance. In brief, we can place ourselves in someone else's shoes, feel what it is like, and discover the meaning of that feeling.

The effects of mirror neurons recently studied in non-human primates are grounded on this sort of arrangement, which combines body simulations and specific kinds of associated memory. So here are two gifts of memory to the human mind. They are less well known and heralded than the patently obvious ones. But in the end they are of no small importance to the construction of personhood.

From ERIC R. KANDEL, *In Search of Memory* (2007)

To be useful, a memory has to be recalled. Memory retrieval depends on the presence of appropriate cues that an animal can associate with its learning experiences. The cues can be external, such as a sensory stimulus in habituation, sensitization, and classical conditioning, or internal, sparked by an idea or an urge. In the *Aplysia* gill-withdrawal reflex, the cue for memory recall is external: namely, the touch to the siphon that elicits the reflex.* The neurons that retrieve the memory of the stimulus are the same sensory and motor neurons that were activated in the first place. But because the

* Kandel experimented on the giant sea-slug, *Aplysia*, and its reaction to repeated stimuli.

strength and number of synaptic connections between these neurons have been altered by learning, the action potential generated by the sensory stimulus to the siphon 'reads out' the new state of the synapse when it arrives at the presynaptic terminals and the recall gives rise to a more powerful response.

In long-term memory, as in short-term memory, the number of changed synaptic connections may be great enough to reconfigure a neural circuit, but this time anatomically. For example, prior to training, a stimulus to a sensory neuron in *Aplysia* might be strong enough to cause motor neurons leading to the gill to fire action potentials, but not strong enough to cause motor neurons leading to the ink gland to fire action potentials. Training strengthens not only the synapses between the sensory neuron and the motor neurons to the gill but also the synapses between the sensory neuron and the motor neurons to the ink gland. When the sensory neuron is stimulated after training, it retrieves the memory of the enhanced response, which causes both gill and ink motor neurons to fire action potentials and causes inking as well as gill withdrawal to take place. Thus, the form of *Aplysia*'s behavior is altered. The touch to the siphon elicits not just a change in the magnitude of the behavior – the amplitude of gill withdrawal – but also a change in the animal's behavioral repertory.

Our studies showing that the brain of *Aplysia* is physically changed by experience led us to wonder: does experience change the primate brain? Does it change the brains of people?

When I was a medical student in the 1950s, we were taught that the map of the somatosensory cortex discovered by Wade Marshall is fixed and immutable throughout life. We now know that idea is not correct. The map is subject to constant modification on the basis of experience. Two studies in the 1990s were particularly informative in this regard.

First, Michael Merzenich at the University of California, San Francisco discovered that the details of cortical maps vary considerably among individual monkeys. For example, some monkeys have a much more extensive representation of the hand than other monkeys. Merzenich's initial study did not separate the effects of experience from those of genetic endowment, so it was possible that the differences in representation were genetically determined.

Merzenich then carried out additional experiments to determine the relative contributions of genes and experience. He trained monkeys to obtain food pellets by touching a rotating disk with their three middle fingers. After several months, the area of the cortex devoted to the middle fingers – especially the tips of the fingers used for touching the disk – had expanded greatly. At the same time, the tactile sensitivity of the middle fingers increased. Other studies have shown that training in visual discrimination of color or form also leads to changes in brain anatomy and improved perceptual skills.

Second, Thomas Ebert and his colleagues at the University of Konstanz in Germany compared images of violinists' and cellists' brains with images of non-musicians' brains. Players of stringed instruments use the four fingers of the left hand to modulate the sound of the strings. The fingers of the right hand, which move the bow, are not involved in such highly differentiated movements. Ebert found that the area of the cortex devoted to the fingers of the right hand did not differ in string players and non-musicians, whereas representations of the fingers of the left hand were much more extensive – by as much as five times – in the brains of string players than in those of non-musicians. Furthermore, musicians who began playing the instrument before age thirteen had larger representations of the fingers of their left hand than musicians who began playing after that age.

These dramatic changes in cortical maps as a result of learning extended the anatomical insights that our studies in *Aplysia* had revealed: the extent to which a body part is represented in the cortex depends on the intensity and complexity of its use. In addition, as Ebert's study showed, such structural changes in the brain are more readily achieved in the early years of life. Thus, a great musician such as Wolfgang Amadeus Mozart is who he is not simply because he has the right genes (although genes help), but also because he began practising the skills for which he became famous at a time when his brain was more pliable.

Moreover, our results in *Aplysia* showed that the plasticity of the nervous system – the ability of nerve cells to change the strength and even the number of synapses – is the mechanism underlying learning and long-term memory. As a result, because each human being is brought up in a different environment and has different experiences, the architecture of each person's brain is unique. Even identical twins with identical genes have different brains because of their different life experiences. Thus, a principle of cell biology that first emerged from the study of a simple snail turned out to be a profound contributor to the biological basis of human individuality.

Our finding that short-term memory results from a functional change and long-term memory from an anatomical change raised even more questions: what is the nature of memory consolidation? Why does it require the synthesis of new protein? To find out, we would have to move into the cell and study its molecular makeup. My colleagues and I were ready for that step.

Memory and Imagination

From *Beowulf,* c.8th century, translated by Harriet Harvey Wood (2007)

Bid the warriors build a barrow after the bright funeral fire, on the promontory above the sea. It shall serve as a reminder to my people, as it towers high on Hronesnesse, so that in future the seafarers shall call it Beowulf's barrow as they urge their ships far over the dark waters.

From ROBERT HENRYSON, *The Testament of Cresseid* (*c*.1470)

Than upon him scho kest up baith hir Ene
And with ane blenk it come into his thocht,
That he sumtime hir face befoir had sene.
But scho was in sic plye he knew hir nocht,
Yit than hir luik into his mynd it brocht
The sweit visage and amorous blenking
Of fair Cresseid sumtyme his awin darling.

Na wonder was, suppois in mynd that he
Tuik hir visage sa sone, and lo now quhy?
The Idole of ane thing, in cace may be
Sa deip Imprentit in the fantasy
That it deludis the wittis outwardly,
And sa appeiris in forme and lyke estait,
Within the mynd as it was figurait.

Ane spark of lufe than till his hart culd spring
And kendlit all his bodie in ane fyre.
With hait Fewir ane sweit and trimbling

Him tuik, quhill he was reddie to expyre.
To beir his Scheild, his Breist began to tyre
Within ane quhyle he changit mony hew,
And nevertheless not ane ane uther knew.

Scho, she; *kest*, cast; *ene*, eyes; *blenk*, blink; *thocht*, mind; *plye*, plight; *luik*, face; *brocht*, brought; *blenking*, expression; *sumtyme*, once; *tuik*, noticed; *visage*, face; *quhy*, why; *Idole*, image; *in cace*, sometimes; *fantasy*, imagination; *wittis*, brain; *sa*, so; *figurait*, imagined; *than*, then; *till*, to; *culd*, did; *kendlit*, kindled; *hait Fewir*, hot fever; *sweit*, sweat; *him tuik*, seized him; *quhill*, till; *quhyle*, instant; *mony*, many; *hew*, colour; *ane*, one; *ane uther*, each other.

VOLTAIRE (FRANÇOIS-MARIE AROUET), 'The Adventure of Memory', in *Romans et Contes* (1773), translated by Harriet Harvey Wood (2004)

The thinking part of the human race, which is to say about the hundred thousandth part of it, had believed for a long time, or at least had often said it did, that we had no ideas except those which came to us through our senses, and that memory was the only instrument by means of which we could join two ideas and two words together.

This is why Jupiter, representing Nature, was in love with Mnemosyne, goddess of memory, from the first moment he saw her; and of their marriage were born the nine Muses, who invented all the arts.

This belief, on which all our knowledge is founded, was universally accepted, and even the Sorbonne embraced it from the moment of its conception, even although it was true.

Some time later there came a theorist[1], half a geometrician and half a dreamer, who argued against the five senses and against memory; and he said to the tiny number of thinking human beings: 'You have been mistaken up to now; your senses are useless to you, since your ideas were innate in you long before any of your senses could act, and you had all the basic knowledge you needed when you came into the world; you knew everything without ever

---

[1] René Descartes.

having perceived anything through your senses; all your ideas, which were born with you, were present to your intelligence, which is called your soul, without the help of memory. Memory is no use for anything.'

The Sorbonne condemned this proposition, not because it was absurd, but because it was new: however, when later an Englishman[2] started to prove at some length that there were no innate ideas, that nothing was more essential than the five senses, and that memory was extremely useful in remembering what was received through the five senses, it denounced its own former opinions because they had become those of an Englishman. Consequently it ordered the human race to believe henceforward in innate ideas, and to dismiss belief in the five senses and memory. The human race laughed at the Sorbonne instead of obeying, which put it into such a fury that it wanted to burn a philosopher: for this philosopher had said that it is impossible to have any complete conception of a cheese without having seen and tasted one; and the scoundrel had even dared to advance the idea that men and women would never have been able to work a tapestry if they had not had needles and fingers to thread them with.

The Jesuits joined with the Sorbonne for the first time ever, and the Jansenists, mortal foes of the Jesuits, joined with them temporarily; they summoned to their aid the old ministers who were eminent philosophers; and all of them, before they died, proscribed memory and the five senses, and the author who had spoken well of these six things.

There was a horse who happened to be present when this judgement was pronounced by these gentlemen, although he was not of the same species, and although between him and them there were various differences in matters such as the tail, the voice, the hair and ears; this horse, I say, which had sense as well as senses, spoke of the matter one day to Pegasus in my stable; and Pegasus went with his customary energy to retail the story to the Muses.

The Muses who for the past hundred years had shown particular favour to the country where these events took place, which before that had for a long time been barbaric, were deeply shocked; they were tenderly attached to Memory or Mnemosyne, their mother, to whom all of these nine daughters owe everything they know.

---

[2] John Locke.

The ingratitude of the human race annoyed them. They did not satirise the old ministers, the Jesuits, the Jansenists and the Sorbonne, because satires do no good to anyone, they irritate fools and make them behave more badly than ever. They devised a method of educating them by punishing them. Men had blasphemed against Memory: the Muses took from them this divine gift so that they might learn once and for all what life would be like without its assistance.

Thus it happened that in the middle of the night every brain was dulled, so that the following morning everyone woke without the slightest recollection of the past. Some of the ministers who were in bed with their wives desired, by a remnant of instinct unconnected with memory, to make love to them; the wives, who very rarely had any instinct to embrace their husbands, tartly repulsed their disgusting caresses. The husbands were furious, the wives wept and most households came to blows.

Gentlemen, finding a square hat, made use of it for certain needs which neither memory nor good sense could relieve. The ladies employed their cosmetic pots for the same purpose; the servants, oblivious of the contract which they had made with their employers, invaded their rooms without realising where they were; but, since man is born inquisitive, they opened all the drawers; and, since man instinctively and without the need of memory loves the sparkle of money and gold, they helped themselves to whatever they found to hand. The masters would have liked to shout 'Robber!'; but since the idea of a robber had deserted their brains, they could not think of the word. Everyone, having forgotten his own language, spoke gibberish. It was far worse than Babel where everyone had instantly invented a new language. The innate instincts of the young jackanapes for pretty women operated so powerfully that these insolent fellows threw themselves carelessly on the first women or girls they came across, whether they were bar-maids or the President's lady; and they, oblivious now of the dictates of modesty, let them have their way freely.

It was time for dinner; but no one knew any longer what they should do about it. No one had been to the market, either to buy or to sell. The servants had adopted the habits of the masters, and the masters those of the servants. Everyone stared around as if they had been stunned. Those who were a little better at getting what they needed (and in general these were the common people) found themselves something to live on; the others went without. The first president and the archbishop went naked, and their grooms were dressed, some in red robes, others in dalmatics: everything was upside down, everyone was perishing from hunger and misery for lack of being able to understand each other.

After several days, the Muses took pity on these poor people: they are good-natured, even if sometimes they become angry with evil-doers, therefore they begged their mother to give the blasphemers back their memory which she had taken from them. Mnemosyne descended to the habitation of the vexatious people who had insulted her with such foolhardiness, and spoke these words to them:

'Imbeciles, I forgive you; but remember that without the senses there is no memory, and without the memory there is no intelligence.'

The ministers thanked her rather coldly and decided to address remonstrances to her. The Jansenists put the whole adventure into their gazette; it was clear that they had not yet entirely recovered. The Jesuits made a court intrigue out of it. Maître Cogé, completely flabbergasted by the whole episode and understanding nothing about it, gave his fifth-year scholars this useful axiom: *Non magis musis quam hominibus infensa est ista quae vocatur memoria* ('no more dangerous to Muses than to men is that which men call memory').

From WILLIAM WORDSWORTH, *The Prelude* (1805)

There are in our existence spots of time,
Which with distinct pre-eminence retain
A vivifying Virtue, whence, depress'd
By false opinion and contentious thought,
Or aught of heavier or more deadly weight,
In trivial occupations, and the round
Of ordinary intercourse, our minds
Are nourished and invisibly repair'd,
A virtue by which pleasure is enhanced

That penetrates, enables us to mount
When high, more high, and lifts us up when fallen.
This efficacious spirit chiefly lurks
Among those passages of life in which
We have had deepest feeling that the mind
Is lord and master, and that outward sense
Is but the obedient servant of her will.
Such moments worthy of all gratitude,
Are scatter'd everywhere, taking their date
From our first childhood: in our childhood even
Perhaps are most conspicuous. Life with me,
As far as memory can look back, is full
Of this beneficent influence. At a time
When scarcely (I was then not six years old)
My hand could hold a bridle, with proud hopes
I mounted, and we rode towards the hills:
We were a pair of horsemen; honest James
Was with me, my encourager and guide.
We had not travell'd long, ere some mischance
Disjoin'd me from my Comrade, and, through fear
Dismounting, down the rough and stony Moor
I led my Horse, and stumbling on, at length
Came to a bottom, where in former times
A Murderer had been hung in iron chains.
The Gibbet-mast was moulder'd down, the bones
And iron case were gone; but on the turf,
Hard by, soon after that fell deed was wrought
Some unknown hand had carved the Murderer's name.
The monumental writing was engraven
In times long past, and still, from year to year,
By superstition of the neighbourhood,
The grass is clear'd away; and to this hour
The letters are all fresh and visible.
Faltering, and ignorant where I was, at length
I chanced to espy those characters inscribed
On the green sod: forthwith I left the spot
And, reascending the bare Common, saw
A naked Pool that lay beneath the hills,
The Beacon on the summit, and more near,
A Girl who bore a Pitcher on her head

And seem'd with difficult steps to force her way
Against the blowing wind. It was, in truth,
An ordinary sight; but I should need
Colours and words that are unknown to man
To paint the visionary dreariness
Which, while I look'd all round for my lost guide,
Did at that time invest the naked Pool,
The Beacon on the lonely Eminence,
The Woman, and her garments vex'd and toss'd
By the strong wind. When, in a blessed season
With those two dear Ones, to my heart so dear,
When in the blessed time of early love,
Long afterwards, I roam'd about
In daily presence of this very scene,
Upon the naked pool and dreary crags,
And on the melancholy Beacon, fell
The spirit of pleasure and youth's golden gleam;
And think ye not with radiance more divine
From these remembrances, and from the power
They left behind? So feeling comes in aid
Of feeling, and diversity of strength
Attends us, if but once we have been strong.
Oh! mystery of Man, from what a depth
Proceed thy honours! I am lost, but see
In simple childhood something of the base
On which thy greatness stands, but this I feel,
That from thyself it is that thou must give,
Else never canst receive. The days gone by
Come back upon me from the dawn almost
Of life: the hiding-places of my power
Seem open; I approach, and then they close;
I see by glimpses now; when age comes on,
May scarcely see at all, and I would give,
While yet we may, as far as words can give,
A substance and a life to what I feel:
I would enshrine the spirit of the past
For future restoration.

From SIR WALTER SCOTT, *Guy Mannering* (1815)

Why is it, he thought, continuing to follow out the succession of ideas which the scene prompted – Why is it that some scenes awaken thoughts, which belong as it were to dreams of early and shadowy recollection, such as my old Bramin Moonshie would have ascribed to a state of previous existence? Is it the visions of our sleep that float confusedly in our memory, and are recalled by the appearance of such real objects as in any respect correspond to the phantoms they presented to our imagination? How often do we find ourselves in society which we have never before met, and yet feel impressed with a mysterious and ill-defined consciousness, that neither the scene, the speakers, nor the subject are entirely new; nay, feel as if we could anticipate that part of the conversation which has not yet taken place! It is even so with me while I gaze upon that ruin; nor can I divest myself of the idea, that these massive towers, and that dark gate-way retiring through its deep-vaulted and ribbed arches, and dimly lighted by the court-yard beyond, are not entirely strange to me. Can it be that they have been familiar to me in infancy, and that I am to seek in their vicinity those friends of whom my childhood has still a tender though faint remembrance, and whom I early exchanged for such severe task-masters? Yet Brown, who I think would not have deceived me, always told me I was brought off from the eastern coast, after a skirmish in which my father was killed; and I do remember enough of a horrid scene of violence to strengthen his account. –

From JOHN KEATS, *The Fall of Hyperion* (1819)

　　　　　. . . Then saw I a wan face,
Not pin'd by human sorrows, but bright blanch'd
By an immortal sickness which kills not;
It works a constant change, which happy death
Can put no end to; deathwards progressing

To no death was that visage; it had pass'd
The lily and the snow; and beyond these
I must not think now, though I saw that face—
But for her eyes I should have fled away.
They held me back, with a benignant light
Soft mitigated by divinest lids
Half closed, and visionless entire they seem'd
Of all external things; they saw me not,
But in blank splendour beam'd like the mild moon,
Who comforts those she sees not, who knows not
What eyes are upward cast. As I had found
A grain of gold upon a mountain side,
And twing'd with avarice strain'd out my eyes
To search its sullen entrails rich with ore,
So at the view of sad Moneta's brow
I ach'd to see what things the hollow brain
Behind enwombed: what high tragedy
In the dark secret chambers of her skull
Was acting, that could give so dread a stress
To her cold lips, and fill with such a light
Her planetary eyes, and touch her voice
With such a sorrow—'Shade of Memory!'
Cried I, with act adorant at her feet,
'By all the gloom hung round thy fallen house,
'By this last temple, by the golden age,
'By great Apollo, thy dear Foster Child,
'And by thyself, forlorn divinity,
'The pale Omega of a withered race,
'Let me behold, according as thou saidst,
'What in thy brain so ferments to and fro!'
No sooner had this conjuration pass'd
My devout lips, than side by side we stood
(Like a stunt bramble by a solemn pine)
Deep in the shady sadness of a vale,
Far sunken from the healthy breath of morn,
Far from the fiery noon and eve's one star.
Onward I look'd beneath the gloomy boughs,
And saw, what first I thought an image huge,
Like to the image pedestal'd so high
In Saturn's temple. Then Moneta's voice

Came brief upon mine ear—'So Saturn sat
When he had lost his Realms'—whereon there grew
A power within me of enormous ken
To see as a god sees, and take the depth
Of things as nimbly as the outward eye
Can size and shape pervade. The lofty theme
At those few words hung vast before my mind,
With half unravel'd web. I set myself
Upon an eagle's watch, that I might see,
And seeing ne'er forget. No stir of life
Was in this shrouded vale, not so much air
As in the zoning of a summer's day
Robs not one light seed from the feather'd grass,
But where the dead leaf fell there did it rest.
A stream went voiceless by, still deaden'd more
By reason of the fallen divinity
Spreading more shade; the Naiad 'mid her reeds
Press'd her cold finger closer to her lips.

From THOMAS DE QUINCEY, 'Suspiria de Profundis' (1845)

And, recollecting it, often I have been struck with the important truth – that far more of our deepest thoughts and feelings pass to us through perplexed combinations of *concrete* objects, pass to us as *involutes* (if I may coin that word) in compound experiences incapable of being disentangled, than ever reach us *directly*, and in their own abstract shapes. It had happened that amongst our nursery collection of books was the Bible illustrated with many pictures. And in long dark evenings, as my three sisters with myself sate by the firelight round the *guard* of our nursery, no book was so much in request amongst us. It ruled us and swayed us as mysteriously as music. One young nurse, whom we all loved, before any candle was lighted, would often strain her eyes to read it for us; and sometimes, according to her simple powers, would endeavour to explain what we found obscure. We, the children, were all constitutionally touched with pensiveness; the fitful gloom and sudden lambencies of the room by fire-light, suited our evening state of feelings; and they suited also the divine revelations of power and mysterious beauty which awed us. Above all, the story of a just man, – man and yet *not* man, real above all things and yet shadowy above all things, who had suffered the passion of death in Palestine, slept upon our minds like early dawn upon the waters. The nurse knew and explained to us the chief differences in Oriental climates; and all these differences (as it happens) express themselves in the great varieties of summer. The cloudless sunlights of Syria – those seemed to argue everlasting summer; the disciples plucking the ears of corn – that *must* be summer; but, above all, the very name of Palm Sunday, (a festival in the English church,) troubled me like an anthem. 'Sunday!' what was *that*? That was the day of peace which masqued another peace deeper than the heart of man can comprehend. 'Palms!' – what were they? *That* was an equivocal word: palms, in the sense of trophies, expressed the pomps of life: palms, as a product of nature, expressed the pomps of summer. Yet still even this explanation does not suffice: it was not merely by the peace and by the summer, by the deep sound of rest below all rest, and of ascending glory, – that I had been haunted. It was also because Jerusalem stood near to these deep images both in time and in place. The great event of Jerusalem was at hand when Palm Sunday came; and the scene of that Sunday was near in place to Jerusalem. Yet what then was Jerusalem? Did I fancy it to be the *omphalos* (navel) of the earth? That pretension had once been made for Jerusalem, and once for Delphi; and both pretensions had become ridiculous, as the figure of the planet became known. Yes; but if not of the earth, for earth's tenant Jerusalem was the *omphalos* of mortality. Yet how? there on the contrary it was, as we infants understood, that mortality had been trampled under foot. True; but for that very reason there it was that mortality had opened its very gloomiest crater. There it was indeed that the human had risen on wings from the grave; but for that reason there also it was that the divine had been swallowed up by the abyss: the lesser star could not rise, before the greater would submit to eclipse. Summer, therefore, had connected itself with death not merely as a mode of antagonism, but also through intricate relations to Scriptural scenery and events . . .

What else than a natural and mighty palimpsest is the human brain? Such a palimpsest is my brain; such a palimpsest, O reader! is yours. Everlasting layers of ideas, images, feelings, have fallen upon your brain softly as light. Each succession has seemed to bury all that went before. And yet in reality not one has been extinguished. And if, in the vellum palimpsest, lying amongst the other *diplomata* of human archives or libraries, there is any thing fantastic or which moves to laughter, as oftentimes there is in the grotesque collisions of those successive themes, having no natural connexion, which by pure accident have consecutively occupied the roll, yet, in our own heaven-created palimpsest, the deep memorial palimpsest of the brain, there are not and cannot be such incoherencies. The fleeting accidents of a man's life, and its external shows, may indeed be irrelate and incongruous; but the organising principles which fuse into harmony, and gather about fixed predetermined centres, whatever heterogeneous elements life may have accumulated from without, will not permit the grandeur of human unity greatly to be violated, or its ultimate repose to be troubled in the retrospect from dying moments, or from other great convulsions.

From ALFRED, LORD TENNYSON, *In Memoriam, XLV* (1850)

The baby new to earth and sky,
   What time his tender palm is prest
   Against the circle of the breast
Has never thought that 'this is I:'

But as he grows he gathers much,
   And learns the use of 'I', and 'me',
   And finds 'I am not what I see,
And other than the things I touch.'

So rounds he to a separate mind
   From whence clear memory may begin,
   As thro' the frame that binds him in
His isolation grows defined.

This use may lie in blood and breath,
   Which else were fruitless of their due,
   Had man to learn himself anew
Beyond the second birth of Death.

ROBERT BROWNING, 'Memorabilia' (1855)

I

Ah, did you once see Shelley plain,
   And did he stop and speak to you,
And did you speak to him again?
   How strange it seems, and new!

II

But you were living before that,
   And also you are living after;
And the memory I started at –
   My starting moves your laughter!

III

I crossed a moor with a name of its own
   And a certain use in the world no doubt,
Yet a hand's-breadth of it shines alone
   'Mid the blank miles round about:

IV

For there I picked up on the heather
   And there I put inside my breast
A moulted feather, an eagle-feather!
   Well, I forget the rest.

From LEWIS CARROLL, *Through the Looking-Glass* (1871)

Alice . . . did her best to get the hair into order. 'Come, you look rather better now!' she said, after altering most of the pins. 'But really you should have a lady's-maid!'

'I'm sure I'll take you with pleasure!' the [White] Queen said. 'Twopence a week, and jam every other day.'

Alice couldn't help laughing, as she said, 'I don't want you to hire *me* – and I don't care for jam.'

'It's very good jam,' said the Queen.

'Well, I don't want any *to-day*, at any rate.'

'You couldn't have it if you *did* want it,' the Queen said. 'The rule is, jam to-morrow and jam yesterday – but never jam to-day.'

'It *must* come sometimes to "jam to-day",' Alice objected.

'No it can't,' said the Queen. 'It's jam every *other* day: to-day isn't any *other* day, you know.'

'I don't understand you,' said Alice. 'It's dreadfully confusing!'

'That's the effect of living backwards,' the Queen said kindly: 'it always makes one a little giddy at first –'

'Living backwards!' Alice repeated in great astonishment. 'I never heard of such a thing!'

'– but there's one great advantage in it, that one's memory works both ways.'

'I'm sure *mine* only works one way', Alice remarked. 'I can't remember things before they happen.'

'It's a poor sort of memory that only works backwards,' the Queen remarked.

From GEORGE ELIOT, *Middlemarch* (1871)

The ride to Stone Court, which Fred and Rosamond took the next morning, lay through a pretty bit of midland landscape, almost all meadows and pastures, with hedgerows still allowed to grow in bushy beauty and to spread out coral fruit for the birds. Little details gave each field a particular physiognomy, dear to the eyes that have looked on them from childhood: the pool in the corner where the grasses were dank and trees leaned whisperingly; the great oak shadowing a bare place in mid-pasture; the high bank where the ash-trees grew; the sudden slope of the old marl-pit making a red background for the burdock; the huddled roofs and ricks of the homestead without a traceable way of approach; the gray gate and fences against the depths of the bordering wood; and the stray hovel, its old, old thatch full of mossy hills and valleys with wondrous modulations of light and shadow such as we travel far to see in later life, and see larger, but not more beautiful. These are the things that make the gamut of joy in landscape to midland-bred souls – the things they toddled among, or perhaps learned by heart standing between their father's knees while he drove leisurely.

Daniel Deronda (1876)

Pity that Offendene was not the home of Miss Harleth's childhood, or endeared to her by family memories! A human life, I think, should be well rooted in some spot of a native land, where it may get the love of tender kinship for the face of earth, for the labours men go forth to, for the sounds and accents that haunt it, for whatever will give that early home a familiar unmistakable difference amidst the future widening of knowledge: a spot where the definiteness of early memories may be inwrought with affection, and kindly acquaintance with all neighbours, even to the dogs and donkeys, may spread not by sentimental effort and reflection, but as a sweet habit of the blood. At five years old, mortals are not prepared to be citizens of the world, to be stimulated by abstract nouns, to soar above preference into impartiality; and that prejudice in favour of milk with which we blindly begin, is a type of the way body and soul must get nourished at least for a time. The best introduction to astronomy is to think of the nightly heavens as a little lot of stars belonging to one's own homestead.

But this blessed persistence in which affection can take root had been wanting in Gwendolen's life.

From HENRY JAMES, *The Art of the Novel* (1884)

Who shall say thus – and I have put the vain question but too often before! – where the associational nimbus of the all but lost, of the miraculously recovered, chapter of experience shall absolutely fade and stop? That would be possible only were experience a chessboard of sharp black-and-white squares. Taking one of these for a convenient plot, I have but to see my particle of suggestion lurk in its breast, and then but to repeat in this connexion the act of picking it up, for the whole of the *rest* of the connexion to loom into life, its parts all clinging together and pleading with a collective friendly voice that I can't pretend to resist: 'Oh but we too, you know; what were *we* but of the experience?' Which comes to scarce more than saying indeed, no doubt, that nothing more complicates and overloads the act of retrospect than to let one's imagination itself work backward as part of the business. Some art of preventing this by keeping that interference out would be here of a useful application; and would include the question of providing conveniently for the officious faculty in the absence of its natural caretakers, the judgment, the memory, the conscience, occupied, as it were elsewhere. These truants, the other faculties of the mind without exception, I surmise, would then be free to remount the stream of time (as an earnest and enquiring band) with the flower of the flock, the hope of the family, left at home or 'boarded out,' say, for the time of the excursion. I have been unable, I confess, to make such an arrangement; the consequence of which failure is that everything I 'find,' as I look back, lives for me again in the light of *all* the parts, such as they are, of my intelligence. Or to express the phenomenon otherwise, and perhaps with still more complacency for it, the effort to reconstitute the medium and the season that favoured the first stir of life, the first perceived gleam of the vital spark, in the trifle before us, fairly makes everything in the picture revive, fairly even extends the influence to matters remote and strange. The musing artist's imagination – thus *not* excluded and confined – supplies the link that is missing and makes the whole occasion (the occasion of the glorious birth to him of still another infant motive) comprehensively and richly *one*.

From WILLIAM JAMES, *The Principles of Psychology* (1890)

Briefly, then, of two men with the same outward experiences and the same amount of mere native tenacity, *the one who* THINKS *over his experiences most*, and weaves them into systematic relations with each other, *will be the one with the best memory*. We see examples of this on every hand. Most men have a good memory for facts connected with their own pursuits. The college athlete who remains a dunce at his books will astonish you by his knowledge of men's 'records' in various feats and games, and will be a walking dictionary of sporting statistics. The reason is that he is constantly going over these things in his mind, and comparing and making series of them. They form for him not so many odd facts, but a concept-system – so they stick. So the merchant remembers prices, the politician other politicians' speeches and votes, with a copiousness which amazes outsiders, but which the amount of thinking they bestow on these subjects easily explains. The great memory for facts which a Darwin and a Spencer reveal in their books is not incompatible with the possession on their part of a brain with only a middling degree of physiological retentiveness. Let a man early in life set himself the task of verifying such a theory as that of evolution, and facts will soon cluster and cling to him like grapes to their stem. Their relations to the theory will hold them fast; and the more of these the mind is able to discern, the greater the erudition will become. Meanwhile the theorist may have little, if any, desultory memory. Unutilizable facts may be unnoted by him and forgotten as soon as heard. An ignorance almost as encyclopædic as his erudition may coexist with the latter, and hide, as it were, in the interstices of its web. Those who have had much to do with scholars and *savants* will readily think of examples of the class of mind I mean.

In a system, every fact is connected with every other by some thought-relation. The consequence is that every fact is retained by the combined suggestive power of all the other facts in the system, and forgetfulness is well-nigh impossible.

The reason why *cramming* is such a bad mode of study is now made clear. I mean by cramming that way of preparing for examinations by committing 'points' to memory during a few hours or days of intense application immediately preceding the final ordeal, little or no work having been performed during the previous course of the term. Things learned thus in a few hours, on one occasion, for one purpose, cannot possibly have formed many associations with other things in the mind. Their brain-processes are led into by few paths, and are relatively little liable to be awakened again. Speedy oblivion is the almost inevitable fate of all that is committed to memory in this simple way. Whereas, on the contrary, the same materials taken in gradually, day after day, recurring in different contexts, considered in various relations, associated with other external incidents, and repeatedly reflected on, grow into such a system, form such connections with the rest of the mind's fabric, lie open to so many paths of approach, that they remain permanent possessions. This is the *intellectual* reason why habits of continuous application should be enforced in educational establishments. Of course there is no moral turpitude in cramming. If it led to the desired end of secure learning it would be infinitely the best method of study. But it does not; and students themselves should understand the reason why.

It will now appear clear that *all improvement of the memory lies in the line of* ELABORATING THE ASSOCIATES *of each of the several things to be remembered. No amount of culture would seem capable of modifying a man's* GENERAL *retentiveness*. This is a physiological quality, given once for all with his organization, and which he can never hope to change. It differs no doubt in disease and health; and it is a fact of observation that it is better in fresh and vigorous hours than when we are fagged or ill. We may say, then, that a man's native tenacity will fluctuate somewhat with his hygiene, and that whatever is good for his tone of health will also be good for his memory. We may even say that whatever amount of intellectual exercise is bracing to the general tone and nutrition of the brain will also be profitable to the general retentiveness. But more than this we cannot say: and this, it is obvious, is far less than most people believe.

It is, in fact, commonly thought that certain exercises systematically repeated, will strengthen, not only a man's remembrance of the particular facts used in the exercises, but his faculty for remembering facts at large. And a plausible case is always made out by saying that practice in learning words by heart makes it easier to learn new words in the same way. If this be true, then what I have just said is false, and the whole doctrine of memory as due to 'paths' must be revised. But I am disposed to think the alleged fact untrue. I have carefully questioned several mature actors on the point, and all have denied that the practice of learning parts has made any such difference as is alleged. What it has done for them is to improve their power of *studying* a part systematically. Their mind is now full of precedents in the way of intonation, emphasis, gesticulation; the new words awaken distinct suggestions and decisions; are caught up, in fact, into a pre-existing net-work, like the merchant's prices, or the athlete's store of 'records,' and are recollected easier, although the mere native tenacity is not a whit improved, and is usually, in fact, impaired by age. It is a case of better remembering by better *thinking*. Similarly when school-boys improve by practice in ease of learning by heart, the improvement will, I am sure, be always found to reside in the *mode of study of the particular piece* (due to the greater interest, the greater suggestiveness, the generic similarity with other pieces, the more sustained attention, etc., etc.), and not at all to any enhancement of the brute retentive power.

From SIGMUND FREUD, 'Screen Memories' (1899)

We are so much accustomed to this lack of memory of the impressions of childhood that we are apt to overlook the problem underlying it and are inclined to explain it as a self-evident consequence of the rudimentary character of the mental activities of children. Actually, however, a normally developed child of three or four already exhibits an enormous amount of highly organised mental functioning in the comparisons and inferences which he makes and in the expression of his feelings; and there is no obvious reason why amnesia should overtake these psychical acts, which carry no less weight than those of a later age.

. . . I have no intention at present of discussing the subject as a whole, and I shall therefore content myself with emphasising the few points which will enable me to introduce the notion of what I have termed 'screen memories'.

The age to which the content of the earliest memories of child-hood is usually referred back is the period between the ages of two and four . . . There are some, however, whose memory reaches back further – even to the time before the completion of their first year; and, on the other hand, there are some whose earliest recollections go back only to their sixth, seventh, or even eighth year . . .

Quite special interest attaches to the question of what is the usual *content* of these earliest memories of childhood. The psychology of adults would necessarily lead us to expect that those experiences would be selected as worth remembering which had aroused some powerful emotion or which, owing to their conse-quences, had been recognised as important soon after their occur-rence. And some indeed of the observations collected by the Henris appear to fulfil this expectation. They report that the most frequent content of the first memories of childhood are on the one hand occasions of fear, shame, physical pain, etc., and on the other hand important events such as illnesses, deaths, fires, births of brothers and sisters, etc. We might therefore be inclined to assume that the principle governing the choice of memories is the same in the case of children as in that of adults. It is intelligible – though the fact deserves to be explicitly mentioned – that the memories retained from childhood should necessarily show evidence of the difference between what attracts the interest of a child and of an adult . . .

Further investigation of these indifferent childhood memories has taught me that they can originate in other ways as well and that an unsuspected wealth of meaning lies concealed behind their apparent innocence. But on this point I shall not content myself with a mere assertion but shall give a detailed report of one partic-ular instance which seems to me the most instructive out of a considerable number of similar ones. Its value is certainly increased by the fact that it relates to someone who is not at all or only very slightly neurotic.

The subject of this observation is a man of university education, aged thirty-eight. Though his own profession lies in a very different field, he has taken an interest in psychological questions ever since I was able to relieve him of a slight phobia by means of psycho-analysis. Last year he drew my attention to his childhood memo-ries, which had already played some part in his analysis. After studying the investigation made by V. and C. Henri, he gave me the following summarised account of his own experience.

'I have at my disposal a fair number of early memories of child-hood which I can date with great certainty. For at the age of three I left the small place where I was born and moved to a large town; and all these memories of mine relate to my birthplace and there-fore date from my second and third years. They are mostly short scenes, but they are very well preserved and furnished with every detail of sense-perception, in complete contrast to my memories of adult years, which are certainly lacking in the visual element. From my third year onwards my recollections grow scantier and less clear; there are gaps in them which must cover more than a year; and it is not, I believe, until my sixth or seventh year that the stream of my memories becomes continuous. My memories up to the time of my leaving my first place of residence fall into three groups. The first group consists of scenes which my parents have repeatedly since described to me. As regards these, I feel uncertain whether I have had the mnemic image from the beginning or whether I only construed it after hearing one of these descriptions. I may remark, however, that there are also events of which I have no mnemic image in spite of them having been frequently retailed by my parents. I attach more importance to the second group. It comprises scenes which have not (so far as I know) been described to me, as I have not met the other participants in them (my nurse and playmates) since their occurrence. I shall come to the third group presently. As regards the contents of these scenes and their consequent claim to being recollected, I should like to say that I am not entirely at sea. I cannot maintain, indeed, that what I have retained are memo-ries of the most important events of the period, or what I should to-day judge to be the most important. I have no knowledge of the birth of a sister, who is two and a half years younger than I am; my departure, my first sight of the railway and the long carriage-drive before it – none of these has left a trace in my memory. On the other hand, I can remember two small occurrences during the railway-journey; these, as you will recollect, came up in the analysis of my phobia. But what should have made most impression on me was an injury to my face which caused a considerable loss of blood and for which I had to have some stitches put in by a surgeon. I can still feel the scar resulting from this accident, but I know of no recollection which points to it, either directly or indirectly. It is true that I may perhaps have been under two years old at the time.

'It follows from this that I feel no surprise at the pictures and scenes of these first two groups. No doubt they are displaced memories from which the essential element has for the most part been omitted. But in a few of them it is at least hinted at, and in others it is easy for me to complete them by following certain pointers. By doing so I can establish a sound connection between the separate fragments of memories and arrive at a clear understanding of what the childish interest was that recommended these particular occurrences to my memory. This does not apply, however, to the content of the third group, which I have not so far discussed. There I am met by material – one rather long scene and several smaller pictures – with which I can make no headway at all. The scene appears to me fairly indifferent and I cannot understand why it should have become fixed in my memory. Let me describe it to you. I see a rectangular, rather steeply sloping piece of meadowland, green and thickly grown; in the green there are a great number of yellow flowers – evidently common dandelions. At the top end of the meadow there is a cottage and in front of the cottage door two women are standing chatting busily, a peasant-woman with a handkerchief on her head and a children's nurse. Three children are playing in the grass. One of them is myself (between the ages of two and three); the other two are my boy cousin, who is a year older than me, and his sister, who is almost exactly the same age as I am. We are picking the yellow flowers and each of us is holding a bunch of flowers we have already picked. The little girl has the best bunch; and, as though by mutual agreement, we – the two boys – fall on her and snatch away her flowers. She runs up the meadow in tears and as a consolation the peasant-woman gives her a big piece of black bread. Hardly have we seen this than we throw the flowers away, hurry to the cottage and ask to be given some bread too. And we are in fact given some; the peasant-woman cuts the loaf with a long knife. In my memory the bread tastes quite delicious – and at that point the scene breaks off.

'Now what is there in this occurrence to justify the expenditure of memory which it has occasioned me? I have racked my brains in vain over it. Does the emphasis lie in our disagreeable behaviour to the little girl? Did the yellow colour of the dandelions – a flower which I am, of course, far from admiring to-day – so greatly please me? Or, as a result of my careering round the grass, did the bread taste so much nicer than usual that it made an unforgettable impression on me? Nor can I find any connection between this

scene and the interest which (as I was able to discover without any
difficulty) bound together the other scenes from my childhood.
Altogether, there seems to me something not quite right about this
scene. The yellow of the flowers is a disproportionately prominent
element in the situation as a whole, and the nice taste of the bread
seems to me exaggerated in an almost hallucinatory fashion. I cannot
help being reminded of some pictures that I once saw in a burlesque
exhibition. Certain portions of these pictures, and of course the
most inappropriate ones, instead of being painted, were built up
in three dimensions – for instance, the ladies' bustles. Well, can
you point out any way of finding an explanation or interpretation
of this redundant memory of my childhood?'

I thought it advisable to ask him since when he had been occupied with this recollection: whether he was of the opinion that it had
recurred to his memory periodically since his childhood, or whether
it had perhaps emerged at some later time on some occasion that
could be recalled. This question was all that it was necessary for me
to contribute to the solution of the problem; the rest was found by
my collaborator himself, who was no novice at jobs of this kind.

'I have not yet considered that point,' he replied. 'Now that you
have raised the question, it seems to me almost a certainty that
this childhood memory never occurred to me at all in my earlier
years. But I can also recall the occasion which led to my recovering this and many other recollections of my earliest childhood.
When I was seventeen, and at my secondary school, I returned for
the first time to my birthplace for the holidays, to stay with a
family who had been our friends ever since that remote date. I
know quite well what a wealth of impressions overwhelmed me at
that time. But I see now that I shall have to tell you a whole big
piece of my history: it belongs here, and you have brought it upon
yourself by your question. So listen. I was the child of people who
were originally well-to-do and who, I fancy, lived comfortably
enough in that little corner of the provinces. When I was about
three, the branch of industry in which my father was concerned
met with a catastrophe. He lost all his means and we were forced
to leave the place and move to a large town. Long and difficult
years followed, of which, as it seems to me, nothing was worth
remembering. I never felt really comfortable in the town. I believe
now that I was never free from a longing for the beautiful woods
near our home, in which (as one of my memories from those days

tells me) I used to run off from my father, almost before I had learnt to walk. Those holidays, when I was seventeen, were my first holidays in the country, and, as I have said, I stayed with a family with whom we were friends and who had risen greatly in the world since our move. I could compare the comfort reigning there with our own style of living at home in the town. But it is no use evading the subject any longer: I must admit that there was something else that excited me powerfully. I was seventeen, and in the family where I was staying there was a daughter of fifteen, with whom I immediately fell in love. It was my first calf-love and suffi-ciently intense, but I kept it completely secret. After a few days the girl went off to her school (from which she too was home for the holidays) and it was this separation after such a short acquaintance that brought my longings to a really high pitch. I passed many hours in solitary walks through the lovely woods that I had found once more and spent my time building castles in the air. These, strangely enough, were not concerned with the future but sought to improve the past. If only the smash had not occurred! If only I had stopped at home and grown up in the country and grown as strong as the young men in the house, the brothers of my love! And then if only I had followed my father's profession and if I had finally married her – for I should have known her intimately all those years! I had not the slightest doubt, of course, that in the circumstances created by my imagination I should have loved her just as passionately as I really seemed to then. A strange thing. For when I see her now from time to time – she happens to have married someone here – she is quite exceptionally indifferent to me. Yet I can remember quite well for what a long time afterwards I was affected by the yellow colour of the dress she was wearing when we first met, whenever I saw the same colour anywhere else.'

That sounds very much like your parenthetical remark to the effect that you are no longer fond of the common dandelion. Do you now suspect that there may be a connection between the yellow of the girl's dress and the ultra-clear yellow of the flowers in your childhood scene?

'Possibly. But it was not the same yellow. The dress was more of a yellowish brown, more like the colour of wallflowers. However, I can at least let you have an intermediate idea which may serve your purpose. At a later date, while I was in the Alps, I saw how certain flowers which have light colouring in the lowlands take on darker shades at high altitudes. Unless I am greatly mistaken, there is frequently to be found in mountainous regions a flower which is very similar to the dandelion but which is dark yellow and would exactly agree in colour with the dress of the girl I was so fond of. But I have not finished yet. I now come to a second occasion which stirred up in me the impressions of my childhood and which dates from a time not far distant from the first. I was seventeen when I revisited my birthplace. Three years later during my holidays I visited my uncle and met once again the children who had been my first playmates, the same two cousins, the boy a year older than I am and the girl of the same age as myself, who appear in the childhood scene with the dandelions. This family had left my birthplace at the same time as we did and had become prosperous in a far-distant city.'

And did you once more fall in love – with your cousin this time – and indulge in a new set of phantasies?

'No, this time things turned out differently. By then I was at the University and I was a slave to my books. I had nothing left over for my cousin. So far as I know I had no similar phantasies on that occasion. But I believe that my father and my uncle had concocted a plan by which I was to exchange the abstruse subject of my studies for one of more practical value, settle down, after my studies were completed, in the place where my uncle lived, and marry my cousin. No doubt when they saw how absorbed I was in my own intentions the plan was dropped; but I fancy I must certainly have been aware of its existence. It was not until later, when I was a newly-fledged man of science and hard pressed by the exigencies of life and when I had to wait so long before finding a post here, that I must sometimes have reflected that my father had meant well in planning this marriage for me, to make good the loss in which the original catastrophe had involved my whole existence.'

Then I am inclined to believe that the childhood scene we are considering emerged at this time, when you were struggling for your daily bread – provided, that is, that you can confirm my idea that it was during this same period that you first made the acquaintance of the Alps.

'Yes, that is so: mountaineering was the one enjoyment that I allowed myself at that time. But I still cannot grasp your point.'

I am coming to it at once. The element on which you put most stress in your childhood scene was the fact of the country-made bread tasting so delicious. It seems clear that this idea, which amounted almost to a hallucination, corresponded to your phantasy of the comfortable life you would have led if you had stayed at home and married this girl [in the yellow dress] – or, in symbolic language, how sweet the bread would have tasted for which you had to struggle so hard in your later years. The yellow of the flowers, too, points to the same girl. But there are also elements in the childhood scene which can only be related to the *second* phantasy – of being married to your cousin. Throwing away the flowers in exchange for bread strikes me as not a bad disguise for the scheme your father had for you: you were to give up your unpractical ideals and take on a 'bread-and-butter' occupation, were you not?

'It seems then that I amalgamated the two sets of phantasies of how my life could have been more comfortable – the "yellow" and the "country-made bread" from the one and the throwing-away of the flowers and the actual people concerned from the other.'

Yes, you projected the two phantasies on to one another and made a childhood memory of them. The element about the alpine flowers is as it were a stamp giving the date of manufacture. I can assure you that people often construct such things unconsciously – almost like works of fiction.

'But if that is so, there was *no* childhood memory, but only a phantasy put back into childhood. A feeling tells me, though, that the scene is genuine. How does that fit in?'

There is in general no guarantee of the data produced by our memory. But I am ready to agree with you that the scene is genuine. If so, you selected it from innumerable others of a similar or another kind because, on account of its content (which in itself was indifferent) it was well adapted to represent the two phantasies, which were important enough to you.

Recollection of this kind, whose value lies in the fact that it represents in the memory impressions and thoughts of a later date whose content is connected with its own by symbolic or similar links, may appropriately be called a *'screen memory'*. In any case you will cease to feel any surprise that this scene should so often recur to your mind. It can no longer be regarded as an innocent one since, as we have discovered, it is calculated to illustrate the most momentous turning-points in your life, the influence of the two most powerful motive forces – hunger and love.

'Yes, it represented hunger well enough. But what about love?'

In the yellow of the flowers, I mean. But I cannot deny that in this childhood scene of yours love is represented far less prominently than I should have expected from my previous experience.

'No. You are mistaken. This essence of it is its representation of love. Now I understand for the first time. Think for a moment! Taking flowers away from a girl means to deflower her. What a contrast between the boldness of this phantasy and my bashfulness on the first occasion and my indifference on the second.'

I can assure you that youthful bashfulness habitually has as its complement bold phantasies of that sort.

'But in that case the phantasy that has transformed itself into these childhood memories would not be a conscious one that I can remember, but an unconscious one?'

Unconscious thoughts which are a prolongation of conscious ones. You think to yourself 'If I had married so-and-so', and behind the thought there is an impulse to form a picture of what the 'being married' really is.

'I can go on with it now myself. The most seductive part of the whole subject for a young scapegrace is the picture of the marriage night. (What does he care about what comes afterwards?) But that picture cannot venture out into the light of day; the dominating mood of diffidence and of respect towards the girl keeps it suppressed. So it remains unconscious –'

And slips away into a childhood memory. You are quite right. It is precisely the coarsely sensual element in the phantasy which explains why it does not develop into a *conscious* phantasy but must be content to find its way allusively and under a flowery disguise into a childhood scene.

THOMAS HARDY, 'The Voice' (1912)

Woman much missed, how you call to me, call to me,
Saying that now you are not as you were
When you had changed from the one who was all to me,
But as at first, when our day was fair.

Can it be you that I hear? Let me view you, then,
Standing as when I drew near to the town
Where you would wait for me: yes, as I knew you then,
Even to the original air-blue gown!

Or is it only the breeze, in its listlessness
Travelling across the wet mead to me here,
You being ever dissolved to wan wistlessness,
Heard no more again far or near?

    Thus I; faltering forward,
    Leaves around me falling,
Wind oozing thin through the thorn from norward,
    And the woman calling.

FREUD ON GOETHE, 'A Childhood Recollection' (1917), translated by James Strachey

'If we try to recollect what happened to us in the earliest years of childhood, we often find that we confuse what we have heard from others with what is really a possession of our own derived from what we ourselves witnessed.' This remark is found on one of the first pages of Goethe's account of his life [*Dichtung und Wahrheit*], which he began to write at the age of sixty. It is preceded only by some information about his birth, which 'took place on 28 August 1749, at mid-day on the stroke of twelve'. The stars were in a favourable conjunction and may well have been the cause of his survival, for at his entry into the world he was 'as though dead', and it was only after great efforts that he was brought to life. There follows on this a short description of the house and of the place in it where the children – he and his younger sister – best liked to play. After this, however, Goethe relates in fact only one single event which can be assigned to the 'earliest years of childhood' (the years up to four?) and of which he seems to have preserved a recollection of his own.

The account of it runs as follows. 'And three brothers (von Ochsenstein by name) who lived over the way became very fond of me; they were orphan sons of the late magistrate, and they took an interest in me and used to tease me in all sorts of ways.

'My people used to like to tell of all kinds of pranks in which these men, otherwise of a serious and retiring disposition, used to encourage me. I will quote only one of these exploits. The crockery-fair was just over, and not only had the kitchen been fitted up from it with what would be needed for some time to come, but minia-ture utensils of the same sort had been bought for us children to play with. One fine afternoon, when all was quiet in the house. I was playing with my dishes and pots in the hall' (a place which had already been described, opening on to the street) 'and, since this seemed to lead to nothing, I threw a plate into the street, and was overjoyed to see it go to bits so merrily. The von Ochsensteins, who saw how delighted I was and how joyfully I clapped my little hands, called out "Do it again!" I did not hesitate to sling out a pot on to the paving-stones, and then, as they kept crying "Another!", one after another all my little dishes, cooking-pots and pans. My neigh-bours continued to show their approval and I was highly delighted to be amusing them. But my stock was all used up, and still they cried "Another!" So I ran off straight into the kitchen and fetched the earthenware plates, which made an even finer show as they smashed to bits. And thus I ran backwards and forwards, bringing one plate after another, as I could reach them in turn from the dresser; and, as they were not content with that, I hurled every piece of crockery I could get hold of to the same destruction. Only later did someone come and interfere and put a stop to it all. The damage was done, and to make up for so much broken earthenware there was at least an amusing story, which the rascals who had been its instigators enjoyed to the end of their lives.'

In pre-analytic days it was possible to read this without finding occasion to pause and without feeling surprised, but later on the analytic conscience became active. We had formed definite opin-ions and expectations about the memories of earliest childhood, and would have liked to claim universal validity for them. It should not be a matter of indifference or entirely without meaning which detail of a child's life had escaped the general oblivion. It might on the contrary be conjectured that what had remained in memory was the most significant element in that whole period of life, whether it had possessed such an importance at the time, or whether it had gained subsequent importance from the influence of later events.

The high value of such childish recollections was, it is true, obvious only in a few cases. Generally they seemed indifferent, worthless even, and it remained at first incomprehensible why just these memories should have resisted amnesia; nor could the person who had preserved them for long years as part of his own store of memories see more in them than any stranger to whom he might relate them. Before their significance could be appreciated, a certain work of interpretation was necessary. This interpretation either showed that their content required to be replaced by some other content, or revealed that they were re-lated to some other unmistakably important experiences and had appeared in their place as what are known as 'screen memories'.

In every psychoanalytic investigation of a life-history it is always possible to explain the meaning of the earliest childhood memories along these lines. Indeed, it usually happens that the very recollection to which the patient gives precedence, which he relates first, with which he introduces the story of his life, proves to be the most important, the very one that holds the key to the secret pages of his mind. But the little childish episode related in *Dichtung und Wahrheit* does not rise to our expectations. The ways and means that with our patients lead to interpretation are of course not available to us here; the episode does not seem in itself to admit of any traceable connection with important impressions at a later date. A mischievous trick with damaging effects on the household economy, carried out under the spur of outside encouragement, is certainly no fitting headpiece for all that Goethe has to tell us of his richly filled life. An impression of utter innocence and irrelevance clings to this childhood memory, and it might be taken as a warning not to stretch the claims of psychoanalysis too far nor to apply it in unsuitable places.

From MELANIE KLEIN, 'The Psychogenesis of Tics' (1924), translated by Hanna Segal (1925)

The tic comprised three phases. At the beginning Felix had a feeling as though the depression in his neck, under the back of his head, were being torn. In consequence of this feeling he felt constrained first to throw his head back and then to rotate it from right to left. The second movement was accompanied by a feeling that something was cracking loudly. The concluding phase consisted of a third movement in which the chin was pressed as deeply as possible downwards. This gave Felix a feeling of drilling into something. For a time he performed these three movements three times over consecutively. One meaning of the 'three' was that in the tic – I shall return to this later in detail – Felix played three roles: the passive role of his mother, the passive role of his own ego, and the active role of his father. The passive roles were represented predominantly by the first two movements; though in the feeling of 'cracking' was contained also the sadistic element representing the active role of the father, an element which came to fuller expression in the third movement, that of drilling into something.

In order to bring the tic within the scope of the analysis, it was necessary to obtain the patient's free associations to his sensations associated with the tic and to the circumstances which gave rise to the tic. It had developed after some time into a symptom that occurred with increasing frequency but at first at irregular intervals. Not until the analysis had succeeded in penetrating the deeper layers of his repressed homosexuality, the material for which had first appeared in his accounts of games and the phantasies associated with them, did its significance begin to emerge. Later his homosexuality found expression in the form of a hitherto unrevealed interest in concerts, particularly in conductors and individual musicians. A love of music came to light and developed into a real and lasting understanding of music.

Felix had already in this third year revealed by his singing an identification with his father. After the trauma this interest, in conformity with the rest of his unfavourable development, became repressed. Its re-emergence in the course of the analysis was preceded by screen memories of early childhood. He remembered as a small boy getting up in the morning and seeing his face reflected in the polished surface of the grand piano, noticing that it was a distorted reflection, and feeling afraid. Another screen memory was that of hearing his father snore in the night and seeing horns growing out of his forehead. His associations led from a dark piano, which he had seen at the house of a friend, to his parents' bed, and showed that the sounds which he had heard emanating from the bed had first contributed largely to his interest in sounds and music and had later caused their inhibition. After attending a concert he complained, during analysis, that the grand piano had completely concealed the artist, and in this connection he produced a memory: the position of his cot at the foot of his parents' bed had been such that the end piece of the bed had obstructed his view of what was taking place, but had not prevented him listening and making observations. It became increasingly clear that his interest in conductors was determined by the equation of the conductor with his father in the act of copulating. The wish to participate actively in what was taking place, while still an onlooker, came to light in the following association: he would very much like to know how the conductor manages to make the players follow his beat with such precision. To Felix that seemed extremely difficult, because while the conductor had a fairly large baton, the musicians use only their fingers.[1] Phantasies of being a musician and playing in time with the conductor constituted an essential part of his repressed masturbation phantasies. The already developing sublimation of his masturbation phantasies into an interest in the rhythmic and motor elements of music became impeded by the premature and violent onset of repression, and in this connection the trauma of the surgical manipulation when he was three was significant. The need for motor activity therefore was discharged in excessive restlessness and, in the course of his development, was expressed in other ways as well, of which I shall speak later.

From E.M. FORSTER, *Aspects of the Novel* (1927)

Memory and intelligence are closely connected, for unless we remember we cannot understand. If by the time the queen dies we have forgotten the existence of the king we shall never make out what killed her. The plot-maker expects us to remember, we expect him to leave no loose ends. Every action or word in a plot ought

---

[1] This desire to keep time was expressed also in other ways, for instance in his emotional reaction when a bigger boy outstripped him in walking.

to count; it ought to be economical and spare; even when complicated it should be organic and free from dead matter. It may be
difficult or easy, it may and should contain mysteries, but it ought
not to mislead. And over it, as it unfolds, will hover the memory
of the reader (that dull glow of the mind of which intelligence is
the bright advancing edge) and will constantly rearrange and recon-
sider, seeing new clues, new chains of cause and effect, and the
final sense (if the plot has been a fine one) will not be of clues or
chains but of something aesthetically compact, something which
might have been shown by the novelist straight away, only if he
had shown it straight away it would never have become beautiful.
We come up against beauty here for the first time in our inquiry:
beauty at which a novelist should never aim, though he fails if he
does not achieve it.

From MARCEL PROUST, *Time Regained* (1927), translated by Andreas Mayor, Terence Kilmartin and D.J. Enright (1992)

I got out of my cab a second time just before it reached the house
of the Princesse de Guermantes and I began once more to reflect
upon the mood of lassitude and boredom in which I had attempted,
the previous day, to note the characteristics of that line which,
in a countryside reputed one of the loveliest of France, had separated upon the trunks of the trees the shadow from the light.
Certainly the reasoned conclusions which I had drawn at the time
did not cause me so much pain today. They were unchanged; but
at this moment, as on every occasion when I found myself torn
from my habits – in a new place, or going out at an unaccustomed hour – I was feeling a lively pleasure. The pleasure seemed
to me today a purely frivolous one, that of going to an afternoon
party given by Mme de Guermantes. But since I knew now that
I could hope for nothing of greater value than frivolous pleasures, what point was there in depriving myself of them? I told
myself again that I had felt, in attempting the description, not a
spark of that enthusiasm which, if it is not the sole, is a primary
criterion of talent. I tried next to draw from my memory other

'snapshots', those in particular which I had taken in Venice, but the mere word 'snapshot' made Venice seem to me as boring as an exhibition of photographs, and I felt that I had no more taste, no more talent for describing now what I had seen in the past, then I had had yesterday for describing what at that very moment I was, with a meticulous and melancholy eye, actually observing. In a few minutes a host of friends whom I had not seen for years would probably ask me to give up being a recluse and devote my days to them. And what reason had I to refuse their request, now that I possessed the proof that I was useless and that literature could no longer give me any joy whatever, whether this was my fault, through my not having enough talent, or the fault of literature itself, if it were true that literature was less charged with reality than I had once supposed?

When I thought of what Bergotte had said to me: 'You are ill, but one cannot pity you for you have the joys of the mind,' how mistaken he had been about me! How little joy there was in this sterile lucidity! Even if sometimes perhaps I had pleasures (not of the mind), I sacrificed them always to one woman after another; so that, had fate granted me another hundred years of life and sound health as well, it would merely have added a series of extensions to an already tedious existence, which there seemed to be no point in prolonging at all, still less for any great length of time. As for the 'joys of the intelligence', could I call by that name those cold observations which my clairvoyant eye or my power of accurate ratiocination made without any pleasure and which remained always infertile?

But it is sometimes just at the moment when we think that everything is lost that the intimation arrives which may save us; one has knocked at all the doors which lead nowhere, and then one stumbles without knowing it on the only door through which one can enter – which one might have sought in vain for a hundred years – and it opens of its own accord.

Revolving the gloomy thoughts which I have just recorded, I had entered the courtyard of the Guermantes mansion and in my absent-minded state I had failed to see a car which was coming towards me; the chauffeur gave a shout and I just had time to step out of the way, but as I moved sharply backwards I tripped against the uneven paving-stones in front of the coach-house. And at the moment when, recovering my balance, I put my foot on a stone which was slightly lower than its neighbour, all my discouragement vanished and in its place was that same happiness which at various epochs of my life had been given to me by the sight of trees which I had thought that I recognised in the course of a drive near Balbec, by the sight of the twin steeples of Martinville, by the flavour of a madeleine dipped in tea, and by all those other sensations of which I have spoken and of which the last works of Vinteuil had seemed to me to combine the quintessential character. Just as, at the moment when I tasted the madeleine, all anxiety about the future, all intellectual doubts had disappeared, so now those that a few seconds ago had assailed me on the subject of the reality of my literary gifts, the reality even of literature, were removed as if by magic.

I had followed no new train of reasoning, discovered no decisive argument, but the difficulties which had seemed insoluble a moment ago had lost all importance. The happiness which I had just felt was unquestionably the same as that which I had felt when I tasted the madeleine soaked in tea. But if on that occasion I had put off the task of searching for the profounder causes of my emotion, this time I was determined not to resign myself to a failure to understand them. The emotion was the same; the difference, purely material, lay in the images evoked: a profound azure intoxicated my eyes, impressions of coolness, of dazzling light, swirled round me and in my desire to seize them – as afraid to move as I had been on the earlier occasion when I had continued to savour the taste of the madeleine while I tried to draw into my consciousness whatever it was that it recalled to me – I continued, ignoring the evident amusement of the great crowd of chauffeurs, to stagger as I had staggered a few seconds ago, with one foot on the higher paving-stone and the other on the lower. Every time that I merely repeated this physical movement, I achieved nothing; but if I succeeded, forgetting the Guermantes party, in recapturing what I had felt when I first placed my feet on the ground in this way, again the dazzling and indistinct vision fluttered near me, as if to say: 'Seize me as I pass if you can, and try to solve the riddle of happiness which I set you.' And almost at once I recognised the vision: it was Venice, of which my efforts to describe it and the supposed snapshots taken by my memory had never told me anything, but which the sensation which I had once experienced as I stood upon two uneven stones in the baptistery of St Mark's had, recurring a moment ago, restored to me complete with all the other sensations linked on that day to that particular sensation, all of which had been waiting in their place – from which with imperious suddenness a chance happening had caused them to emerge – in the series of forgotten days. In the same way the taste of the little madeleine had recalled Combray to me. But why had the images of Combray and of Venice, at these two different moments, given me a joy which was like a certainty and which sufficed, without any other proof, to make death a matter of indifference to me?

Still asking myself this question, and determined today to find the answer to it, I entered the Guermantes mansion, because always we give precedence over the inner task that we have to perform to the outward role which we are playing, which was, for me at this moment, that of guest. But when I had gone upstairs, a butler requested me to wait for a few minutes in a little sitting-room used as a library, next to the room where the refreshments were being served, until the end of the piece of music which was being played, the Princess having given orders for the doors to be kept shut during its performance. And at that very moment a second intimation came to reinforce the one which had been given to me by the two uneven paving-stones and to exhort me to persevere in my task. A servant, trying unsuccessfully not to make a noise, chanced to knock a spoon against a plate and again that same species of happiness which had come to me from the uneven paving-stones poured into me; the sensation was again of great heat, but entirely different: heat combined with a whiff of smoke and relieved by the cool smell of a forest background; and I recognised that what seemed to me now so delightful was that same row of trees which I had found tedious both to observe and to describe but which I had just now for a moment, in a sort of daze – I seemed to be in the railway carriage again, opening a bottle of beer – supposed to be before my eyes, so forcibly had the identical noise of the spoon knocking against the plate given me, until I had had time to remember where I was, the illusion of the noise of the hammer with which a railwayman had done something to a wheel of the train while we stopped near the little wood. And then it seemed as though the signs which were to bring me, on this day of all days, out of my disheartened state and restore to me my faith in literature, were thronging eagerly about me, for, a butler who had long been in the service of the Prince de Guermantes having recognised me and brought to me in the library where I was waiting, so that I might not have to go to the buffet, a selection of petits fours and a glass of orangeade, I wiped my mouth with the napkin which he had given me; and instantly, as though I had been the character in the *Arabian Nights* who unwittingly accomplished the very rite which can cause to appear, visible to him alone, a docile genie ready to convey him to a great distance, a new vision of azure passed before my eyes, but an azure that this time was pure and saline and swelled into blue and bosomy undulations, and so strong was this impression that the moment to which I was transported seemed to me to be the present moment: more bemused than on the day when I had wondered whether I was really going to be received by the Princesse de Guermantes or whether everything round me would not collapse, I thought that the servant had just opened the window on to the beach and that all things invited me to go down and stroll along the promenade while the tide was high, for the napkin which I had used to wipe my mouth had precisely the same degree of stiffness and starchedness as the towel with which I had found it so awkward to dry my face as I stood in front of the window on the first day of my arrival at Balbec, and this napkin now, in the library of the Prince de Guermantes's house, unfolded for me – concealed within its smooth surfaces and its folds – the plumage of an ocean green and blue like the tail of a peacock. And what I found myself enjoying was not merely these colours but a whole instant of my life on whose summit they rested, an instant which had been no doubt an aspiration towards them and which some feeling of fatigue or sadness had perhaps prevented me from enjoying at Balbec but which now, freed from what is necessarily imperfect in external perception, pure and disembodied, caused me to swell with happiness.

From F.A. POTTLE, 'The Power of Memory in Boswell and Scott' (1945)

It may be felt that the comparison [between the sensibility of Boswell and the sensibility of Scott] is rendered futile at the start by the fact that Scott was a writer of fiction, Boswell a biographer and journalist. And indeed, unless one is willing to grant the fundamental assumption of the Crocean position – that all expression is art, and that the difference between a novel and a journal like Boswell's is a difference of degree and not of kind – there will seem to be no justification for the present study. It is precisely that assumption that will be made in what follows: that in analysing Boswell's journal we are concerned not merely with perception and memory, but also with imagination. To distinguish Scott from Boswell merely in the workings of the imagination is useful, but I should like to go farther back and see if even more interesting results could not be obtained if we began at the level of perception and continued on through the stage of memory. It may well be that memory will prove to be the most useful differential of all.

Did Boswell and Scott perceive the same sort of world to begin with? We have, as it happens, documents which should be capable of answering the question. They are Boswell's *Journal of a Tour to the Hebrides* and the journal of the tour to the Shetlands, Orkneys, and Hebrides which Scott made in 1814. The material is all similar in nature, and some of it – rather less than one would have expected – is quite parallel . . .

The fact is that the two journals show much less difference in immediate perception of the world than one would have predicted. Boswell favours conversation (and would have even if Johnson had not been his companion), Scott favours scenery. But the central interests are so similar that not merely sentences but whole paragraphs could be interchanged without being detected by a casual reader. The two journals do not show respectively a typically 'neoclassic' and a typically 'romantic' perception of the world. Scott's throughout has the shrewd, humane, humorous tone of common sense that we associate with the eighteenth century . . .

It is only when we turn to the *uses* that Scott made of his perceptions that we discern a sharp and striking difference between his mind and Boswell's. His memory works very differently. It will be easier to show this if we say something of Boswell first. The nature of Boswell's memory has been made the subject of a brilliant investigation by Geoffrey Scott, unfortunately in a work of limited circulation. In what follows I shall draw freely on his conclusions, not pausing to indicate the places where I have modified and extended them.

Given the right kind of jog to his memory, Boswell had something that looks like total recall. If he failed to make a written record soon after a series of events, he seems to have lost those events permanently, or at least to have had no greater power of recall than the next person. But given his written clue, and given time and patience, he could reconstruct accurately and in minute detail an account of practically everything that ever happened to him. The clues he relied on (when he did not write a full journal immediately) were rough and abbreviated notes jotted down on odd scraps of paper, often on the backs of envelopes. In these notes, which are in the highest degree fragmentary and cryptic, there appears to be no attempt to select what is important. Boswell simply jots down whatever rises first to his consciousness, knowing that one sort of hint will serve as well as another. Once fixed in this fashion, the events may be recalled at will, the fullness of the recovery depending less upon the interval of time than upon his patience and ability to concentrate his attention.

The journal is generally written from these notes, after a lapse of time varying from days to years. When the notes and journal are compared (which is seldom possible, for Boswell's usual practice was to destroy his notes as soon as they had served their purpose), it will generally be found that something – sometimes a great deal – turns up for which there was no sort of hint in the notes, and not infrequently that some hints in the notes are ignored. Suppressions of this kind in the journal I take to be due to several causes: inability to read the note; lack of time or patience to bring the scene back fully; deliberate rejection of remembered material as not worth recording. The material which turns up in the journal without warrant in the notes I can only conclude to have been *remembered*. It is of exactly the same sort as the material for which the notes furnish hints, and is just as circumstantial. When the circumstances are of a sort that will permit verification, they prove to be correct.

The process of recollection does not stop with the journal, but is still going on in the *Life of Johnson*. For one thing, the greater part of the extended Johnsonian conversations in which several speakers take part seems never to have been expanded in the journal at all. The only record Boswell had was frequently the rough note written many years before. And even when he had before him a journal version which could have been transferred almost without change into the *Life*, one constantly finds additions which can only be explained, in my opinion, by assuming that even here he relived the scene as he copied it and recollected matter which had eluded him at the time he wrote the journal, or which he had then suppressed.

The qualities which make the recall of Boswell remarkable are its wealth of detail and its circumstantial accuracy. Memory in people of education, particularly in artists, is usually a very inaccurate affair and deals cavalierly with circumstances. Very few people, moreover, can distinguish between what they have actually witnessed and what they have been told. Adults, no less than children, frequently convince themselves that they were spectators of events which for a time they were content to relate on the authority of others.

Yet the kind of memory here ascribed to Boswell, if it were merely a matter of detail and accuracy, would be no very rare thing. We have all met people who could remember everything, and we have shunned them. Who does not number among his acquaintance a narrator who bores his audience with interminable circumstantial detail, often of events of the remote past? . . . But accuracy of that sort is tedious. What we want, as we say, is for him to come to his *point*. We want selection; that is, we want him to pick out a few important things and sink the rest. To repeat, the memory which is tenacious of circumstantial detail is not uncommon, but it is usually associated with a low order of intelligence or a primitive culture.

The really remarkable feat of Boswell is that he has combined the full recall of the savage or the moron with the selectivity of the artist. His record, by its wealth of circumstantial detail, convinces us of its firm basis in reality, while by coming to the point he keeps us interested: that is, persuades us that what he is saying is significant.

What gives the peculiar quality of solidity and trustworthiness to Boswell's accounts is that he always presents his scenes in terms of average or normal experience. It begs the question to say that he presents things as they really were. There is a certain area in which all minds agree or in which agreement is ideally possible. The circumstantial detail which we have mentioned falls in this area. A particular conversation occurred on Thursday 3 June 1784 in the Oxford coach, or it did not; the ladies who accompanied

Johnson were named Beresford, were Americans, were going to Worcestershire, or they were not ... We may not always be able to verify things like this, but we shall agree that they are capable of verification and that only one answer is right. This is selection ... but it is not interpretation. When it comes to what Johnson *said* on any subject, if it was a matter of more than a sentence or two, it is obvious that Boswell gives us not merely selection but also interpretation, for you cannot condense or epitomise speech without deciding what, on the whole, it means. Boswell's interpretation moves on the plane of average or normal experience, with the result that in him we seem to see the past through no kind of medium at all, or at most through plate glass. The style that can achieve this result is one of the rarest things in literature. Much more common is the medium which colours or distorts – Carlyle's, let us say, or Scott's.

From EDWIN MUIR, *An Autobiography* (1954)

The day I remember best was the day when Freddie Sinclair chased me home: it was after we had gone to Helye, and his road lay in the same direction as mine. He was the boy I had fought over the knife, and this day he wanted to fight me again, but I was afraid. The road from the school to Helye lay on the crown of the island, and as I ran on, hollow with fear, there seemed to be nothing on either side of me but the sky. What I was so afraid of I did not know; it was not Freddie, but something else; yet I could no more have turned and faced him than I could have stopped the sun revolving. As I ran I was conscious only of a few huge things, monstrously simplified and enlarged: Wyre, which I felt under my feet, the other islands lying round, the sun in the sky, and the sky itself, which was quite empty. For almost thirty years afterwards I was so ashamed of that moment of panic that I did not dare to speak of it to anyone, and drove it out of my mind. I was seven at the time, and in the middle of my guilty fears. On that summer afternoon they took the shape of Freddie Sinclair, and turned him into a terrifying figure of vengeance. I felt that all the people of

Wyre, as they worked in their fields, had stopped and were watching me, and this tempered my fear with some human shame. I hoped that none of my family had noticed me, but when they came in from the fields at tea-time Sutherland said, 'Weel, boy, I see thu can run!' I had got over my panic by then, and pretended that Freddie and I had been merely having a race. Sutherland laughed. 'Ay, a fine race, man, a fine race!' He called me 'man' when he wanted to be sarcastic.

I got rid of that terror almost thirty years later in a poem describing Achilles chasing Hector round Troy, in which I pictured Hector returning after his death to run the deadly race over again. In the poem I imagined Hector as noticing with intense, dreamlike precision certain little things, not the huge simplified things which my conscious memory tells me I noticed in my own flight. The story is put in Hector's mouth:

> The grasses puff a little dust
> Where my footsteps fall,
> I cast a shadow as I pass
> The little wayside wall.
>
> The strip of grass on either hand
> Sparkles in the light,
> I only see that little space
> To the left and to the right,
>
> And in that space our shadows run,
> His shadow there and mine,
> The little knolls, the tossing weeds,
> The grasses frail and fine.

That is how the image came to me, quite spontaneously: I wrote the poem down, almost complete, at one sitting. But I have wondered since whether that intense concentration on little things, seen for a moment as the fugitive fled past them, may not be a deeper memory of that day preserved in a part of my mind which I cannot tap for ordinary purposes. In any case the poem cleared my conscience. I saw that my shame was a fantastically elongated shadow of a childish moment, imperfectly remembered; an untapped part of my mind supplied what my conscious recollection left out, and I could at last see the incident whole by seeing it as happening, on a great and tragic scale, to some one else. After I had written the poem the flight itself was changed, and with that my feelings towards it. A psychologist would say that this was because I had suppressed my knowledge of my cowardice, and that it could trouble me only so long as I suppressed it. That may be so, but what it was that made me stop suppressing it is another question. I think there must be a mind within our minds which cannot rest until it has worked out, even against our conscious will, the unresolved questions of our past; it brings up these questions when our will is least watchful, in sleep or in moments of intense contemplation. My feeling about the Achilles and Hector poem is not of a suppression suddenly removed, but rather of something which had worked itself out. Such events happen again and again in everyone's life; they may happen in dreams; they always happen unexpectedly, surprising us if we are conscious of them at the time. It is an experience as definite as conviction of sin; it is like a warning from a part of us which we have ignored, and at the same time like an answer to a question which we had not asked, or an unsolicited act of help where no help was known to be. These solutions of the past projected into the present, deliberately announced as if they were a sibylline declaration that life has a meaning, impress me more deeply than any other kind of experience with the conviction that life does have a meaning quite apart from the thousand meanings which the conscious mind attributes to it: an unexpected and yet incontestable meaning which runs in the teeth of ordinary experience, perfectly coherent, yet depending on a different system of connected relations from that by which we consciously live.

From E.H. GOMBRICH, *Art and Illusion* (1960)

According to Meder, it was Rousseau who first held forth in *Emile* in 1763 against the traditional way of teaching the elements of drawing. Emile should never be taught to copy other men's work, he should copy only nature. This is one of those programmes which may be said to be charged with explosive ignorance. True, similar things had been said before of or by Lysippus and Caravaggio, but in the eighteenth century the demand had a new ring. It is the time of 'original genius' and of nature worship. And so the break in tradition is heralded, which foreshadows the modern dilemma.

No artist embodies this dilemma more clearly than John Constable, with whose work I began these chapters. Nearly all his utterances betray this ambivalence towards tradition. 'I remember to have heard him say,' Leslie writes, 'when I sit down to make a sketch from nature the first thing I try to do is to forget that I have ever seen a picture.' The psychologist who hears of someone's 'trying to forget' will prick up his ears. In fact there is a strange irony in this manifesto of unconditional originality, for in itself it is not original. Cochin records a similar saying by Chardin and this, in its turn, may merely represent a variation on a theme intoned by the great traditionalist Poussin. Not that we need doubt that all these artists really strove to forget the formula. But the sober observer will realise there is all the difference in the world between trying to forget something and never having known it. The cynic may even be reminded of the sad story of the confidence man who promised his dupe a wonderful treasure-trove at a certain spot at midsummer midnight. There is only one condition attached to it – on no account must he think of a white crocodile while digging, or the treasure will vanish. The way to visual treasure-trove cannot lie that way. Nobody knew this better than Constable himself, who said that an artist who is self-taught is taught by a very ignorant person indeed. But the worship of tradition which he found prevalent among the public sometimes led him to talk as if the artist could ever do without it: 'In Art as in Literature, there are two modes by which men aim at distinction; in the one the Artist by careful application to what others have accomplished, imitates their works, or selects and combines their various beauties; in the other he seeks excellence at its primitive source NATURE. The one forms a style upon the study of pictures, and produces either imitative or eclectic art, as it has been termed; the other by a close observation of nature discovers qualities existing in her, which have never been portrayed before, and thus forms a style which is original.'

From CARL JUNG, 'Confrontation with the Unconscious', from *Memories, Dreams, Reflections* (1961)

I was in a region like the Alyscamps near Arles. There they have a lane of sarcophagi which go back to Merovingian times. In the dream I was coming from the city, and saw before me a similar lane with a long row of tombs. They were pedestals with stone slabs on which the dead lay. They reminded me of old church burial vaults, where knights in armour lie outstretched. Thus the dead lay in my dream, in their antique clothes, with hands clasped, the difference being that they were not hewn out of stone, but in a curious fashion mummified. I stood still in front of the first grave and looked at the dead man, who was a person of the eighteen-thirties. I looked at his clothes with interest, whereupon he suddenly moved and came to life. He unclasped his hands; but that was only because I was looking at him. I had an extremely unpleasant feeling, but walked on and came to another body. He belonged to the eighteenth century. There exactly the same thing happened: when I looked at him, he came to life and moved his hands. So I went down the whole row, until I came to the twelfth century – that is, to a crusader in chain mail who lay there with clasped hands. His figure seemed carved out of wood. For a long time I looked at him and thought he was really dead. But suddenly I saw that a finger of his left hand was beginning to stir gently.

Of course, I had originally held to Freud's view that vestiges of old experiences exist in the unconscious.[1] But dreams like this, and my actual experiences of the unconscious, taught me that such contents are not dead, outmoded forms, but belong to our living being. My work had confirmed this assumption, and in the course of years there developed from it the theory of archetypes.

The dreams, however, could not help me over my feeling of disorientation. On the contrary, I lived as if under constant inner pressure. At times this became so strong that I suspected there was some psychic disturbance in myself. Therefore I twice went over all the details of my entire life, with particular attention to childhood memories; for I thought there might be something in my past which I could

---

[1.] Freud speaks of 'archaic vestiges.'

not see and which might possibly be the cause of the disturbance. But this retrospection led to nothing but a fresh acknowledgment of my own ignorance. Thereupon I said to myself, 'Since I know nothing at all, I shall simply do whatever occurs to me.' Thus I consciously submitted myself to the impulses of the unconscious.

The first thing that came to the surface was a childhood memory from perhaps my tenth or eleventh year. At that time I had had a spell of playing passionately with building blocks. I distinctly recalled how I had built little houses and castles, using bottles to form the sides of gates and vaults. Somewhat later I had used ordinary stones, with mud for mortar. These structures had fascinated me for a long time. To my astonishment, this memory was accompanied by a good deal of emotion. 'Aha,' I said to myself, 'there is still life in these things. The small boy is still around, and possesses a creative life which I lack. But how can I make my way to it?' For a grown man it seemed impossible to me that I should be able to bridge the distance from the present back to my eleventh year. Yet if I wanted to re-establish contact with that period, I had no choice but to return to it and take up once more that child's life with his childish games. This moment was a turning point in my fate, but I gave in only after endless resistances and with a sense of resignation. For it was a painfully humiliating experience to realise that there was nothing to be done except play childish games.

Nevertheless, I began accumulating suitable stones, gathering them partly from the lake shore and partly from the water. And I started building: cottages, a castle, a whole village. The church was still missing, so I made a square building with a hexagonal drum on top of it, and a dome. A church also requires an altar, but I hesitated to build that.

Preoccupied with the question of how I could approach this task, I was walking along the lake as usual one day, picking stones out of the gravel on the shore. Suddenly I caught sight of a red stone, a four-sided pyramid about an inch and a half high. It was a fragment of stone which had been polished into this shape by the action of the water – a pure product of chance. I knew at once: this was the altar! I placed it in the middle under the dome, and as I did so, I recalled the underground phallus of my childhood dream. This connection gave me a feeling of satisfaction.

I went on with my building game after the noon meal every day, whenever the weather permitted. As soon as I was through eating,

I began playing, and continued to do so until the patients arrived; and if I was finished with my work early enough in the evening, I went back to building. In the course of this activity my thoughts clarified, and I was able to grasp the fantasies whose presence in myself I dimly felt.

Naturally, I thought about the significance of what I was doing, and asked myself, 'Now, really, what are you about? You are building a small town, and doing it as if it were a rite!' I had no answer to my question, only the inner certainty that I was on the way to discovering my own myth. For the building game was only a beginning. It released a stream of fantasies which I later carefully wrote down.

This sort of thing has been consistent with me, and at any time in my later life when I came up against a blank wall, I painted a picture or hewed stone. Each such experience proved to be a *rite d'entrée* for the ideas and works that followed hard upon it. Everything that I have written this year[2] and last year, 'The Undiscovered Self,' 'Flying Saucers: A Modern Myth,' 'A Psychological View of Conscience,' has grown out of the stone sculptures I did after my wife's death.[3] The close of life, the end, and what it made me realise, wrenched me violently out of myself. It cost me a great deal to regain my footing, and contact with stone helped me.

From ESTHER SALAMAN, *A Collection of Moments: A Study of Involuntary Memories* (1970)

A vast amount of information is stowed away in our brain; that much we know for certain. There is a great variety in the faculty of memory: verbal, musical, mathematical, sculptural, a memory for chess configurations, for faces, names, habits, customs, and so on. Very often a person excels in one and not in the others. From observation alone we can tell that children of very similar IQ have very different kinds of memory. The memory for experiences is as common as any of the other kinds, but varies from person to person. Let anyone confine himself to a particular period, preferably to one before he settled down, in youth, adolescence, or childhood,

---

[2.] 1957.
[3.] 27 November, 1955.

and he will find a number of memories available to him. If he concentrates he will find that many more come back, and even make him wonder how he could have forgotten them . . .

To show how elusive involuntary memories are I will go for further examples to my own experience of them in youth, when they were comparatively frequent. They puzzled me then, but later they afforded me material to work on. I left Russia in 1920, and a couple of years later, when I was a student in Berlin, I began to suffer homesickness: to be exact I was visited by it. But there was no longer any home in Russia: my father had died of typhus and the rest of the family had left the country.

I had known homesickness as a child. I remember it coming over me at twilight when I was staying with an aunt. The house was very quiet. I felt that I was in a mist – she never lit the lamps until it was quite dark – the sunlit hours had vanished as if they had never existed, and the *now* felt endless in memory. I pined for home, as if stretching out towards it.

My new homesickness, in Berlin, did not resemble the old one in the least: it did not come at twilight, or at any definite time; I did not pine: on the contrary it was as if something came to me, bringing a sense of mystery, magic, and loss. For years I did not know how to describe this kind of homesickness.

The next thing I noticed (there seems an infinity of time between the two observations, as there must seem to the baby between rolling over and crawling) was that my homesickness did not come when I might well have expected it: sitting with Russians round the samovar, reminiscing nostalgically about lilac and syringa, school outings in May and wild strawberries and cream, teachers of literature and essays on Turgenev's women, or moved to tears by a line in a Russian song. Such purposeful journeys in chosen company were not at all like my unpredictable, sudden homesickness, my feelings of something precious in the past, reassuring by its mere existence, a fleeting joy, not to be held even for a moment in the mind. It was then that I used to say, being still in my early twenties, that I would give ten years of my life to revisit Russia. In time it dawned on me that some of the Russian *émigrés* I met, whose childhood had been a paradise, did not seem to know my kind of homesickness. So why did I, whose childhood had been full of darkness as well as light, have these intimations of a paradise lost? . . .

To sum up my experiences of involuntary memories in Berlin: they always came suddenly, they brought me great joy, and more often than not I lived in the 'then' and forgot the 'now'. In *Contre Sainte-Beuve*, where Proust described his real experience of involuntary memories, he says that it happens that we come upon an object and a lost sensation thrills in us, but we cannot give it a name. Still more elusive was an element of fear and it was years before I found this confirmed in Proust's experiences recorded in *Jean Santeuil*.

So elusive are these experiences of involuntary memories that Aksakov goes so far as to say that when involuntary memories came back to him in childhood the moment was 'imperceptible to consciousness'.

Often one notices nothing more than a change of mood. If I had not been the kind of person who is drawn to his memories like a musical person to sounds, and had not re-created many of them in words, nothing more than fragments would have been left of my experience of involuntary memories in youth. One thing I remember clearly: saying to myself that they helped me to live; yes, they sustained me and gave me courage, which I needed in the utter insecurity in which I, like so many *émigrés* and refugees, found myself.

It was years before I realised that my homesickness in Berlin had been for the past, that people who have never left their country have similar experiences: we are all exiles from our past. It was then that I was surprised, indeed amazed, that my involuntary memories in Berlin had not reminded me of similar experiences which I had had before I left home: memories of a pale blue figured-velvet outfit, a little yellow magic stick, colours changing in the neck of a drake, for these and other fragments had brought me indescribable joys when I was still a schoolgirl.

Looking back I can see now what made confusion worse confounded. As well as being unpredictable, elusive, and desultory, my involuntary memories did not always bring me joy: some brought only great distress. Some had the glory and freshness of a dream, but others were nightmares. I had a memory of my sister who died before she was four of diphtheria. I was nine years old, the eldest, and she the fourth. I had memories of her, playing with Father, unafraid of him, and delighting me as she did him. But the memory of her dying, which came back to me while I was still a child suddenly and unexpectedly, did something terrible to me. I am standing in the doorway, she is lying on her back on the bed, and her face in agony is in a pool of morning sunlight coming from the window opposite. My father on one side, my mother on the other, are desperately trying to help her. Death was not new to me: my grandfather died in our house not many months earlier, neighbours' children had died. I cannot separate the components in my unmitigated horror when this memory suddenly hit me, and I know for certain it happened more than once, but I do remember trying to shake off the memory as one tries to wake from a nightmare.

No, not all involuntary memories bring joy. Aksakov went to boarding-school at nine. His mother had made the need of his going clear to him – they could not afford a tutor. He would have managed the separation from her, and the teasing of other children, but for the headmaster's dislike of him: 'I don't like your silent, solitary child,' he told the master who was kind to the boy. Aksakov began to break down – he describes his illness fully in *A Russian Schoolboy*. Suddenly there would come back to him memory of his home, Aksakovo. One day, when he was preparing a lesson, a pigeon suddenly perched on the windowsill and began to turn around and coo – at once he was reminded of his pet pigeon at home, and immediately his chest constricted and he had a fainting fit. This happened again and again. At the time nobody could discover the cause of these attacks, but Aksakov is convinced that every one of these fits was due to a sudden memory of the past appearing to him with the 'vividness and brightness of a dream'. This might happen when he was thinking of something quite different, or learning a lesson: 'suddenly the sound of a voice, probably resembling a voice I had heard before; a patch of sunlight on the window or wall, such as had before lit up familiar objects; or a fly buzzing and beating against a window pane, which I had often watched in my childhood – suddenly and for one instant, though imperceptible to consciousness, evoked the forgotten past and gave a shock to my overstrung nerves'. He got worse, and his mother came and fetched him away.

From ITALO CALVINO, *Invisible Cities* (1972), translated by William Weaver (1975)

Leaving there and proceeding for three days towards the east, you reach Diomira, a city with sixty silver domes, bronze statues of all the gods, streets paved with lead, a crystal theatre, a golden cock that crows each morning on a tower. All these beauties will already be familiar to the visitor, who has seen them also in other cities. But the special quality of this city for the man who arrives there on a September evening, when the days are growing shorter and the multicoloured lamps are lighted all at once at the doors of the food stalls and from a terrace a woman's voice cries ooh!, is that he feels envy towards those who now believe they have once before lived an evening identical to this and who think they were happy, that time.

From CHARLES RYCROFT, *The Innocence of Dreams* (1991)

Since the physiological evidence suggests that we all dream for about a fifth of the time that we are asleep, the majority of dreams dreamt must be forgotten. Indeed, since some people claim never to dream, it must be possible for people to forget all their dreams. On the face of it, therefore, the fact that some dreams are remembered and others are forgotten, and that some people remember dreams frequently, some people remember dreams seldom, and yet others remember them never, constitutes a problem.

Curiously enough, this problem is almost always raised in connection with forgetting dreams, the tacit assumption being that dreams are experiences analogous to events or happenings, that events are normally remembered, and that it must therefore require some special explanation to account for forgetting dream events. On this view of the matter, forgetting dreams is as remarkable as, and is the same kind of phenomenon as, forgetting the whole of one's childhood, losing one's memory, or forgetting about things that are of importance in one's everyday life – all of which are instances of forgetting that are, in principle, pathological, since they impoverish

one's sense of self and interfere with one's capacity to function efficiently; there is obviously something amiss if one has forgotten
one's origins, if one has lost one's memory and no longer knows
who one is, or if one fails to remember things that one has to do
or facts that have a bearing on one's life. So, if dreams really were
events, forgetting them would be a form of amnesia, a forgetting
of what in health would be remembered, and is due to some conflict,
inhibition or repression which prevents the emergence into
consciousness of wishes, thoughts and recollections that would
disturb the dreamer's waking equanimity and received conception
of himself.

Now, although the forgetting of many dreams must be explicable in this way – just as many instances of forgetting things in
waking life are patently due to the wish to forget them, e.g. forgetting to pay bills, to keep dreaded appointments, forgetting the
names of people one dislikes, or wishes to snub, or who remind
one of events of which one is ashamed – consideration of the nature
and function of memory and of the quantitative relationship existing
between the past and the present[1] will show that it cannot possibly
be true that in a state of ideal health people would be able to
remember every thought and image of which they have ever been
conscious, whether in their sleep or while awake, – and that the
assumption that they could is an example of misapplying ideas
derived from pathology.

According to biological and neurological theory, the function of
memory is to enable each organism or individual to base his actions
on a wider range of experience than would be available to him if
he had no memory; to enable him to interpret the present in terms
of past experience and to make decisions which take account of
the past as well as of the immediate present. And an efficient
memory is one which makes available to its owner information

---

[1]. Since there is so much more of the past than there is of the present and remembering
is an activity that takes time and can itself be remembered, there is something absurd
about the idea that all experiences could be remembered in the form in which they were
experienced. Recall would take up more time than was available for it and infinite regresses
(remembering oneself remembering oneself remembering . . .) would clutter up the system.
What in fact happens is, of course, that all experiences, including events, imaginings,
reflections and dreams are subject to a continuous process of selection, abstraction, gener-
alisation, distillation. When Proust set out on his *A la Recherche du Temps Perdu*, what
he discovered was not a serial account of the time he had lost (not forgotten (*oublié*), a
point which the English translation, *Remembrance of Things Past*, misses) but a distillation of it.

relevant to his present and future without distracting him by irrelevancies. In other words, when memory is functioning harmoniously, information (memories) relevant to work will be available when working, information relevant to home will be available at home, information relevant to childhood will be available when in the company of children, information relevant to food will be available when hungry, and so on – and information which would be distracting will be unavailable.

It follows from this that memory is not, as it were, an inbuilt audio-visual tape of one's past thoughts and experiences, all parts of which should ideally be instantly available, but a selective process by which the present self is continuously fed with relevant memories from its past and protected from distraction and confusion by some barrier to remembering the irrelevant. It follows from this too that there are three categories of past experience that can loosely be described as forgotten: those which will never have any bearing on the present and never are or need be retrieved, e.g. half-formed thoughts which never crystallise out into a definite idea or decision, or the intermediate stages of a calculation the final result of which may be retrievable; those which remain dormant or latent because situations on which they might have bearing are not being presently encountered, e.g. a language once learnt but not at present being used; and those which do have bearing on the present but are rendered unavailable by conflict, inhibition and repression, e.g. memories of childhood events which have a bearing on aspects of the self with which the present self is not in contact, and, more dramatically, fugue states (loss of memory) in which the individual forgets who he is.

From TERRY PRATCHETT, *Reaper Man*
(1991)

The sun was near the horizon.

The shortest-lived creatures on the Disc were mayflies, which barely make it through twenty-four hours. Two of the oldest zigzagged aimlessly over the waters of a trout stream, discussing history with some younger members of the evening hatching.

'You don't get the kind of sun now that you used to get,' said one of them.

'You're right there. We had proper sun in the good old hours. It were all yellow. None of this red stuff.'

'It were higher, too.'

'It was. You're right.'

'And nymphs and larvae showed you a bit of respect.'

'They did. They did,' said the other mayfly vehemently.

'I reckon, if mayflies these hours behaved a bit better, we'd still be having proper sun.'

The younger mayflies listened politely.

'I remember,' said one of the oldest mayflies, 'when all this was fields, as far as you could see.'

The younger mayflies looked around.

'It's still fields,' one of them ventured, after a polite interval.

'I remember when it was *better* fields,' said the old mayfly sharply.

'Yeah,' said his colleague. 'And there was a cow.'

'That's right! You're right! I remember that cow! Stood right over there for, oh, forty, fifty minutes. It was brown, as I recall.'

'You don't get cows like that these hours.'

'You don't get cows at all.'

'What's a cow?' said one of the hatchlings.

'See?' said the oldest mayfly triumphantly. 'That's modern Ephemeroptera for you.' It paused. 'What were we doing before we were talking about the sun?'

'Zigzagging aimlessly over the water,' said one of the young flies. This was a fair bet in any case.

'No, before that.'

'Er . . . you were telling us about the Great Trout.'

'Ah. Yes. Right. The Trout. Well, you see, if you've been a good mayfly, zigzagging up and down properly –'

'– taking heed of your elders and betters –'

'– yes, and taking heed of your elders and betters, then eventually the Great Trout –'

Clop

Clop

'Yes?' said one of the younger mayflies.

There was no reply.

'The Great Trout what?' said another mayfly, nervously.

They looked down at a series of expanding concentric rings on the water.

'The holy sign!' said a mayfly. 'I remember being told about that! A Great Circle in the water! Thus shall be the sign of the Great Trout!'

The oldest of the young mayflies watched the water thoughtfully. It was beginning to realise that, as the most senior fly present, it now had the privilege of hovering closest to the surface.

'They say,' said the mayfly at the top of the zigzagging crowd, 'that when the Great Trout comes for you, you go to a land flowing with . . . flowing with . . .' Mayflies don't eat. It was at a loss. 'Flowing with water,' it finished lamely.

'I wonder,' said the oldest mayfly.

'It must be really good there,' said the youngest.

'Oh? Why?'

''Cos no one ever wants to come back.'

From MARTIN AMIS, *Experience* (2000)

This is strenuous moonshine. He wasn't coming back. Words and memories were leaving him: like banks of lights and switches, sighing as they closed down.

– I feel a bit . . . You know.

– What Dad?

– You know.

– Anxious? Uneasy?

– Not really. Just a bit . . . *You* know.

I know? In his choice of words my father is not a delegator, particularly in accounts of his own state of mind. But here he is, smiling trustingly and, it seems, calmly, and lost for words. I now see that this was an alternate-world Kingsley, an anti-Kingsley, confined from now on to a regime of tautologies and commonplaces. What his brain was doing was the *opposite of writing* . . . his hands today are all over the place, waving, interclasping, and again waving. Should I regale him with his description of the critic and writer John Berger?

'All this with my hands, it's nothing sinister.'

I am impressed by the rare and immediate success with the adjective ('Or is that a complement, Dad?' I once asked him. 'Yes but it's *first-and-foremost* an adjective,' he said, momentarily enraged by a competing pedantry.)

– It's just so I know where they are, he says.

– Gives them somewhere to be.

– Exactly.

Then I went through with something I had planned to say. I said.

– Do you remember the book you wrote called *Ending Up*? They did it on TV with John Mills and Michael Hordern and Wendy Hiller and Googie Withers. Remember? Anyway, one of the characters in the book you wrote, a nice old boy called George Zeyer, suffers from nominal aphasia. He can't remember common nouns, he can't remember the names of common objects. In the book you wrote this gives him the chance to be very entertainingly *boring* in three different ways. In the first phase he's incredibly boring because he just stumbles along improvising as he goes. Like: 'This chap's got a thing, you drive around in it. It's got a, you know, it turns round.' In the second phase he's incredibly boring because he tries to get over the difficulty with rehearsal formulas and paraphrases. Like: 'They hit him with a screwing-up job and the iron thingummy for the fire.' In the third phase he's incredibly boring because he's cured! He's completely back to normal and he can't stop displaying his mastery of the common noun. Like: 'table, sheet chair, glass, bottle, spoon.' All this, Dad, in the book *you wrote*.

He is contemplating me with delighted admiration.

– Do you remember?

– *No*, he said.

HARUKI MURAKAMI, from an interview with Mick Brown, *Daily Telegraph Magazine* (16 August 2003)

By a good story I mean that the reader will arrive at a different place from where they started – a good place. It's not necessarily that the story has a moral, or a happy ending; not saying this is

right, this is wrong. The difference must be that it leaves a kind
of memory. I believe memory is a kind of petrol in your life, in
your body, in your will to live. My memories help me a lot to live
on, to survive.

From MILAN KUNDERA, *The Curtain* (2007)

The perpetual activity of forgetting gives our every act a ghostly,
unreal, hazy quality. What did we have for lunch the day before
yesterday? What did my friend tell me yesterday? And even: what
was I thinking about, three seconds ago? All of that is forgotten
and (what's a thousand times worse!) it deserves no better. Against
our real world, which, by its very nature, is fleeting and worthy
of forgetting, works of art stand as a different world, a world that
is ideal, solid, where every detail has its importance, its meaning,
where everything in it – every word, every phrase – deserves to be
unforgettable and was conceived to be such.

Still, the perception of art does not escape the force of forgetting
either. Though it should be said that each art has a different relation to forgetting. From that standpoint poetry is privileged. A person
reading a Baudelaire sonnet cannot skip a single word. If he loves
it he will read it several times and perhaps aloud. If he adores it,
he will learn it by heart. Lyric poetry is a fortress of memory.

The novel, on the other hand, is a very poorly fortified castle.
If I take an hour to read twenty pages, a novel of four hundred
pages will take me twenty hours, thus about a week. Rarely do we
have a whole week free. It is more likely that, between sessions of
reading, intervals of several days will occur, during which forgetting will immediately set up its worksite. But it is not only in the
intervals that forgetting does its work; it participates in the reading
continuously, with never a moment's lapse; turning the page, I
already forget what I just read; I retain only a kind of summary
indispensable for understanding what is to follow, but all the details,
the small observations, the admirable phrasings are already gone.
Erased. Someday, years later, I will start to talk about this novel
to a friend, and we will find that our memories have retained only
a few shreds of the text and have reconstructed very different books
for each of us.

And yet the novelist writes his novel as if he were writing a sonnet. Look at him! He is amazed at the composition he sees taking shape before him: the least detail is important to him, he makes it into a motif and will bring it back in dozens of repetitions, variations, allusions, like a fugue. And so he is sure that the second half of his novel will be even finer, stronger, than the first; for the farther one progresses through the castle's halls, the more the echoes of phrases already pronounced, themes already set out, will multiply and, brought together into chords, they will resonate from all sides.

False Memories

From FORD MADOX FORD, *Memories and Impressions* (1911)

Just a word to make plain the actual nature of this book: it contains impressions. When some parts of it appeared in serial form, a distinguished critic fell foul of one of the stories that I told. My impression was and remains that I heard Thomas Carlyle tell how at Weimar he borrowed an apron from a waiter and served tea to Goethe and Schiller, who were sitting in eighteenth-century court dress beneath a tree. The distinguished critic of a distinguished paper commented upon this story, saying that Carlyle never was in Weimar, and that Schiller died when Carlyle was aged five. I did not write to this distinguished critic, because I do not like writing to the papers, but I did write to a third party. I said that a few days before that date I had been talking to a Hessian peasant, a veteran of the war of 1870. He had fought at Sedan, at Gravelotte, before Paris, and had been one of the troops that marched under the Arc de Triomphe. In 1910 I asked this veteran of 1870 what the war had been all about. He said that the Emperor of Germany, having heard that the Emperor Napoleon had invaded England and taken his mother-in-law, Queen Victoria, prisoner – that the Emperor of Germany had marched into France to rescue his distinguished connection. In my letter to my critic's friend I said that if I had related this anecdote I should not have considered it as a contribution to history, but as material illustrating the state of mind of a Hessian peasant. So with my anecdote about Carlyle. It was intended to show the state of mind of a child of seven brought into contact with a Victorian great figure. When I wrote the anecdote I was perfectly aware that Carlyle never was in Weimar while Schiller was alive, or that Schiller and Goethe would not be likely to drink tea, and that they would not have worn eighteenth-century court dress at any time when Carlyle was alive. But as a boy I had that pretty and romantic impression, and so I presented it to the world – for what it was worth. So much I communicated to the distinguished critic in question. He was kind enough to reply to my friend, the third party, that whatever I might say, he was right and I was wrong. Carlyle was only five when Schiller died, and so on. He proceeded to comment upon my anecdote of the Hessian peasant to this effect: at the time of the Franco-Prussian War there was no emperor of Germany; the Emperor Napoleon never invaded England; he never took Victoria prisoner, and so on. He omitted to mention that there never was and never will be a modern emperor of Germany.

I suppose that this gentleman was doing what is called 'pulling my leg,' for it is impossible to imagine that any one, even an English literary critic or a German professor or a mixture of the two, could be so wanting in a sense of humour – or in any sense at all. But there the matter is, and this book is a book of impressions.

From W. G. SEBALD, *Vertigo* (1990), translated by Michael Hulse (2001)

In mid-May of the year 1800 Napoleon and a force of 36,000 men crossed the Great St Bernard pass, an undertaking that had been regarded until that time as next to impossible. For almost a fortnight, an interminable column of men, animals and equipment proceeded from Martigny via Orsières through the Entremont valley and from there moved, in a seemingly never-ending serpentine, up to the pass two and a half thousand metres above sea level, the heavy barrels of the cannon having to be dragged by the soldiery, in hollowed-out tree trunks, now across snow and ice and now over bare outcrops and rocky escarpments.

Among those who took part in that legendary transalpine march, and who were not lost in nameless oblivion, was one Marie Henri Beyle. Seventeen years old at the time, he could now see before him the end of his profoundly detested childhood and adolescence and, with some enthusiasm, was embarking on a career in the armed services which was to take him the length and breadth of Europe. The notes in which the 53-year-old Beyle, writing during a sojourn at Civitavecchia, attempted to relive the tribulations of

those days afford eloquent proof of the various difficulties entailed
in the act of recollection. At times his view of the past consists of
nothing but grey patches, then at others images appear of such
extraordinary clarity he feels he can scarce credit them – such as
that of General Marmont, whom he believes he saw at Martigny
to the left of the track along which the column was moving, clad
in the royal- and sky-blue robes of a Councillor of State, an image
which he still beholds precisely thus, Beyle assures us, whenever
he closes his eyes and pictures that scene, although he is well aware
that at that time Marmont must have been wearing his general's
uniform and not the blue robes of state.

Beyle, who claims at this period, owing to a wholly misdirected
education which had aimed solely at developing his mental faculties, to have had the constitution of a fourteen-year-old girl, also
writes that he was so affected by the large number of dead horses
lying by the wayside, and the other detritus of war the army left
in its wake as it moved in a long-drawn-out file up the mountains,
that he now has no clear idea whatsoever of the things he found
so horrifying then. It seemed to him that his impressions had been
erased by the very violence of their impact. For that reason, the
sketch below should be considered as a kind of aid by means of
which Beyle sought to remember how things were when the part
of the column in which he found himself came under fire near the
village and fortress of Bard. *B* is the village of Bard. The three Cs

on the heights to the right signify the fortress cannon, firing at the
points marked with Ls on the track that led across the steep slope,
P. Where the *X* is, at the bottom of the valley and beyond all hope
of rescue, lie horses that plunged off the track in a frenzy of fear.
H stands for Henri and marks the narrator's own position. Yet, of
course, when Beyle was in actual fact standing at that spot, he will

not have been viewing the scene in this precise way, for in reality, as we know, everything is always quite different.

Beyle furthermore writes that even when the images supplied by memory are true to life one can place little confidence in them. Just as the magnificent spectacle of General Marmont at Martigny before the ascent remained fixed in his mind, so too, after the most arduous portion of the journey was done, the beauty of the descent from the heights of the pass, and of the St Bernard valley unfolding before him in the morning sun, made an indelible impression on him. He gazed and gazed upon it, and all the while his first words of Italian, taught him the day before by a priest with whom he was billeted – *quante miglia sono di qua a Ivrea* and *donna cattiva* – were going through his head. Beyle writes that for years he lived in the conviction that he could remember every detail of that ride, and particularly of the town of Ivrea, which he beheld for the first time from some three-quarters of a mile away, in light that was already fading. There it lay, to the right, where the valley gradually opens out into the plain, while on the left, in the far distance, the mountains arose, the Resegone di Lecco, which was later to mean so much to him, and at the furthest remove, the Monte Rosa.

It was a severe disappointment, Beyle writes, when some years ago, looking through old papers, he came across an engraving entitled *Prospetto d'Ivrea* and was obliged to concede that his recollected picture of the town in the evening sun was nothing but a copy of that very engraving. This being so, Beyle's advice is not to purchase engravings of fine views and prospects seen on one's travels, since before very long they will displace our memories completely, indeed one might say they destroy them. For instance, he could no longer recall the wonderful Sistine Madonna he had seen in Dresden, try as he might, because Müller's engraving after it had become superimposed in his mind; the wretched pastels by Mengs in the same gallery, on the other hand, of which he had never set eyes on a copy, remained before him as clear as when he first saw them.

From ELIZABETH F. LOFTUS, 'When a Memory May Not Be a Memory' (March 1994)

'But I don't want to go among abused people,' Alice remarked.

'Oh, you can't help that,' said the Therapist: 'We were all abused here. I was abused. You were abused.'

'How do you know I was abused?' said Alice.

'You must have been,' said the Therapist, 'or you wouldn't have come here.'

If Lewis Carroll were writing today, he might decide to have Alice talk to the Therapist rather than the Cat. It is hard to exist in the modern, media-fed world without hearing about adults remembering for the first time that they were sexually abused as children. Any discussion of this topic must begin with an acknowledgement of the horrible reality of child sexual abuse. Harrison Pope and James Hudson estimate the prevalence to be 27–51 per cent of children for narrowly defined childhood sexual abuse by an older perpetrator and 31–67 per cent if non-contact experiences are included.[1] Many factors contribute to the variability of these estimates. We can all agree that even the most conservative of these estimates tells us that child abuse is a serious social problem.

One subset of the large class of abuse memories involves memories that emerged after a long period of 'repression'. Roseanne Barr Arnold is one of many celebrities who have recently remembered incest. Her earliest memories were of her mother abusing her from the time she was an infant. Later memories involved abuse by both parents that continued until she was six or seven years old.[2] Roseanne's public accusations caused her parents and siblings to denounce her in an equally public way.

Those interested in the details of Roseanne's allegations and how she recovered her memory can find clues in a long interview Roseanne gave to *Playboy* magazine. Implied in the article, Roseanne accused her mother of putting soap in her vagina; her father allegedly fondled his penis, made Peeping Tom photos, and chased her with his dirty underwear.[3] Roseanne's memories of abuse came after

[1] H.G. Pope and J.I. Hudson, 'Is childhood sexual abuse a risk factor for bulimia nervosa?', *American Journal of Psychiatry* (1922).

[2] 'A star cries incest', *People Magazine* (7 October 1991). N. Darton, 'The Pain of the Last Taboo', *Newsweek* (7 October 1993).

[3] Interview with Roseanne and Tom Arnold, *Playboy* (June 1993).

therapy: 'When I first started to have therapy and recall my memories, I really couldn't handle anything.' But later she would go public with her accusations. Why? She may have several reasons. 'There's tons of abuse going on. Hardly anything is being done about child sexual abuse and the way it's handled in the courts, in the media, everywhere. That's what I feel I was put on earth for, and I'm going to do it.' But elsewhere she tells *Playboy*, 'I say what I say because my fans want to hear it.'

Did the abuse happen? Roseanne says it happened not only to her, but also to her sister, Stephanie. She says that she and her sister talked about it every day for hours and hours. Stephanie denies anything ever happened, and traces Roseanne's charges to an 'overheated imagination'.

Roseanne appears completely uninterested in exploring the veracity of her claims: 'To question any victim is hideously immoral.' Roseanne and I would agree if she changed one word in her plea: 'to question *all* victims is hideously immoral.' But that is not what is being done.

This article is not about the child who has gonorrhoea of the throat. This is not about the woman who suffered silently her whole life with memories of abuse and first got the courage to tell a talented and trusted therapist about it decades later. We know that many tortured individuals need time to bring the dark secret of their abuse to light. This is not about those long-held memories. This is about one small class of 'memories': those that emerge in adulthood after extensive 'memory work' – age regression or body memory interpretation or suggestive questioning or guided visualisation or sexualised dream interpretation or aggressive sodium amytal interviews or any of many other suspect techniques. These techniques have led to the surfacing of 'memories' of child molestation. Sometimes, what have surfaced are endless numbers of violent traumas spanning years of one's life. This happens even when patients begin therapy thinking they had happy childhoods.

In cases such as Roseanne's, the traumatic events supposedly happened in the first six months of life, sometimes even earlier. In one case a woman sued her mother's former boyfriend for child molestation. The woman also claimed that the therapist had helped her recall prenatal memories.[4] There is not one piece of empirical

4. *Mateu v. Hagen*, No. 91-2-08053-5 (Washington 1993).

work in human memory to support the idea that adults have concrete episodic memories of events from the first year of their lives. Research on later childhood amnesia raises many questions about some claims of repressed memory.

John Kihlstrom has written: 'While the notion of repression is intuitively plausible, the evidence for the delayed recovery of valid repressed memories of incest and other forms of abuse is rather thin.'[5]

As adults we are occasionally asked, 'What is your earliest memory?' There is enormous variability in the age of earliest memory – from two years to eight years, and occasionally later. One thing is true for most of us: there is a period from which no events can be remembered, and this period is sometimes called 'childhood amnesia'. The inverse of childhood amnesia is the onset of auto-biographical memory. Most cognitive psychologists place the end of childhood amnesia at age three or four. One study suggested that some people might have a memory for a hospitalisation or the birth of a sibling that occurred at age two. Even these 'memories' could well have been educated guesses, general knowledge about what must have happened, or external information acquired after the age of two. Anyone who is familiar with the literature on childhood amnesia cannot help but feel some scepticism about adults who 'remember' events from infancy.

What about repression of memories? It would not be surprising if something that really happened to a small infant, no matter how traumatic, was not remembered later in life. One need not invoke the idea of repression to understand this failure, for it is most parsimoniously understood as ordinary childhood amnesia.

What about repression of memories for events that occur later in life? Of course the answer to this question depends completely on how you define repression. Repression, often called 'the queen of defences', most generally refers to '. . . a warding off of any conscious experience of a frightening memory, wish, or fantasy, or of unwanted emotions'. The literature is full of case histories and some experimental studies that support the idea that people sometimes fail to remember horrifying experiences from their past. One study of concentration camp survivors, for example, shows the

5. J.F. Kihlstrom, *The recovery of memory in the laboratory and the clinic.*' Unpublished MS, University of Arizona (1993).

extent to which forgetting of horrors is possible. One person was beaten so badly he was unable to walk for several days. Interviewed 40 years later, he remembered receiving only an occasional kick.[6] But just because something horrible is forgotten does not mean it was 'repressed'; repression is supposed to involve something beyond ordinary forgetting.

When repression is discussed in childhood sexual abuse, the extent of banishment from consciousness is virtually total. John Briere calls this 'total repression', Richard Ofshe and Margaret Singer call it 'robust repression'.[7] The concept of total or robust repression is being invoked to explain how endless numbers of traumatic events spanning years of one's life can be banished completely from awareness, leaving an individual who professes to have had a relatively happy childhood.

Claims about the commonness of repressed memories are freely made; they give the sense of a phenomenon that is extraordinarily prevalent. For example, E. Sue Blume, a social worker who works with incest survivors, claims that 'half of all incest survivors do not remember that the abuse occurred'. B. Engel, a licensed marriage, family, and child counsellor, and a leading expert in the treatment of adults who were sexually abused as children, maintains that 'many victims of childhood sexual abuse have entirely repressed the horrifying memory of the abuse'.[8] Renée Fredrickson, a psychotherapist with 18 years of experience, claims that 'Millions of people have blocked out frightening episodes of abuse, years of their life, or their entire childhood.' Later she tells readers that 'sexual abuse is particularly susceptible to memory repression'.[9] In a case in which I recently testified, one book recommended to a client by her therapist tells readers that a noted expert who is named in the book believes that 'as high as 70 percent of women have no conscious awareness of a molestation that occurred in their past'.[10]

With psychotherapists advancing these claims, it is hardly surprising to find them in the popular media. John Bradshaw tells

---

[6.] W.A. Wagenaar, *Identifying Ivan* (1988), 29.

[7.] J. Briere, *Child Abuse Trauma: Theory and Treatment of the Lasting Effects* (1992), 117; R.J. Ofshe and M.T. Singer, 'Recovered memory therapies and robust repression: a collective error'. Unpublished MS, University of California, Berkeley (1993).

[8.] B. Engel, *The Right to Innocence* (1989), 20.

[9.] Renée Fredrickson, *Repressed Memories* (1992), 15, 23.

[10.] J. Frank, *A Door of Hope: Recognizing and Resolving the Pains of your Past* (1987), 41.

readers of *Lear's Magazine*: 'About 60 percent of all incest victims don't remember the sexual abuse for many years after the fact. This characteristic – the delayed emergence of long-repressed memories – has been widely reported in incest cases . . .'[11] These claims are being made despite a review of 60 years of controlled studies showing virtually no support for the idea that an event can be accurately reproduced in memory after a long period of robust repression.

Several recent studies confirm that sexual abuse survivors sometimes report memory difficulties. In one study, 59 per cent claimed that there was a period of time between the first forced sexual experience and their eighteenth birthday when they could not remember the forced sexual experience. But, if the first experience occurred before the offset of childhood amnesia, the memory difficulty would be completely normal and unsurprising. In another study, 26 per cent were classified by their therapists as having severe memory defects.[12] But these deficits could also be due to ordinary childhood amnesia. Moreover, there is no evidence that these particular cases were validated.

Not everyone accused is innocent, of course. Certainly we must accept the reality of childhood traumas that can be highly damaging. But at the moment, we do not have the means for reliably distinguishing true memories about the guilty from false memories about the innocent. We cannot get to the truth about the past by remembering alone. Until we can, it seems prudent to be cautious about how one goes about piercing some presumed amnesic barrier. Is it unfair to the truly victimised to make this point? Definitely not. For uncritical acceptance of every claim of sexual abuse, no matter how dubious, is bound to have another chilling consequence: it will make trivial the true and ruthless cases of abuse and increase the suffering of genuine victims.

[11.] J. Bradshaw, 'Incest: When you wonder if it happened to you', *Lear's Magazine* (August 1992).
[12.] J. Briere and J. Conte, 'Self-reported Amnesia for Abuse in Adults Molested as Children', *Journal of Traumatic Stress* 6 (1993); J.L. Herman and E. Schatzow, 'Recovery and Verification of Memories of Childhood Sexual Trauma', *Psychoanalytic Psychology* (1987).

From IAN HACKING, *Rewriting the Soul* (1995)

Does it matter whether what we seem to remember really happened, more or less as we remember it? In daily life it matters most of the time. I thought I left my wallet in my raincoat pocket; it's not there. Panic. I (seem to) remember loaning you my copy of Putnam's book. Oh, I'm sorry, I loaned it to Lisa; I was confused. But what about seeming memories of long ago? They matter when our beliefs affect other people. That is the point of the false memory polemics. If someone cuts off all contact with her family, because she wrongly has come to believe that her father abused her and her mother knew but kept silent, then incalculable harm has been done to the family. In that case, the false beliefs, which seem to be memories, have terrible effects. But what about false beliefs that do not affect other people? What is wrong with mistaken memories that do no harm? I shall suggest an answer in terms of what I call false consciousness.

I mean something quite ordinary by false consciousness: the state of people who have formed importantly false beliefs about their character and their past. I argue that false consciousness is a bad state to be in even if one is not responsible for being in that state. False memory – something of a contradiction in terms – is only a small part of false consciousness. This is because 'false memory syndrome' usually refers to a pattern of memories of events in one's own past that never took place. It is not that the events are remembered inaccurately (for most events are). It is rather that nothing remotely like those events occurred. Indeed, the so-called syndrome might be called contrary-memory syndrome, for the seeming memories are not merely false but contrary to all reality. In the prototypical example, a 'recanter' says that she seemed to remember being regularly raped by her uncle, but now she realizes that nothing of the sort ever occurred. Nobody ever raped her. Her uncle was gentle and caring. Her seeming memory that the abuser was her uncle does not cast him as a stand-in for someone else, for no one ever abused her. That is what I call a contrary-memory. That is the sort of 'memory' that the False Memory Syndrome Foundation advertises. A person with contrary-memories of her own most intimate life would, in my terminology, have false consciousness. But there is more to false consciousness than that.

A merely-false-memory, in the same ballpark as the above example of a contrary-memory, would be one in which the uncle is, in memory, a screen for the father, the real perpetrator. Thus the memory is not contrary to all reality, but the past has been radically remolded. Another possibility is that the uncle did not rape her when she was six, but did fondle her improperly. The false memory syndrome people have expressed little interest in merely-false-memories like that. But such seeming memories could certainly feed what I call a false consciousness – for example, if the victim seems to remember vile treatment from her uncle, who was sweetness and light, in order to shield her father, and her own self-image.

Another relevant defect in memory could be called wrong-forgetting. That is the suppression of central items from one's past that are integral to one's character or nature. I say suppression, not repression. Repression is a postulated mechanism whereby incidents are lost to conscious memory and drives or tendencies are lost to conscious desire. Part of the postulate is that the repression is itself not a deliberate and conscious act on the part of any moral agent. A purist, especially a psychoanalytic purist, might say that a person who has not worked through the past and liberated repressed memory suffers from false consciousness. Well, maybe a person with five years of free time and a great deal of money, who declines analysis out of fear, is afflicted with false consciousness. But ordinary mortals bringing up a family, and supplying its needs of love, care, and sustenance, are not suffering from false consciousness, in any important way, if repressing their memories keeps them on an even keel. If, however, some memories have been suppressed, deliberately, by whomever and by whatever means, then we may begin to think of false consciousness.

Contrary-memory, merely-false-memory, and wrong-forgetting by no means exhaust the possibilities. Let me group these and other possibilities under the heading of deceptive-memory. I am inventing compound words with hyphens to flag the fact that, strictly speaking, we are concerned not with memories but with seeming memories or the absence of memories. In deceptive-memory I include seeming memories, or absence of memory, of definite facts about the past. I am not referring to the indeterminacies about past human action discussed in the previous chapter. But of course if there is what I called semantic contagion, then a person may arrive at definitely false beliefs that seem to be incorporated in memory. If she passes from redescribing a past action as sexual abuse (an adult's obsessive attention to her genitalia when washing her as a child) to the seeming memory that her mother constantly forced a rubber duck into her orifices while bathing her, we have semantic contagion and deceptive-memory.

Since memoro-politics has largely succeeded, we have come to think of ourselves, our character, and our souls as very much formed by our past. Hence, in our times, false consciousness will often involve some deceptive-memories. It need not do so. The Delphic injunction 'Know thyself!' did not refer to memory. It required that we know our character, our limits, our needs, our propensities for self-deception. It required that we know our souls. Only with the advent of memoro-politics did memory become a surrogate for the soul. Even today there are plenty of kinds of false consciousness that have nothing to do with memory. We all know those who genuinely believe that they are generous and sensitive, when in fact they are self-centered and indifferent. Kant held the maxim 'He who wills the end wills the means,' yet I know someone who is a living refutation of Kant. For he sincerely strives for worthy ends, but he is lacking in self-understanding and sensibility for other people; hence he does not comprehend what could serve as means to the ends for which he strives. He wills the end but seems incapable of willing the means. That too is a kind of false consciousness. Every reader will furnish other examples close to home, or closer: readers who are sure that they are free of any taint of false consciousness are perhaps the falsest of all.

Here, however, we are concerned with remembering, and hence with false consciousness that feeds on deceptive-memories. I say that it feeds on them, because it is not enough that we have deceptive-memories. In order for there to be false consciousness we must use the deceptive-memories as part of our sense of who we are. They must be part of the story that we tell about ourselves. They must be part of the way in which we constitute ourselves, or see our selves as constituted.

So much impassioned rubbish is now spoken and written about 'false memory' – that is, contrary-memory – that we shall have a cleaner slate if we think instead about wrong-forgetting No one, I think, so systematically cultivated deceptive-memory as Pierre Janet. He did so from the highest motives. His patients were in torment. Their symptoms were caused by ill-remembered trauma. His cures often relied on eliciting the trauma by discussion and by hypnosis. Once the cause of the distress had been brought to light, he hypnotized the patient into thinking that the events never happened. To recall two cases discussed earlier, Marie had been traumatized by her terror of her first menstrual period, and by standing in a barrel of freezing water in order to stop it. Her periods did cease, for a while, but later on she endured hysterical hypothermia, terrible fits of freezing cold every month. She did not understand why, and more and more hysterical symptoms appeared. When Marguerite was six she had to sleep beside a girl with a disgusting facial skin disease and had been made to put her hand on it to show she was not frightened by it. As an adult, she developed rashes, paralyses, insensitivity, and blindness on that side of her face and body. Janet hypnotized these women into believing that the events never occurred. Marie had never, on the occasion of her first menstrual period, stood for hours in a freezing water barrel. Marguerite had never had to sleep beside a girl with an appalling skin disease on her face. In both cases the hysterical symptoms vanished.

Marie and Marguerite did not suppress their memories, but Janet did. Hence, by my definition, they have wrongly-forgotten a critical event in their lives. Should we say that these women suffered from false consciousness? Not on the basis of what Janet told us. Marguerite's trauma is, so far as Janet has informed us, an accident, a mere incident in her life that repelled her. We may well suspect that a great deal has been left out. Why was she made to sleep beside the sick girl? Why did she have to touch the repugnant skin? What cruel mother or aunt did this to her? What else did that person do to her? What sort of family was this, anyway? Likewise with Marie we wonder why she was so terrified of her periods, why she took such desperate measures. There is a great deal to learn about both lives. We may suspect that after treatment by Janet both women were living in a state of thoroughly false consciousness. But we cannot prove that. It is a counsel of perfection that everyone should understand themselves to the core.

Now turn to another historical example of what was probably wrong-forgetting. Goddard's nineteen-year-old Bernice had an alter aged four, the obnoxious Polly. Bernice repeatedly told Goddard about incest with her father. Goddard convinced her, and I think hypnotized her, into believing this was a fantasy. Let us suppose that Bernice's memories of incest were pretty much correct. (That is only a hypothesis on my part, but assume it for this analysis.) Let us suppose also that Goddard succeeded in suppressing Bernice's memory. (This is dubious; we know, from letters written by the superintendent of the Columbus State Hospital for the Insane, that Goddard lied when he ended his account of Bernice by saying that he sent her off effectively cured.) I use these two suppositions not to present a 'Real Person,' in Kathleen Wilkes's sense, but to provide an example that in many ways resembles a real-life incident. Under the first supposition, Goddard induced wrong-forgetting. Under the second supposition, Bernice believed that she was not molested in any way by her father or anyone else. But, under the first supposition, she was.

This only slightly imagined Bernice certainly has deceptive-memory. Unlike Marguerite and Marie, I think that she also has false consciousness. For she has not forgotten an incident or pattern of behavior that we, or she, or people in her community, in 1921, would take to be a mere incident in her life. The incest was something deeply important about her growing up, her family, her young life.

But is there anything wrong with the false consciousness that Goddard induced and to which Bernice succumbed? There might be obvious, utilitarian, things wrong with it. It might have had terrible consequences. For example, in historical fact, in 1921 Bernice had a number of younger siblings, including a three-year-old sister, Betty Jane. Her father had died of tuberculosis three years earlier; her mother also died of TB soon afterward, and the family was broken up. Betty Jane was adopted by an upright family in the community, even changing her surname. Now if the father had not died when Bernice was sixteen – when Betty Jane was an infant – many experienced social workers would bet their bottom dollar that father would have been after Betty Jane in a while. If so, Goddard would have achieved an evil consequence. Bernice, who might have given the alarm, is now silenced. She no longer remembers what once she knew. But for the utilitarian, the false consciousness is not what is wrong. It is the fact that Bernice was deprived of a crucial piece of information that would have mattered to young Betty Jane.

False beliefs about one's past can have less dramatic bad consequences. Most of us find it embarrassing to be contradicted, even in matters of no significance. But in the story as told, there were no survivors to contradict Bernice. Even a twin sister, who may well have been assaulted, died at the age of eleven. In this story that I am adapting from historical fact, Bernice was simply insulated from all contradiction. It would have been different if all this had happened thirty years later. Bernice, aged nineteen in 1951 (rather than 1921), comes to believe that the incest never occurred. But by 1981, when she is forty-nine, she can hardly escape the media coverage of child sexual abuse and incest. We can certainly envisage a severe midlife crisis, to say the least, as she dimly feels her mind torn by a vague sense that something awful happened to her long ago.

In the story that is closer to the historical situation, however, Betty Jane is safe (we hope) in her adoptive home, and almost everyone else is dead. Given Bernice's health record, I expect that she died before incest became front-page news. There was no occasion for any cognitive dissonance. Thus I am deliberately telling a story in which there may be no utilitarian argument to show that Bernice's false consciousness in 1930, say, was a bad thing. There were no bad consequences. But perhaps we can find utilitarian objections to Bernice's state of affairs. There were still dangers. For example, the dead father may have been a member of a cult. That cult might go on harming children, and Bernice, with memories suppressed, would not be able to blow the whistle. Or even in 1930 there was the risk that Bernice's suppressed memories might, after all, resurface. Then, lacking adequate support, she might endure dreadful psychological self-torture. Janet himself was well aware of this danger and sometimes found it necessary to re-hypnotize his patients into re-forgetting their trauma. Only half in jest he said that he hoped he would outlive his patients, for without him to make the resurfaced memories go away again, they would be in trouble.

The utilitarian has to work harder and harder to find anything to object to in false consciousness. That is not surprising, for false consciousness is (I say) objectionable in itself, not in its consequences – and what utilitarians must object to is consequences. Suppose Goddard's therapy had worked. Bernice issued as a relatively whole person, able to carry on a life, perform light secretarial work (she was not a very well person), able to fulfill the societal norms of her day, marry, raise a family. What's wrong with that if there were no bad consequences?

Bernice, as imagined, certainly violates the ancient injunction 'Know thyself.' There is a sense in which she really does not know herself, how she came to be as she is, the dreadful episodes with her father that (according to today's etiology of dissociation) brought about her breakdown. So what? Bernice has achieved a coherent soul. It works, or so we are told. What better truth for her is needed? The therapist will say, perhaps, none. He is glad to get Bernice back to an almost normal life. There is a slight inconsistency in Goddard's reporting. He ended his article published in 1926 by saying that Bernice is quite happy working half-days. In the book published the next year, and closer to the historical truth, we learn that 'it will be some time before she will be strong enough to earn her own living.' Leave that aside. Suppose Bernice carried on well enough after Goddard released her. The pragmatist may say that there is no need for some 'historical' truth: Bernice's soul worked.

I am not satisfied. We do have another vision of the soul and self-knowledge. What is its basis? It comes from deeply rooted convictions and sensibilities about what it is to be a fully developed human being. They are parts of the Western moral tradition – that of Bernice, Goddard, and myself. First, there is an old sense of teleology, fostered by Aristotle, a sense of the ends for which a person exists: to grow into a complete and self-aware person. Second, there is the nominalism, represented by John Locke, according to which memory is a criterion for personal identity, perhaps the essential one. Third, there is the idea of autonomy, that we are responsible for constructing our own moral selves; that is perhaps the most enduring aspect of Kant's ethics. Fourth, memoro-politics has recently taught us or coerced us to believe that a person, or in older language the soul, is constituted by memories and character. Any type of amnesia results in something's being stolen from oneself; how much worse if it is replaced by deceptive-memories, a non-self.

The third part of this inheritance is especially interesting in the example of Bernice and many other damaged women. Consider the kind of material that was and was not in the false consciousness of Miss Bernice R. She was reconstructed and built into the male-dominated world of Dr Goddard, in which few fathers molest their daughters, and in which unwell young women are cured if they work as part-time secretaries. Bernice becomes a tidy and polite half-day clerk. Any possible autonomy of this already much weakened woman has been effectively annihilated.

Such a critique of what Goddard did has strong feminist overtones. But it also arises from basic 'modern' moral theory, whether we take that to be characterised by Kant or by Rousseau or, for that matter, by Michel Foucault. The thought of those men was dominated by the ideas of autonomy and freedom. They demanded awareness of how to take responsibility for one's own character, one's own growth, one's own morality. Those philosophers had overcome the ancient Greek idea that we, like all else in nature, have a fully defined end to which we as human beings naturally tend. No: in the modern image, it is we ourselves who must choose the ends. That is a stern creed: we can be fully moral beings only when we understand why we choose the ends. To be realistic, we do not expect Bernice to have been strong enough to satisfy the demands envisaged by Rousseau or Kant or Foucault. But Goddard absolutely precluded Bernice's having any freedom at all. He brutally reconstructed her and suppressed her past. He did so using patriarchal strategies, but one need have no special feminist alignment to see that what he did was wrong.

We should be under no illusions. Autonomy is not comfortable. A 1990s Bernice would not have her memories of incest simply quashed. Things are not so great today, either, for someone like Bernice. But at least with the consciousness that she would acquire now, and some serious sisterly support, there would be some possibility that she would find a self to which it would be worth her while to be true. Beware, however, of cant. One has no confidence that a 1990s Bernice is going to lead a happier or even better life in the rough-and-tumble of fuller knowledge than did my quasi-historical Bernice seventy years earlier. A truer consciousness may be a bed of thistles compared to which the real Bernice's false consciousness was a thorny rose garden.

Self-knowledge is a virtue in its own right. We value the way in which people can fulfill their own natures by gaining an unsentimental self-understanding. We think it is good to grow, for all our vices, into someone who is mature enough to face the past and the present, someone who understands how character, in its weaknesses as well as its strengths, is made of interlocking tendencies and gifts that have grown in the course of a life. The image of growth and maturing is Aristotelian rather than Kantian. These ancient values are ideals that none fully achieve, and yet they are modest, not seeking to find a meaning in life beyond life, but finding excellence in living and honoring life and its potentialities. Those values imply that false consciousness is bad in itself.

From MICHAEL FRAYN, *Copenhagen* (1998)

Margrethe: Then the Nazis came to power . . .
Bohr: And it got more and more difficult. When the war broke out – impossible. Until that day in 1941.
Margrethe: When it finished forever.
Bohr: Yes, why did he do it?
Heisenberg: September, 1941. For years I had it down in my memory as October.
Margrethe: September. The end of September.
Bohr: A curious sort of diary memory is.
Heisenberg: You open the pages, and all the neat headings and tidy jottings dissolve around you.
Bohr: You step through the pages into the months and days themselves.
Margrethe: The past becomes the present inside your head.

From OLIVER SACKS, 'A Symposium on Memory' (2005)

In 1993, approaching my sixtieth birthday, I started to experience a curious phenomenon – the spontaneous, unsolicited rising of early memories into my mind, memories which had lain dormant for upwards of fifty years. Not merely memories, but frames of mind, thoughts, atmospheres, and passions associated with them – memories, especially, of my boyhood. Moved by these, I wrote two little memoirs, one about the grand Science Museums in South Kensington, which were so much more important than school to me when I was growing up in London; the other about Humphry Davy, an early-nineteenth-century chemist who had been a hero of mine in those far-off days, and whose vividly described experiments excited me and inspired me to emulation. I think a more general autobiographical impulse was stimulated rather than sated by these brief writings, and late in 1997 I launched on a three-year project of dredging, reclaiming memories, reconstructing, refining, seeking for unity and meaning, which finally became my book, *Uncle Tungsten.*

I expected deficiencies of memory – partly because the events I was writing of had occurred fifty or more years earlier, and most of those who might have shared their memories, or checked my facts, were now dead; partly because, in writing about the first fifteen years of my life, I could not call on the letters, notebooks, etc., which I started to keep assiduously from the age of eighteen or so; and, of course, because of the weakness and fallibility of memory itself. I accepted that I must have forgotten or lost a great deal. But I assumed that the memories I did have, especially those which were very vivid, concrete, and circumstantial, were essentially valid and reliable, and it was a shock to me when I found that some of them were not.

A striking example of this, the first that came to my notice, came up in relation to the two bomb incidents that I describe in *Uncle Tungsten,* both of which occurred in the winter of 1940–41, when London was bombarded in the Blitz:

> One night, a thousand-pound bomb fell into the garden next to ours, but fortunately it failed to explode. All of us, the entire street, it seemed, crept away that night (my family to a cousin's flat) – many of us in our pajamas – walking as softly as we could (might vibration set the thing off?). The streets were pitch dark, for the blackout was in force, and we all carried electric torches dimmed with red crepe paper. We had no idea if our houses would still be standing in the morning.
>
> On another occasion, an incendiary bomb, a thermite bomb, fell behind our house and burned with a terrible, white-hot heat. My father had a stirrup pump, and my brothers carried pails of water to him, but water seemed useless against this infernal fire – indeed, made it burn even more furiously. There was a vicious hissing and sputtering when the water hit the white-hot metal, and meanwhile

the bomb was melting its own casing and throwing blobs and jets of molten metal in all directions.

A few months after the book was published, I spoke of these bombing incidents to my brother, Michael. Michael is five years my senior and had been with me at Braefield, the boarding school to which we had been evacuated at the beginning of the war (and in which I was to spend four miserable years, beset by bullying schoolmates and a sadistic headmaster). My brother immediately confirmed the first bombing incident, saying, 'I remember it exactly as you described it.' But regarding the second bombing, he said, 'You never saw it. You weren't there.'

I was staggered at Michael's words. How could he dispute a memory I would not hesitate to swear on in a court of law and had never doubted as real?

'What do you mean?' I objected. 'I can see the bomb in my mind's eye now, Pop with his pump, and Marcus and David with their buckets of water. How could I see it so clearly if I wasn't there?'

'You never saw it,' Michael repeated. 'We were both away at Braefield at the time. But David [our older brother] wrote us a letter about it. A very vivid, dramatic letter. You were enthralled by it.' Clearly, I had not only been enthralled, but must have constructed the scene in my mind, from David's words, and then taken it over, appropriated it, and taken it for a memory of my own.

After Michael said this, I tried to compare the two memories – the primary one, whose direct experiential stamp was not in doubt, with the constructed or secondary one. With the first incident, I could feel myself into the body of the little boy, shivering in his thin pajamas – it was December, and I was terrified – and because of my shortness compared to the big adults all around me, I had to crane my head upwards to see their faces.

The second image, of the thermite bomb, was equally clear, it seemed to me – very vivid, detailed, and concrete. I tried to persuade myself that it had a different quality from the first, that it bore evidences of its appropriation from someone else's experience and its translation from verbal description into image. But although I now know, intellectually, that this memory was 'false', secondary, appropriated, translated, it still seems to me as real, as intensely my own, as before. Had it, I wondered, become as real, as personal, as strongly embedded in my psyche (and, presumably, my nervous system) as if it had been a genuine primary memory? Would psychoanalysis, or, for that matter, brain imaging, be able to tell the difference?

The Threepenny Review, Winter 2005.

Public Memory

WILFRED OWEN, 'Anthem for Doomed Youth' (1917)

What passing-bells for those who die as cattle?
    – Only the monstrous anger of the guns.
    Only the stuttering rifles' rapid rattle
Can patter out their hasty orisons.
No mockeries now for them; no prayers nor bells;
    Nor any voice of mourning save the choirs, –
The shrill, demented choirs of wailing shells;
And bugles calling for them from sad shires.

What candles may be held to speed them all?
    Not in the hands of boys, but in their eyes
Shall shine the holy glimmers of goodbyes.
    The pallor of girls' brows shall be their pall;
Their flowers the tenderness of patient minds,
And each slow dusk a drawing-down of blinds.

From PAUL FUSSELL, *The Great War and Modern Memory* (1975)

Everyone who remembers a war first-hand knows that its images remain in the memory with special vividness. The very enormity of the proceedings, their absurd remove from the usages of the normal world, will guarantee that a structure of irony sufficient for ready narrative recall will attach to them. And the irony need not be Gravesian and extravagant: sometimes a very gentle irony emerging from anomalous contrasts will cause, as Stephen Hewett finds, 'certain impressions [to] remain with one – a sunrise when the Huns are quiet, a sunset when they are raising a storm, a night made hideous by some distant cannonades, the nightingales in the warm darkness by a stagnant weedy river, and always the march back from the trenches to reserve-billets in some pretty village full of shady trees.' One remembers with special vividness too because military training is very largely training in alertness and a special kind of noticing. And one remembers because at the front the well-known mechanisms of the psychology of crisis work to assign major portent to normally trivial things like single poppies or the scars on a rifle-stock or 'the smell of rum and blood.' When a man imagines that every moment is his next to last, be observes and treasures up sensory details purely for their own sake. 'I had a fierce desire to rivet impressions,' says Max Plowman, 'even of commonplace things like the curve of a roof, the turn of a road, or a mere milestone. What a strange emotion all objects stir when we look upon them wondering whether we do so for the last time in this life.' Fear itself works powerfully as an agent of sharp perception and vivid recall. Oliver Lyttelton understands this process in highly mechanical terms:

> Fear and its milder brothers, dread and anticipation, first soften the tablets of memory, so that the impressions which they bring are clearly and deeply cut, and when time cools them off the impressions are fixed like the grooves of a gramophone record, and remain with you as long as your faculties. I have been surprised how accurate my memory has proved about times and places where I was frightened.

By contrast, 'How faded are the memories of gaiety and pleasure.' Subsequent guilt over acts of cowardice or cruelty is another agent of vivid memory: in recalling scenes and moments marking one's own fancied disgrace, one sets the scene with lucid clarity to give it a verisimilitude sufficient for an efficacious self-torment.

Revisiting moments made vivid for these various reasons becomes a moral obligation. Owen registers it in an extreme form, but everyone who has shared his circumstances shares his obsession to some degree. He writes his mother in February, 1918: 'I confess I *bring on* what few war dreams I now have, entirely by *willingly* considering war of an evening. I do so because I have my duty to perform towards War.' Revisiting the battlefields in memory becomes as powerful a ritual obligation as visiting the cemeteries. Of the silent battlefields of Vimy and Souchez, Reginald Farrer says, 'They draw and hold me like magnets: I have never had enough.' 'I still loaf into the past,' says Tomlinson, 'to the Old Front Line, where now there is only silence and thistles. I like it; it is a phase of my lunacy.'

From CEES NOOTEBOOM, *Rituals* (1980), translated by Adrienne Dixon (1983)

Had he been set thinking after all? Then it was obviously infectious. As long as you did not do anything yourself, your life was determined by the people and the things that occurred in it. Their presence set into motion a slow stream of events you had to drag along with you: dead fathers, foreign mothers, boarding schools, guardians, and now also an aunt and a skiing champion. With a certain satisfaction he reflected that once again there had been no need for him to do anything himself. But how was it, then, that while he had the feeling that he had done nothing himself and that everything had only happened to him, his life seemed so long? He had already been here for thousands of years, and if he had studied zoology, it would have been millions. Small wonder, with such a past, that you could not remember everything, and yet at the same time it was surprising what you did remember. And stranger still was the equivalence of these recollections, in which the announcement of his father's death was on a par with all kinds of other annexed events, such as Thalassa Thalassa, the Crucifixion, and the burning of the Reichstag. All of it was you, in effect, for although you had not yourself experienced it all, it had woven itself into your life. Ultimately, it was your body that remembered these things for you. Strange chemical processes in your brain had seen to it that you were aware of the Paleozoic, which therefore, somehow or other, had become part of your experience, so that you yourself were connected with unimaginably distant times to which you would belong until you died, by virtue of that same mysterious mechanism. Consequently, your life was stretched out infinitely – that was not to be denied. He suddenly felt very old.

From JACQUES LE GOFF, *History and Memory* (1986), translated by Bridget Patterson

The evolution of societies in the second half of the twentieth century makes clear the importance of the stake represented by collective memory. Extending beyond history both as a science and as a public cult, firstly as a (shifting) reservoir of history, rich in archives, monuments and documents, at the same time as being, further down the line, a resonant (and living) echo of historical work, collective memory is one of the huge forces at play in developed and developing societies, amongst those who wield power and those who are subject to it, all of whom are struggling for power or for life, for survival and for advancement.

André Leroi-Gourhan's words are truer than ever: 'From the moment *homo sapiens* existed, organising a structure for social memory was predominant amongst the problems of human evolution' and furthermore: 'Tradition is as vital biologically to the human species as genetic conditioning is to insect societies: ethnic survival depends on routine, the dialogue which becomes established creates a balance between routine and progress, routine symbolising the assets necessary for the group's survival, progress the intervention of individual innovations for a better survival'. Memory is an essential element of what was subsequently called individual or collective *identity*, the feverish and anguished search for which is one of the fundamental activities of today's individuals and societies. But collective memory is not only a conquest, it is also an instrument and objective of power. It is in societies where social memory is primarily oral, or where they are in the process of collating a collective written memory, that the struggle for the control of recollection and tradition, effectively a manipulation of memory, can best be understood.

The case of Etruscan historiography is perhaps an example of a collective memory so inextricably linked to a dominant social class that the identification of this class with the nation resulted in an absence of memory when the nation disappeared: 'We only know the Etruscans, in a literary context, through the Greeks and Romans: no historical connection, even if one existed, has been handed down to us. It may be that their historical or parahistorical traditions disappeared with the aristocracy, which appears to have been the repository for the moral, legal and religious heritage of their nation. When this ceased to exist as an autonomous nation, it would seem that the Etruscans lost all consciousness of their past, and therefore of themselves'.*

From TONI MORRISON, *Beloved* (1987)

'What were you praying for, Ma'am?'
  'Not *for* anything. I don't pray anymore. I just talk.'
  'What were you talking about?'
  'You won't understand, baby.'
  'Yes, I will.'
  'I was talking about time. It's so hard for me to believe in it. Some things go. Pass on. Some things just stay. I used to think it was my rememory. You know. Some things you forget. Other things you never do. But it's not. Places, places are still there. If a house burns down, it's gone, but the place – the picture of it – stays, and not just in my rememory, but out there, in the world. What I remember is a picture floating around out there outside my head. I mean, even if I don't think it, even if I die, the picture of what I did, or knew, or saw is still out there. Right in the place where it happened.'
  'Can other people see it?' asked Denver.
  'Oh, yes. Oh, yes, yes, yes. Someday you be walking down the road and you hear something or see something going on. So clear. And you think it's you thinking it up. A thought picture. But no. It's when you bump into a rememory that belongs to somebody else. Where I was before I came here, that place is real. It's never going away. Even if the whole farm – every tree and grass blade of it dies. The picture is still there and what's more, if you go there – you who never was there – if you go there and stand in the place where it was, it will happen again; it will be there for you, waiting for you. So, Denver, you can't never go there. Never. Because even though it's all over – over and done with – it's going to always be there waiting for you. That's how come I had to get all my children out. No matter what.'

* G. Mansuelli, *Les Civilisations de l'Europe ancienne*. Paris 1967, pp. 139–40.

Denver picked at her fingernails. 'If it's still there, waiting, that must mean that nothing ever dies.'

Sethe looked right in Denver's face. 'Nothing ever does,' she said.

From DANIEL ARASSE, *Anselm Kiefer* (2001), translated by Mary Whittall (2001)

Constructed in Munich in 1935 by Paul Ludwig Troost, the two 'temples' ['Temples of the Nordic Heroes of the Eternal Guard'] were the setting for the 'most sacred' of all Nazi rites: the commemoration of the deaths of twenty-three of Hitler's companions in the failed putsch of 1923, who became the martyrs of the national renewal ten years later and whose coffins were preserved inside the temples, beneath an open sky. As Hitler declared in 1935: 'These temples are not vaults but an Eternal Guard. They are there for Germany and watch over our people.' This context allows us to reconstruct Kiefer's possible strategy in the Unknown Painter series. First of all, it is very likely that the 'unknown painter' designates Hitler. Not only did he believe himself a painter – a very important fact in the regime's propaganda and ideology – but Nazi terminology also contrived to identify him with the 'unknown soldier', raised from the dead of the First World War to usher in the new Germany. To loyal Nazis, he was a painter and a soldier in one. At a deeper level, Hitler is the 'unknown painter' because Nazi political theory closely compared the Führer to an artist. In 1936, Ernst Schindler, a professor at Munich University, proclaimed: 'Art is the leader [*Führer*], guiding and accompanying our life. In the form of myth, it shows us where we come from and where we are going. It is a symbol of ourselves, it provides the image of the goal of our will. With its songs, it goes everywhere with us until the grave.'

However repugnant we find them, these words deserve close attention. They lend substance to the statements of Gerdy Troost, wife of the architect of the Temples of the Heroes, who described the Führer's buildings (those directly supervised by Hitler, who sometimes provided the preliminary sketches) as 'the self-representation of the most original powers of *Kultur*'. All these texts also shed light on the meaning of the work of memory to which Kiefer unreservedly devoted himself. By changing the *image* that the Nazis installed in their most sacred commemorative *place*, replacing the coffins beneath an open sky with the palette of the 'unknown painter', he made manifest, and visually committed to memory, the intimate alliance of the cults of death and art under Nazism, which considered itself the product of 'two thousand years of German *Kultur*'.

This theme was a leitmotiv of Kiefer's work in the early 1980s. One of the most successful works to come of it was the picture *Shulamith* (1983), which was also the last in the series focusing on Nazi architecture. Following the usual mnemonic principles, the work has two points of reference which share a particularly incongruous relationship. The name Shulamith refers both to the bride in the Song of Songs ('Shulamite', 'black but comely' in the King James version) and to Paul Celan's poem *Todesfuge*, where the Jewess Shulamith with her ashen hair is the counterpart of the Aryan Margarete with her golden hair. In the picture, Shulamith is designated by her name, in the upper left-hand corner, and represented metaphorically by the *image* of the seven flames shown at the vanishing point, in the centre of the picture, a clear allusion to the seven-branched candlestick of the temple of Jerusalem. At the same time, however, the architectural *place* sites the allusion mnemonically, by 'quoting' the funerary crypt of the Soldier's Hall built in Berlin in 1939 by Wilhelm Kreis. In this way, Kiefer's art of memory transforms a space dedicated to the Nazi cult of the dead into a memorial to the victims of the Holocaust, while the strictly constructed perspective reveals even more tellingly, as Andreas Huyssen emphasised, 'fascism's genocidal telos in its own celebratory memorial spaces'.

So, by constructing a memory of German history for himself, by appropriating the past in order to turn this history into 'an immense archive of memory, whose contents are not arranged once and for all, definitively, but are available for continually new combinations', and by practising a 'therapy of memory' to counter the 'pathology of history', Kiefer is adopting a Nietzschean attitude with his own unique stamp. Taking a stand against the 'costly superfluity' of history as a branch of learning, which hampers life and its 'plastic power', Nietzsche invited the young to use history as a remedy against itself, and, in particular, to approach it critically 'in the service of life'.

From TZVETAN TODOROV, *The Abuses of Memory* (1995), translated by Bridget Patterson

Twentieth century totalitarian regimes have revealed the existence of a danger undreamt of until now: that of the obliteration of memory. It is not that ignorance has not existed since time immemorial, nor even the systematic destruction of documents and statues: we know, to take an example distant from us in time and space, that at the beginning of the fifteenth century, the Aztec emperor Itzcoatl had ordered the destruction of all stela [inscribed stones] and all books in order to be able to reinvent tradition in his own way. A century later, the Spanish conquistadors devoted themselves in their turn to erasing and burning all traces of anything testifying to the former greatness of those they had defeated. But as these were not totalitarian regimes, they only attacked official depositories of memory, allowing many other forms to survive, such as oral recitations or poetry. Having understood that the conquest of land and people is filtered through that of information and communication, twentieth-century tyrannies have systematised their annexation of memory and have been determined to control its most secret recesses. Sometimes these attempts have failed, but there is no doubt that in other cases (which by definition cannot be documented), traces of the past have been successfully eliminated.

There are countless and well-known examples of a less than perfect appropriation of memory. 'The entire history of the "millennium Reich" can be re-read as a war against memory', as Primo Levi rightly wrote; but the same could be said of the USSR or Communist China. The traces of what used to exist have either been thoroughly obliterated, or well-disguised and transformed; lies and inventions take the place of reality; it is forbidden to search for and disseminate the truth: any method is acceptable to gain their objective. Bodies in concentration camps have been disinterred, burned and their ashes scattered; photographs, supposedly showing a true picture, have been cleverly manipulated to avoid awkward reminders; History has been rewritten with each change of leader and readers of the encyclopedia ordered to cut out themselves the pages which have become undesirable; it is said that the seagulls in the Solovki islands were shot so that they could not carry messages from prisoners. The necessary concealment of actions nevertheless deemed essential led to paradoxical situations, like the one encapsulated by Himmler's famous phrase about the 'final solution': 'It is a glorious page in our history which has never been written and never will be.'

From MILAN KUNDERA, *The Book of Laughter and Forgetting* (1978), translated by Aaron Asher (1996)

In [Kafka's] novel, Prague is a city without memory. The city has even forgotten its name. No one there remembers or recalls anything, and Josef K. even seems not to know anything about his own life previously. No song can be heard there to evoke for us the moment of its birth and link the present to the past.

The time of Kafka's novel is the time of a humanity that has lost its continuity with humanity, of a humanity that no longer knows anything and no longer remembers anything and lives in cities without names where the streets are without names or with names different from those they had yesterday, because a name is continuity with the past and people without a past are people without a name.

Prague, as Max Brod said, is the city of evil. When the Jesuits, after the defeat of the Czech Reformation in 1621, tried to re-educate the people in the true Catholic faith, they swamped Prague with the splendor of Baroque cathedrals. The thousands of petrified saints gazing at you from all sides and threatening you, spying on you, hypnotizing you, are the frenzied occupation army that invaded Bohemia three hundred fifty years ago to tear the people's faith and language out of its soul . . .

Wandering the streets that do not know their names are the ghosts of monuments torn down. Torn down by the Czech Reformation, torn down by the Austrian Counter-Reformation, torn down by the Czechoslovak Republic, torn down by the Communists; even the statues of Stalin have been torn down. In place of those destroyed monuments, statues of Lenin are nowadays springing up in Bohemia by the thousands, springing up like weeds among ruins, like melancholy flowers of forgetting.

If Franz Kafka is the prophet of a world without memory, Gustav Husak is its builder. After T.G. Masaryk, who was called the Liberator President (every last one of his monuments has been destroyed), after Benes, Gottwald, Zapotocky, Novotny, and Svoboda, he is the seventh president of my country, and he is called the President of Forgetting.

The Russians put him in power in 1969. Not since 1621 has the Czech people experienced such a devastation of culture and intellectuals. Everyone everywhere thinks that Husak was merely persecuting his political enemies. But the struggle against the political opposition was instead the perfect opportunity for the Russians to undertake, with their lieutenant as intermediary, something much more basic.

I consider it very significant from this standpoint that Husak drove one hundred forty-five Czech historians from the universities and research institutes. (It's said that for each historian, as mysteriously as in a fairy tale, a new Lenin monument sprang up somewhere in Bohemia.) One day in 1971, one of those historians, Milan Hübl, wearing his extraordinarily thick-lensed eyeglasses, came to visit me in my studio apartment on Bartolomejska Street. We looked out the window at the towers of Hradcany Castle and were sad.

'You begin to liquidate a people,' Hübl said, 'by taking away its memory. You destroy its books, its culture, its history. And then others write other books for it, give another culture to it, invent another history for it. Then the people slowly begins to forget what it is and what it was. The world at large forgets it still faster.'

'And the language?'

'Why bother taking it away? It will become a mere folklore and sooner or later die a natural death.'

Was that just hyperbole dictated by excessive gloom?

Or is it true that the people will be unable to survive crossing the desert of organized forgetting?

None of us knows what is going to happen. One thing, however, is certain. In moments of clear-sightedness, the Czech people can see the image of its own death near at hand. Neither as a fact nor as an inescapable future, but nonetheless as a quite concrete possibility. Its death is right there with it.

From EVA HOFFMANN, *Shtetl* (1998)

Why remember, to what end, and in what way? In the post-Holocaust era, we have taken the obligation to preserve memory as sacred – as indeed, when rightly understood, it is. But if they are merely recited or needed without active understanding, the injunctions never to forget can become formulaic, an invitation to a ritual rather than to a moral act. How we remember, how much effort and pressure of intelligence and imagination we bring to the process, also matters. On the Polish side, the great pitfalls in relation to the wartime past have been amnesia on the one hand, and the wilfully tendentious uses of memory on the other. But this also needs to be admitted: several decades after the Holocaust, there is a danger, for those of us who did not live through it, of a kind of automatism of Jewish memory; of reiterating narratives of tragedy without any longer bothering to think about them; of identifying with martyrdom without having earned the right to it; of remaining fixated on the most awful moment so that we don't have to look back to the more ambiguous past – or forward to the troublingly uncertain future.

At this point, the task is not only to remember but to remember strenuously – to explore, decode, and deepen the terrain of memory. Moreover, what is at stake is not only the past but the present. In Poland, the lacunae in collective consciousness, the blank spots, as Poles themselves call them, have had harmful and disturbing consequences. In the last few years, together with a revival of interest in Jewish history and culture, there has been a resurgence of anti-Semitic rhetoric in Poland, which is particularly insidious in that it is rhetoric without a real object. It is as if, with the lifting of Communist repression, the prewar prejudices have reemerged from their Pandora's box in an unreconstructed – because unprocessed – form. The contents of the Pandora's box, the demons and ghosts haunting the Polish psyche, need urgently to be confronted and examined.

In the United States, where Poles and descendants of Polish Jews come into direct contact, visions of the past have a vital impact on the continuing, still highly charged dialogue between the two groups. In a sense, that dialogue is a particularly painful example of multi-cultural debate on the whole; and possibly, in its very intensity, it offers a model of both the hazards and the possibilities of cross-ethnic conversations in general.

In its worst-case version, the Polish-Jewish dialogue has taken the form of a moral war and has proceeded in escalating rounds of accusation and counter-accusation, exaggeration and denial. The Polish participants in such exchanges discern in all Jewish statements an attack on their country and its ideals. The Jewish respondents read the entire past as an agon between oppressors and victims. After a while both positions harden, as each side, in response to rising attacks, pulls up the drawbridge to protect its moral fortress.

Such forms of cross-cultural encounter are unfortunately all too familiar. But the patterns of suspicion and grievance not only prevent us from looking at the actual object of inquiry; they also perpetuate damaging patterns of thinking about multicultural relationships, even if they are relationships between majority and minority groups. The history of Poles and Jews was hardly a tale of pure good intentions on the Polish side, but neither was it a one-sided struggle between brute Polish power and passive Jewish powerlessness. Nor, starting from the other end, was the past a narrative of Polish martyrdom and Jewish selfishness. The various forms of Jewish attachment to Poland and participation in historical events cannot be reduced to disloyalty or a simple lack of patriotism. In any case, such categories as 'Poles' and 'Jews,' as we have learned from looking at other groups and areas of the world, are too large to be anything but fictitious and dangerously misleading. If cross-cultural discussions of difficult histories are to be at all fruitful, they need to start with acknowledgement of complexity rather than insistence on reductiveness.

Ideally, in such encounters, both partners would feel enough equality and strength to supplant accusation with self-examination, and to talk fully and openly about their own histories *to each other*. It is of course necessary in such a conversation for the majority culture to admit its history of dominance or injustice; but the dialogue cannot proceed if the minority group continues to hold the majority moral hostage in perpetuity, or if the history of powerlessness is taken as proof of moral superiority. And it is unproductive, always, to counter prejudice by denying facts, It does not help to respond to a Jewish interlocutor who claims that 'all Poles are anti-Semitic' with the equally absurd statement that 'there was never any anti-Semitism in Poland.' Conversely, it is unhelpful, because untrue, to meet the Polish thesis that 'Jews were harmful to the interests of Poland because they wouldn't assimilate' with the retort that Jewish separateness was entirely a function of Polish anti-Semitism. It is tempting, and all too commonplace, to resort to such strategies, if only so as not to give our opponent the satisfaction of exposing our weaknesses. But if we are to come to a better understanding of a shared – if embattled – past, it is necessary to abolish the double standard for 'internal' and 'external' self-presentation, and to admit even shameful intra-tribal problems, so to speak, into the discussion. It is the better part of dignity to be able to take such risks, but it is also the beginning of perceiving one's own history and one's present more three-dimensionally. For a Polish participant in a dialogue to admit irrational prejudices; for a Jewish person to acknowledge that an ethos of separateness has its price; this may be the beginning of a more probing self-exploration. In that sense, how we remember is crucial not only for the sake of those who have perished, but for our own sake as well.

In memories, too, begin responsibilities.

All acts of memory are to some extent imaginative; we can no longer reconstruct 'the full truth' of the Shoah or of a long and various past. But one thing is sure: the truth and the past were far more striated, textured, and many-sided than either nostalgia or bitterness would admit. This book is a modest attempt to reach into the past without assuming too many partisan positions or stereotypes. It is primarily the story of one Polish shtetl called Brańsk. Situated near the Russian border, Brańsk had about 4,600 inhabitans before the war, over half of whom were Jewish. Today there are no Jews left there. Therefore, this is a book of memory and about memory – or rather, of and about multiple layers of memory. On the more immediate level, this book springs primarily from several quests and encounters. There is the quest of Marian Marzynski, who made the documentary film *Shtetl* from which this book is partly derived. For Mr Marzynski, who survived the war as a Jewish child in Poland, the attempt to find out what happened in Brańsk was, as he indicates in his film, a way of investigating his own past from a bearable distance. Many members of his large, extended family lived in a shtetl very much like Brańsk. Most of them perished during the war. His film, then, springs from a need to fill in a lacuna in personal knowledge. But the lacuna is public as well as private – what happened during the war in the small, remote towns of Poland is still often obscure and unrecorded. In a sense Mr Marzynski's documentary is a race against time, an effort to capture on camera faces and images that still connect us to the life and death of the shtetl before they disappear forever.

From PAUL RICOEUR, *Memory, History, Forgetting* (2000), translated by Bridget Patterson (2007)

A third cause of fragility is the legacy of founding violence.* It is a fact that no historic community exists which does not have its origins in war. What we celebrate under the heading of founding events are essentially violent acts, legitimised after the fact by a State of questionable legality; events legitimised, ultimately, by their very antiquity, their timeworn custom. The same events, therefore, signify glory for some, but humiliation for others. One side's rejoicing corresponds to the other's execration. This is how real and symbolic wounds are stored in the archives of collective memory. Here, the third reason for the fragility of identity merges into the second. What remains to be seen is the device by which forms of misuse of memory can be grafted onto the claiming of identity, whose innate fragility we have just demonstrated.

From OLLIVIER DYENS, 'The Sadness of the Machine' (2001)

In a very touching book titled *The Man Who Mistook His Wife for a Hat*, the neuropsychologist Oliver Sacks recounts several stories of men and women who, due to lesions, deformities, and other cerebral illnesses, see the world in very strange ways. These patients, of whom Sacks paints a very moving picture, are unusual and unique not because of their physical appearance, but because their

---

* Ricoeur's first cause of fragility is a shifting sense of identity over time. The second is confrontation with others, experienced as threat.

representation of the world is profoundly different from our own. Sacks' patients are complete but different human beings. Their relationship to humanity is less vertical than horizontal, for they position themselves parallel to the majority.

These men and women do not live in our world of categorized universal representations. Instead, each of them inhabits a real, but entirely individual realm, to which no one else has access (one patient suddenly begins to mistrust his sense of smell, another constantly hears childhood songs playing in his head, a third discovers the use of his hands after sixty years, etc.). These human beings, whose brains were somehow damaged by illness or accident, are not prisoners in their worlds any more than we are in our own, but living in *our* world, one so foreign to them, forces them into withdrawal. These people share their bodies, knowledge, and 'souls' with us, but are unable to share the world itself. They are strangers in our universe, cognitive immigrants suffering from a terminal case of homesickness . . .

Sacks' book clearly illustrates that the existence of the world is intimately anchored to representations. This is not to say that the physical world does not exist, a victim of torture is undeniable proof of its materiality . . . The world definitely exists, *but the brain alone gives it its soul*, and because we all share a nearly identical brain, we are able to posit universal representations. But if the brain gives the world its 'soul', then it can also pervert it to such a point that the resulting phenomenology is incompatible with that of the majority. A different brain, a diseased and incomplete one, produces a representation of the world that it cannot share with other brains. This is what has happened to Sacks' patients.

This multiplication and 'personalization' of representation is particularly interesting in light of the entanglement of technologies and human beings. *Technologies transform phenomenology*. This, I believe, is undeniable. Technologies give access to different, multiple, and unknown levels of reality, and by its mere presence, this access alters the encoding of our world. Of course, this is not a new phenomenon (technologies are as old as living beings). However, what is new is the proliferation of technologies and their adaptability to very particular and specific needs. New technologies are drawing closer to us. They adapt to us as much as we adapt to them. With current technologies, each of us may choose how to live, die, and pray – even how to give birth and create life. New technologies enable each of us to erect a world that responds to our particular perception and understanding. We are turning into Oliver Sacks' patients: explorers of worlds that are ours alone, worlds that have tastes, colors, and realities unique to each of us. Sacks' patients are, to some extent, prototypes of the cultural being.

We are moving from a world where human beings diversified themselves according to their absolutes (shared absolutes), to one where human beings *diversify absolutes themselves*. Like Sacks' patients, we are physically very similar to one another, but are separated by worlds (technologically specific worlds) that are increasingly dissimilar. We are not witnessing the end of great ideological stories but their infinite proliferation, and to such a point that formerly unwavering representations like time, space, life, and death are also mutating and multiplying. Like head trauma victims, we are now seeing space, perceiving time, experiencing life, and considering death according to 'languages' which are not and cannot be universal. Because of technology, the world has become a series of exclusive and personal realms.

> One of the radical spirits in current thought has defined the task of this somber age as 'learning anew to be human'.[1]

The brain not only reads the surrounding world (leaving traces of itself in it), it also bestows meaning on it, and this meaning originates from memories. Memories are extended emotions that allow us to exist within various levels of time and space. The brain does not create the world, for the world already exists. But the world created by the brain is one whose meaning and richness is produced by memory-laced representations.

How can one have a memory without memories? asks Michel Serrault to his secretary as she works on her computer (in Claude Sautet's film *Nelly and Mr Arnaud*). This whimsical reflection conceals an important phenomenon: memory and memories are confused as we are entrusting our memories, rather than the ability to remember, to our machines. But what will happen once memories, which endow us with conscience and existence, survive only in databases? How will this transform us? Some years ago, Susan

[1.] George Steiner, *Real Presences* (1989) p. 4.

Sontag studied the impact of an excessive use of representations where, for example, the photograph of an event became more important than the event itself. This living by proxy, Sontag suggested, profoundly alters our experience of the world.

Today our memories almost never originate from our own decoding but are almost exclusively machine-recorded events. How will that affect our structuring of both the world and our individual psyche? How will we be remodeled by our multiplying worlds and relinquished memories? Is this what theoreticians of technological culture are talking about? When we examine the entanglement of biology and culture, are we witnessing the off-loading of our phenomenology onto technology?

What are we becoming as we empty more of our memories into culture and technology? How will we perceive the world when even our most intimate memories become device-dependent?

Clearly, we already share a great number of memories that are recorded, interpreted, and archived by machines alone. Memory banks are already easily accessible. *Memory withdrawal* from those banks is something we already often do to structure our understanding not only of world history, but more ominously, of our own personal history. The images of the Chinese student facing a tank during the Tiananmen Square crisis or those of the Kennedy assassination and, of course the live images of the World Trade Center terror are good examples of machine-recorded events with deep global and personal meaning. The recorded voices and images of Neil Armstrong and of Martin Luther King are yet other examples of the same phenomenon. Such memories have been extracted from the minds of individual men and women and have become universal, permanently frozen in their recording, and protected from the ravages of time, history, and human forgetfulness. They now belong to a collective human memory, available to all in a sort of supermarket of memories, where (as Susan Sontag said) it is the recording of the event that becomes the memory, where *memory* (in the computer sense) becomes *memories*. We have fewer and fewer individual memories, and most of the ones we now have are shared with an ever-increasing number of men and women. But memories are the colors and material of our human universe.

What will happen as more and more representations of the surrounding world are produced, while the cultural springs from which we draw these representations become weaker and weaker?

Memories and their emotions are not only that which gives us our essence. They are also a universal language. One of the most interesting elements of Oliver Sacks' book is his patients' extreme responsiveness to the emotions embodied in art. Whether a poem, music, play, song, or dance, all of Sacks' patients are transformed, even reborn (almost literally), when they come into contact with works of art. Suddenly, each is rid of his handicap(s), and seems to dive into a different and universal realm to which all humans have access. In art, Sacks' patients rediscover meaning and direction. Relieved of their handicaps for the duration of the artistic experience, they reintegrate normal human society. Artistic emotion opens their individual world to the community of men and women that surrounds them.

Born of human memories and emotions, art is a universal current.

Melancholy, sadness, joy, terror, anger, and the like constitute an Esperanto that every human being – every mammal – can read, understand, and share. *But emotion and art are nothing other than memories.* Living beings remember, and this is how they are able to consciously exist in time and space. Memory is fundamental to the emergence of both order and complexity. Without memories, a being cannot learn and adapt to the demands of the environment. Without memories, a being cannot evaluate the condition of his body (since this evaluation depends upon an interaction between before and now), and is thereby unable to emerge as a conscious being. Memories of pleasure, pain, sadness, and joy, are the common thread that unites all human beings. Memories are our existence, and art is their system of replication.

When I listen to a symphony, when I read a poem or watch a film, I do not only see, hear, or read specific words, images, or sounds. What I also (and I would suggest mostly) perceive is a sort of universal human 'memory' that unites beings to one another. Memory is a matrix; it is a moving, unstable, and ephemeral language that is continually renewed but eternally recognized and decoded.

Memories are at the core of most of today's fundamental changes. We live in a world that is riddled, inundated, and infested with memories of both men and machines. We live in a world where memories *no longer belong exclusively to us.* The memories that we now have are ahuman, created and manipulated events, preserved outside ourselves. Our current memories, those that give us form and identity, are fabricated productions; their recording, storage, recall, and modification are all operations performed by machines. We live in a world of mostly inhuman memories. If there is a memory of the world today, it is a memory of machines. Without them, I do not exist, for without them, I, personally, have no memories. Our existence, in its most intimately human structure, now belongs to machines. Machines create my past. Machines create my melancholy. Relationships among human beings are now inseparable from machines and technology, and contemporary works of art reflect that. Worlds multiply, and in the most fundamental paths of human presence, machines find their place. When I am nostalgic about a remembered event of my life, I can only be so through a machine's recording and filtering of it. We fall in love with our technologies, not simply because machines possess augmented and multiplied senses (they see and hear 'better', they run faster, are stronger, etc.), but because they control our memories and emotions. Human identity now dwells within machines and machine-made memories. The hunger to become machine, a fantasy so prevalent today, illustrates a thirst, not to locate, but to rediscover memories. Machines control our memories, they own the fundamental materials that shape us, and they manage the structures that generate human meaning and perspective. We long for our humanity.

This longing is, I believe, one of the foundations of postmodernism. In its multiplicity, in its infinite exploration of surfaces, meanings, and contradictions, postmodernity searches for human emotions. It is not only a cognitive map that needs to be redrawn (as Jameson suggests), but also a *map of memories*; a map whose trails pass resolutely through the territory of machines. When theoreticians of technological culture explore the phenomenon of the post-human and of post-biology, when they explore the concepts of life and artificial intelligences, they not only examine the emergence of a new being that is half-organic and half-machine; they also point to a new ontology defined by the common memories of men and machines.

The representations of postmodernity, referred to as *Panic Bodies, Retrofuture*, or *Inverted Millennarism*, illustrate a need to find emotions and memories that each can call his own. This need for human emotional and mnemonic specificity is found in art as well as in commerce, in war and in fashion, in history and in poverty. Machines, technologies, institutions, and commercial phenomena are so fertile with memories and emotions (and human beings have off-loaded onto machines so many of them) that sociological meaning must come from their interplay. That is what postmodernity illustrates. Like so many of Oliver Sacks' patients, we are devoid of memories. Like them, we move in and out of countless worlds and experiences in the hope of finding memories, any memory at all. But only in the machine-made realm are those memories now available.

One cannot be surprised, then, that protagonists of so many contemporary films fall in love with their machines. For only within those machines can one find love, pain, and pleasure. Whether in *Blade Runner*, where the androids ponder their life, death, and existence (whereas humans only, almost mechanically, corrupt), or in *Robocop*, where the cyborg is the film's only moral being, or even in *Terminator 2*, where the robot played by Schwarzenegger emerges as the only loving father a young boy can have, machines, not humans, are the new artistic imprints of humanity, sensibility, and morality.[2]

Humanity is flowing away from humans and toward machines. Marvin Minsky and Hans Moravec suggest that today's robots are our cognitive children. Let's be more specific here and speak of machines, robots, and technologies, not as cognitive children, but as *emotion children, representational children, and memory children.*

[2.] There is a fundamental difference between *Do Androids Dream of Electric Sheep?* by Philip K. Dick and *Blade Runner,* the film that Ridley Scott adapted from Dick's novel. Whereas it is the cyborgs that exhibit sensitivity and empathy in Scott's film, Dick's novel, written several years before its cinematic adaptation, paints the opposite picture. For Dick, it is machines that are inhuman, cruel, vicious, amoral, and manipulative, while humans suffer, question their existence, and see themselves slowly dying away. In *Do Androids Dream of Electric Sheep?* human beings are still human, even if they share their world with machines. For Ridley Scott, however, human beings are no longer human. In his film, cyborgs must be exterminated, not because they are a danger to society, but because they are more human than the humans themselves. In *Blade Runner,* cyborgs long for love, life, and understanding: they long for beauty and spirituality. In contrast to Dick's novel, human beings have now become amoral, vicious, dangerous, manipulative, and cruel. The reversal is complete: In Scott's film, just as in Cameron's (*Terminator 2*) and Verhoeven's (*Robocop*), human beings are more dangerous than their machines. In these films, machines are rich with humanity, they are moral beings endowed with compassion, sensitivity, and empathy. Suddenly, machines are the ones who, like a curse, carry the weighty burden of human kindness . . .

From the Digital Preservation Coalition action plan, House of Commons (27 February 2002)

The broadcaster and author Loyd Grossman (Chairman of the Campaign for Museums and a commissioner for Resource: the Council for Museums, Archives and Libraries) spoke in support of the digital heritage and our memory institutions. He also gave examples of digital preservation challenges.

'Last year marked the 30th anniversary of email. But it is salutary that we do not have the first email message, and no knowledge of its contents other than it was in upper case. Contrast this with how much we know about the first telegram (now digitised and on the web) or telephone message. Email took many years to become today's pervasive form of communication and we are now beginning to realise how digital materials are more ephemeral than traditional materials and sometimes the significance of key developments in new technologies may take several years to be recognised. The implications for our intellectual and cultural record and for their preservation are profound.

'The BBC Domesday Project of the mid-eighties is another particularly good example of the digital preservation challenges that face our institutions. BBC Domesday was launched to celebrate the 900th anniversary of the original Domesday Book with the idea of capturing a massive range of information on the social, environmental, cultural and economic make-up of the UK. Contributions from researchers and thousands of schoolchildren from across the country were recorded on to two 12" discs which could be viewed using a special BBC Microcomputer. The project was a landmark in terms of both its scale and its technological achievements. As a multimedia resource and interactive learning tool it was unsurpassed.

'Yet despite those achievements, the problems of hardware and software dependence have now rendered the system obsolete. While the 12" video discs are likely to remain in good condition for many years to come, the 1980s computers which read them and the BBC Micro software which interprets the digital data have a finite lifetime. With few working examples left, the information on this incredible historical object will soon disappear for ever.'

He stressed the importance of an urgent and collaborative approach to the challenges being faced:

'We cannot continue to rely on heroic efforts alone to safeguard our digital heritage: it must become a mainstream service for our institutions at national, regional and local level. We must work urgently to preserve our heritage of digital information before we leave a "digital gap" in history.'

Forgetting

From CICERO, *De Oratore* (55 BC), translated by E.W. Sutton (1942)

We are told that the famous Athenian Themistocles was endowed with wisdom and genius on a scale quite surpassing belief; and it is said that a certain learned and highly accomplished person went to him and offered to impart to him the science of mnemonics, which was then being introduced for the first time; and that when Themistocles asked what precise result that science was capable of achieving, the professor asserted that it would enable him to remember everything; and Themistocles replied that he would be doing him a greater kindness if he taught him to forget what he wanted than if he taught him to remember. Do you observe what mental force and penetration the man possessed, what power and range of intellect? inasmuch as his answer brings home to us that nothing that had once been introduced into his mind had ever been able to pass out of it, inasmuch as he would rather have been able to forget something that he did not wish to remember than to remember everything that he had once heard or seen. But this reply of Themistocles must not cause us to neglect the training of the memory . . .

From MICHEL DE MONTAIGNE, *Essays* (1588), translated by John Florio (1603)

For, memorie representeth unto us, not what we chuse, but what pleaseth her. Nay, there is nothing so deeply imprinteth any thing in our remembrance, as the desire to forget the same.: It is a good way to commend to the keeping, and imprint any thing in our minde, to solicite her to lose the same.

From WILLIAM SHAKESPEARE, *King Lear* (1606), IV. vii

Pray, do not mock me:
I am a very foolish fond old man,
Fourscore and upward, not an hour more nor less;
And, to deal plainly,
I fear I am not in my perfect mind.
Methinks I should know you, and know this man;
Yet I am doubtful: for I am mainly ignorant
What place this is; and all the skill I have
Remembers not these garments; nor I know not
Where I did lodge last night.

From SIR THOMAS BROWNE, *Religio Medici* (1642)

I am no way facetious, nor disposed for the mirth and galliardize of company; yet in one dream I can compose a whole Comedy, behold the action, apprehend the jests, and laugh my self awake at the conceits thereof. Were my memory as faithful as my reason is then fruitful, I would never study but in my dreams; and this time also would I chuse for my devotions: but our grosser memories have then so little hold of our abstracted understandings, that they forget the story, and can only relate to our awaked souls, a confused and broken tale of that that hath passed.

From SAMUEL JOHNSON, *The Idler*, no. 73

It would add much to human happiness, if an art could be taught of forgetting all of which the remembrance is at once useless and afflictive, if that pain which never can end in pleasure could be driven totally away, that the mind might perform its functions without incumbrance, and the past might no longer encroach upon the present.

Little can be done well to which the whole mind is not applied; the business of every day calls for the day to which it is assigned, and he will have little leisure to regret yesterday's vexations who resolves not to have a new subject of regret to-morrow.

But to forget or to remember at pleasure, are equally beyond the power of man. Yet as memory may be assisted by method, and the decays of knowledge repaired by stated times of recollection, so the power of forgetting is capable of improvement. Reason will, by a resolute contest, prevail over imagination, and the power may be obtained of transferring the attention as judgment shall direct.

The incursions of troublesome thoughts are often violent and importunate; and it is not easy to a mind accustomed to their inroads to expel them immediately by putting better images into motion; but this enemy of quiet is above all others weakened by every defeat; the reflection which has been once overpowered and ejected, seldom returns with any formidable power.

Employment is the great instrument of intellectual dominion. The mind cannot retire from its enemy into total vacancy, or turn aside from one object but by passing to another. The gloomy and the resentful are always found among those who have nothing to do, or that do nothing. We must be busy about good or evil, and he to whom the present offers nothing will be looking backward on the past.

From FRANCOIS-RENÉ DE CHATEAUBRIAND, *Mémoires d'outre-tombe* (1849–50)

What should we be without memory? We should forget our friendships, our loves, our pleasures, our work; the genius would be unable to collect his thoughts; the most ardent lover would lose his tenderness if he could remember nothing. Our existence would be reduced to the successive moments of a perpetually fading present; there would no longer be any past. Poor creatures that we are, our life is so vain that it is nothing but a reflection of our memory.

From WILLIAM JAMES, *The Principles of Psychology* (1890)

In the practical use of our intellect, forgetting is as important a function as recollecting.

Locke says, in a memorable page of his dear old book:

> The memory of some men, it is true, is very tenacious, even to a miracle; but yet there seems to be a constant decay of all our ideas, even of those which are struck deepest, and in minds the most retentive; so that if they be not sometimes renewed by repeated exercise of the senses, or reflection on those kinds of objects which at first occasioned them, the print wears out, and at last there remains nothing to be seen. Thus the ideas, as well as the children, of our youth, often die before us; and our minds represent to us those tombs to which we are fast approaching; where, though the brass and marble remain, yet the inscriptions are effaced by time, and the imagery moulders away. The pictures drawn in our minds are laid in fading colours; and, if not sometimes refreshed, vanish and disappear. How much the constitution of our bodies, and the make of our animal spirits, are concerned in this; and whether the temper of the brain makes this difference, that in some it retains the characters drawn on it like marble, in others like freestone, and in others little better than sand, I shall not here inquire, though it may seem probable that the constitution of the body does sometimes influence the memory; since we oftentimes find a disease quite strip the mind of all its ideas, and the flames of a fever in a few days calcine all those images to dust and confusion, which seemed to be as lasting as if graven in marble.[1]

This peculiar mixture of forgetting with our remembering is but one instance of our mind's selective activity. Selection is the very keel on which our mental ship is built. And in this case of memory its utility is obvious. If we remembered everything, we should on most occasions be as ill off as if we remembered nothing. It would take as long for us to recall a space of time as it took the original time to elapse, and we should never get ahead with our thinking. All recollected times undergo, accordingly, what M. Ribot calls

---

[1.] *Essay Concerning Human Understanding*, II x. 5.

foreshortening; and this foreshortening is due to the omission of an enormous number of the facts which filled them.

> As fast as the present enters into the past, our states of conscious-ness disappear and are obliterated. Passed in review at a few days' distance, nothing or little of them remains: most of them have made shipwreck in that great nonentity from which they never more will emerge, and they have carried with them the quantity of duration which was inherent in their being. This deficit of surviving conscious states is thus a deficit in the amount of represented time. The process of abridgment, of foreshortening, of which we have spoken, presup-posed this deficit. If, in order to reach a distant reminiscence, we had to go through the entire series of terms which separate it from our present selves, memory would become impossible on account of the length of the operation. We thus reach the paradoxical result that one condition of remembering is that we should forget. Without totally forgetting a prodigious number of states of consciousness, and momentarily forgetting a large number, we could not remember at all. Oblivion, except in certain cases, is thus no malady of memory, but a condition of its health and its life.[2]

There are many irregularities in the process of forgetting which are as yet unaccounted for. A thing forgotten on one day will be remembered on the next. Something we have made the most stren-uous efforts to recall, but all in vain, will, soon after we have given up the attempt, saunter into the mind, as Emerson somewhere says, as innocently as if it had never been sent for. Experiences of bygone date will revive after years of absolute oblivion, often as the result of some cerebral disease or accident which seems to develop latent paths of association, as the photographer's fluid develops the picture sleeping in the collodion film. The oftenest quoted of these cases is Coleridge's:

> In a Roman Catholic town in Germany, a young woman, who could neither read nor write, was seized with a fever, and was said by the priests to be possessed of a devil, because she was heard talking Latin, Greek, and Hebrew. Whole sheets of her ravings were written out, and found to consist of sentences intelligible in themselves, but

[2.] Théodule Ribot, *Les Maladies de la Mémoire* (1881) p. 46.

having slight connection with each other. Of her Hebrew sayings, only a few could be traced to the Bible, and most seemed to be in the Rabbinical dialect. All trick was out of the question; the woman was a simple creature; there was no doubt as to the fever. It was long before any explanation, save that of demoniacal possession, could be obtained. At last the mystery was unveiled by a physician, who determined to trace back the girl's history, and who, after much trouble, discovered that at the age of nine she had been charitably taken by an old Protestant pastor, a great Hebrew scholar, in whose house she lived till his death. On further inquiry it appeared to have been the old man's custom for years to walk up and down a passage of his house into which the kitchen opened, and to read to himself with a loud voice out of his books. The books were ransacked, and among them were found several of the Greek and Latin Fathers, together with a collection of Rabbinical writings. In these works so many of the passages taken down at the young woman's bedside were identified that there could be no reasonable doubt as to their source.[3]

Hypnotic subjects as a rule forget all that has happened in their trance. But in a succeeding trance they will often remember the events of a past one. This is like what happens in those cases of 'double personality' in which no recollection of one of the lives is to be found in the other. We have already seen . . . that the sensibility often differs from one of the alternate personalities to another, and we have heard M. Pierre Janet's theory that anaesthesias carry amnesias with them. In certain cases this is evidently so; the throwing of certain functional brain-tracts out of gear with others, so as to dissociate their consciousness from that of the remaining brain, throws them out for both sensorial and ideational service. M. Janet proved in various ways that what his patients forgot when under

---

3. *Biographia Literaria*, 1847 edn, I, 117 (quoted in Carpenter's *Mental Physiology*, Chapter 10, which see for a number of other cases, all unfortunately deficient, like this one, in the evidence of exact verification which 'psychical research' demands). Compare also Th. Ribot, *Diseases of Memory*, Chapter 4. The knowledge of foreign words, etc., reported in trance mediums, etc., may perhaps often be explained by exaltation of memory. An hystero-epileptic girl, whose case I quoted in *Proceedings of the American Society for Psychical Research,* automatically writes an 'Ingoldsby Legend' in several cantos, which her parents say she 'had never read'. Of course she must have read or heard it, but perhaps never *learned* it. Of some macaronic Latin-English verses about a sea-serpent which her hand also wrote unconsciously, I have vainly sought the original (see ibid., p. 553).

anaesthetic they remembered when the sensibility returned. For instance, he restored their tactile sense temporarily by means of electric currents, passes, etc., and then made them handle various objects, such as keys and pencils, or make particular movements, like the sign of the cross. The moment the anaesthesia returned they found it impossible to recollect the objects or the acts. 'They had had nothing in their hands, they had done nothing,' etc. The next day, however, sensibility being again restored by similar processes, they remembered perfectly the circumstance, and told what they had handled or had done.

From FRIEDRICH NIETZSCHE, *Beyond Good and Evil* (1886), translated by R. J. Hollingdale (1961)

Blessed are the forgetful: for they get over their stupidities too.

From MAX SAUNDERS, Conrad's reminiscences (1924) in *Ford Madox Ford: A Dual Life* (1996)

In the 'Author's Note' for the 1924 Collected Edition of *Tales of Unrest*, Conrad's reminiscence suggests an allegory of his collaboration with Ford. Conrad muses on the continuity of style between *An Outcast of the Islands* and his story 'The Lagoon'; 'there has been no change of pen, figuratively speaking.' This was literally true too: 'It was the same pen: a common steel pen':

> I thought the pen had been a good pen and that it had done enough for me, and so, with the idea of keeping it for a sort of memento on which I could look later with tender eyes [like Ford, Conrad too wanted to 'have remembrance now'], I put it into my waistcoat pocket. Afterwards it used to turn up in all sorts of place[s . . .] till at last it found permanent rest in a large wooden bowl containing some loose keys, bits of sealing-wax, bits of string, small broken chains, a few buttons, and similar minute wreckage that washes out

of a man's life into such receptacles. I would catch sight of it from time to time with a distinct feeling of satisfaction till, one day, I perceived with horror that there were two old pens in there. How the other pen found its way into the bowl instead of the fireplace or the wastepaper basket I can't imagine, but there the two were, lying side by side, both encrusted with ink and completely undistinguishable from each other. It was very distressing, but being determined not to share my sentiment between two pens or run the risk of sentimentalising over a mere stranger, I threw them both out of the window into a flower-bed – which strikes me now as a poetical grave for the remnants of one's past.[1]

From ALPHONSE DAUDET, *In the Land of Pain* (written *c.*1887, published 1930), translated by Julian Barnes (2002)

Last night, in my study, around ten o'clock, I had a couple of minutes of pure anguish.

I was fairly calm, writing an unimportant letter. The page was very white, with all the light from a *lampe anglaise* concentrated upon it; the table and the study were plunged in darkness.

A servant came in and put a book or something on the table. I raised my head, and from that moment I lost all sense of everything for two or three minutes. I must have looked completely stupid, because the servant, taking my blank face as a question, explained what he'd come for. I didn't understand his words and no longer remember them.

What was horrible was that I didn't recognise my own study: I knew that's where I was, but had lost all sense of it as a place. I had to get up and find my bearings, running my hand along the bookcase and the doors and saying to myself, 'That's where he came in.' Gradually, my brain began to work again, my faculties returned. But I remember my vivid sense of the whiteness of the letter I was writing, the way it shone forth from the blackness of the table.

A kind of hypnotic effect, compounded by fatigue.

[1.] *The Works of Joseph Conrad* (1921) I, viii–ix.

This morning, hurrying to write all this down, I remembered being in a cab a couple of years ago: I shut my eyes for a few moments, and when I opened them I found myself on the lamplit *quais* of a Paris I simply couldn't identify. I ended up leaning right out of the cab door, staring at the river and a row of grey houses opposite. I was bathed in a sweat of fear. Then, as we came to a bridge, I suddenly recognized the Palais de Justice and the Quai des Orfèvres, and the bad dream faded away.

From CYRIL CONNOLLY, *The Unquiet Grave* (1944)

Our memories are card-indexes consulted, and then put back in disorder by authorities whom we do not control.

PHILIP LARKIN, 'The Winter Palace' (1978)

Most people know more as they get older:
I give all that the cold shoulder.

I spent my second quarter-century
Losing what I had learnt at university

And refusing to take in what had happened since.
Now I know none of the names in the public prints,

And am starting to give offence by forgetting faces
And swearing I've never been in certain places.

It will be worth it, if in the end I manage
To blank out whatever it is that is doing the damage.

Then there will be nothing I know.
My mind will fold into itself, like fields, like snow.

From ROLAND BARTHES, *Camera Lucida,*
translated by Richard Howard (1981)

Now, one November evening shortly after my mother's death, I was going through some photographs . . .

And here the essential question first appeared: did I *recognise* her?

According to these photographs, sometimes I recognised a region of her face, a certain relation of nose and forehead, the movement of her arms, her hands. I never recognised her except in fragments, which is to say that I missed her *being*, and that therefore I missed her altogether. It was not she, and yet it was no one else. I would have recognised her among thousands of other women, yet I did not 'find' her. I recognised her differentially, not essentially. Photography therefore compelled me to perform a painful labour; straining toward the essence of her identity, I was struggling among images partially true and therefore totally false. To say, confronted with a certain photography, 'that's *almost* the way she was!', was more distressing than to say, confronted with another, 'that's not the way she was at all'. The *almost*: love's dreadful regime, but also the dream's disappointing status, which is why I hate dreams. For I often dream about her (I dream only about her), but it is never quite my mother: sometimes in the dream, there is something misplaced, something excessive: for example, something playful or casual – which she never was; or again I *know* it is she, but I do not *see* her features (but do we *see* in dreams, or do we *know*?): I dream about her, I do not dream *her*. And confronted with the photograph, as in the dream, it is the same effort, the same Sisyphean labour: to reascend, straining toward the essence, to climb back down without having seen it, and to begin all over again.

From BILLY COLLINS, 'Forgetfulness' (1991)

The name of the author is the first to go
followed obediently by the title, the plot,
the heartbreaking conclusion, the entire novel
which suddenly becomes one you have never read, never even
    heard of.

It is as if, one by one, the memories you used to harbor
decided to retire to the southern hemisphere of the brain,
to a little fishing village where there are no phones.

Long ago you kissed the names of the nine Muses goodbye
and watched the quadratic equation pack its bag,
and even now as you memorize the order of the planets,

something else is slipping away, a state flower perhaps,
the address of an uncle, the capital of Paraguay.

Whatever it is you are struggling to remember
it is not poised on the tip of your tongue,
not even lurking in some obscure corner of your spleen.

It has floated away down a dark mythological river
whose name begins with an *L* as far as you can recall,
well on your own way to oblivion where you will join those
who have even forgotten how to swim and how to ride a
    bicycle.

No wonder you rise in the middle of the night
to look up the date of a famous battle in a book on war.
No wonder the moon in the window seems to have drifted
out of a love poem that you used to know by heart.

Acknowledgements

The editors would like to acknowledge the following publishers, individuals, agencies and institutions for their kind permission to reproduce copyright material, as listed below. Where the edition used differs from that of the publishers acknowledged this is indicated in brackets, with the publication date. Every effort has been made to trace and contact all copyright holders, and the publishers would be pleased to rectify any omissions brought to their notice at the earliest opportunity.

DANIEL L. ALKON: *Memory's Voice: Deciphering the Mind–Brain Code* (© 1991 Daniel L. Alkon), HarperCollins Publishers Inc.; Blackwell Publishing; MARTIN AMIS: *Experience* (Jonathan Cape, 2000), Random House UK and the Wylie Agency, Inc.; ANON: *Rhetorica ad Herrenium*, translated by Harry Caplan, from *Cicero*: Volume 1, LCL 403 (© 1954 by the President and Fellows of Harvard College), Harvard University Press and the Trustees of the Loeb Classical Library; DANIEL ARASSE: *Anselm Kiefer*, translated by Mary Whittall (2001), Thames & Hudson, London and Editions du Regard, Paris; OWEN BARFIELD: *History in English Words* (Faber and Faber 1962), the Owen Barfield Literary Estate; ROLAND BARTHES: *Camera Lucida*, translated by Richard Howard, (1981) Editions du Seuil, Paris and Farrar, Straus & Giroux; JULIAN BARNES: translation of Alphonse Daudet, *In The Land Of Pain* (Jonathan Cape, 2002), Random House UK, Random House inc., and PFD (The Peters Fraser & Dunlop Group); F.C. BARTLETT: *A Theory of Remembering* (1932:1995), Cambridge University Press; SAMUEL BECKETT: *Happy Days* (1987), Faber and Faber and Grove/Atlantic Inc.; COLIN BLAKEMORE: *Mechanics of the Mind* (1977), Cambridge University Press; JORGE LUIS BORGES: 'Funes the Memorious', translated by James E. Irby, from *Labyrinths* (King Penguin 1981) © 1962, 1964, New Directions Publishing Corporation, New York and Pollinger Ltd., London; ITALO CALVINO: *Invisible Cities* translated by William Weaver (1974; Vintage Classics 1997), Random House UK, Inc. and Vintage Canada; MARY J. CARRUTHERS: 'Hugh of St Cher's Bear', *The Book of Memory* (1992), Cambridge University Press; MARY J. CARRUTHERS and JAN M. ZIOLKOWSKI, ed.: 'Thomas Bradwardine' *The Medieval Craft of Memory* (2002), University of Pennsylvania Press; JEAN-PIERRE CHANGEUX AND PAUL RICOEUR: *What Makes us Think* (2000), Princeton University Press; RICHARD COE: *When the Grass was Taller: Autobiography and the Experience of Childhood* (1984), Yale University Press; R.G. COLLINGWOOD: *Speculum Mentis* (Clarendon Press, 1924), Oxford University Press; BILLY COLLINS: 'Forgetfulness', *Questions about Angels* (1991), by kind permission of the author and Pittsburgh University Press; FRANCIS CRICK: *The Astonishing Hypothesis: The Scientific Search for the Soul* (© 1994 by the Francis H. C. Crick and Odile Crick Revocable Trust), Scribner, an imprint of Simon & Schuster Adult Publishing Group; RICHARD DAWKINS: *The Selfish Gene* (1989), Oxford University Press; BRIAN DILLON: *In the Dark Room* (2006), Penguin Group UK; OLLIVIER DYENS: 'The Sadness of the Machine' (11.2.2001), *CTheory*, University of Victoria, Canada; ECONOMIST: 'Sleeping on it', © *The Economist Newspaper*, London, 4.2.2006; G.M. EDELMAN: 'Building a Picture of the Brain', from *The Brain*, ed. G. M. Edelman and Jean-Pierre Changeux, © 2001 Transaction Publishers, Piscataway, New Jersey; FORD MADOX FORD: *Memories and Impressions* (Bodley Head, 1911), David Higham Associates; E.M. FORSTER: *Aspects of the Novel* (1927), The Provost and Scholars of King's College, Cambridge, and The Society of Authors as the Literary Representatives of the Estate of E.M. Forster; MICHAEL FRAYN: *Copenhagen* (Methuen Drama 1998), PFD (The Peters Fraser & Dunlop Group); SIGMUND FREUD: *Screen Memories* and other works, Random House UK; PAUL FUSSELL, *The Great War and Modern Memory* (1976), Oxford University Press Inc; JACQUES LE GOFF: *Histoire et mémoire*, (Gallimard, 1988), Einaudi; E.H. GOMBRICH: *Art and Illusion* (1960, 2000), Princeton University Press; HENRY GREEN: *Pack My Bag* (Hogarth Press, 1940), © The Estate of Henry Green), Random House UK and New Directions Publishing Corporation, New York; IAN HACKING: *Rewriting the Soul: Multiple Personality and the Science of Memory* (1998 edition), Princeton University Press; NICHOLAS HARBERD: *Seed to Seed* (2006), Bloomsbury Publishing; CYRIL HARE: *He Should Have Died Hereafter* (1958), AP Watt Ltd on behalf of Charles Gordon Clark; SUDHIR HAZAREESINGH: 'Guard Dog of Good Deeds' (21.3.03), *Times Literary Supplement*; EVA

HOFFMAN: *Shtetl* (Chatto & Windus, 1997), by kind permission of the author and Random House UK; TED HUGHES: 'Fingers', *Birthday Letters* (1998), Faber and Faber, and Farrar, Straus and Giroux Inc.; ABU ALI AHMAD IBN MUHAMMAD MISKAWAYH in H.F. Amedroz and D.S. Margliouth: *The Eclipse of the 'Abbasid Caliphate* (Oxford University Press, 1920–21), ROBERT IRWIN: *Night and Horses and Desert: An Anthology of Classical Arabic Literature* (1999, © Robert Irwin 1999), Penguin Group UK and Overlook Press; GEORGE JOHNSON: *In the Palaces of Memory: How We Build the World Inside Our Heads* (Vintage, 1992, © George Johnson 1991), Alfred A. Knopf, a division of Random House Inc.; C.G. JUNG: *Memories, Dreams, Reflections*, edited by Aniela Jaffe, translated by Richard & Clara Winston (© 1961, 1962, 1963 and renewed 1989, 1990, 1991), Pantheon Books, a division of Random House, Inc.; ERIK R. KANDEL: *In Search of Memory* (2007), W.W. Norton & Company, Inc., New York; FRANK KERMODE: 'Palaces of Memory', *Index on Censorship* (Vol. 30, 1/ 2001); MELANIE KLEIN: 'The Psychogenesis of Tics', *Love, Guilt, Reparation and other works 1921–1945* (1975), Simon & Schuster; MILAN KUNDERA: *The Book of Laughter and Forgetting*, translated by A. Asher (1996), and *The Curtain*, translated by Linda Asher (2007) by kind permission of the author, Faber and Faber, London, and HarperCollins Publishers Inc.; PHILIP LARKIN: 'The Winter Palace', *Collected. Poems*, ed. A. Thwaite (1988), Faber and Faber, and Farrar, Straus & Giroux Inc.; PENELOPE LIVELY: *Going Back* (1975), David Higham Associates; ELIZABETH F. LOFTUS: *The Champion Magazine* (March 1994), National Association of Criminal Defense Lawyers, Washington DC; KONRAD LORENZ: *King Solomon's Ring* translated by Marjorie Kerr Wilson (1949, 2001 Routledge edition), Taylor & Francis books UK; *The Foundations of Ethology* (Simon and Schuster, 1982), Springer Verlag, Vienna/New York; A.R. LURIA: *The Mind of a Mnemonist* (Basic Books, 1968), by kind permission of Michael Cole; JOHN McCRONE: 'Not-so Total Recall', *New Scientist*, 3 May 2003; HILARY MANTEL: *Giving up the Ghost* (2003), HarperCollins Publishers UK; 'Father Figured', © *Daily Telegraph* 23 April 2005; GABRIEL GARCÍA MÁRQUEZ: *Living To Tell The Tale* (2003), Carmen Balcells Agency, Barcelona; WILLIAM MAXWELL: *So Long, See You Tomorrow* (Vintage, 1980), Alfred A. Knopf and Random House UK; TONI MORRISON: *Beloved* (Chatto & Windus, 1987), International Creative Management Inc., New York, and

Random House UK; EDWIN MUIR: *An Autobiography*, (Methuen University Paperbacks, 1964), Random House UK; HARUKI MURAKAMI: interview with Mick Brown (16.8.2003), *Daily Telegraph Magazine*; VLADIMIR NABOKOV: *Speak Memory: An Autobiography Revisited* (Gollancz, 1951), Smith/Skolnik Literary Management, Plainfield, New Jersey; CEES NOOTEBOOM: *Rituals*, translated by Adrienne Dixon (Harvill Press, 1996), Random House UK and Harcourt Inc.; I.P. PAVLOV: *Lectures on Conditioned Reflexes*, translated by W. Horsley Gantt (1927), International Publishers, New York; STEVEN PINKER: *The Language Instinct: The New Science of Language and Mind* (© Steven Pinker 1994), Penguin Group UK; F.A. POTTLE: 'The Power of Memory in Boswell and Scott' in *Essays on the Eighteenth Century* (1945), Oxford University Press; ANTHONY POWELL: 'Infants of the Spring' from *To Keep the Ball Rolling* (Heinemann, 1921), David Higham Associates; TERRY PRATCHETT: *Reaper Man* (1991), HarperCollins Publishers; MARCEL PROUST: *Time Regained* (1927), translated by Andreas Mayor, Terence Kilmartin & D.J. Enright (1992), Random House UK; VILAYANUR RAMACHANDRAN: *The Emerging Mind* (2003), Profile Books Ltd.; GWEN RAVERAT: *Period Piece* (1952), Faber and Faber; PAUL RICOEUR: *La mémoire, l'histoire, l'oublie* (2000), Editions du Seuil, Paris; CHARLES RYCROFT: *The Innocence of Dreams* (Hogarth Press 1979), Random House UK and Pantheon; OLIVER SACKS: 'A Symposium on Memory', (*Threepenny Review*, January 2005 © Oliver Sacks 2005), the Wylie Agency Inc.; ESTHER SALAMAN: *A Collection of Moments*, (Longman, 1970), Pearson Education; MAX SAUNDERS: *Ford Madox Ford: A Dual Life* (1997), Oxford University Press; DAVID SHENK: *The Forgetting*, (Flamingo, 2003) HarperCollins Publishers; W.G. SEBALD: *Vertigo*, translated by Michael Hulse (Harvill Press, 2000), Random House UK and Eichborn Verlag; NICHOLAAS TINBERGEN: *The Study of Instinct* (Clarendon Press, 1989), Oxford University Press, 1989; TZVETAN TODOROV: *Les Abus de la Mémoire* (1998), Arlea, Paris; MARY WARNOCK: *Memory* (1987), Faber and Faber; WELLCOME TRUST: 'Magic Memories' (www. Wellcome.ac.uk 21.1.2007), The Wellcome Trust, London; LUDWIG WITTGENSTEIN: *Philosophical Investigations* (1958), Blackwell Publishing, Oxford; LEONARD WOOLF: *Sowing: An Autobiography of the years 1880–1904* (Hogarth Press, 1960, © Leonard Woolf 1960, renewed 1988 by M.T. Parsons), Random House UK and Harcourt Inc.; VIRGINIA

WOOLF: *Moments of Being* (Hogarth Press 1985 edition), © 1976 Quentin Bell and Angelica Garnett, Random House UK and Harcourt Inc.; FRANCES A. YATES: *The Art of Memory* (1966), University of Chicago Press and Random House UK; J.Z. YOUNG: *Programs of the Brain* (1978), Oxford University Press; SEMIR ZEKI: 'Art and the Brain', *Daedalus* 127:2 (Spring 1988), © 1988 American Academy of Arts and Sciences; STEFAN ZWEIG: 'Buchmendel', *Fantastic Night and other Stories* (2004), Pushkin Press.

Index